M000091939

brief contents

contents

preface

In college, after a horrible holiday experience working for a major clothing retailer, I swore I'd find a better summer job. Having been a camp counselor as a teenager, I found myself working at a tech camp. There I taught kids of all ages to make video games, build websites, and write code. It was rewarding to see how the kids entered a week of camp with little technical knowledge and left with a working project to show off.

Ever since, I've been passionate about teaching, mentoring, and sharing knowledge. I was lucky in my early career to work for a company that encouraged these skills. As an engineering leader, I now have the opportunity to mentor many software engineers.

Despite this desire to teach and share, I never set out to write a book. It seems, however, that writing blog posts and speaking at conferences naturally lead to other opportunities. Several months after speaking at Strange Loop, I was approached by Manning to see if I'd write a book on isomorphic app development. Here was a chance to take everything I'd learned as a maker of web apps and share it with others. This was the perfect opportunity to teach a much wider audience.

At Vevo, when we first started building an isomorphic app, I thought it was overly complex. But as we continued and I could see the long-term benefits, I became convinced of the value that isomorphic architecture adds for apps. This book explains that value and demystifies the complexity of building an isomorphic app. It distills what I've learned over the past few years about both real-world React apps and real-world isomorphic development. Wherever possible, I've related the concepts to situations you'll run into when building production apps.

I hope this book expands your thinking and gives you a new architecture tool. It took me some time to "think isomorphically." Once I did, I improved both my architecture skills and my understanding of the entire web stack. By sharing this knowledge with you, I hope you'll be able to grow in these areas as well.

acknowledgments

I knew that this book would involve a significant amount of work, but I couldn't fully appreciate what writing a book on top of working full-time would mean. Several people made it possible for me to successfully undertake this endeavor. I'd like to take this time to thank them.

First and most important, I thank you Max, my husband, for your continuous support, especially during the most stressful moments (sometimes even reminding me to eat and sleep). Your willingness to sacrifice so I could work on this project means the world to me. And I love that you acted as a technical consultant too! I also thank the rest of my family for putting up with my limited availability and distractedness throughout the process.

This book never would have made it without my developmental editor, Helen Stergius. I'm grateful for her ongoing positivity and dedication to making the manuscript the best it could be. And her patience and understanding during this process made it easier to believe I could and would finish the book.

In addition, thanks to everyone else at Manning who worked on this book. I've learned so much from this process. Two people stand out: Brian Sawyer, for giving me the opportunity to write this book, and Doug Warren, technical development editor, whose thoroughness and attention to detail made the book better for the reader.

Thanks also go to the reviewers who took time to read the manuscript at various stages and provide helpful feedback: Adil Mezghouti, Bojan Djurkovic, Casey Childers, Christian Nunciato, Evan Wallace, James Anaipakos, Madhav Ayyagari, Michael Jensen, Pearl Latteier, Peter Perlepes, Rahul Sharma, and Stephen Byrne.

I also couldn't have done this without the support of all my awesome colleagues at Vevo. Everyone has been extremely supportive! I especially want to thank Alex Nunes and Scott Dale for supporting me throughout this project.

I'm lucky to have a community of friends and mentors who supported me in writing this book. I'd like to acknowledge Jeff Carnegie for introducing me to isomorphic development and for always believing in me. Additionally, I'd like to thank Jun Heider and David Hassoun, who showed me what it means to be part of a developer community. I'd also like to thank Yomi Fashoro, Ryan Kahn, Arthur Klepchukov, Grant Schofield, and Natalie Serebryakova.

about this book

The main purpose of the book is to teach you to think in a way that will make you successful when working with isomorphic architecture. Given React's presence in the web community and the support React provides for server-side rendering, it's the logical choice for teaching how to build an isomorphic app.

The book starts by explaining what isomorphic apps are and why you'd want to build one. Then it shows a complete example from a 10,000-foot view. Next, it moves into several chapters on the core technologies used in a React app, followed by chapters on how to implement isomorphic code and related advanced topics including testing, managing environments, and performance.

Who should read this book

This book is aimed at web developers with professional experience. It's not for beginners. If you're looking to expand your architectural tool set and better understand ways to build web apps, this is a good book for you. It can also help you decide whether you should build an isomorphic app for a particular project.

The book assumes readers already have a solid understanding of JavaScript, CSS, and HTML. You don't need to know up front any of the technologies or libraries introduced in the book, including React, Redux, webpack, or Node.js with Express.

How this book is organized: a roadmap

This book has four parts divided into 13 chapters. Part 1, "First steps," explains why you'd want to use an isomorphic application and teaches you what an isomorphic app is:

- Chapter 1 goes over what an isomorphic app is and why you'd want to build it (including challenges and trade-offs). It also briefly introduces the major technologies used throughout the book.

- Chapter 2 goes through a complete isomorphic example. This provides a 10,000-foot view of a (simple) working application.

Part 2, "Isomorphic app basics," teaches the foundational pieces of a React app: React, React Router, Redux, and webpack/Babel:

- Chapter 3 is an introduction to React. Topics include the virtual DOM, writing components with JSX, using properties, and implementing state.
- Chapter 4 builds on that introduction to React by introducing React Router. It also covers the React component lifecycle and advanced concepts on React component architecture.
- Chapter 5 focuses on build tools: webpack and Babel. It explains the basics of using both tools, including how to use Babel in both the server and browser environments.
- Chapter 6 teaches you to use Redux, including how to hook it up to a React app.

Part 3, "Isomorphic architecture," covers in detail how to implement an isomorphic app, as well as several advanced topics:

- Chapter 7 implements the server for an isomorphic app using Express. It also introduces the concepts that make it possible to server-render your application with Redux and React.
- Chapter 8 picks up where chapter 7 leaves off and handles the isomorphic handoff between server and browser as well as getting the single-page application flow up and running with React.
- Chapter 9 covers testing and debugging isomorphic apps. The first part of the chapter focuses on various testing strategies and libraries you can use. The second part introduces several useful development debugging tools.
- Chapter 10 goes over real-world challenges and how to handle them, including working with code that runs only in either the server or the browser, updating metatags for SEO on the server, and creating a consistent approach to working with user-specific information such as the user agent.
- Chapter 11 focuses on performance on both the server and the browser, caching strategies, and handling user sessions.

Part 4, "Applying isomorphic architecture with other tools," applies the concepts taught in part 3 to other frameworks and includes a chapter focused on what to learn after completing this book:

- Chapter 12 introduces alternative options for building isomorphic apps via Ember, Angular, and a React isomorphic framework called Next.js.
- Chapter 13 provides suggestions for expanding your skill set in ways that will support you in building isomorphic apps and make you more employable.

The first part of the book (chapters 1 and 2) provides an overview of isomorphic concepts and explains why it matters. Everyone should read these chapters. The next part introduces each of the major technologies used in building a React isomorphic app. If you have experience building React apps and working with webpack, you can skip these chapters or read them as needed for refreshers.

If you don't have experience with React apps, make sure to read chapters 3–6. Some reviewers found it helpful to read these chapters before chapter 2 if they had little or no experience with React, Redux, and webpack.

The third part teaches the isomorphic implementation and then goes over several advanced topics such as testing, managing environments, and performance. The advanced chapters (10 and 11) may be read straight through or ad hoc as needed.

Finally, the fourth part is optional. You can explore additional frameworks and consider suggestions for expanding your skill set.

About the code

This book contains many examples of source code, both in numbered listings and in line with normal text. In both cases, source code is formatted in a `fixed-width font like this` to separate it from ordinary text. Sometimes code is also **`in bold`** to highlight changes from previous steps in the chapter, such as when a new feature adds to an existing line of code.

In many cases, the original source code has been reformatted; we've added line breaks and reworked indentation to accommodate the available page space in the book. In rare cases, even this was not enough, and listings include line-continuation markers (➥). Additionally, comments in the source code have often been removed from the listings when the code is described in the text. Code annotations accompany many of the listings, highlighting important concepts.

The code for this book is split into several GitHub repositories. The full list can be found at https://github.com/isomorphic-dev-js. I've also provided a list mapping chapters to their repos:

- Chapter 2: https://github.com/isomorphic-dev-js/chapter2-a-sample-isomorphic-app
- Chapter 3: https://github.com/isomorphic-dev-js/chapter3-react-overview
- Chapters 4 and 7–11: https://github.com/isomorphic-dev-js/complete-isomorphic-example
- Chapter 5: https://github.com/isomorphic-dev-js/chapter5-webpack-babel
- Chapter 6: https://github.com/isomorphic-dev-js/chapter6-redux
- Chapter 12: https://github.com/isomorphic-dev-js/chapter12-frameworks

Most of the repos use branches to help teach you the concepts. In each chapter that uses branches, I indicate what branch goes with each section. Each branch provides the base code for the section you're working on, but not the complete solution for that section. The complete solution is found in the next section's branch as well as in the branches labeled with a `-complete`. The idea is to check out the branch, add the code from the section of the book you're working on, and end up with a working example. The "complete" branches are provided in case you get lost or stuck.

Code versions

The code in the book assumes the following versions of libraries and tools are being used. You're welcome to try to upgrade versions on your own, but I make no guarantees about future versions of libraries working smoothly.

- Node.js v6.9.2 is what everything in the book was developed and tested on. Newer versions of Node through at least 8 will also work.
- Express v4.15.3.
- React v15.6.1. The code in the book was built with React 15, but I've verified that all the examples will also work with React 16 (which came out too late to update the code for this edition).
- React Router v3.0.5. I've provided a set of appendices that go over how to use React Router 4. The original examples in the book are still in React Router 3. Each chapter that has React Router 3 provides a note about which appendix provides the relevant information on accomplishing the same task in React Router 4.
- Redux v3.7.2.
- Webpack v3.4.1.
- Babel v6.25.0.
- Angular v4.0.0 (casually referred to as Angular 2, as opposed to Angular 1).
- Ember v2.13.2.
- Next.js v2.4.4.

Many other libraries are introduced throughout the book. Please refer to the package .json in each chapter's repo for a complete list of versions.

Book forum

Purchase of *Isomorphic Web Applications* includes free access to a private web forum run by Manning Publications where you can make comments about the book, ask technical questions, and receive help from the author and from other users. To access the forum, go to https://forums.manning.com/forums/isomorphic-web-applications. You can also learn more about Manning's forums and the rules of conduct at https://forums.manning.com/forums/about.

Manning's commitment to our readers is to provide a venue where a meaningful dialogue between individual readers and between readers and the author can take place. It is not a commitment to any specific amount of participation on the part of the author, whose contribution to the forum remains voluntary (and unpaid). We suggest you try asking the author challenging questions lest her interest stray! The forum and the archives of previous discussions will be accessible from the publisher's website as long as the book is in print.

about the author

ELYSE KOLKER GORDON is an engineering leader who builds effective client apps in consumer spaces such as sports and music. She is passionate about developing engineers, building cohesive teams, and creating great consumer apps. Currently, she runs the growth engineering team at Strava. Previously, she was the director of web engineering at Vevo, where she regularly solved challenges with isomorphic apps. She speaks and writes regularly about web development topics. She is also an avid musician who plays the drums and dabbles with other instruments. When she isn't at work, you can find her hanging out with her husband and dog, either at home or at the beach.

about the cover illustration

The figure on the cover of *Isomorphic Web Applications* is a "Gran Visir," the Prime Minister to the Sultan in a medieval Arabic country. While the exact meaning of his position and his national origin are lost in historical fog, there is no doubt that we are facing a man of stature and authority. The illustration is taken from a Spanish compendium of regional dress customs first published in Madrid in 1799. The book's title page states:

> *Coleccion general de los Trages que usan actualmente todas las Nacionas del Mundo desubierto, dibujados y grabados con la mayor exactitud por R.M.V.A.R. Obra muy util y en special para los que tienen la del viajero universal*

Translated as literally as possible, this means the following:

> *General Collection of Costumes currently used in the Nations of the Known World, designed and printed with great exactitude by R.M.V.A.R. This work is very useful especially for those who hold themselves to be universal travelers.*

Although nothing is known of the designers, engravers, and workers who colored this illustration by hand, the "exactitude" of their execution is evident in this drawing. The "Gran Visir" is just one of many figures in this colorful collection that reminds us vividly of how culturally apart the world's towns and regions were just 200 years ago. Dress codes have changed since then and the diversity by region, so rich at the time, has faded away. It is now often hard to tell the inhabitant of one continent from another. Perhaps we have traded a cultural and visual diversity for a more varied personal life—certainly a more varied and interesting world of technology.

At a time when it can be hard to tell one computer book from another, Manning celebrates the inventiveness and initiative of the computer business with book covers based on the rich diversity of regional life of two centuries ago—brought back to life by the picture from this collection.

Part 1

First steps

Understanding what an isomorphic app is and why you'd want to build one is an important first step in learning about isomorphic architecture. The first part of this book explores the why and how of isomorphic apps with a bird's-eye view, giving you the context you need in order to comprehend the specific implementation details presented in later sections.

In chapter 1, you'll learn all the reasons to build an isomorphic app. This chapter also gives you an overview of the All Things Westies app you'll build later in the book. In chapter 2, you'll work through building an example app with the technologies used in the book: React, Node.js, webpack, and Babel. Instead of covering all the small details, this chapter allows you to see how the pieces fit together.

1 Introduction to isomorphic web application architecture

This chapter covers

- Differentiating between isomorphic, server-side rendered, and single-page apps
- Server rendering and the steps involved in transitioning from a server-rendered to a single-page app experience
- Understanding the advantages and challenges of isomorphic web apps
- Building isomorphic web apps with React's virtual DOM
- Using Redux to handle the business logic and data flow
- Bundling modules with dependencies via webpack

This book is intended for web developers looking to expand their architectural toolset and better understand the options available for building web apps. If you've ever built a single-page or server-rendered web app (say, with Ruby on Rails), you'll have an easier time following the content in this book. Ideally, you're comfortable with JavaScript, HTML, and CSS. If you're new to web development, this book isn't for you.

Historically, web apps and websites have come in two forms: server-rendered and single-page apps (SPAs). *Server-rendered apps* handle each action the user takes by making a new request to the server. In contrast *SPAs* handle loading the content and responding to user interactions entirely in the browser. *Isomorphic web apps* are a combination of these two approaches.

This book aspires to take a complex application architecture and break it into repeatable and understandable bits. By the end of this book, you'll be able to create a content site or an e-commerce web app with the following techniques:

- Render any page on the server by using React to achieve fast perceived performance and fully render pages for search engine optimization (SEO) crawlers (such as Googlebot).
- Choose not to render certain features on the server. Understand how to use the React lifecycle to achieve this.
- Handle user sessions on both the server and the browser.
- Implement single-direction data flow with Redux, making prefetching data on the server and rendering in the browser feasible.
- Use webpack and Babel to enable a modern JavaScript workflow.

1.1 Isomorphic web app overview

My team and I had a big problem: our SEO rendering system was brittle and eating up valuable time. Instead of building new features, we were troubleshooting why Googlebot was seeing a different version of our app from what our users were seeing. The system was complex, involved a third-party provider, and wasn't scaling well for our needs, so we moved forward with a new type of app—an isomorphic one.

An *isomorphic app* is a web app that blends a server-rendered web app with a single-page application. On the one hand, we want to take advantage of fast perceived performance and SEO-friendly rendering from the server. On the other hand, we want to handle complex user actions in the browser (for example, opening a modal). We also want to take advantage of the browser push history and XMLHttpRequest (XHR). These technologies prevent us from making a server request on every interaction.

To get started understanding all of this, you're going to use an example web app called All Things Westies (you'll build this app later in the book, starting in chapter 4). On this site, you can find all kinds of products to buy for your Westie (West Highland white terrier—a small, white dog). You can purchase dog supplies and buy products featuring Westies (socks, mugs, shirts, and so forth). If you're not a pet owner, you might find this example ridiculous. As a dog owner, even I thought it was over the top. But it turns out that dog products such as mugs are a huge thing. If you don't believe me, search Google for "pug mugs."

Because this is an e-commerce app, we care about having good SEO. We also want our customers to have a great experience with performance in the app. This makes it an ideal use case for isomorphic architecture.

1.1.1 Understanding how it works

Look at figure 1.1, which is a wireframe for the All Things Westies app. There's a standard header with some main site navigation on the right. Below the header, the main content areas promote products and the social media presence.

The first time you come to the site, the app content is rendered on the server using server-rendered techniques with Node.js. After being server-rendered, the content is sent to the browser and displayed to the user. As the user navigates around the pages, looking for a dog mug or supplies, each page is rendered by the JavaScript running in the browser and using SPA techniques.

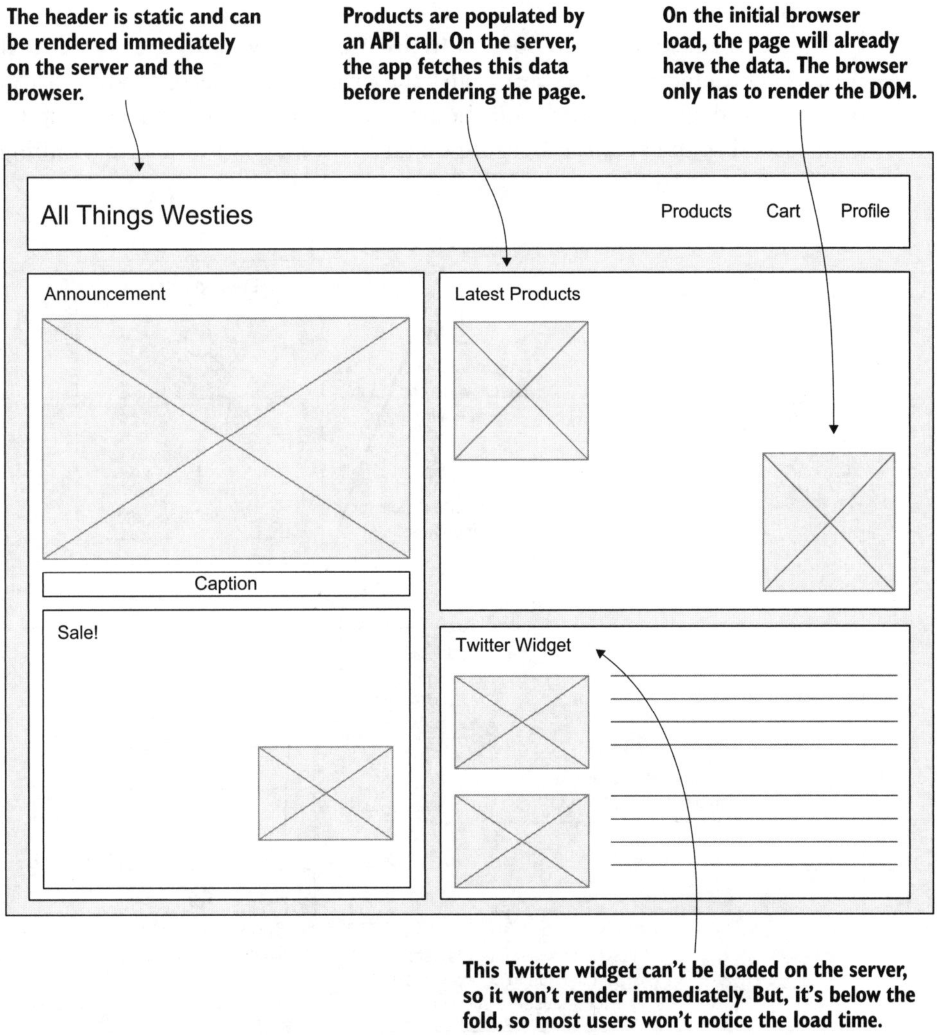

The header is static and can be rendered immediately on the server and the browser.
Products are populated by an API call. On the server, the app fetches this data before rendering the page.
On the initial browser load, the page will already have the data. The browser only has to render the DOM.
All Things Westies
Products
Cart
Profile
Announcement
Latest Products
Caption
Sale!
Twitter Widget
This Twitter widget can't be loaded on the server, so it won't render immediately. But, it's below the fold, so most users won't notice the load time.

Figure 1.1 A wireframe showing the homepage for All Things Westies, an isomorphic web app

The All Things Westies app relies on reusing as much code as possible between the server and the browser. The app relies on JavaScript's ability to run in multiple environments: JavaScript runs in browsers and on the server via Node.js. Although JavaScript can run in other environments as well (for example, on Internet of Things devices and on mobile devices via React Native), the focus here is on web apps that run in the browser.

Many of the concepts in this book could be applied without writing all the code in JavaScript. Historically, the complexity of running an isomorphic app without being able to reuse code has been prohibitive. Although it's possible to server-render your site with Java or Ruby and then transition to a single-page app, it isn't commonly done because it requires duplicating large portions of code in two languages. That requires more maintenance.

To see this flow in action, look at figure 1.2. It shows how the code for All Things Westies gets deployed to the server and the browser. The server code is packaged and run on a Node.js web server, and the browser code is bundled into a file that's later downloaded in the browser. Because we take advantage of JavaScript running in both

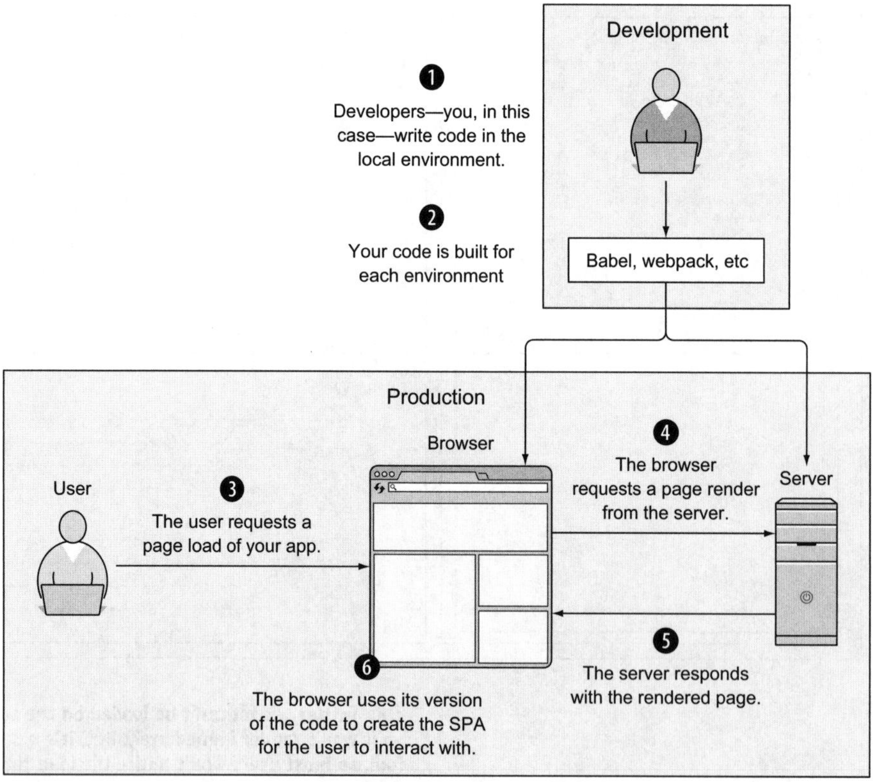
Development
1
Developers—you, in this case—write code in the local environment.
2
Your code is built for each environment
Babel, webpack, etc
Production
Browser
User
3
The user requests a page load of your app.
4
The browser requests a page render from the server.
Server
5
The server responds with the rendered page.
6
The browser uses its version of the code to create the SPA for the user to interact with.

Figure 1.2 Isomorphic apps build and deploy the same JavaScript code to both environments.

environments, the same code that runs in the browser and talks to our API or data source also runs on the server to talk to our back end.

1.1.2 Building our stack

Building an app such as All Things Westies requires putting together several well-known technologies. Many of the concepts in this book are executed with open source libraries. Although you could build an isomorphic app using few or no libraries, I highly recommend taking advantage of the JavaScript communities' efforts in this area.

> **TIP** Make sure any libraries you include in an isomorphic app support running in both the server and browser environments. Check out chapter 10 for what to watch for and how to handle differences in environments. If you intend to use a library only on the server, you don't need to check for browser compatibility.

The HTML components that display the products (the view) will be built with React (in chapter 12, you'll explore how to use other popular frameworks, including Angular 2 and Ember, to implement isomorphic architecture). You'll use a single-direction data flow via Redux, the current community standard data management in React apps. You'll use webpack to compile the code that runs in the browser and to enable running Node.js packages in the browser.

On the server side, you'll build a Node.js server using Express to handle routing. You'll take advantage of React's ability to render on the server and use it to build up a complete HTML response that can be served to the browser. Table 1.1 shows how all these pieces fit together.

Table 1.1 The technologies used in an isomorphic app and the environments they run in

Library (version)	Server	Browser	Build tool
Node.js (6.9.2)	✓		
Express (4.15.3)	✓		
React (15.6.1)	✓	✓	
React Router (3.0.5)	✓	✓	
Redux (3.7.2)	✓	✓	
Babel (6.25.0)	✓	✓	✓
webpack (3.4.1)		✓	✓

To make our application work everywhere, you'll build in data prefetching for your routes using React Router. You'll also handle differences in environments by building separate code entry points for the server and browser. If code can be run only in the browser, you'll gate the code or take advantage of the React lifecycle to ensure that the code won't run on the server. I introduce React in chapter 3 and the specifics of the server logic in chapter 7.

1.2 Architecture overview

Earlier in this chapter, I told you that an isomorphic application is the result of combining a server-rendered application and a single-page application. To get a better understanding of how to connect the concepts of a server-rendered application and a single-page application, see figure 1.3. This figure shows all the steps involved in getting an isomorphic app rendered and responding to user input, like a single-page application, starting when the user enters the web address.

1.2.1 Understanding the application flow

Every web app session is initiated when a user navigates to the web app or types the URL into the browser window. For allthingswesties.com, when a user clicks a link to the app from an email or from searching on Google, the flow on the server goes through the following steps (the numbers match those in figure 1.3):

1. The browser initiates the request.
2. The server receives the request.
3. The server determines what needs to be rendered.
4. The server gathers the data required for the part of our application being requested. If the request is for allthingswesties.com/product/mugs, the app requests the list of gift items for sale through the site. This list of mugs, along with all the information to be displayed (names, descriptions, price, images), is collected before moving on to the render step.
5. The server generates the HTML for our web page using the data collected for the mugs page.
6. The server responds to the request for allthingswesties.com/product/mugs with the fully built HTML.

The next part of the application cycle is the initial load in the browser. We differentiate the first time the user loads the app from subsequent requests because several things that will happen only once per session happen during this first load.

> **DEFINITION** *Initial load* is the first time the user interacts with your website. This means the first time the user clicks a link to your site in a Google search or from social media, or types it directly into the web address bar.

The first load on the browser begins as soon as the HTML response from the server is received and the DOM is able to be processed. At this point, single-page application flow takes over, and the app responds to user input, browser events, and timers. The user can add products to their cart, navigate around the site, and interact with forms.

7. The browser renders the markup received from the server.
8. The application is now able to respond to user input.
9. When the user adds an item to their cart, the code responds and runs any business logic necessary.
10. If required, the browser talks to the back end to fetch data.

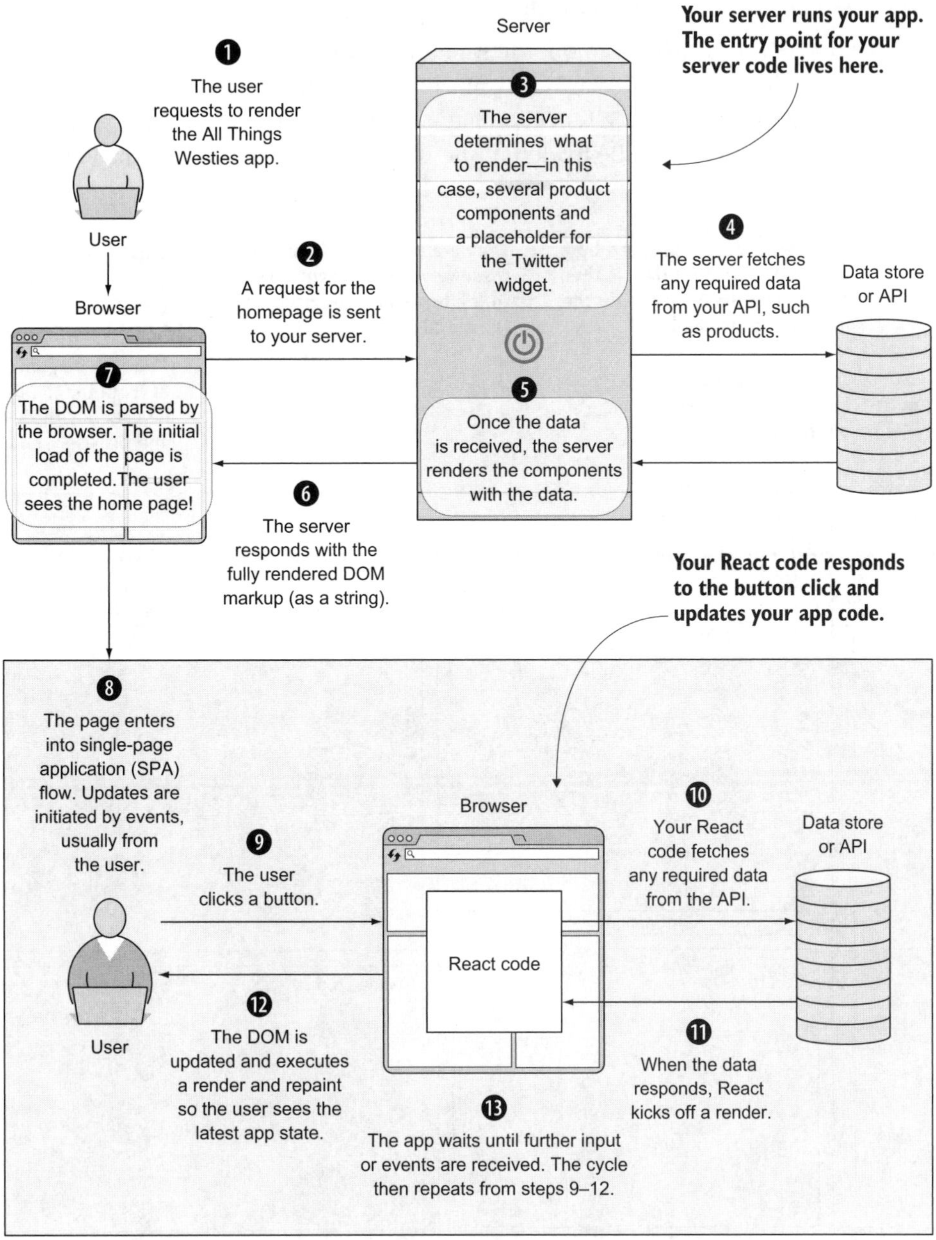
Server
Your server runs your app. The entry point for your server code lives here.
1
The user requests to render the All Things Westies app.
User
Browser
2
A request for the homepage is sent to your server.
3
The server determines what to render—in this case, several product components and a placeholder for the Twitter widget.
4
The server fetches any required data from your API, such as products.
Data store or API
5
Once the data is received, the server renders the components with the data.
6
The server responds with the fully rendered DOM markup (as a string).
7
The DOM is parsed by the browser. The initial load of the page is completed. The user sees the home page!
Your React code responds to the button click and updates your app code.
8
The page enters into single-page application (SPA) flow. Updates are initiated by events, usually from the user.
Browser
9
The user clicks a button.
10
Your React code fetches any required data from the API.
Data store or API
React code
User
11
When the data responds, React kicks off a render.
12
The DOM is updated and executes a render and repaint so the user sees the latest app state.
13
The app waits until further input or events are received. The cycle then repeats from steps 9–12.

Figure 1.3 The isomorphic app flow from initial browser request to SPA cycle

11. React renders the components.
12. Updates are made, and any repaints are executed. For instance, the user's cart icon updates to show that an item has been added.
13. Each time the user interacts with the app, steps 9–12 repeat.

1.2.2 *Handling the server-side request*

Now let's take a closer look at what happens when the server receives the initial request to render the page. Look at what part of the site renders on the server. Figure 1.4 is similar to figure 1.1, except that it doesn't render the Twitter widget. The Twitter widget is designed to be loaded in the browser, so it doesn't render on the server.

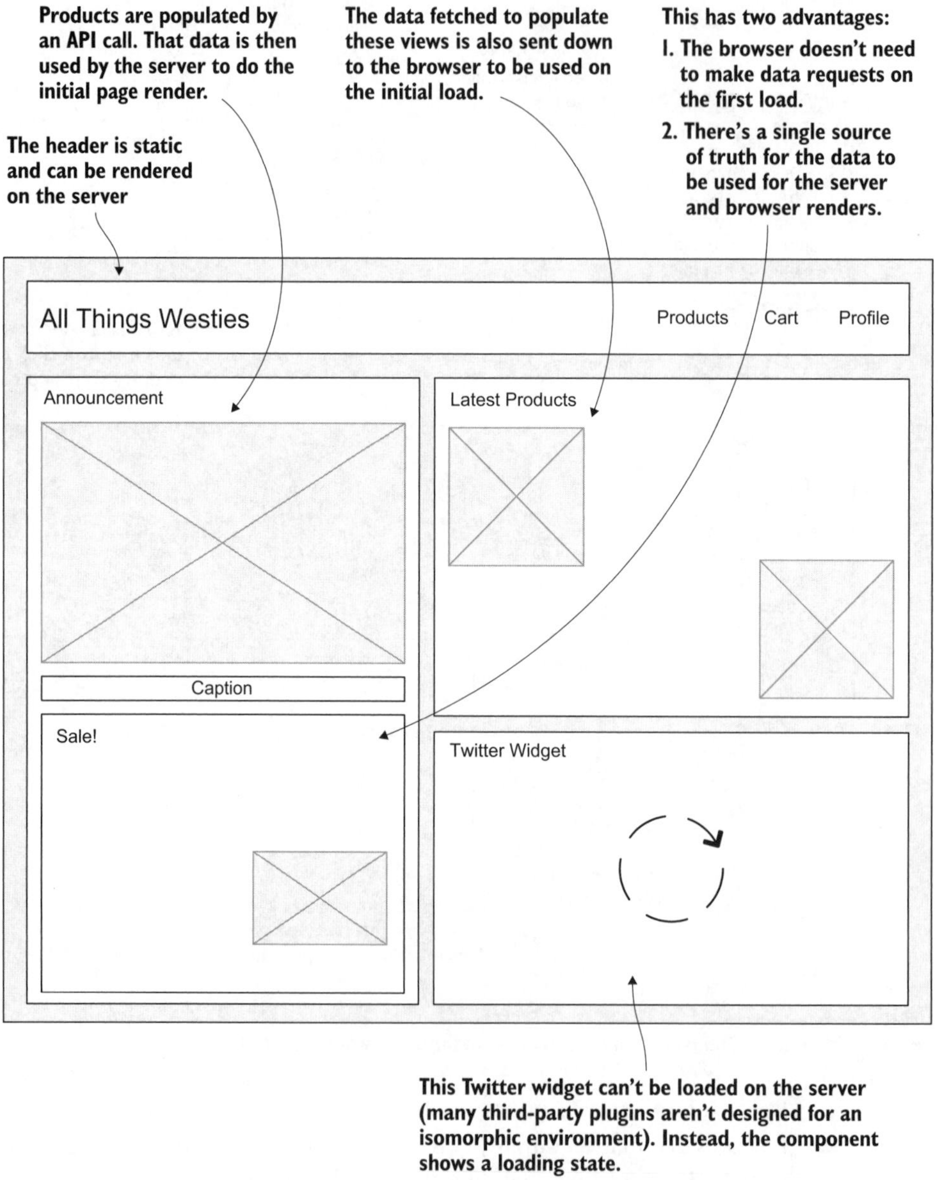
Products are populated by an API call. That data is then used by the server to do the initial page render.
The data fetched to populate these views is also sent down to the browser to be used on the initial load.
This has two advantages:
1. The browser doesn't need to make data requests on the first load.
2. There's a single source of truth for the data to be used for the server and browser renders.
The header is static and can be rendered on the server
All Things Westies
Products
Cart
Profile
Announcement
Latest Products
Caption
Sale!
Twitter Widget
This Twitter widget can't be loaded on the server (many third-party plugins aren't designed for an isomorphic environment). Instead, the component shows a loading state.

Figure 1.4 The server-rendered version of the All Things Westies homepage

The server does three important things. First, it fetches the data required for the view. Then it takes that data and uses it to render the DOM. Finally, it attaches that data to the DOM so the browser can read in the app state. Figure 1.5 shows the flow on the server.

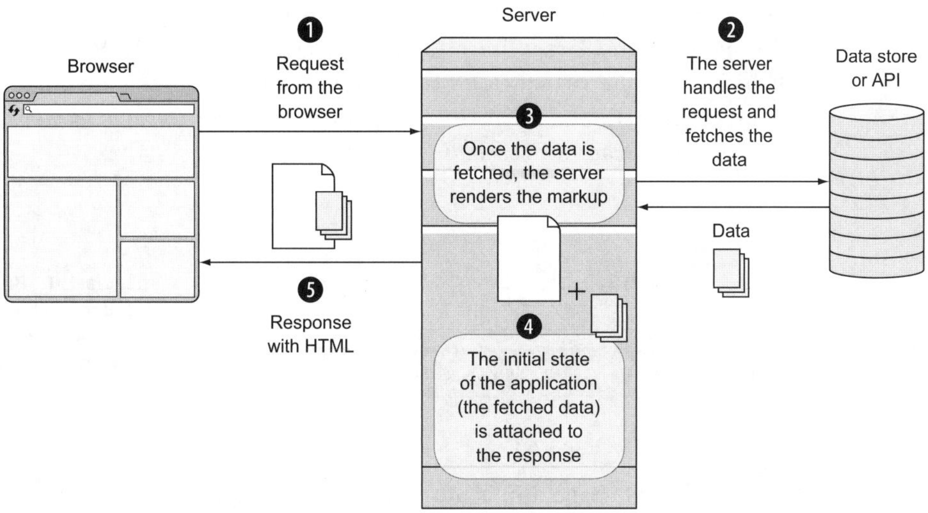
Server
1
Request from the browser
Browser
2
The server handles the request and fetches the data
Data store or API
3
Once the data is fetched, the server renders the markup
Data
5
Response with HTML
4
The initial state of the application (the fetched data) is attached to the response

Figure 1.5 App flow for the initial server render

Let's step through the flow:

1. The server receives a request.
2. The server fetches the required data for that request. This can be from either a persistent data store such as a MySQL or NoSQL database or from an external API.
3. After the data is received, the server can build the HTML. It generates the markup with React's virtual DOM via React's `renderToString` method.
4. The server injects the data from step 2 into your HTML so the browser can access it later.
5. The server responds to the request with your fully built HTML.

1.2.3 *Rendering in the browser*

Now let's look more closely at what happens in the browser. Figure 1.6 shows the flow in the browser, from the point the browser receives the HTML to the point it bootstraps the app:

1. The browser starts to render the mugs page immediately because the HTML sent by the server is fully formed with all the content you generated on the

server. This includes the header and the footer of your app along with the list of mugs for purchase. *The app won't respond to user input yet. Things like adding a mug to the cart or viewing the detail page for a specific mug won't work.*

2 When the browser reaches the JavaScript entry for our application, the application bootstraps.
3 The virtual DOM is re-created in React. Because the server sent down the app state, this virtual DOM is identical to the current DOM.
4 Nothing happens! React finds no differences between the DOM and the virtual DOM it built (the virtual DOM is explained in depth in chapter 3). The user is already being shown the list of mugs in the browser. *The application can now respond to user input, such as adding a mug to the cart.*

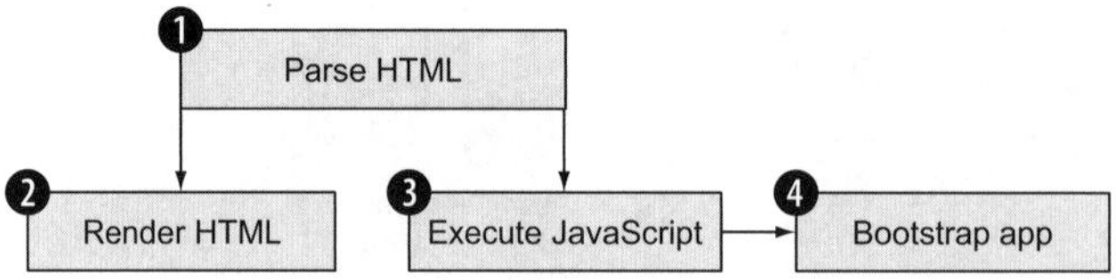
1
Parse HTML
2
Render HTML
3
Execute JavaScript
4
Bootstrap app

Figure 1.6 Browser render and bootstrap—between steps 1 and 4, the app won't respond to user input.

This is when the single-page application flow kicks in again. This is the most straightforward part. It handles user events, makes XHR calls, and updates the application as needed.

1.3 Advantages of isomorphic app architecture

At this point, you may be thinking this sounds complicated. You may be wondering why this approach to building a web app would ever be worth it. There are several compelling reasons to go down this path:

- Simplified and improved SEO—bots and crawlers can read all the data on page load.
- Performance gains in user-perceived performance.
- Maintenance gains.
- Improved accessibility because the user can view the app without JavaScript.

Isomorphic app architecture also has challenges and trade-offs. There's increased complexity in managing and deploying code running in multiple environments. Debugging and testing are more complicated. Server-rendered HTML via Node.js and React can be slow for views that have many components. For example, a page that displays many items for sale might quickly end up with hundreds of React components. As this number increases, the speed at which React can build these components on the server declines. First, I'll cover the benefits of building an isomorphic app. Let's start by discussing SEO.

1.3.1 SEO benefits

Our example app, All Things Westies, is an e-commerce site, so to be successful it needs shoppers! And it needs good SEO to maximize the number of people who come to the app from search engines. Single-page applications are difficult for search-engine bots to crawl because they don't load the data for the app until after the JavaScript has run in the browser. Isomorphic apps also need to bootstrap after JavaScript is run, but because their content is rendered by the server, neither users nor bots have to wait for the application to bootstrap in order to see the content of the site.

> **DEFINITION** *Bootstrapping* an application means running the code required to get everything set up. This code is run only once on the initial load of the application and is run from the entry point of the browser application.

On the All Things Westies app, you want to make sure all the SEO-relevant content is fetched on the server so you don't rely on the SEO crawlers to try to render your page. Crawlers (both searchbots such as Google or Bing and sharebots such as Facebook) either can't run all this code or don't want to wait long enough for this code to run. For example, Google will try to run JavaScript but penalizes sites that take too long for the content to load. That can be seen in the warning shown in figure 1.7. This warning shows up when you enter a URL for a single-page application into the Google PageSpeed Insights tool.

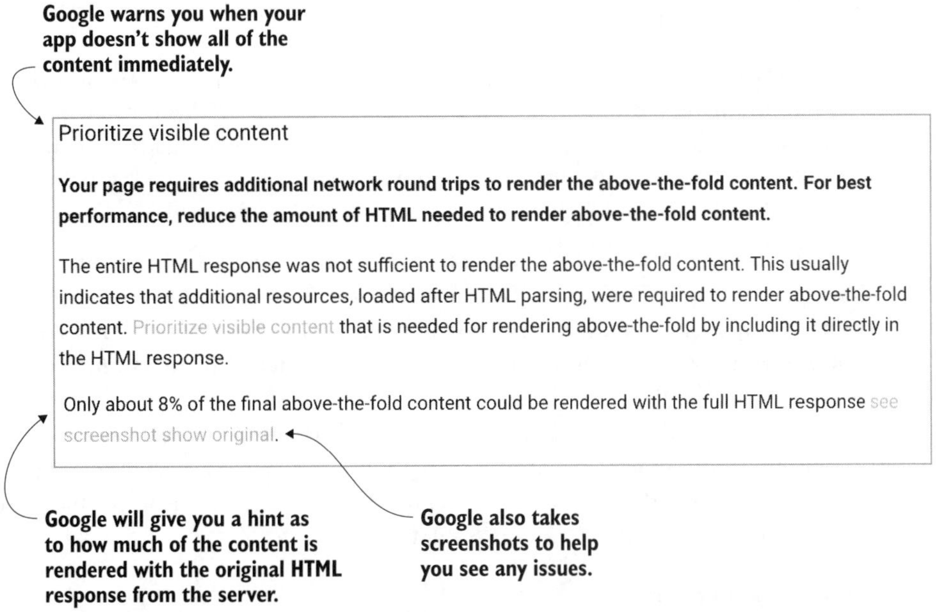
Google warns you when your app doesn't show all of the content immediately.
Prioritize visible content
Your page requires additional network round trips to render the above-the-fold content. For best performance, reduce the amount of HTML needed to render above-the-fold content.
The entire HTML response was not sufficient to render the above-the-fold content. This usually indicates that additional resources, loaded after HTML parsing, were required to render above-the-fold content. Prioritize visible content that is needed for rendering above-the-fold by including it directly in the HTML response.
Only about 8% of the final above-the-fold content could be rendered with the full HTML response see screenshot show original.
Google will give you a hint as to how much of the content is rendered with the original HTML response from the server.
Google also takes screenshots to help you see any issues.

Figure 1.7 Google PageSpeed Insights presents a warning for a single-page application. The application makes too many AJAX calls to fetch visible content after the initial load of the page.

> **Google PageSpeed Insights tool**
>
> Google's PageSpeed Insights tool helps measure how your page is doing on a scale of 0 to 100. You get a score for both speed-related issues (size of images, size of JavaScript, magnification, round trips made, and so forth) and UI (size of click areas, for example). Test it on your web app at https://developers.google.com/speed/pagespeed/insights.
>
> Google also has the Lighthouse tool (available as a Chrome extension or command-line tool), which will run an in-depth analysis of pages on your site. It makes recommendations on everything from performance, to using service workers to allow offline use, to improved accessibility for screen readers. You can learn more about Lighthouse at https://developers.google.com/web/tools/lighthouse/.

If you don't deal with this warning, you may end up with a lower ranking and fewer customers. Also, there's no guarantee that any page content that relies on API calls will be run by the crawler. Whole services have popped into existence to solve this problem for single-page apps. Dev teams pour time into developing systems to crawl and prerender their pages. They then redirect bots to these prerendered pages. These systems are complex and brittle to maintain.

Personally, I can't wait for the day when crawlers and bots will be able to get to all our content regardless of when the data is fetched (on the server or in the browser). Until that day, server-rendering the initial content gives a big advantage over single-page application rendering. This is especially true for above-the-fold content and any other content that has SEO benefits.

> **DEFINITION** *Above-the-fold* is a term that comes from the newspaper business. It refers to all the content that shows on the front page when a newspaper is folded in half and sitting on a newsstand. For web apps, this term is used to refer to all the content that's in the viewable area of a user's screen when the app loads. To see below-the-fold content, the user must scroll.

In addition to SEO crawlers, many social sites and apps that allow inline website previews (for example, Facebook, Twitter, Slack, or WhatsApp), also use bots that don't run JavaScript. These sites assume that all content that's available to build a social card or inline preview will be available on the server-rendered page. Isomorphic apps are ideal for handling the social bot use case.

At the beginning of this section, I mentioned that both bots and users don't need to wait for the isomorphic application to bootstrap to see the dynamic content. Another way to say that is that the perceived performance of isomorphic web apps is fast. The next section describes this in detail.

1.3.2 Performance benefits

Users want to see the content of All Things Westies right away. Otherwise, they'll get impatient and leave before seeing all the products and information being offered.

Loading an SPA can be a slow experience for a user (especially on mobile phones). Even though the browser may connect quickly to your application, it takes time to run the startup code and fetch the content, which leaves the user waiting. In the best-case scenario, SPAs display loading indicators and messaging for the user. In the worst-case scenario, there's no visual feedback, and the user is left wondering whether anything is happening.

Figure 1.8 shows what All Things Westies would look like during the initial rendering if it were a single-page application. Instead of seeing all content immediately, you'd see loading spinners in all of the content areas.

A server-rendered page displays its content (all the HTML, images, CSS, and data for your site) to the user as soon as the browser receives and renders the HTML. This leads to content being seen by the user several seconds faster than in an SPA.

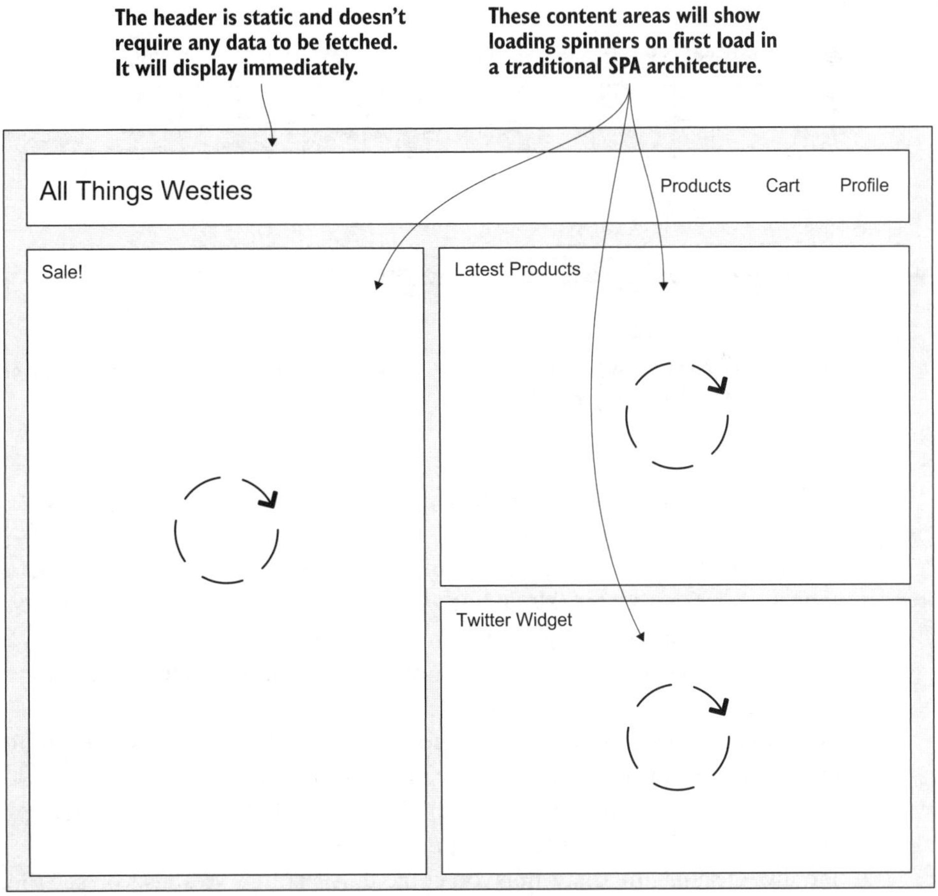
The header is static and doesn't require any data to be fetched. It will display immediately.
These content areas will show loading spinners on first load in a traditional SPA architecture.
All Things Westies
Products
Cart
Profile
Sale!
Latest Products
Twitter Widget

Figure 1.8 In a single-page app version of All Things Westies, spinners would be shown during the first load instead of the real content.

Although the site still requires JavaScript to be loaded and executed before user interactions can take place, this fast load allows the user to start visually processing your content quickly. This is called *perceived performance.* The app content is presented to the user quickly. The user isn't aware that JavaScript is being run in the background.

When this process is executed well, the user will never know that the JavaScript loaded after the view rendered. For all practical purposes, your user has a great experience because they believe the app loaded fast. This greatly reduces the need for loading spinners or other waiting states on the first load of the app. This leads to happier users. Figure 1.9 demonstrates the differences between SPA and isomorphic apps.

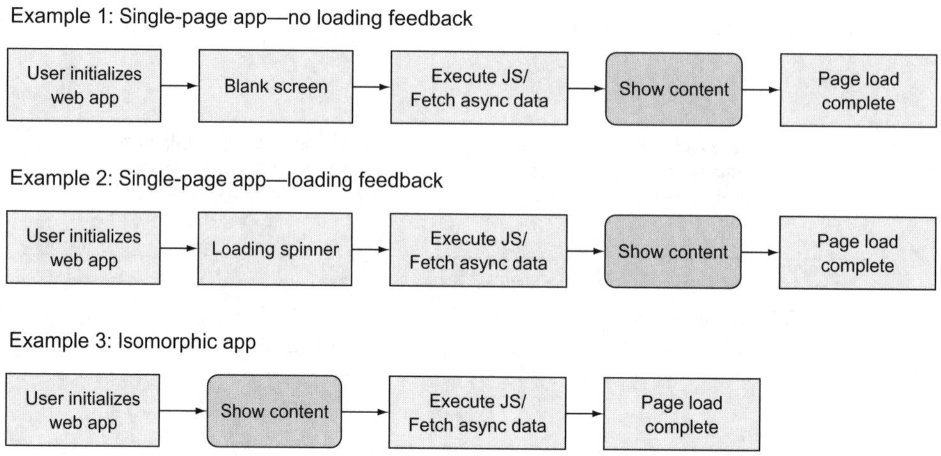
Example 1: Single-page app—no loading feedback
User initializes web app
Blank screen
Execute JS/ Fetch async data
Show content
Page load complete
Example 2: Single-page app—loading feedback
User initializes web app
Loading spinner
Execute JS/ Fetch async data
Show content
Page load complete
Example 3: Isomorphic app
User initializes web app
Show content
Execute JS/ Fetch async data
Page load complete

Figure 1.9 Comparison of when the user sees the content of a web app. An isomorphic app displays its content much sooner than a single-page app.

Now I'll walk you through the single-page app and isomorphic scenarios in detail. You can see these flows in figure 1.9 as well.

First, look at example 1. Imagine going to our example web app and being shown a blank screen for six seconds. What would you do? How likely are you to get frustrated and give up on using that web app? If you were looking to buy a pair of Westie socks, you'd be inclined to give up on All Things Westies and take your business elsewhere.

Now imagine that the web app still took six seconds to load (as in example 2), but this time it showed you a basic structure (a loading spinner) to let you know that the web app is doing something but you can't interact with it yet, just as in figure 1.8 previously. Are you willing to wait for this site to load?

Finally, let's imagine that when you come to All Things Westies, you see the content in under two seconds, as shown in example 3. This flow matches that of figure 1.1 at the beginning of the chapter. This time, your brain starts processing the information as soon as it's displayed. You don't feel like you had to wait. In the background, the app is still loading and working to get everything set up, but you don't have to wait for this to finish before being able to see the content.

Notice that the app is able to show content much earlier in the page-load flow. Although the page-load time as measured by performance metrics will be the same in all three approaches, the user *perceives* the performance of an isomorphic app to be much faster.

1.3.3 No JavaScript? No problem!

Another user-facing benefit of isomorphic app architecture is that you can serve portions of your site without requiring JavaScript. Users who can't or don't want to run JavaScript can still benefit from using your site when it's built isomorphically. Because you serve a complete page to the browser, users can at least see your content despite not being able to interact with the app.

This allows you to use progressive enhancement to better provide for users across a spectrum of browsers and devices. Although it may be unlikely to encounter a user with no JavaScript running, there are other good reasons for loading a full page from the server. For example, if you support older browsers or devices, isomorphic apps are good tools for providing the best experience possible across a multitude of browser/device/OS combinations.

We've covered the user-facing benefit of isomorphic apps. Next we'll look at the developer benefits that come with this architecture.

1.3.4 Maintenance and developer benefits

When building an isomorphic app, most of the code can be run on both the server and the browser. If you want to render a view, you need to write your code only once. If you want to have helper functions for a common task in the app, you need to write this logic only once, and it'll run in both places.

This is an advantage over apps that have server-side code written in one language and browser code written in JavaScript. Developers can keep their focus without having to switch between languages. Builds, environment management, and dependencies are all simplified, which makes your overall workflow cleaner.

This isn't to say that building isomorphic apps is easy. Writing everything in one language comes with its own set of problems.

1.3.5 Challenges and trade-offs

Choosing to build an app with isomorphic web architecture isn't without trade-offs. For one, it requires a new way of thinking, which takes time to adjust to. The good news is that's what you'll learn in this book. Some of the challenges include the following:

- Handling the differences between Node.js and the browser
- Debugging and testing complexity
- Managing performance on the server

HANDLING THE DIFFERENCES BETWEEN THE SERVER AND THE BROWSER

Node.js has no concept of a window or document. The browser doesn't know about Node.js environment variables and has no idea what a request or response object is. Both environments know about cookies, but they handle them in different ways. In chapter 10, you'll look at strategies for dealing with these environment tensions.

DEBUGGING AND TESTING COMPLEXITY

All your code needs to be tested twice: loaded directly off the server and as part of the single-page flow. Debugging requires mastery of both browser and server debugging tools and knowing whether a bug is happening on the server, on the browser, or in both environments. Additionally, a thorough unit-testing strategy is needed, where tests are written and run in the appropriate environments. Server-only code should be tested in Node.js, but shared code should be tested in all the environments where it'll eventually be run.

MANAGING PERFORMANCE ON THE SERVER

Performance on the server also presents a challenge as the React-provided `renderToString` method is slow to execute on complex pages with many components. In chapter 11, I'll show you how to optimize your code as much as possible without breaking React best practices. We'll also discuss caching as a tool to minimize issues with server performance.

At this point, you understand the benefits and trade-offs that come with isomorphic app architecture. Next let's take an in-depth look at how to execute an isomorphic app.

1.4 Building the view with React

React is one of the pieces that makes building an isomorphic web app possible. *React* is a library, open sourced by Facebook, for creating user interfaces (the view layer in your app). React makes it easy to express your views via HTML and JavaScript. It provides a simple API that's easy to get up and running but that's designed to be composable in order to facilitate building user interfaces quickly and efficiently. Like many other view libraries and implementations, React provides a template language (JSX) and hooks into commonly used parts of the DOM and JavaScript.

React also takes advantage of functional concepts by adhering to single-direction data flows from the top-level component down to its children. What makes it appealing for isomorphic apps is how it uses a virtual DOM to manage changes and updates to the application.

React isn't a framework like Angular or Ember. It only provides the code you use to write your view components. It can fit easily into a Model-View-Controller (MVC) style architecture as the view. But there's a recommended way to build complex React apps, which is covered throughout the book.

The *virtual DOM* is a representation of the browser DOM written with JavaScript. At its core, React is composed of React elements. Since React introduced the virtual DOM to the web community, this idea has started to show up in many major libraries and frameworks. Some people are even writing their own virtual DOM implementations.

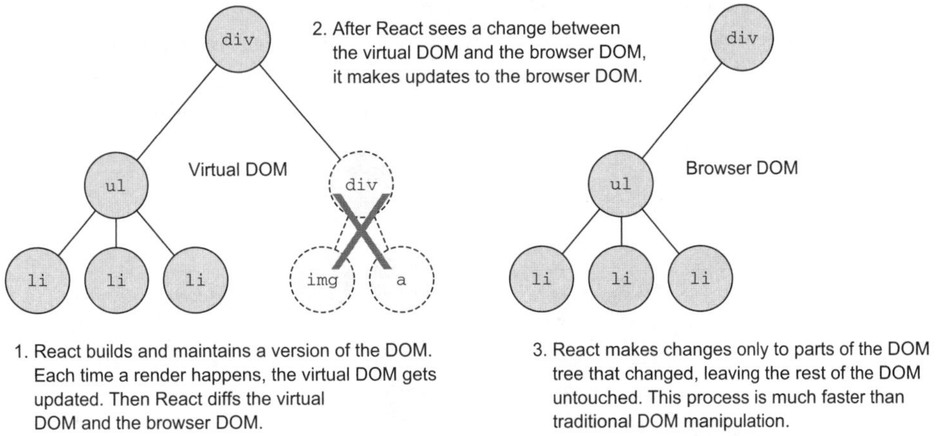
2. After React sees a change between the virtual DOM and the browser DOM, it makes updates to the browser DOM.
div
ul
Virtual DOM
div
li
li
li
img
a
div
ul
Browser DOM
li
li
li
1. React builds and maintains a version of the DOM. Each time a render happens, the virtual DOM gets updated. Then React diffs the virtual DOM and the browser DOM.
3. React makes changes only to parts of the DOM tree that changed, leaving the rest of the DOM untouched. This process is much faster than traditional DOM manipulation.

Figure 1.10 Comparing the DOM trees: the virtual DOM changes are compared to the browser DOM. Then React intelligently updates the browser DOM tree based on the calculated diff.

Like the browser DOM, the virtual DOM is a tree comprising a root node and its child nodes. After the virtual DOM is created, React compares the virtual tree to the current tree and calculates the updates it needs to make to the browser DOM. If nothing has changed, no update is made. If changes have occurred, React updates only the parts of the browser's DOM that have changed. Figure 1.10 shows what happens at this point. On the left, the virtual DOM has been updated to remove the right subtree with the `<div>` tag whose children are an `<img>` tag and an `<a>` tag. This results in these same children being removed from the browser DOM.

React uses JavaScript to represent DOM nodes. In JavaScript, this is written as follows:

```
let myDiv = React.createElement('div');
```

When a React render occurs, each component returns a series of React elements. Together they form the virtual DOM, a JavaScript representation of the DOM tree.

Because the virtual DOM is a JavaScript representation of the browser DOM and isn't dependent on browser-provided objects such as the window and document (although certain code paths may depend on these items), it can be rendered on the server. But rendering a DOM on the server wouldn't work. Instead, React provides a way to output the rendered DOM as a string (`ReactDOM.renderToString`). This string can be used to build a complete HTML page that's served from your server to the user.

1.5 Business logic and model: Redux

In real-world web apps, you need a way to manage the data flow. Redux provides an application state implementation that works nicely with React. It's important to note that you don't have to use Redux with React, or vice versa, but their concepts mesh well because they both use functional programming ideas. Using Redux and React together is also a community best practice.

Like React, Redux follows a single-direction flow of data. Redux holds the state of your app in its store, providing a single source of truth for your application. To update this store, *actions* (JavaScript objects that represent a discrete change of app state) are dispatched from the views. These actions, in turn, trigger reducers. *Reducers* are pure functions (a function with no side effects) that take in a change and return a new store after responding to the change. Figure 1.11 shows this flow.

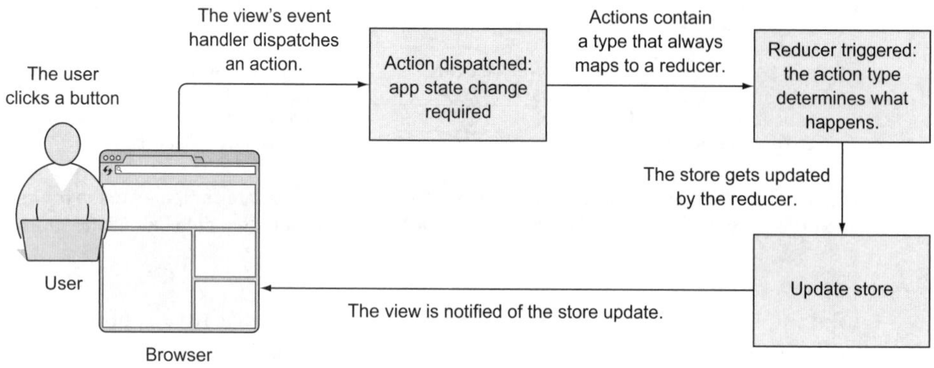
The view's event handler dispatches an action.
Actions contain a type that always maps to a reducer.
The user clicks a button
Action dispatched: app state change required
Reducer triggered: the action type determines what happens.
The store gets updated by the reducer.
User
Update store
The view is notified of the store update.
Browser

Figure 1.11 The view (React) uses Redux to update the app state when the user takes an action. Redux then lets the view know when it should update based on the new app state.

The key thing to remember about Redux is that only reducers can update the store. All other components can only read from the store. Additionally, the store is immutable. This is enforced via the reducers. I cover this again in chapter 2 and do a full Redux explanation in chapter 6.

The ability to transfer state between server and browser is important in an isomorphic app. Redux's store provides top-level state. By relying on a single root object to hold your application state, you can easily serialize your state on the server and send it down to the browser to be deserialized. Chapter 7 covers this topic in more detail. The final piece of the app is the build tool. The next section gives an overview of webpack.

1.6 Building the app: webpack

Webpack is a powerful build tool that makes packaging code into a single bundle easy. It has a plugin system in the form of loaders, allowing simple access to tools such as Babel for ES6 compiling or Less/Sass/PostCSS compiling. It also lets you package Node.js module code (npm packages) into the bundle that will be run in the browser.

> **DEFINITION** There are many names for current and future JavaScript versions (ES6, ES2015, ES2016, ES7, ES Next). To keep things consistent, I refer to modern JavaScript that's not yet 100% adopted in browsers as *ES6*.

This is key for our isomorphic app. By using webpack, you can bundle all your dependencies together and take advantage of the ecosystem of libraries available via npm, the Node package manager. This allows you to share nearly all the code in your app with both environments—the browser and the server.

> **NOTE** You won't use webpack for our Node.js code. That's unnecessary, as you can write most ES6 code on Node.js, and Node.js can already take advantage of environment variables and npm packages.

Webpack also lets you use environment variables inside your bundled code. This is important for our isomorphic app. Although you want to share as much code between environments as possible, some code from the browser can't run on the server, and vice versa. On a Node.js server, you can take advantage of an environment variable like this:

```
if (NODE_ENV.IS_BROWSER) { // execute code }
```

But this code won't run in the browser because it has no concept of Node.js environment variables. You can use webpack to inject a `NODE_ENV` object into your webpacked code, so this code can run in both environments. Chapter 5 covers this concept in depth.

Summary

In this chapter, you learned that isomorphic web apps are the result of combining server-rendered HTML pages with single-page application architecture. Doing so has several advantages but does require learning a new way of thinking about web app architecture. The next chapter presents a high-level overview of an isomorphic application.

- Isomorphic web apps blend server-side architecture and single-page app architecture to provide a better overall experience for users. This leads to improved perceived performance, simplified SEO, and developer benefits.
- Being able to run JavaScript on the server (Node.js) and in the browser allows you to write code once and deploy it to both environments. React's virtual DOM lets you render HTML on the server.
- Redux helps you manage application state and easily serialize this state to be sent from the server to the browser.
- By building your app with webpack, you can use Node.js code in the browser and flag code to run only in the browser.

2 A sample isomorphic app

This chapter covers

- Setting up your build to work on the server and the browser
- Rendering the views
- Fetching data with Redux
- Handling the request on the server
- Serializing the data on the server
- Deserializing the data on the browser

In this chapter, I'm going to walk you through all the key parts of an isomorphic app built with React, Redux, Babel, and webpack. Think of this chapter as an opportunity to dip your feet in before taking the full plunge. You won't need to understand all the details, but by the end you'll have a sense of how all the pieces fit into the app, and that will provide you context for working through the rest of the book.

If you're already proficient in building React apps, this chapter along with chapters 7 and 8 will get you started. If you're not already comfortable with React, I'll take you through React and the other building blocks for the app in chapters 3 through 6.

2.1 What you'll build in this chapter: recipes example app

First, let's look at the app you'll build in this chapter. Figure 2.1 shows the recipes app you'll construct. In this chapter, you'll build the homepage for the app, which will show a list of top recipes and a featured recipe. Getting all the pieces of your first isomorphic app together is an involved process, so for your first pass at building an isomorphic app, I'll keep the end goal simple.

This app will have a single route and won't handle any user interaction. Isomorphic architecture is overly complex for such a simple app, but the simplicity will allow me to present the core concepts. In later chapters (starting in chapter 4), I'll teach you how to build a more complex app with routing and user interaction.

In chapter 1, we went over the three main steps in an isomorphic app: server render, initial browser render, and single-page application behavior. In this chapter, you'll learn how to create an application that can take advantage of this render flow. You'll build the

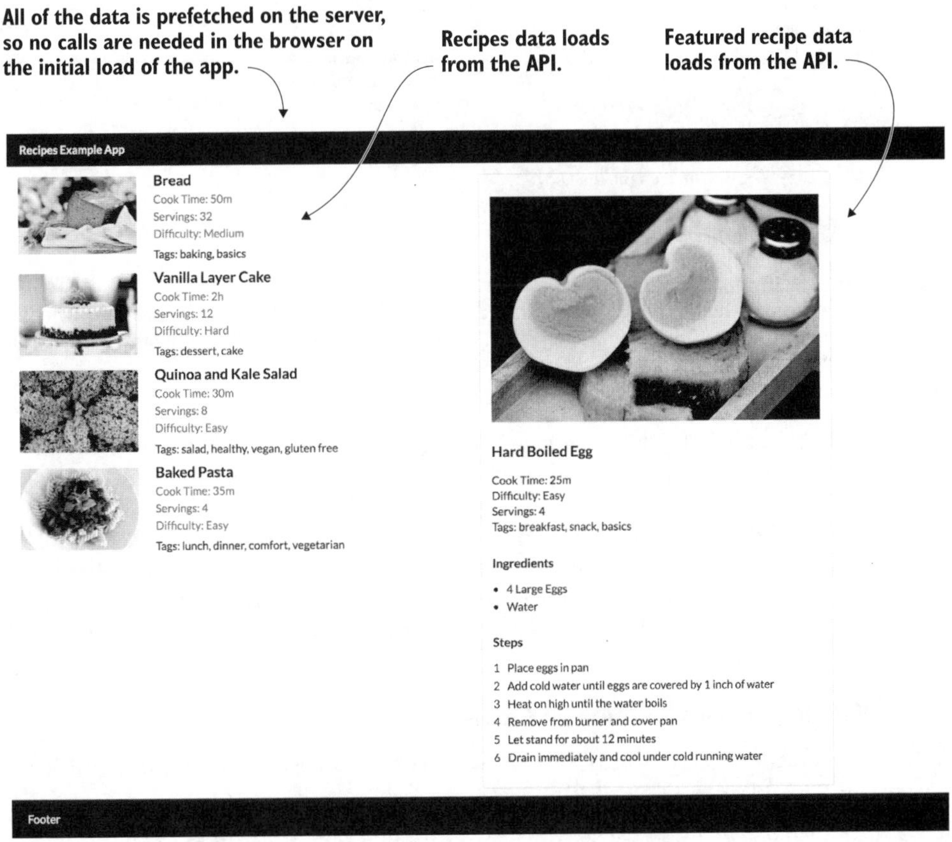
All of the data is prefetched on the server, so no calls are needed in the browser on the initial load of the app.
Recipes data loads from the API.
Featured recipe data loads from the API.
Recipes Example App
Bread
Cook Time: 50m
Servings: 32
Difficulty: Medium
Tags: baking, basics
Vanilla Layer Cake
Cook Time: 2h
Servings: 12
Difficulty: Hard
Tags: dessert, cake
Quinoa and Kale Salad
Cook Time: 30m
Servings: 8
Difficulty: Easy
Tags: salad, healthy, vegan, gluten free
Baked Pasta
Cook Time: 35m
Servings: 4
Difficulty: Easy
Tags: lunch, dinner, comfort, vegetarian
Hard Boiled Egg
Cook Time: 25m
Difficulty: Easy
Servings: 4
Tags: breakfast, snack, basics
Ingredients
4 Large Eggs
Water
Steps
1 Place eggs in pan
2 Add cold water until eggs are covered by 1 inch of water
3 Heat on high until the water boils
4 Remove from burner and cover pan
5 Let stand for about 12 minutes
6 Drain immediately and cool under cold running water
Footer

Figure 2.1 The home screen for the recipes app you'll build in this chapter

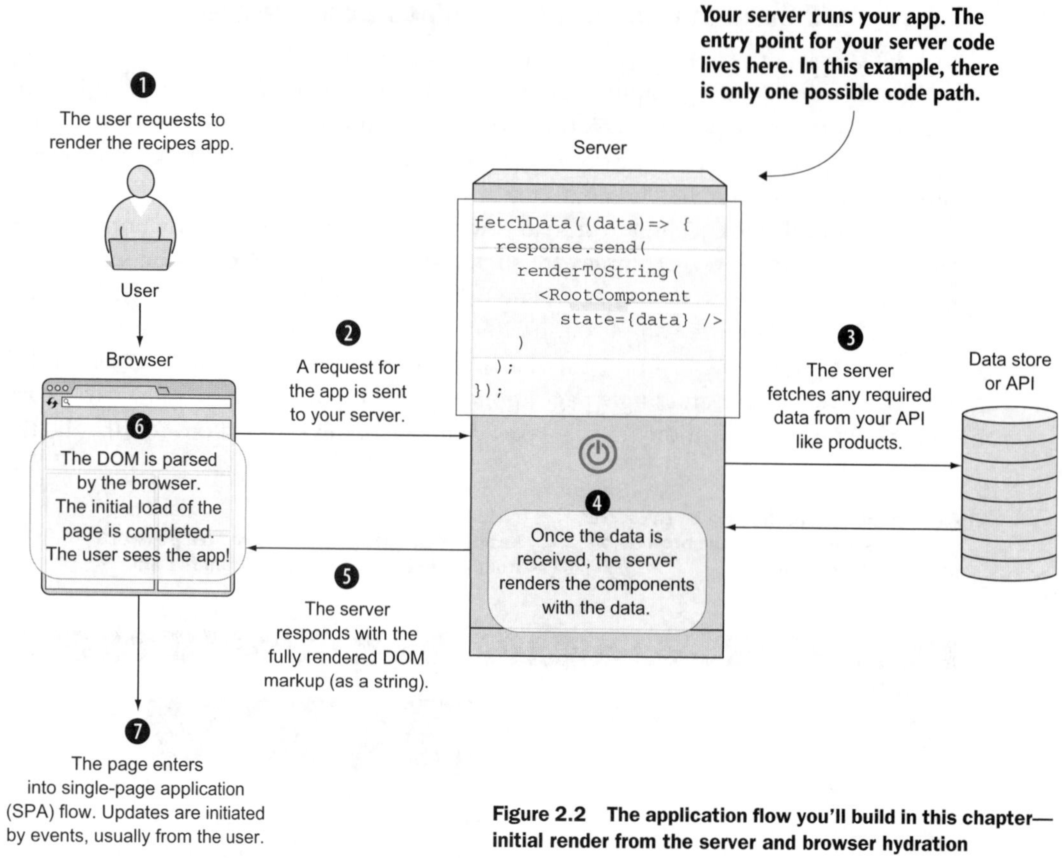

Your server runs your app. The entry point for your server code lives here. In this example, there is only one possible code path.
1
The user requests to render the recipes app.
User
Browser
Server
fetchData((data)=> {
response.send(
renderToString(
<RootComponent
state={data} />
)
);
});
2
A request for the app is sent to your server.
3
The server fetches any required data from your API like products.
Data store or API
6
The DOM is parsed by the browser. The initial load of the page is completed. The user sees the app!
4
Once the data is received, the server renders the components with the data.
5
The server responds with the fully rendered DOM markup (as a string).
7
The page enters into single-page application (SPA) flow. Updates are initiated by events, usually from the user.

Figure 2.2 The application flow you'll build in this chapter—initial render from the server and browser hydration

server, serialize the data, hydrate the data on the browser, and render the browser view. Figure 2.2 shows how the pieces that you'll build in this chapter fit together.

> **DEFINITION** *Serializing* occurs when you take JSON and turn it into a string. This string is easy to send between applications and can be sent to the browser as part of the server response. *Hydrating* (or *deserializing*) the data means taking the string and converting it back into a JSON object that can be used by the app in the browser.

2.1.1 Building blocks: libraries and tools

To write the recipes app and make it run as an isomorphic app, you'll use several JavaScript libraries:

- *Babel and webpack*—Compilation and build tools. Babel will compile the code into a version understood by the JavaScript compiler regardless of browser implementation. Webpack will allow you to bundle code for the browser, including libraries that are installed via npm (Node packet manager).

- *Express*—Enables simple server-side routing for rendering the view.
- *React and Redux*—The view and the business logic. You'll write your React components using a template language called JSX, which is the standard for React. It looks a lot like HTML but allows you to insert logic and variables into your view code.
- *Semantic UI*—Simplify the CSS by providing a standard set of classes. The focus of this book isn't CSS, so this will make following along in the various examples easier.

Semantic UI for layout and CSS

Semantic UI is a CSS library that provides basic styling and predefined layouts, components, and grids. I've used Semantic UI's CSS for the layout in the view for the recipes example app. Documentation on Semantic UI can be found at http://semantic-ui.com.

Before you get started building and running the code, let's look at what parts of the code run on the server, on the browser, and on both environments. Figure 2.3 maps the various parts of the app (React components, Redux actions and reducers, entry points for the server and browser) to the environments they run in. Some code (for example, React and Redux) will run in both environments. Other code is specific to either the server or browser (for example, Express for the server).

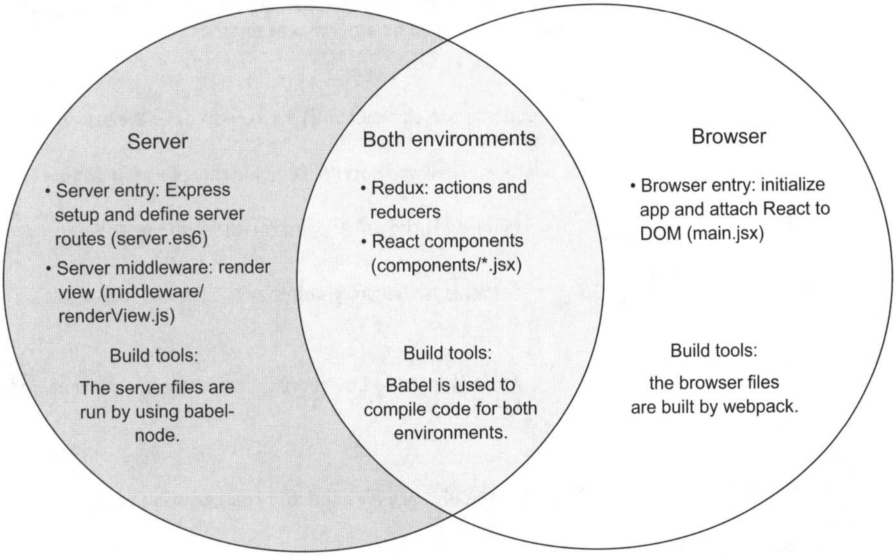
Server
• Server entry: Express setup and define server routes (server.es6)
• Server middleware: render view (middleware/renderView.js)
Build tools:
The server files are run by using babel-node.
Both environments
• Redux: actions and reducers
• React components (components/*.jsx)
Build tools:
Babel is used to compile code for both environments.
Browser
• Browser entry: initialize app and attach React to DOM (main.jsx)
Build tools:
the browser files are built by webpack.

Figure 2.3 An overview of how the various libraries and build tools are used across the two environments the code runs in (server and browser). The files listed here can be found in the code example. See the next section for instructions on downloading the code.

The diagram also demonstrates what build tools are used for which environments. Webpack will be used to build only the browser code. The server code will be built with npm scripts. Babel is used in both environments.

2.1.2 Download the example code

You can download the code for this example from GitHub at https://github.com/isomorphic-dev-js/chapter2-a-sample-isomorphic-app.git. I recommend you do so, as all the required packages and code are already set up for you, and you can easily follow along.

To check out the code from GitHub, run the following command inside the directory you want to clone the project into:

```
$ git clone https://github.com/isomorphic-dev-js/chapter2-a-sample-
    isomorphic-app.git
```

> **TIP** If you need help getting started with Git, *Learn Git in a Month of Lunches* by Rick Umali (Manning, 2015) is a good resource.

Look at the key folders and files in the app. Figure 2.4 shows the core folder structure of the app (other files and folders are also in the repo, but the figure calls out what's relevant for this chapter). You can map this to the environments shown in figure 2.3. The entry points for the server (app.es6) and the browser (main.jsx) are of particular importance because all the code that's environment specific will go in these files.

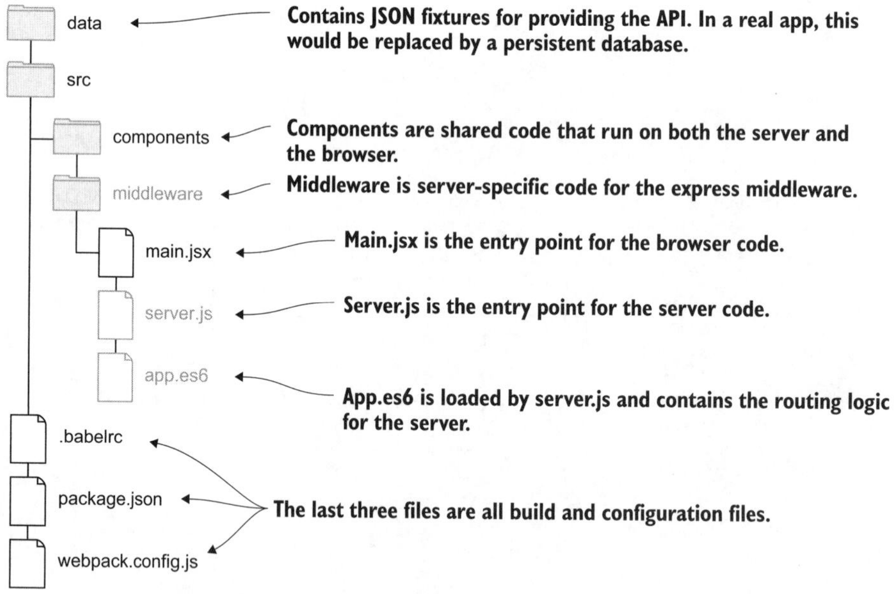
data
Contains JSON fixtures for providing the API. In a real app, this would be replaced by a persistent database.
src
components
Components are shared code that run on both the server and the browser.
middleware
Middleware is server-specific code for the express middleware.
main.jsx
Main.jsx is the entry point for the browser code.
server.js
Server.js is the entry point for the server code.
app.es6
App.es6 is loaded by server.js and contains the routing logic for the server.
.babelrc
package.json
webpack.config.js
The last three files are all build and configuration files.

Figure 2.4 Folder organization and top-level build and configuration files. A subset view of the folder structure for the recipes app that shows what files pertain to build and tools, the server, and the browser.

2.2 Tools

After you've cloned the repo, it's time to run the app. The code for this chapter includes a simple Node.js server that will render the recipes app homepage. The Node.js server will also serve up the data for the recipes. For this example, the recipes will be loaded from a JSON file. In the real world, you'd want to use a database or API to be able to persist the data.

To get everything up and running for the recipes app, you'll learn about the following:

- Setting up the development environment and installing packages with npm
- Compiling and running the server code with Babel
- Building the browser code with webpack
- Handling multiple code entry points

2.2.1 Setting up the environment and installing packages

You'll be using Node.js to run the web server. It's suitable for many use cases but especially good for isomorphic apps, as it allows you to write the entire stack of the application in JavaScript.

Node.js download and docs

This chapter assumes that you have basic familiarity with Node.js and have already installed it on your machine. To get the latest version of Node.js and stay up-to-date on the docs, visit https://nodejs.org. Node.js comes with npm.

I'm running Node.js version 6.9.2. If you run a major version lower than 6, you may need additional Babel packages that aren't covered in this book. If you run a major version higher than 6, you may not need all the Babel packages included.

Before you get started running the server, you need to install all the npm packages for this example. You'll find a list of all npm packages as well as documentation for the packages listed in tables 2.1 and 2.2 at www.npmjs.com. The packages needed for the recipes app are already provided in the package.json of the project. To install them, run the following command in your terminal:

```
$ npm install
```

Two groups of packages get installed:

- devDependencies includes build tools such as Babel and webpack. Packages in the devDependencies section of package.json don't get installed when the `NODE_ENV` variable is set to `production`. See table 2.1 for additional information.
- dependencies include any libraries that are required to run the application. See table 2.2 for additional information.

Table 2.1 List of devDependencies (for building and compiling the app)

Package	Description
babel-core	The main Babel compiler package. More information at https://babeljs.io.
babel-cli	The Babel command-line tool. Used to compile the server code.
babel-loader	Webpack loader for using Babel with webpack.
babel-preset-es2015, babel-preset-react, babel-plugin-transform-es2015-destructuring, babel-plugin-transform-es2015-parameters, babel-plugin-transform-object-rest-spread	Babel has many preset options, so we include the ones relevant to this project. These packages include rules for React, ES6, and compiling JSX.
css-loader	Webpack loader for using CSS inside webpacked files.
style-loader	Webpack loader for using CSS inside webpacked files.
webpack	A build tool for compiling JavaScript code. Enables the use of ES6 and JSX in the browser as well as the use of packages written for Node.js (as long as they're isomorphic). More information at https://webpack.js.org.

Table 2.2 Core dependencies for the recipes app

Package	Description
express	A Node.js web framework that provides routing and route-handling tools via middleware. More information at https://github.com/expressjs.
isomorphic-fetch	Enables the use of the fetch API in the browser and the server.
react	The main React package. More information at https://facebook.github.io/react/.
react-dom	The browser- and server-specific DOM-rendering implementations.
redux	Core Redux code.
react-redux	Provides support to connect React and Redux.
redux-thunk	Redux middleware.
redux-promise-middleware	Redux middleware that supports promises.

Open the code in your editor and find the package.json file. You'll see all the libraries listed in the preceding tables. Now that you understand the dependencies of the example app, you can set up and run the server.

2.2.2 *Running the server*

To get the server running (so you can test the API, as shown in figure 2.5), you first need to build the server code using Babel. You're probably wondering why you need to compile code for a language that's interpreted at runtime. This step is required for two reasons:

- *Writing the latest and greatest code with ES6 language features*—JavaScript is also known as ECMAScript (ES). ES6 is a recent version that adds many language features, including classes, maps, and promises. Most of the ES6 spec already runs on Node.js 6.9.2 or later. But if you want to use upcoming features from ES7 (the next version of JavaScript) or use the `import` statement instead of `require` statements, a compile is still required. The examples in the book take advantage of `import` statements.
- *Because the server will render components, you'll need to run JSX on the server*—JSX is the template language that React uses to declare the view. Node.js doesn't understand how to run JSX, so you'll need to compile the JSX into JavaScript before using it on the server. I discuss JSX later in the chapter.

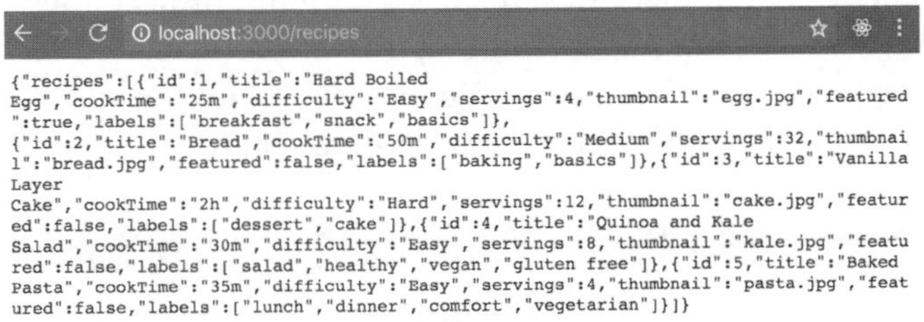
localhost:3000/recipes
{"recipes":[{"id":1,"title":"Hard Boiled
Egg","cookTime":"25m","difficulty":"Easy","servings":4,"thumbnail":"egg.jpg","featured
":true,"labels":["breakfast","snack","basics"]},
{"id":2,"title":"Bread","cookTime":"50m","difficulty":"Medium","servings":32,"thumbnai
l":"bread.jpg","featured":false,"labels":["baking","basics"]},{"id":3,"title":"Vanilla
Layer
Cake","cookTime":"2h","difficulty":"Hard","servings":12,"thumbnail":"cake.jpg","featur
ed":false,"labels":["dessert","cake"]},{"id":4,"title":"Quinoa and Kale
Salad","cookTime":"30m","difficulty":"Easy","servings":8,"thumbnail":"kale.jpg","featu
red":false,"labels":["salad","healthy","vegan","gluten free"]},{"id":5,"title":"Baked
Pasta","cookTime":"35m","difficulty":"Easy","servings":4,"thumbnail":"pasta.jpg","feat
ured":false,"labels":["lunch","dinner","comfort","vegetarian"]}]}

Figure 2.5 Expected output from the recipes API endpoint after the server is running

> **NOTE** I use two extensions for files in the project instead of .js. For files written with ES6, I use the extension .es6 to indicate the need to compile the file with Babel. For files that include React components, I use .jsx to indicate the presence of a JSX template. This lets us pass only the files we want to the Babel compiler and also makes it easy to distinguish between working and compiled files. The .jsx extension is also picked up by some editors and IDEs as a signal to use different syntax highlighting.

To build and run the server, you use the Babel tools and configuration that are set up in the npm packages. Two additional pieces of code are required to make this all work. First, to use Babel, you need a Babel configuration. The best way to do that is to create a .babelrc configuration file. Inside .babelrc, I've called out two presets for the compiler to use: `es2015` and `react`. The following listing shows this code, which is already included in the repo.

Listing 2.1 Babel configuration—babelrc

```
{
  "presets": ["es2015", "react"],
  "plugins": [
    "transform-es2015-destructuring",
    "transform-es2015-parameters",
    "transform-object-rest-spread"
  ]
}
```

- **Packages that contain groups of plugins, making configuration easier and quicker** (presets)
- **Plugins are the base unit in Babel, and each plugin is responsible for one type of update.** (plugins)
- **Three plugins allow use of spread operator (...) so you can easily work with and update objects.**

The presets listed here map to the preset packages you installed earlier in the chapter. This will ensure that ES6 code and JSX template code are compiled properly.

> **NOTE** The babel-cli and related tools are powerful and flexible. Visit https://babeljs.io to find out what else Babel can do. For example, Babel supports sourcemaps for compiled files. Also, if you prefer different build tools, you can use Babel with most of the popular JavaScript build tools.

As for the other required piece of code, I've set up this project to use Babel inline in development mode on the server. You don't have to precompile any of the code to have it run on the server. The server.js file is just two lines of code. The following listing shows the code, which is already included in the repo.

Listing 2.2 Running the server with Babel—src/server.js

```
require('babel-register');
require('./app.es6');
```

- **Include Babel—it will parse all code that comes after it (not recommended for production use).** (line 1)
- **Include root application code for server.** (line 2)

With everything configured and set up, all you have to do to start the Node.js server is run the following:

```
$ npm start
```

The Node.js server is now running on localhost at port 3000. Load http://localhost:3000/recipes and you'll see a JSON object with several recipes. Sample output will look like the JSON object in figure 2.5. Remember, the server plays two roles in the recipes app: it renders the initial view and provides the data API.

Next, we'll explore how webpack uses Babel to create the browser code.

2.2.3 Building the code for the browser with webpack

Every time I learn a new build tool, I spend hours being frustrated, wondering why I'm ramping up on yet another library that may or may not give me long-term workflow improvements. Although webpack has a steep learning curve, the time I invested to learn it has been well worth it. Each time I've run into something new that I need to do with build scripts, I've found that webpack can get the job done. Additionally, it has a strong community and has become one of the top choices for modern web apps.

Webpack is a build tool that you can run from the command line and configure via a JavaScript configuration file. It supports a wide range of features:

- Using loaders to compile ES6 and JSX code and load static assets via loaders
- Code splitting for smart bundling of code into smaller packages
- Ability to build code for the server or the browser
- Out-of-the-box sourcemaps
- The webpack dev server
- Built-in watch option

You're going to use webpack to build the browser bundle. Unlike on Node.js, browser support for the latest version of JavaScript is inconsistent. To write code with ES6, I need to compile it into a format the browser can read (ES5). Also, as on the server, JSX must be compiled into a format that the JavaScript compiler can understand. To do that, you'll take advantage of the webpack config and then run that config via the npm script you saw in the previous section. To run the webpack script, you also run this:

```
$ npm start
```

The package.json includes a prestart script that runs the command for webpack.

> **NOTE** Although it's possible to build your Node.js server with webpack, that will present challenges for building and testing later and require you to run two Node.js servers. It's preferable to use webpack only for building the browser code.

As on the server, you'll use Babel to compile the code. The webpack configuration file is located at the top level of the project and is a JavaScript module. The code is already included in the repo. The following listing explains how it works.

Listing 2.3 Webpack configuration—webpack.config.js

```
module.exports = {
  entry: "./src/main.jsx",            <- Defines input starting point or entry path—file runs only on browser
  output: {
    path: __dirname + '/src/',        <- Output folder—the dist directory where we build all other files
    filename: "browser.js"            <- Output filename
  },
  module: {
    rules: [
      {
        test: /\.(jsx|es6)$/,         <- Regular expression that tells loader what files to apply loader to
        exclude: /node_modules/,      <- Excludes node_modules because these files are already compiled and production ready
```

```
          loader: "babel-loader"
        },
      ]
    },
    resolve: {
      extensions: ['.js', '.jsx', '.css', '.es6']
    }
  };
```

Defines loader to apply to matched files, for Babel to compile ES6 and JSX

Supported file extensions—empty file extension allows import statements with no extension (your src files have one extension but your compiled files have a different one)

You can also load any CSS you need via files included in webpack. To do that, you need to define a loader that will handle any `require` statements that include a .css extension. Because our app is isomorphic and you aren't using webpack for the server, it's important to include CSS only in files that will be loaded in the browser. In this case, the CSS include will be in main.jsx:

```
{test: /\.css$/,loaders: ['style-loader', 'css-loader']}
```

That's all you need for now. For a full intro to webpack, make sure to read chapter 5.

2.3 The view

This section and the following pieces explore the specific technologies that will be used to wire the app together. Figure 2.6 shows how each piece fits into the app lifecycle.

The key takeaway here is that the app lifecycle is single directional. Anytime the app state is updated, the view receives an update and displays it to the user (step 4). When the view receives user input, it notifies the app state (Redux) to make an update (step 2). The view doesn't worry about the implementation of the business logic, and app state doesn't worry about how it'll be displayed.

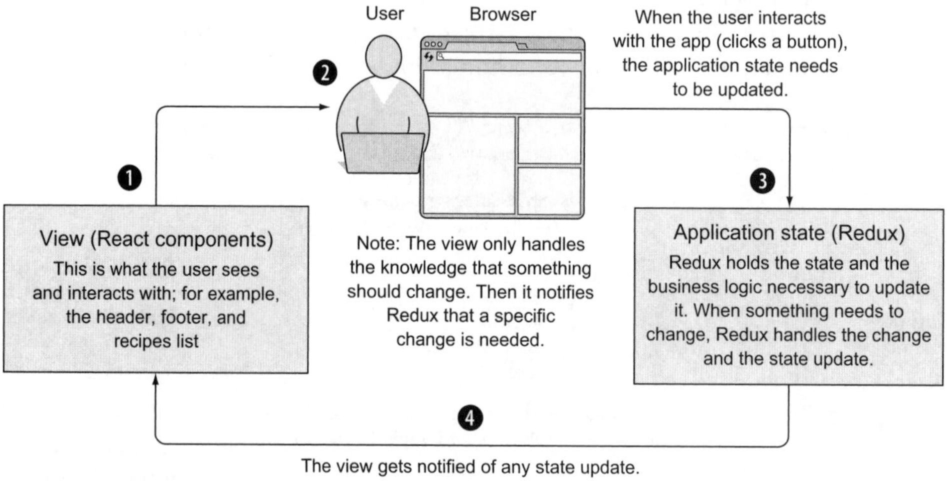
User
Browser
When the user interacts with the app (clicks a button), the application state needs to be updated.
2
1
3
View (React components)
This is what the user sees and interacts with; for example, the header, footer, and recipes list
Note: The view only handles the knowledge that something should change. Then it notifies Redux that a specific change is needed.
Application state (Redux)
Redux holds the state and the business logic necessary to update it. When something needs to change, Redux handles the change and the state update.
4
The view gets notified of any state update.

Figure 2.6 How React and Redux fit into the application flow

2.3.1 React and components

When building apps, the user interface is the most important piece. I enjoy building apps with great UIs. In these apps, users easily find what they're looking for and can interact with the app without frustration. React makes this process easier. I find that its concepts map well to the way I think about piecing together good UIs.

To build the view for the recipes app, I'll show you how to take advantage of React to implement a declarative view that can be used to render both on the server and the browser. React offers a render cycle that allows you to easily separate which code will run on both the server and browser and which will run on only the browser. Additionally, React comes with built-in methods for constructing the DOM on both the server and the browser.

First let's talk about the idea of components. Look at the example app in figure 2.7. You could write this whole app as just one block of HTML, but it's best practice to break this UX into small components. In the figure, you can see how you'd break up

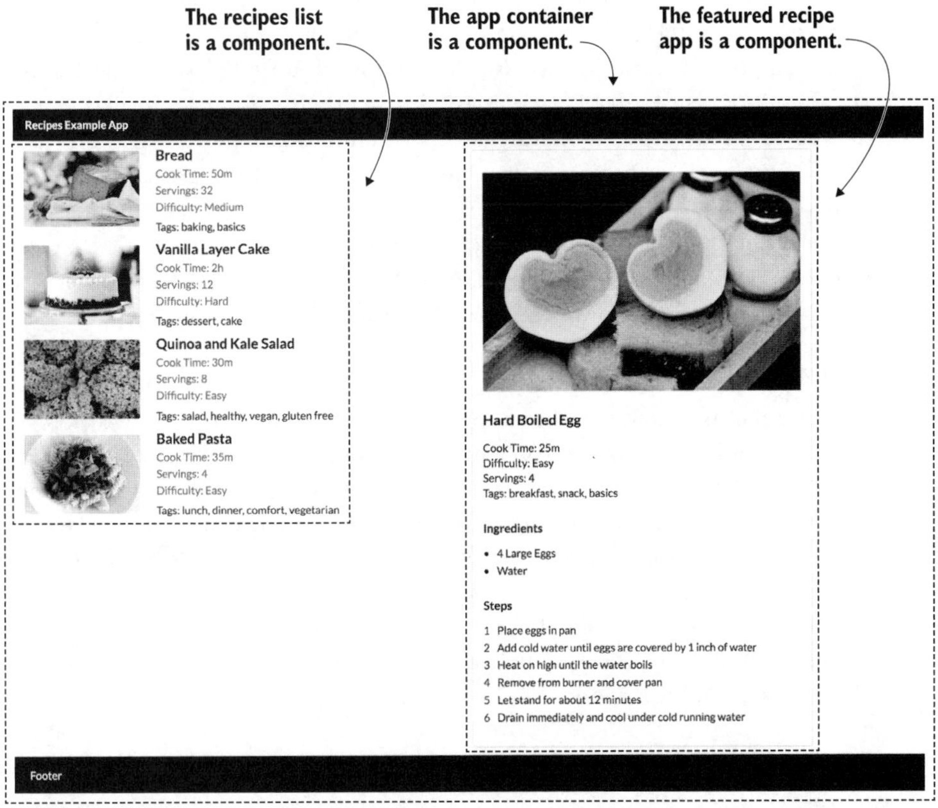
The recipes list is a component.
The app container is a component.
The featured recipe app is a component.
Recipes Example App
Bread
Cook Time: 50m
Servings: 32
Difficulty: Medium
Tags: baking, basics
Vanilla Layer Cake
Cook Time: 2h
Servings: 12
Difficulty: Hard
Tags: dessert, cake
Quinoa and Kale Salad
Cook Time: 30m
Servings: 8
Difficulty: Easy
Tags: salad, healthy, vegan, gluten free
Baked Pasta
Cook Time: 35m
Servings: 4
Difficulty: Easy
Tags: lunch, dinner, comfort, vegetarian
Hard Boiled Egg
Cook Time: 25m
Difficulty: Easy
Servings: 4
Tags: breakfast, snack, basics
Ingredients
4 Large Eggs
Water
Steps
1 Place eggs in pan
2 Add cold water until eggs are covered by 1 inch of water
3 Heat on high until the water boils
4 Remove from burner and cover pan
5 Let stand for about 12 minutes
6 Drain immediately and cool under cold running water
Footer

Figure 2.7 The recipes app is divided into three main components. By composing them together, the app is created.

the recipes app into components. To keep it simple, I've created only three components. In a real app, one with many views, I'd create even smaller components to increase my ability to compose components together. This also reduces code duplication and speeds up development.

The way you build components with React is by writing JavaScript modules and declaring your view in JSX. The next section provides an introduction to JSX.

2.3.2 Using JSX

React uses a template language called JSX. For the most part, JSX looks and acts like normal HTML, which makes it easy to learn and use. JSX consists of HTML tags (which can also be additional React components) and sections of code that are JavaScript. The syntax is presented here:

Use className instead of class — **Wrap JavaScript in {}.**

```
<div className="counter">{props.value}</div>
```

You can see that at the point where you reference JavaScript, you must wrap your code in { }. This indicates to the compiler that the code inside the brackets is executable. JSX is compiled by Babel into pure JavaScript. You could write your components with the base React functions, but that's slower and less readable.

Components can display data passed in via their properties, called *props*. Props are similar to HTML attributes and can be written in the opening tag of any JSX element. You'll find more information in chapter 3, which covers JSX and React properties and state.

The recipe app has four React components: the component that renders the HTML wrapper (used only on the server), the app wrapper component (the root of the React tree), and two view components called Featured and Recipes.

2.3.3 App wrapper component

First, we'll look at main.jsx and app.jsx to get the root of the app setup. If you want to follow along in this section, you can switch branches to the react-components branch (`git checkout react-components`). The starting branch for a section provides a skeleton sample that you'll add the code listings into. If you'd like to see the complete code for this section, you can switch to the react-components-complete branch (`git checkout react-components-complete`).

To render the components in the browser, you need to set up React in main.jsx code. The following listing shows you what to add to make the components render in the browser. Add the code to src/main.jsx.

Listing 2.4 Browser entry point—src/main.jsx

```
import React from 'react';
import ReactDOM from 'react-dom';
import App from './components/app.jsx';
```

Imports React dependencies (first two lines)

Includes root App component (third line)

```
require('./style.css');                     ◁ Includes styles

ReactDOM.render(
  <App />,
  document.getElementById('react-content')
);
```

Includes styles

Renders the App component into the DOM—second parameter indicates the DOM element React should be rendered into

App is a container component. It knows about the business rules and data required by its children. More importantly, it's aware of the application state. In this case, that means it will be connected to Redux later in the chapter. The following listing shows the App component. Replace the placeholder code in the repo (in src/components/app.jsx) with the code from the listing.

Listing 2.5 App (top-level component) —src/components/app.jsx

```
import React from 'react';
import Recipes from './recipes';
import Featured from './featured';

class App extends React.Component {

  render() {
      return (
          <div>
            <div className="ui fixed inverted menu">
              <div className="ui container">
                <a href="/" className="header item">
                  Recipes Example App
                </a>
              </div>
            </div>
            <div className="ui grid">
              <Recipes {...this.props}/>
              <Featured {...this.props.featuredRecipe}/>
            </div>
            <div className="ui inverted vertical footer segment">
            Footer
            </div>
          </div>
      );
  }
}

export default App;
```

To declare a React component that uses state, create a class that extends the base component class.

Every component that has a render function, must return either null or valid JSX.

A component defines the layout of its children.

The App component renders the header and footer but also has two additional React components that it includes as children. Recipes displays the list of recipes returned from the /recipes endpoint. Featured displays just the featured recipe you get back from the server via /featured. These child components require information from the parent, which is passed down in the form of properties.

The data being passed down is from the API and is fetched by Redux and stored in the app state. Run `npm start` after adding the app.jsx code and you'll see the header, footer, and some placeholder strings for Recipes and Featured at http://localhost:3000/index.html.

2.3.4 Building child components

The two child components display the properties that are passed into them. They don't have any awareness of other parts of the application such as Redux. This makes them reusable and loosely coupled to the business logic in the app. The following listing shows the Featured recipe component. Add this code to src/components/featured.jsx, replacing the placeholder code.

Listing 2.6 Featured component—src/components/featured.jsx

```
import React from 'react';

const Featured = (props) => {
  const buildIngredients = (ingredients) => {
    const list = [];

    ingredients.forEach((ingredient, index) => {
      list.push(
        <li className="item"
            key={`${ingredient}-${index}`}>
          {ingredient}
        </li>
      );
    });

    return list;
  }

  const buildSteps = (steps) => {
    const list = [];

    steps.forEach((step, index) => {
      list.push(
        <li className="item"
            key={`${step}-${index}`}>
          {step}
        </li>
      );
    });

    return list;
  }

  return (
    <div className="featured ui container segment six wide column">
      <div className="ui large image">
```

Function converts an array of ingredients into an array of list items; this is called from the render function. (annotates `const buildIngredients`)

Function takes in the steps array and converts it to a list item, called from render function. (annotates `const buildSteps`)

```
        <img src={`http://localhost:3000/assets/${props.thumbnail}`} />
      </div>
      <h3>{props.title}</h3>
      <div className="meta">
        Cook Time: {props.cookTime}
      </div>
      <div className="meta">
        Difficulty: {props.difficulty}
      </div>
      <div className="meta">
        Servings: {props.servings}
      </div>
      <div className="meta">
         Tags: {props.labels.join(', ')}
      </div>
      <h4>Ingredients</h4>
      <div className="ui bulleted list">
        {buildIngredients(props.ingredients)}
      </div>
      <h4>Steps</h4>
      <div className="ui ordered list">
        {buildSteps(props.steps)}
      </div>
    </div>
  );
}

Featured.defaultProps = {
  labels: [],
  ingredients: [],
  steps: []
}

export default Featured;
```

Featured component is a container that renders information about the featured recipe; it renders a recipe passed in via props.

Function converts an array of ingredients into an array of list items; this is called from the render function.

Function takes in the steps array and converts it to a list item, called from render function.

Set properties that are arrays to defaults so if there's no data, the component can still render.

After adding this code, you'll see the featured recipe displayed but without data (you haven't hooked it up to any data yet). There's one more step to show the complete homepage: adding the Recipes component code.

The next Recipes component handles more complex data than Featured. It's similar in that it only displays recipes data and has no awareness of the rest of the application. The following listing shows the Recipes list component. You'll add this code to src/components/recipes.jsx, replacing the placeholder code.

Listing 2.7 Recipes component—src/components/recipes.jsx

```
import React from 'react';

const Recipes = (props) => {

  const renderRecipeItems = () => {
    let items = [];
```

Function called from JSX in return statement

```
    if (!props.recipes) {
      return items;
    }
    props.recipes.forEach((item, index) => {
      if (!item.featured) {
        items.push(
          <div key={item.title+index} className="item">
            <div className="ui small image"><img src="" /></div>
            <div className="content">
              <div className="header">{item.title}</div>
              <div className="meta">
                <span className="time">{item.cookTime}</span>
                <span className="servings">{item.servings}</span>
                <span className="difficulty">{item.difficulty}</span>
              </div>
              <div className="description">{item.labels.join(' ')}</div>
            </div>
          </div>
        )
      }
    });
    return items;
  }

  return (
    <div className="recipes ui items six wide column">
      {renderRecipeItems()}
    </div>
  );
}

export default Recipes;
```

Because you can't write loops directly in JSX, build an array of items that can be rendered by JSX.

Each recipes item is rendered here; data for recipes is passed down via props.

The render function is a wrapper for the recipes list and has no state, like featured component.

In both components, the properties are passed in from the parent component. These components are updated only if their parent component receives an update. That ties into the single-direction flow discussed at the beginning of this section. As top-level components receive updates from the app state, they can then pass these changes down to their children. Because there's no data in the app, you won't see a visual change at this point—there are no recipes to render!

2.3.5 HTML container

The final React component is the one that the server uses to render the full HTML markup. It's mostly standard HTML tags but has a couple of spots to insert the rendered markup and the data. The following listing shows the full HTML component. Add this code to src/components/html.jsx so you have a container to render into on the server.

Listing 2.8 HTML template component (server only)—src/components/html.jsx

```
import React from 'react';

export default class HTML extends React.Component {
  render() {
    return (
      <html>
        <head>
          <title>Chapter 2 - Recipes</title>
          <link rel="stylesheet"
                href="https://cdn.jsdelivr.net/semantic-ui/2.2.2/
      semantic.min.css" />
        </head>
        <body>
          <div id="react-content"
            dangerouslySetInnerHTML={{
                                                __html: this.props.html
                                            }}/>
          <script
            dangerouslySetInnerHTML={{
                                                __html: this.props.data
                                            }}/>
          <script src="/browser.js"/>
        </body>
      </html>
    );
  }
}
```

Component creates a valid HTML page—html, head, body tags included.

CSS referenced from head tag.

Component receives rendered HTML as prop.

Prop being passed in here is data, a stringified JSON object representing the current state of the app on the server—otherwise the handoff from server to browser can't happen.

`dangerouslySetInnerHTML` is used because it's a prerendered string. Normally, you can't put HTML in a React component. This special property allows you to bypass this restriction. It's named that way as a reminder to be cautious and intentional with HTML in components.

Now that all the React components for the app have been created, you'll set up the business logic for the recipes app.

2.4 App state: Redux

In this section, I'll show you how to use Redux to build the business logic for the recipes app. The recipes app doesn't have much user interaction because it's so simple. But Redux will still be responsible for fetching the data for the app. Chapter 6 presents a complete look at Redux, including handling user interactions.

2.4.1 Understanding Redux

The flow of Redux loosely follows the flow originally defined by Facebook's Flux architecture. All updates to the app state are single directional. When a change is requested, it's processed by the business logic (actions), updated in the app state (reducers), and finally returned to the view as part of a brand-new copy of the app state. Figure 2.8 shows how this works.

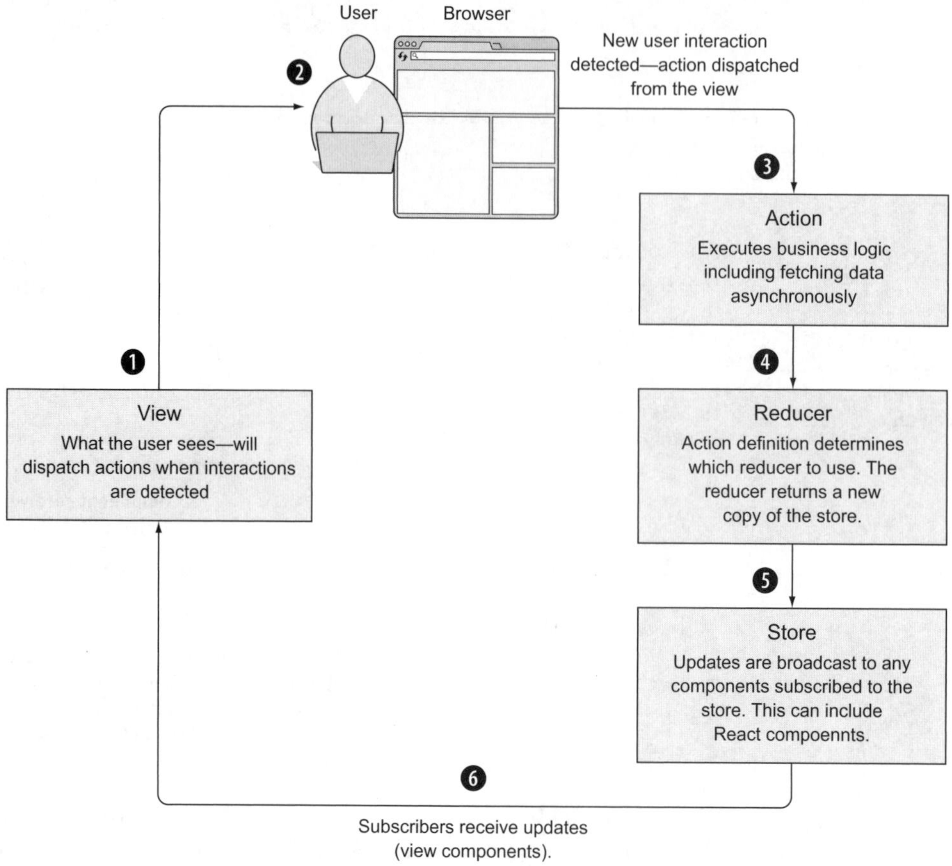
User
Browser
New user interaction detected—action dispatched from the view
Action
Executes business logic including fetching data asynchronously
View
What the user sees—will dispatch actions when interactions are detected
Reducer
Action definition determines which reducer to use. The reducer returns a new copy of the store.
Store
Updates are broadcast to any components subscribed to the store. This can include React compoennts.
Subscribers receive updates (view components).

Figure 2.8 Redux overview: flow of user interaction to store update to view update

THE STORE

Redux is based on the idea of a single root state object for the entire application, commonly referred to as the *store*. This state can be a combination of multiple deeply nested objects. The recipes app is simple, so it will have just a single root object called *recipes*.

The store is immutable, meaning changes to the state object always return a new state rather than modifying the existing state. I like to think of this as the model of the application, where the data is stored.

> **DEFINITION** *Immutable objects* are read-only. To update an immutable object, you need to clone it. In JavaScript, when you change an object, it affects all references to that object. Mutable changes can have unintended side effects. By enforcing immutability in your store, you prevent this from happening in your app.

ACTIONS

To make updates to state, you dispatch actions. *Actions* are where most of our business logic takes place. I like to think of actions as the controllers of the app.

An action can be anything in your app. Actions can be used to fetch data (such as `getRecipes` or `getFeatured`). They can also be used to update the app state—for example, keeping track of items added to a shopping cart. Think of these actions as discrete messages that describe a single state update. Actions are synchronous by default, but we can include middleware in Redux that allows asynchronous actions.

Actions (which are JavaScript objects) are usually wrapped in action *creators*, which are JavaScript functions that return or dispatch an action. They're helper methods that give your code more reusability by centralizing the creation of action objects.

REDUCERS

Actions are handled by reducers. A *reducer* takes the input from the action, including any data fetched asynchronously from the server or an API, and inserts it into the proper place in the store. Reducers are responsible for enforcing the immutable requirement of the state object. By using reducers, the actions and the store are decoupled, which gives greater flexibility to the app.

I'll walk you through setting up Redux and adding actions, reducers, and the code that makes Redux and React work together.

2.4.2 Actions: fetching the recipes data

First, we'll look at the recipes data that you need to fetch to populate the view. For this one-page app, you'll need only asynchronous actions. To learn more about actions and action creators, see chapter 6 for a full explanation. If you'd like to check out the code for this section, change to the redux branch (`git checkout redux`). To see all the code for this section in final working form, check out redux-complete (`git checkout redux-complete`).

In the action-creators file in the recipes app, you'll add two action creators. One will fetch the list of all the recipes, and the other will fetch the featured recipe. Listing 2.9 shows the implementation for the actions. Add the code in this listing to the src/action-creators.es6 file.

> **NOTE** I've included a library called isomorphic-fetch to help make XHR calls. It provides an implementation of the fetch API for both Node.js and in the browser. You can find more information and the documentation at https://developer.mozilla.org/en-US/docs/Web/API/Fetch_API and https://github.com/matthew-andrews/isomorphic-fetch.

Listing 2.9 Action creators for recipes and featured data—src/action-creators.es6

```
export const GET_RECIPES = 'GET_RECIPES';
export const GET_FEATURED_RECIPE = 'GET_FEATURED_RECIPE';
```

Best practice is to create constants for all your actions so action creators (functions listed here) and reducers can use them. Then you won't have discrepancies between strings.

```
export function fetchRecipes() {
  return dispatch => {
    return fetch('http://localhost:3000/recipes', {
      method: 'GET'
    }).then((response) => {
      return response.json().then((data) => {
        return dispatch({
          type: GET_RECIPES,
          data: data.recipes
        });
      });
    })
  }
}

export function fetchFeaturedRecipe() {
  return dispatch => {
    return fetch('http://localhost:3000/featured', {
      method: 'GET'
    }).then((response) => {
      return response.json().then((data) => {
        return dispatch({
          type: GET_FEATURED_RECIPE,
          data: data.recipe
        });
      });
    })
  }
}

export function getHomePageData() {
  return (dispatch, getState) => {
    return Promise.all([
      dispatch(fetchFeaturedRecipe()),
      dispatch(fetchRecipes())
    ])
  }
}
```

fetchRecipes, the first action creator, handles logic for making a request to the server for recipes data.

Implements fetch API for making GET request to appropriate endpoint.

Dispatch action.

Attach JSON data to action payload on a property called data.

On a successful response, get JSON from the response—using a promise to get JSON response is standard with the fetch API.

Type is the only required property of every action, set it using string constants declared at the top of the module.

The second action creator handles the logic for requesting the featured recipe from the server.

Dispatch action.

Attach JSON data to action payload on a property called data.

This action creator composes the other two action creators—making it easier for view and server to request related data.

By themselves, these actions won't do anything. All they're responsible for is determining what will be updated in the app state. They then send the action to the reducers. The reducers take in the objects from the action creators in `fetchRecipes` and `fetchFeaturedRecipe`. They return a new copy of the store (maintaining state as an immutable object), with the updated data. Figure 2.9 shows this flow.

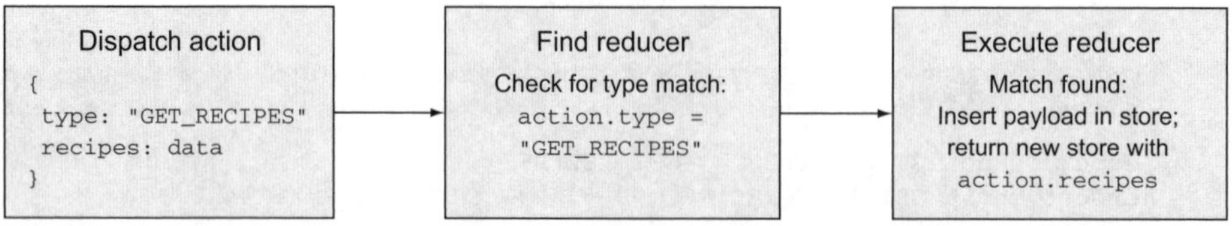
Dispatch action
{
type: "GET_RECIPES"
recipes: data
}
Find reducer
Check for type match:
action.type =
"GET_RECIPES"
Execute reducer
Match found:
Insert payload in store;
return new store with
action.recipes

Figure 2.9 Dispatching an action triggers a lookup in the reducer followed by an update to the store.

The following listing shows the recipes reducers in the app. It also demonstrates how to keep the app state immutable. Add this code to src/recipe-reducer.es6.

Listing 2.10 Reducers—src/recipe-reducer.es6

```
import {
          GET_RECIPES,
          GET_FEATURED_RECIPE
        } from './action-creators';

export default function recipes(state = {}, action) {
  switch (action.type) {
    case GET_RECIPES:
      return {
        ...state,
        recipes: action.data
      };
    case GET_FEATURED_RECIPE:
      return {
        ...state,
        featuredRecipe: action.data
      };

    default:
      return state
  }
}
```

- Include the constants from action creators.
- A reducer is a JavaScript function that takes in the current state and an action.
- Using a switch statement is recommended because many reducers end up with > 4 cases to handle—this switch uses a type property to determine how to handle each action.
- Using the spread operator to clone the state object maintains an immutable store.
- Use data from the action to override the current state so the new app state is the old app state with the modified data.
- If a reducer is triggered but no case matches, return the current store state—no changes required, no need to create new object.

Now that you have action creators and reducers, you need to initialize and configure Redux. Because both the browser and the server will be initializing Redux, you'll abstract the code into a module called init-redux. You add the code from the following listing to src/init-redux.es6.

Listing 2.11 Using `initialState` to start Redux—src/init-redux.es6

```
import {
  createStore,
  combineReducers,
  applyMiddleware,
  compose } from 'redux';
import recipes from './recipe-reducer';
import thunkMiddleware from 'redux-thunk';

export default function () {
  const reducer = combineReducers({
    recipes
  });

  let middleware = [thunkMiddleware];

  return compose(
    applyMiddleware(...middleware)
  )(createStore)(reducer);
}
```

- Include the Redux functions used to create the Redux store.
- Include the recipes reducer you created earlier.
- Include Thunk middleware. It lets you write action creators that can dispatch additional actions and use promises.
- Use the combineReducers function to create one root reducer (in bigger apps, you'll have many reducers).
- Use the functions imported from Redux to initialize the store and pass in middleware options—compose takes functions and combines them from right to left.

Redux is completely wired up, but the view still doesn't have access to the data. The next section covers connecting React and Redux.

2.4.3 React and Redux

You still have a couple of steps before you can get React and Redux working together properly and have the browser code ready to go. You'll use an npm package called react-redux to hook up your React components to Redux. This package provides a React component called Provider that you use to wrap all your other React components. These wrapped components can then optionally subscribe to updates from the Redux store using another component that the library has, called *connect*. The following listing shows how to include the Provider in the browser entry point file. Update src/main.jsx with the code in bold.

Listing 2.12 Redux and React setup—src/main.jsx

```
import { Provider } from 'react-redux';
import initRedux from './init-redux.es6';
require('./style.css');

const store = initRedux();

ReactDOM.render(
  <Provider store={store}>
    <App />
  </Provider>,
  document.getElementById('react-content')
);
```

- Include the Provider component that sets up a Redux store in the app so you can use the connect wrapper in your components.
- Include the module you just added that initializes Redux in application.
- Call initRedux to set up the Redux store.
- Wrap root app component with the react-redux Provider component and pass in the newly created store to the Provider component.

The Provider component acts as the stateful top-level component. It knows when the store updates and passes that change down to its children. Individual components can also subscribe to the store as needed. The following listing shows the code to add to the root component (src/components/app.jsx) so that it becomes a Redux connected component.

Listing 2.13 Connecting the app component to Redux—src/components/app.jsx

```
import React from 'react';
import { connect } from 'react-redux';
import { bindActionCreators } from 'redux';
import Recipes from './recipes';
import Featured from './featured';
import * as actionCreators from '../action-creators';

class App extends React.Component {
```

- Import the Redux dependencies and action creators you added previously.

```
  componentDidMount() {
    this.props.actions.getHomePageData();
  }

  render() {}
}

function mapStateToProps(state) {
  let { recipes, featuredRecipe } = state.recipes;
  return {
    recipes,
    featuredRecipe
  }
}

function mapDispatchToProps(dispatch) {
  return { actions: bindActionCreators(actionCreators, dispatch) }
}

export default connect(
                        mapStateToProps,
                        mapDispatchToProps
                      )(App)
```

With the component configured to use Redux, you can dispatch actions from the view.

Function lets you convert app state to properties on your component.

This component requires data fetched from server, so you need to get recipes and featuredRecipe objects out of the current app state.

Return values you want to access directly on this.props in your component.

Function lets you make actions simpler to call from the component—instead of calling dispatch(action) each time, the view can call the action without knowing about dispatch.

Instead of exporting App component, export connect component, which takes in two helper functions and App component as parameters.

Connect allows you to tap into the app state from components that need to know about how to display the data and where to get it from. Now the App component has access to all the properties needed to make the view work. At this point, if you restart the app, the view will be populated with data! Next, we'll walk through the server code.

2.5 Server rendering

Now that you have your views and business logic set up, it's time to look at server-rendering the homepage. You're going to add a single route for the homepage. This isn't very "real-world"—chapter 7 introduces a more robust way of handling the server, including using React Router on the server.

If you're following along and want to check out the code so far, you can switch to the server-browser-rendering branch (`git checkout server-browser-rendering`). Note that in this section, you'll no longer be loading index.html. Instead, load the app at http://localhost:3000.

2.5.1 Setting up a basic route on the server with middleware

This route will use Express middleware to handle and render the request. The middleware will also fetch the necessary data.

DEFINITION *Express middleware* is made up of chainable functions that each do a single job. Middleware can terminate the request by sending a response or can transform requests and do other business logic, including error handling.

The line of code in the Listing 2.14 needs to be added to src/app.es6. This code adds a handler for the root route. Make sure you add it so that server rendering will work. (I added the other code for you so the data endpoints would work in all the other examples.)

Listing 2.14 Set up the root route—src/app.es6

```
import renderViewMiddleware
➥ from './middleware/renderView';

app.get('/featured', (req, res) => {});

// handle the isomorphic page render
app.get('/', renderViewMiddleware);

// start the app
app.listen(3000, () => {
  console.log('App listening on port: 3000');
});
```

Add an Express route to get the homepage using renderViewMiddleware.

2.5.2 Fetching the data

Next, let's look at `renderViewMiddleware` and see how it fetches the data and renders the view. Remember, you have only one route in the recipes app, so you're able to assume what Redux action needs to be dispatched. The following listing shows how the middleware to render the view works. Replace the code in src/middleware/renderView.jsx with this code.

Listing 2.15 Isomorphic view middleware data fetching—src/middleware/renderView.jsx

```
import initRedux from '../init-redux';
import * as actions from '../action-creators';

export default function renderView(req, res, next) {

  const store = initRedux();

  store.dispatch(actions.getHomePageData())
    .then(() => {
      console.log(store.getState());
      res.send("It worked!!!");
    });
}
```

Middleware function definition—express middleware receives a request object, a response object, and the next callback for passing control to next middleware in the chain.

Set up Redux reducers and compose store—on the server, it starts with an empty store.

Dispatch required action and wait for it to resolve before moving on to render.

At this point, if you run `npm start` and load the app at http://localhost:3000, you'll get a message: "It worked!!!". In the terminal output, you should see the current state, including an array of recipes and the featured recipe. You've set up the data fetching, but you still need to render the view. The next section covers adding the React server rendering code to renderView.jsx.

2.5.3 Rendering the view and serializing/injecting the data

For this single route, the rendering logic is simple. The one weird bit is that you end up doing two React renders on the server. When I first started building isomorphic apps, we used a different server-side templating language to build the index HTML. But this had a lot of downsides, including additional knowledge that each developer on the team had to have before understanding the full render flow. Then we switched to rendering the components for the route into a React component that represented the full-page markup. One less skill to master!

This is to remove the need to have another view template language in use on the server. The following listing shows how to implement the render logic. Add the bold code to the `renderView` middleware.

Listing 2.16 Isomorphic view middleware view render—src/middleware/renderView.jsx

```
import React from 'react';
import ReactDOM from 'react-dom/server';
import { Provider } from 'react-redux';
import initRedux from '../init-redux';
import * as actions from '../action-creators';
import HTML from '../components/html';
import App from '../components/app';

export default function renderView(req, res, next) {

const store = initRedux();

store.dispatch(actions.getHomePageData())
  .then(() => {
      let html;
      const dataToSerialize = store.getState();

      html = ReactDOM.renderToString(
        <Provider store={store}>
          <App />
       </Provider>
      );

      const renderedHTML = ReactDOM.renderToString(
        <HTML data={`window.__INITIAL_STATE =
          ${JSON.stringify(dataToSerialize)}`}
              html={html} />
      )
```

Serialize the data so you can pass the state down to the browser.

Render components by rendering app.jsx and injecting the data you fetched in the previous step.

Render the full HTML page by rendering html.jsx with the previously rendered components and serialized data.

```
      res.send(renderedHTML)
    });
  }
```

The other key piece of logic that must happen during your view render is getting the app state attached to the DOM response. You can see this in the code in the listing—it's necessary so the browser can do its initial render with the exact same app state as was used on the server.

2.6 Browser rendering

The code for browser rendering is one of the most straightforward parts of the whole isomorphic app flow, but it's also one of the most important pieces to get right. If you don't render the app in the same state as on the server, you'll break the isomorphic render and ruin all the performance gains you've earned.

2.6.1 Deserializing the data and hydrating the DOM

The server did all that hard work to get the data to the browser. To grab that data, all the browser needs to do is point at the window object the server set up via a script tag. You do that in main.jsx. Add the code in the next listing to main.jsx.

Listing 2.17 Add code for main.jsx—src/main.jsx

```
import React from 'react';
import ReactDOM from 'react-dom';
import App from './components/app.jsx';
import { Provider } from 'react-redux';
import initRedux from './init-redux.es6';
require('./style.css');

console.log("Browser packed file loaded");

const initialState = window.__INITIAL_STATE;
const store = initRedux(initialState);

console.log("Data to hydrate with", initialState);

ReactDOM.render(
  <Provider store={store}>
    <App />
  </Provider>,
  document.getElementById('react-content')
);
```

Include the Provider component, which will become the root component, as on the server.

Include Redux initialization module.

Grab server serialized state off the window object.

Instead of starting Redux with an empty initial state on the server, pass server data into the Redux setup.

Then, inside the `initRedux` function, the data from the server gets used. Listing 2.18 shows the configuration of Redux and how `initialStore` can be passed into it. You need to add the following code to the init-redux file.

Listing 2.18 Using `initialState` to start redux—src/init-redux.es6

```
import {
  createStore,
  combineReducers,
  applyMiddleware,
  compose } from 'redux';
import recipes from './recipe-reducer';
import thunkMiddleware from 'redux-thunk';

export default function (initialStore={}) {
  const reducer = combineReducers({
    recipes
  });

      let middleware = [thunkMiddleware];

  return compose(
    applyMiddleware(thunkMiddleware)
  )(createStore)(reducer, initialStore);
}
```

initialStore has the value that was passed in from main.jsx (defaults to empty object when none is passed in).

initialStore value is passed into the Redux createStore function—the store is now hydrated with data from server.

Now the app is ready to listen for user interaction and to continually update without talking to the server (the SPA flow). For the recipes app, if you wanted to expand the functionality and add detail pages for recipes, the server wouldn't be involved in loading the detail page when the user clicks it from the homepage. In the GitHub repo, you can see the complete app on the server-browser-rendering-complete or master branches.

Summary

In this chapter, you learned to build a complete isomorphic app. Congrats—you covered a lot of ground by building this example! The next few chapters take a deeper dive into the various parts of isomorphic apps. You learned the following in this chapter:

- Babel and webpack enable JavaScript code to be compiled. Webpack allows npm packages to be used with browser code.
- React components make up the view portion of the application. JSX is used to declare the components.
- Redux acts as the controller and the model of the isomorphic app.
- The Node.js server uses Express middleware to respond to requests. Custom middleware for rendering React is needed for isomorphic apps. This middleware also sends down the initial serialized state of the application.
- The browser uses a separate entry point to load in the initial state and start the app.

Part 2

Isomorphic app basics

If you've spent much time in the front-end web world over the last few years, you've probably experienced "JavaScript fatigue." That malaise happens because there's a constant stream of libraries, tools, and new ideas to learn about. Being exposed to this stream of information can become overwhelming.

This part of the book provides an overview of each of the libraries and tools you need in order to build a best-practice React application that will work in a production environment. Several building blocks are required, including React, React Router, webpack, Babel, and Redux. The four chapters in this part explore these topics in depth and keep you focused on a small slice of the currently available JavaScript tools and libraries that are important for application development.

In chapter 3, you'll learn React, starting with the basics of JSX and the virtual DOM and moving into using properties and state to create React components. In chapter 4, you'll learn how to use React Router to add multiple routes to your application. That chapter also introduces the React component lifecycle and covers advanced React concepts, including component composition and higher-order components. (Three appendices have been added to help you learn React Router 4.) It's the first chapter that has you writing code for the All Things Westies app. In chapter 5, you'll learn all about the build tools: webpack and Babel. In chapter 6, we'll cover Redux in depth—you'll learn to write actions, create reducers, and use the store.

3 React overview

This chapter covers

- How the virtual DOM works
- React's functional nature
- Using JSX to declare React components
- Using React state to handle user interaction

React is a library for creating user interfaces, invented and used by Facebook. The React ecosystem has expanded rapidly over the last few years. It's now possible to use React in many types of applications and architectures. This chapter will teach you what you need to know about React to build an isomorphic application. I'll start by teaching you some React basics. The next chapter covers React component patterns and introduces React Router.

> **NOTE** Before getting started with this chapter, I recommend installing the React Developer tools for Chrome or Firefox. This will make debugging your React code much easier. I use React 15.6.1 for the examples in this chapter. Chapter 9 includes a detailed explanation of the React Developer tools.

For a complete view into React, you can explore the many books on the subject, such as *React Quickly* by Azat Mardan (Manning, 2017). Feel free to skip over this chapter if you already have experience using React.

A note on the code and libraries used for this chapter: you can download the code from the GitHub repo at https://github.com/isomorphic-dev-js/chapter3-react-overview. To get up and running with the example, see README.md. To ensure that you have everything set up, make sure you run the following commands:

```
$ npm install
$ npm install -g @kadira/storybook
$ npm run storybook
```

The examples run at http://localhost:9001. This repo is organized into folders that are named according to chapter and example numbers. For most sections, you'll refer to the components/Chapter_3_X folder.

> **NOTE** At the time of publishing, the code in this chapter runs only with React 15. But Storybook will be upgraded at some point. When Storybook is compatible with React 16, you can choose to use React 16 with the examples in this chapter.

3.1 Overview of React

Let's walk through setting up an HTML page that loads React and renders a single React component. The code for this section can be found in the GitHub repo in the html/Chapter_3_1/ path.

React replaces the view in web apps. It provides a simple API that's easy to get up and running but that's designed to be composed to facilitate building complex user interfaces. React works best when you build lots of small components and put them together to make your complete UI.

Here are the steps to get up and running with React on a static HTML page. If you're familiar with React rendering, you can move on to the next section:

1. Set up an HTML page
2. Include the React library
3. Include a script that renders a React component into the page

To get started, you're going to render Hello World with React. This first render will output only the string "My first react component" into the browser. You can see this in figure 3.1.

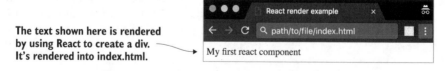

The text shown here is rendered by using React to create a div. It's rendered into index.html.

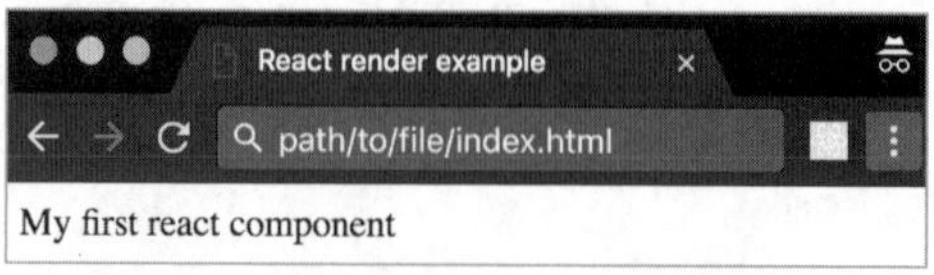
React render example
path/to/file/index.html
My first react component

Figure 3.1 A basic React component's output when loaded into the browser

First, you need your index.html. This HTML file, shown in listing 3.1, will include all the required React dependencies as well as the code that creates a React component and places it on the DOM. For this first example, the HTML page is as bare-bones as possible. To see the output from figure 3.1, open the index.html file in the browser.

Listing 3.1 First React render—html/Chapter_3_1/index.html

```
<html>
  <head>
    <title>React render example</title>
    <script
      src="https://npmcdn.com/react@15.3.1/dist/react.js">
    </script>
    <script src="https://npmcdn.com/react-dom@15.3.1/dist/react-dom.js">
     </script>
  </head>
  <body>
    <div id="render-react-into-me"></div>
    <script type="text/javascript">
      ReactDOM.render(
        React.createElement(
                    div,
                    null,
                    "My first React component"
                   ),
          document.getElementById('#render-react-into-me')
        );
    </script>
  </body>
</html>
```

React and React DOM dependencies, loaded off a CDN for simplicity.

div is where the React code will be rendered.

The script tag has code for rendering a React element into the DOM.

Call the render method of ReactDOM with two parameters: the React element to render and the DOM node to attach to.

Call React.createElement to create div with text.

HTML element where React should attach rendered output

The JavaScript in index.html renders a single React element into the empty `<div>` in the <body>. To do that, you use two of React's methods. `React.createElement` comes from the core library (react.js) and creates a React element. `ReactDOM.render` comes from the React DOM library (react-dom.js), takes the React element created by `React.createElement`, and renders it into the DOM.

That example was simple, so let's look at a slightly more complex one. In listing 3.2, there's a button inside the <div> instead of just text. Figure 3.2 shows this button.

This button is rendered using React to create a nested HTML structure.

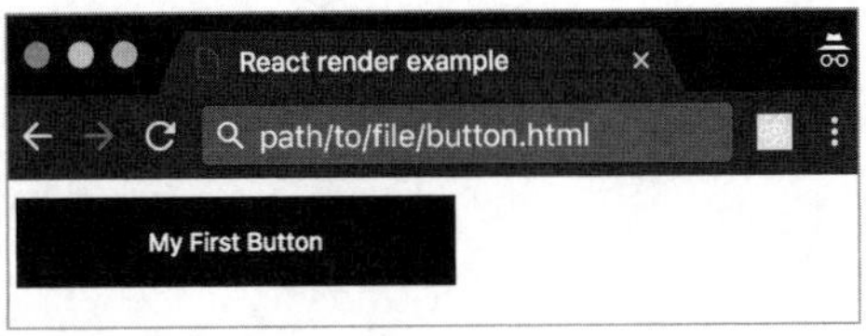
React render example
path/to/file/button.html
My First Button

Figure 3.2 Rendering multiple HTML tags with React

To render this button, you replace the text with a new React element. The following listing shows you how to update the script tag to render the button.

Listing 3.2 Rendering multiple HTML tags—html/Chapter_3_1/button.html

```
<script type="text/javascript">
      ReactDOM.render(
        React.createElement("div", null,
        React.createElement(
                             "button",
                             null,
                             "My First Button"
                           )
        ),
        document.getElementById('render-react-into-me')
      );
    </script>
```

Instead of putting text into <div>, you can nest React elements—here you create an HTML button with text.

This button example shows how to nest HTML elements and use React's declarative style to state your app structure. But React's real power lies in its ability to update the DOM as elements change. Next, I'll introduce the virtual DOM to you.

3.2 Virtual DOM

Before I discuss the virtual DOM, I want to make sure you have a clear picture of the browser DOM (*DOM* stands for Document Object Model). The DOM is a markup representation of a web page. The browser interprets the DOM to determine how to render the web page. You could think of this as a plan, or map, that the browser reads to determine how to build your page. For example, the rendered output of the nested elements in the button example in the previous section is shown in the following listing.

Listing 3.3 DOM markup for button example

```
<div id="render-react-into-me">
  <div data-reactroot="">
    <button>My First Button</button>
  </div>
</div>
```

div placeholder that React renders into

Root component

Button created by React.createElement

This code results in a blueprint for the browser that instructs it to render two divs with a button inside. Along with a little CSS, it results in the button in figure 3.2.

The virtual DOM is a lightweight representation of the DOM that can be traversed and updated much faster. It's a JavaScript representation of the DOM. For the button example, React keeps a version of the component structure in JavaScript.

Traditionally, manipulating the DOM has been slow. When a change needs to be made, the entire page has to be traversed, and updates are inserted and then re-rendered. Imagine that you want to update a list of items in HTML. You'd have to find the list, traverse it, and make updates and insertions as needed. As your app grows and you have more items and more lists, this process gets slower. Enter the virtual DOM.

Figure 3.3 shows the startup flow of a React application. When the initial JavaScript is run, React generates the base virtual DOM from the React components in your app. Then React attaches the DOM tree to the browser DOM.

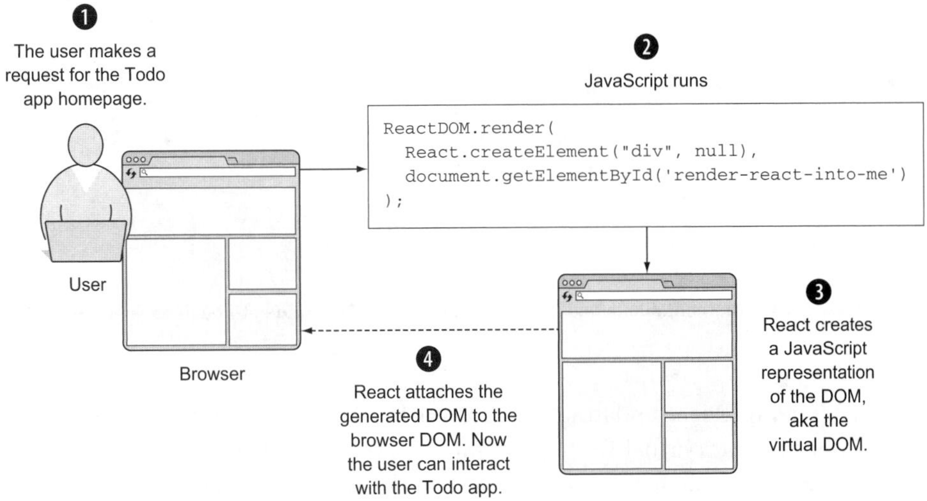
1
The user makes a request for the Todo app homepage.
User
Browser
2
JavaScript runs
ReactDOM.render(
React.createElement("div", null),
document.getElementById('render-react-into-me')
);
3
React creates a JavaScript representation of the DOM, aka the virtual DOM.
4
React attaches the generated DOM to the browser DOM. Now the user can interact with the Todo app.

Figure 3.3 React's virtual DOM when the app starts up

React takes this virtual DOM and does a diff between the previous state and the updated state. React compares the old version of the virtual DOM with the new version and calculates anything that has changed. It then uses an algorithm optimized for web apps to determine where to make updates to the DOM. Figure 3.4 illustrates this process.

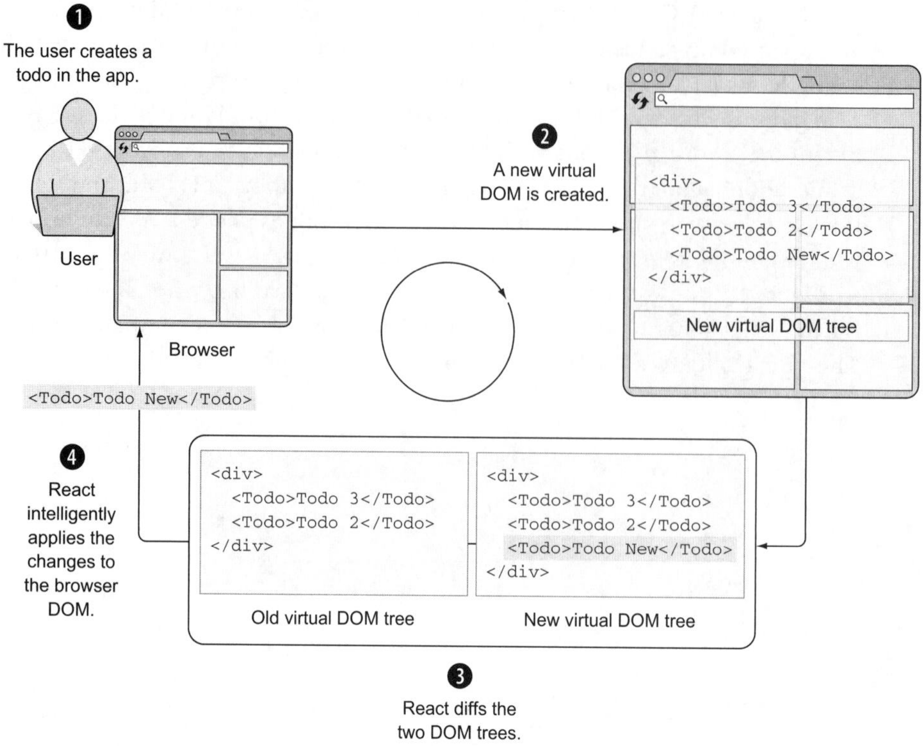
1
The user creates a todo in the app.
User
Browser
2
A new virtual DOM is created.
<div>
<Todo>Todo 3</Todo>
<Todo>Todo 2</Todo>
<Todo>Todo New</Todo>
</div>
New virtual DOM tree
<Todo>Todo New</Todo>
4
React intelligently applies the changes to the browser DOM.
<div>
<Todo>Todo 3</Todo>
<Todo>Todo 2</Todo>
</div>
Old virtual DOM tree
<div>
<Todo>Todo 3</Todo>
<Todo>Todo 2</Todo>
<Todo>Todo New</Todo>
</div>
New virtual DOM tree
3
React diffs the two DOM trees.

Figure 3.4 The continuous update and diff cycle that React goes through to keep the DOM up-to-date

Ultimately, React updates only those parts that are absolutely necessary so that the internal state (virtual DOM) and the view (real DOM) are the same. For example, if there's a `<p>` element and you augment the text via the state of the component, only the text will be updated (`innerHTML`), not the element itself. This results in increased performance compared to re-rendering entire sets of elements or, even more so, entire pages (server-side rendering).

In figure 3.5, you can see an example of what happens when an update is made. React looks at the component tree and figures out which parts need to be updated. Then it intelligently updates the browser DOM to match the current state of the application. In this case, one list item is removed, and one list item is added. The third list item remains unchanged. React is able to optimize for these changes and update the DOM quickly.

NOTE If you want to learn more about the virtual DOM, you can find additional resources online. Codecademy has a good overview (www.codecademy.com/articles/react-virtual-dom), and Hackernoon does a deep dive into the topic (https://hackernoon.com/virtual-dom-in-reactjs-43a3fdb1d130).

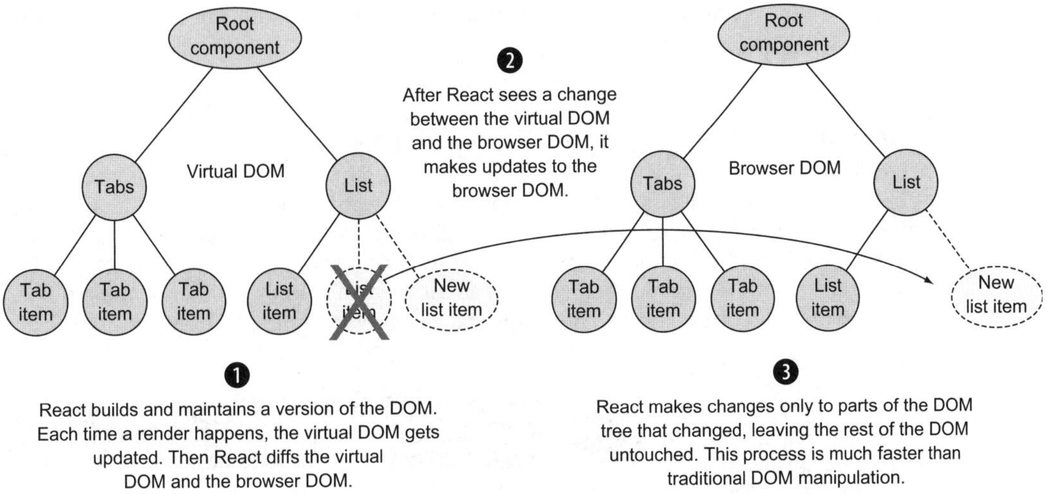
Root component
Virtual DOM
Tabs
List
Tab item
Tab item
Tab item
List item
New list item
1
React builds and maintains a version of the DOM. Each time a render happens, the virtual DOM gets updated. Then React diffs the virtual DOM and the browser DOM.
2
After React sees a change between the virtual DOM and the browser DOM, it makes updates to the browser DOM.
Root component
Browser DOM
Tabs
List
Tab item
Tab item
Tab item
List item
New list item
3
React makes changes only to parts of the DOM tree that changed, leaving the rest of the DOM untouched. This process is much faster than traditional DOM manipulation.

Figure 3.5 The virtual DOM updates the browser DOM based on the diff algorithm that React runs on state changes.

3.3 Todo app overview

In this section, you'll build a Todo app. This single-page application (SPA) will enable users to store lists of todos, mark them as complete, and see what todos are left to be done. Figure 3.6 shows this app. To keep you focused on learning React, this isn't an isomorphic app.

Chapter 5 shows how to set up webpack and ES6 for isomorphic apps. In the meantime, I'll use a library called Storybook throughout this chapter to help you get started with React code. I want you to focus on React—Storybook lets you get started with lit-

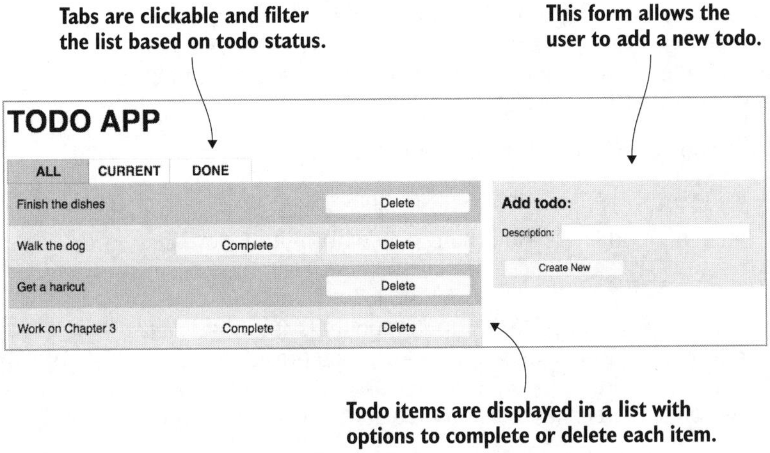
Tabs are clickable and filter the list based on todo status.
This form allows the user to add a new todo.
TODO APP
ALL
CURRENT
DONE
Finish the dishes
Delete
Walk the dog
Complete
Delete
Get a haricut
Delete
Work on Chapter 3
Complete
Delete
Add todo:
Description:
Create New
Todo items are displayed in a list with options to complete or delete each item.

Figure 3.6 A wireframe for the Todo app you'll build in this chapter

tle setup. If you'd like to see more of how this works, you can check out the stories folders in the repo as well as the nearby sidebar.

Using Storybook for previewing React components

The npm package Storybook by Kadira (https://github.com/kadirahq/react-storybook) is a tool for building React components without having to hook up the component to your application to see how it works. Storybook makes no assumptions about your application. Instead, it can render any React component that you want to see in isolation. It can even render full user interfaces composed of multiple components if you provide the correct inputs. Here's Storybook running in the browser:

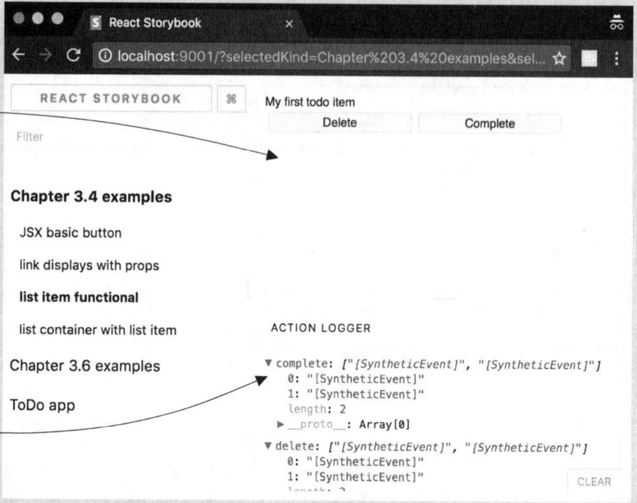

React Storybook
localhost:9001/?selectedKind=Chapter%203.4%20examples&sel...
REACT STORYBOOK
Filter
My first todo item
Delete
Complete
Chapter 3.4 examples
JSX basic button
link displays with props
list item functional
list container with list item
Chapter 3.6 examples
ToDo app
ACTION LOGGER
complete: ["[SyntheticEvent]", "[SyntheticEvent]"]
0: "[SyntheticEvent]"
1: "[SyntheticEvent]"
length: 2
__proto__: Array[0]
delete: ["[SyntheticEvent]", "[SyntheticEvent]"]
0: "[SyntheticEvent]"
1: "[SyntheticEvent]"
CLEAR

The output from the current story is shown here. In this case, the output is the result of the "list item functional" story.

The stories are listed in the left column. Clicking a title switches the content shown in the output frame.

The Action Logger shows any storybook event logs. In the case, clicking Delete or Complete logs an event in the action logger.

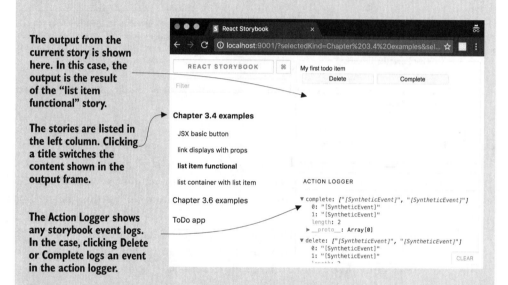

The library takes advantage of iframes to isolate each component so that you can easily flip between components. Storybook uses webpack's hot module loading to build and monitor code changes, autorefreshing changes in the browser as you edit your code.

To use Storybook, you must install it globally:

```
$ npm install -g @kadira/storybook
```

Then in the command line inside the repo, you run the following:

```
$ npm run storybook
```

To write a story, you add code to the components/stories folder. There's a file for each chapter section that uses stories. Storybook provides two functions: `storiesOf` and `add`. The first function, `storiesOf`, adds a new story to Storybook, which shows on the left (Chapter examples and Todo app). The section function (`add`) adds a specific example to the story (link displays with props, list item functional). To see this in action, review the following code:

```
import React from 'react';
import { storiesOf, action } from '@kadira/storybook';

storiesOf('My first story', module)
  .add('list item functional', () => (
    //...code
  ));
```

Then Storybook renders these components at localhost:9001. If you click the button in example 2, the action logger will log `button clicked`. That's how you test whether a component is properly calling the expected actions or callbacks that have been passed into it.

Storybook offers manual assertion testing and visual rendering without the complexity of hooking the component into the app. This makes writing the view portion of your app faster and lets you test components independent of your business logic.

3.4 Your first React component

At this point, you should understand why you want to use React and the basics of rendering. Now you'll learn the following best practice development skills:

- JSX basics
- Pure components
- Using properties
- Conditionals and looping
- React classes
- User interactions

By the end of this section, you'll be able to build a user interface for a Todo application (see figure 3.1) with user interactions. You'll have used all the React features necessary for building isomorphic applications. To follow along with the examples in this chapter, check out the react-components branch in the GitHub repository (`git checkout react-components`).

NOTE You'll find the files for this section in components/Chapter_3_4 and components/stories/chapter_3_4.js.

React follows basic core tenets. First, it provides a standard, simple interface for building views. Second, it uses a declarative style to handle updates and state changes. In React, components don't worry about how their children function. They're concerned only with the data that needs to be passed into the children. For example, to create the list view in the Todo app, you tell React to render a list item for each entry in the list of todos. The list view doesn't worry about how React implements the underlying logic to update the browser DOM. It worries only about the data needs of the list items. To see this in action, you'll learn to write the Todo app button component with React's template language, JSX.

3.4.1 JSX basics

So far, you've seen how to render React components by writing them in JavaScript. But React uses a template language called JSX that makes writing components almost like writing HTML. JSX is designed to be compiled into JavaScript and allows you to mix component declarations, HTML, and JavaScript.

The Todo app has a lot of buttons, so you're going to create a button that can be reused for various button use cases. Figure 3.7 shows what this looks like.

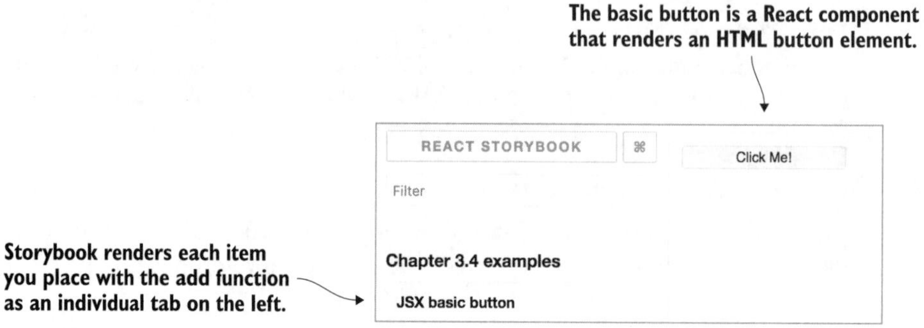
The basic button is a React component that renders an HTML button element.
REACT STORYBOOK
⌘
Click Me!
Filter
Chapter 3.4 examples
JSX basic button
Storybook renders each item you place with the add function as an individual tab on the left.

Figure 3.7 The button component rendered inside Storybook

A basic button in JSX is written like this:

```
<button>Click Me!</button>
```

At this point, you've written what looks to be some HTML. Declaring HTML elements is identical to how you'd write them in an HTML file (`div`, `a`, `ul`, `img`, `video`, and so forth). But because you'll compile the JSX into JavaScript, JSX provides syntax for indicating where to execute JavaScript expressions.

To illustrate this point, let's imagine you want to turn the button label into a variable. Listing 3.4 shows the code for your first React component. Replace the code in buttonBasic.jsx with the code from the listing. I've already set up the story for you. After you've added the code from the listing, you can view it at http://localhost:9001 under the JSX basic button tab, as shown in figure 3.7.

Listing 3.4 JSX Button component—Chapter_3_4/buttonBasic.jsx

```
import React from 'react';

const Button = (props) => {
```

Include React, required in every React component.

```
  let label = "Click Me!";
  return <button>{label}</button>;
}

export default Button;
```

Declare button label as a variable.

Use JSX {} syntax to indicate a JavaScript expression to compiler.

Export component so it can be included in other components.

This JSX will be compiled and will know that `label` is a JavaScript expression. You can put any valid JavaScript inside the `{}`. The curly brackets indicate JavaScript to be executed. That can be a variable, ternary, function, or other valid JavaScript code.

To make sure you understand how JSX compiles to JavaScript, let's revisit the render example from earlier in the chapter, where you render "My first React component" into the DOM:

```
ReactDOM.render(
  React.createElement("div", null, "My first React component"),
  document.getElementById('render-react-into-me')
);
```

Let's rewrite this bit of JavaScript by using what you've learned so far about JSX. I find this second example much easier to process. It reads like HTML:

```
ReactDOM.render(
  <div>My first React component</div>,
  document.getElementById('render-react-into-me')
);
```

In the first example, you have to understand what each parameter is doing. You need to know the details of how `React.createElement` works, including what parameters to pass in. In the second example, you can immediately see that React will render a div that will display "My first React component" because you already know how to read HTML.

Similarly, the compiled version of the button component uses `React.createElement` and passes in a set of parameters indicating what to render. In the button example, an extra parameter is passed: the JavaScript expression, or in this case, the variable called `label`:

```
let label = "Click Me!";
React.createElement( "div", null, label)
```

This example shows the compiled JavaScript version of the JSX. Notice that because the JSX is now plain JavaScript, the variable is readable by the JavaScript interpreter. That's the power of JSX. It lets you mix the view declaration with JavaScript logic.

If you're thinking this seems a bit strange, I encourage you to give it five minutes (see https://signalvnoise.com/posts/3124-give-it-five-minutes). The first time I saw JSX, I thought it was terrible. It reminded me of writing server-side languages like PHP.

After I started to use JSX, I found that it's one of the better, if not the best, inline view options available for web applications. I now enjoy writing JSX! It's about as close to writing HTML as you can get without just writing HTML. It has the added benefit of being easy to read and easy to write. Plus, it enables you to write your view logic and your view structure side by side. That lets you remove unnecessary boilerplate and makes the developer experience better; it's just more readable than other options. JSX gets bonus points for making unit testing your views relatively painless.

COMMON JSX GOTCHAS

For the most part, JSX plays by normal JavaScript rules. But you should be aware of a few exceptions.

> **NOTE** I don't have space to go over every JSX gotcha. The good news is that Facebook keeps its documentation up-to-date. For a full list of JSX gotchas, visit the JSX gotchas page and the JSX in-depth page on the React docs: https://facebook.github.io/react/docs/jsx-gotchas.html and https://facebook.github.io/react/docs/jsx-in-depth.html.

When adding CSS classes in JSX, the compiler will ignore the word `class` because it's a reserved word in JavaScript. Remember that the JSX code will get compiled to JavaScript. Instead, you need to use the attribute `className` to add a class:

```
<div className="blue">I'm blue</div>
```

React will also ignore custom attributes. If you need to add a custom attribute, use the `data-` prefix instead:

```
<div data-custom-id="1234"></div>
```

Finally, JSX looks like HTML, but it's not HTML. You can't write `<!--HTML Comment-->`. If you do, you'll get compile errors. But you can still add regular JavaScript comments; just put them inside an expression { }:

```
{/*JavaScript comment renders here*/}
```

Now that you have some experience with JSX, let's build the ListItem component for the To do app.

3.4.2 Building a reusable component

So far, I've shown you only how to render into the DOM directly and how to write JSX. Now you'll write complete components. The Todo app can be broken into small, reusable components such as Button, ListItem, and Tab. Take a look at the visual representation of the Todo app's component parts in figure 3.8.

In a React view, each repeatable element can become a component. Other components wrap the smaller composable components and determine the layout. In figure 3.8, the wrapper components such as AddItem and List contain smaller, reusable components.

The smaller components such as ListItem and Button are repeated throughout the user interface. React lets you write these once and then use them over and over. That

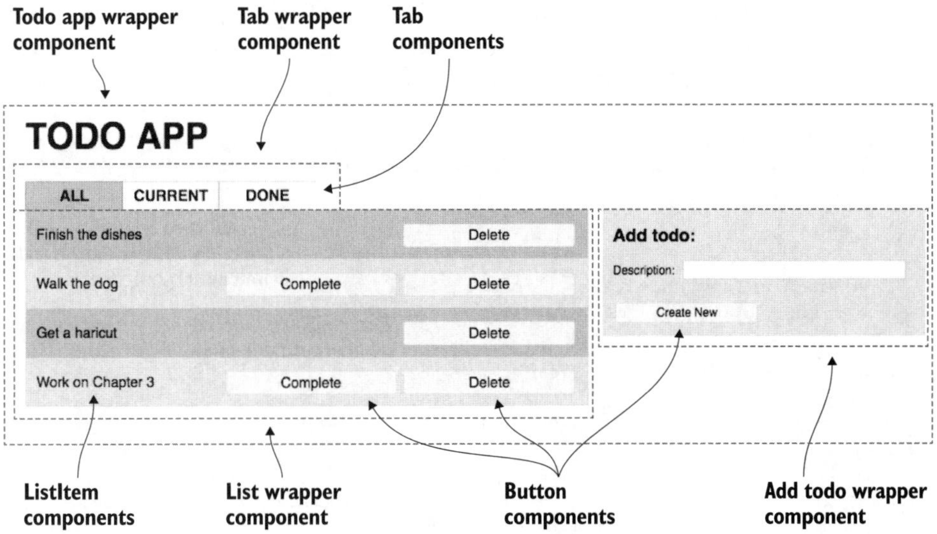
Todo app wrapper component
Tab wrapper component
Tab components
TODO APP
ALL
CURRENT
DONE
Finish the dishes
Delete
Walk the dog
Complete
Delete
Get a haricut
Delete
Work on Chapter 3
Complete
Delete
Add todo:
Description:
Create New
ListItem components
List wrapper component
Button components
Add todo wrapper component

Figure 3.8 Each rectangle encloses an individual component. Some components are nested; for example, the Button component is nested inside the ListItem component, which is inside the List component.

simplifies your code, making it more maintainable and readable. It also lets you write the view in a declarative style.

The first reusable component you'll build will be the ListItem component for the Todo app. (Reusable components are considered best practice because they speed up development time.) Figure 3.9 shows the ListItem output.

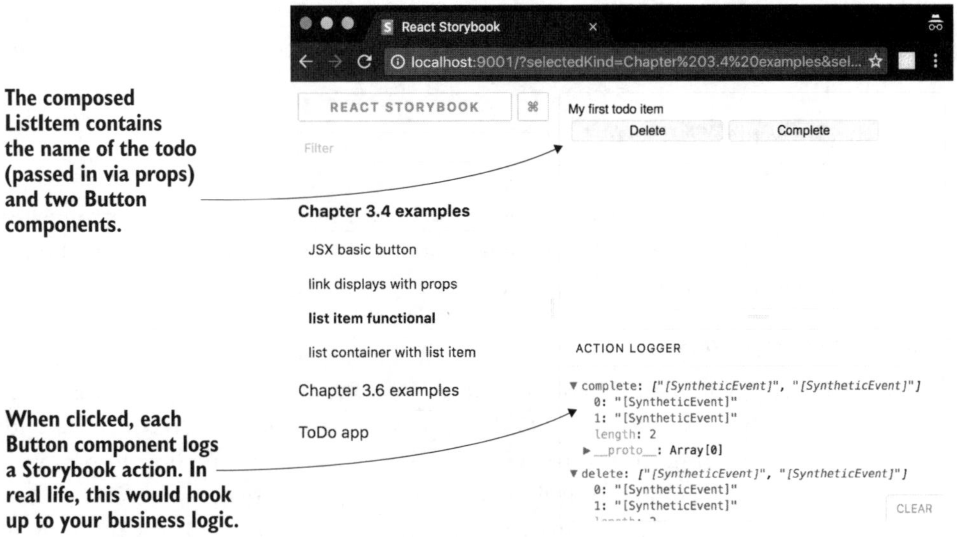
The composed ListItem contains the name of the todo (passed in via props) and two Button components.
When clicked, each Button component logs a Storybook action. In real life, this would hook up to your business logic.
React Storybook
localhost:9001/?selectedKind=Chapter%203.4%20examples&sel...
REACT STORYBOOK
Filter
My first todo item
Delete
Complete
Chapter 3.4 examples
JSX basic button
link displays with props
list item functional
list container with list item
Chapter 3.6 examples
ToDo app
ACTION LOGGER
complete: ["[SyntheticEvent]", "[SyntheticEvent]"]
0: "[SyntheticEvent]"
1: "[SyntheticEvent]"
length: 2
__proto__: Array[0]
delete: ["[SyntheticEvent]", "[SyntheticEvent]"]
0: "[SyntheticEvent]"
1: "[SyntheticEvent]"
CLEAR

Figure 3.9 View of the todo item in Storybook with action logging

This component is created with the code in the following listing. This code replaces the placeholder code in the listItemFunctional.jsx file. After you've added it, you can see it in Storybook, as the story already exists.

Listing 3.5 List item—components/Chapter_3_4/listItemFunctional.jsx

```
import React from 'react';
import Button from './button.jsx';

const ListItemFunctional = (props) => {
  return (
    <div>
      <div>{props.name}</div>
      <Button key='Delete'
              clickHandler={props.deleteCallback}
              label='Delete'></Button>
      <Button key='Complete'
              clickHandler={props.completeCallback}
              label='Complete'></Button>
    </div>
  )
}

export default ListItemFunctional;
```

Create the component with a JavaScript function declaration—creates pure or functional component.

Return JSX to be rendered—must be a single root node or you'll get error.

Parent component passes in the properties ListItem uses, including name and the click handler callback.

If multiple elements of the same type are siblings, give them unique keys so React knows the difference between them on subsequent renders.

It's important to note the use of the `key` attribute in this example. The `key` attribute must be used anytime you have two sibling elements that are the same type. In the listing, there are two buttons. React won't know which one has changed unless you provide a key. If it doesn't know which one has changed, it'll replace both items. With a `key` attribute, React will know which element to update and can be much more efficient in making DOM changes.

The ListItem component in listing 3.5 is rendered using two important React concepts:

- Properties (`props`)
- Pure functional components

In the next section, we'll explore how to use React's concept of properties to turn components into reusable templates that take in properties to display. Then we'll look at declaring pure functional components.

3.4.3 Using properties

With React, you want to build reusable components. For example, a ListItem that can be reused for any todo item that the app needs to display would come in handy. This is where React properties shine. With *properties*, you can define how to pass in the information that a component will need. React properties make it possible to create reusable components. They contain all the information that makes a component's usage unique.

To use a property, you can pass in the `name` property with value `Cleanup my desk`, like this:

```
<ListItem name="Cleanup my desk"/>
```

The component can then access this value on the `props` object:

```
<div>{props.name}</div>
```

That, in turn, would render the following `div` in the browser DOM tree:

```
<div>Cleanup my desk</div>
```

If the property changes, a render is triggered and the component will update. We'll talk more about the component lifecycle in chapter 4.

Think of properties as unchangeable values within an element. They allow elements to have different aspects or properties, hence the name.

Properties are immutable within their components. A parent assigns properties to its children upon their creation. The child element isn't supposed to modify its properties (in development, React will throw errors if you do that).

> **DEFINITION** A *child* is an element that's nested inside another element (for example, `<Button/>` is a child of `<ListItem/>`). The parent is the component that wraps the child. Components may have many children, and these children may have children.

SPREAD OPERATOR

One more thing about passing `props` into components: let's say you have a parent component that has a whole bunch of properties. This might include the current route information, application state, and application data. Rather than writing out each property, you can take advantage of the spread operator (`...`) to pass all the properties. The spread operator takes each key on an object and "spreads" them out into individual properties.

Let's revisit our ListItem component from earlier. Say you have several properties to pass in. Using the spread operator, you'll make each property available on `props` for the child component:

```
<ListItem {...this.props}/>
```

Then in the component code, you can access each prop individually:

```
<div>{props.name}</div>
<Button clickHandler={props. deleteCallback} label='name'></Button>
```

This becomes useful as you build up multiple levels of nested children. The root component may need to pass a property to a great-great-great-grandchild. Each component can pass all the `props` down as needed to help achieve this. But you want to be cautious, because indiscriminately passing all the properties down the tree can also lead to unnecessary renders and performance issues.

You've seen how to use properties in React components; now let's take a look at the functional React component.

3.4.4 Functional components

The simplest React components follow the pure function concept: given a set of inputs, the component will return a predictable output (making them easy to test). A basic addition function illustrates this concept. Given two integer inputs, the `add` function will always return the same value:

```
function add(a, b) { // a = 3, b = 2
  return a + b; // returns 5
}
```

This Link component needs to be told only how to build the link. You can accomplish that via properties. Figure 3.10 shows the Link component rendered inside Storybook.

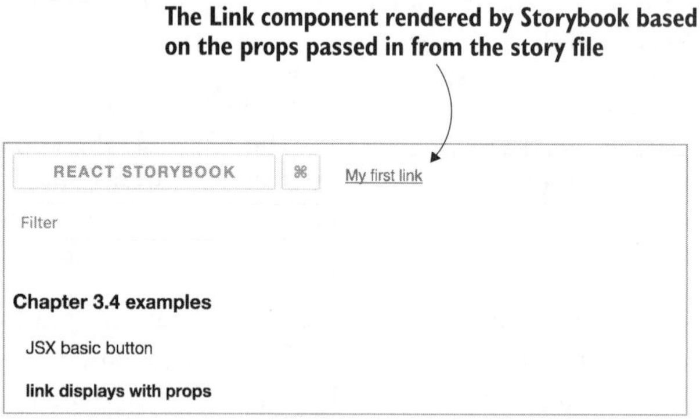
The Link component rendered by Storybook based on the props passed in from the story file
REACT STORYBOOK
⌘
My first link
Filter
Chapter 3.4 examples
JSX basic button
link displays with props

Figure 3.10 Link component rendered inside Storybook

The following listing shows the code that creates the Link component, which is a simple functional component that returns a link created with the props passed into it. Add this code to the link.jsx file. After you've done that, you'll be able to see it, as shown in figure 3.10.

Listing 3.6 Link component—components/Chapter_3_4/link.jsx

```
import React from 'react';

const Link = (props) => {
  return <a href={props.link}
            target={props.target}>
            {props.displayName}
          </a>
  }
export default Link;
```

Pure functions can be declared with JavaScript function declaration (ES6 style used here).

Link component returns a component that has no state and doesn't use any React lifecycle methods—given a set of inputs (props), returns predictable result.

The approach of building pure functional components has benefits for performance, testing (see chapter 9), maintainability, and developer speed.

NOTE This functional component approach shouldn't be confused with `PureComponent`, introduced in React 15. `React.PureComponent` gives you some performance boosts in specific uses cases but is otherwise just like `React.Component`. More information can be found at https://facebook.github.io/react/docs/react-api.html#react.purecomponent.

Many of your components will be reusable display components. React encourages "drying up" your code by breaking it into small, reusable bits. Over time, this enables building new, more complex components quickly, because most of the pieces are already available.

DEFINITION *DRY* is an acronym for *don't repeat yourself.* React allows you to break your user interface into small, repeatable, reusable chunks so you don't repeat yourself.

Given these two concepts, properties and pure functional components, you can build a good portion of your application. Eventually, you'll need to add more complexity. In the next section, you'll build the List component and add conditional logic to the ListItem.

3.4.5 Conditionals and looping

In the previous section, you built a ListItem using foundational React concepts. In this section, you'll add complex JavaScript expressions such as ternaries and loops to JSX. You'll build a List component that uses the ListItem component to display several todo items. The List component you'll build in this section is displayed in figure 3.11.

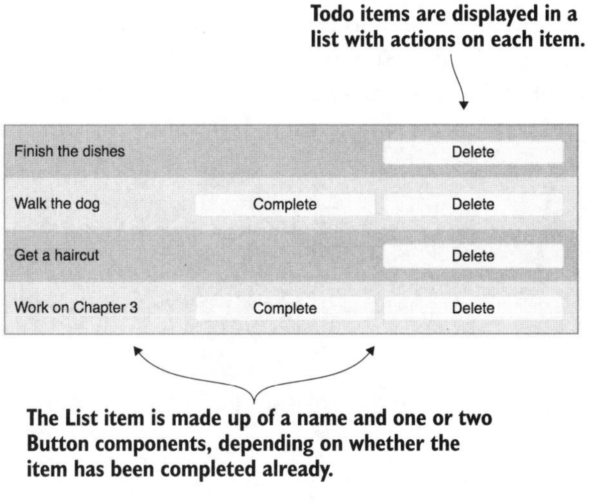
Todo items are displayed in a list with actions on each item.
Finish the dishes
Delete
Walk the dog
Complete
Delete
Get a haircut
Delete
Work on Chapter 3
Complete
Delete
The List item is made up of a name and one or two Button components, depending on whether the item has been completed already.

Figure 3.11 The List component renders multiple list items based on the data it receives.

First, you'll use conditionals to display the Complete button only for items that aren't done. Then you'll use loops to display the list of items.

CONDITIONALS

Let's take the List item you built earlier. Remember, you added two buttons to it: a Delete button todo and a Complete button. But in the Todo app, you're going to show these items in different states: Current or Done. You don't want to show the Complete button if the todo item has already been completed (see figure 3.12).

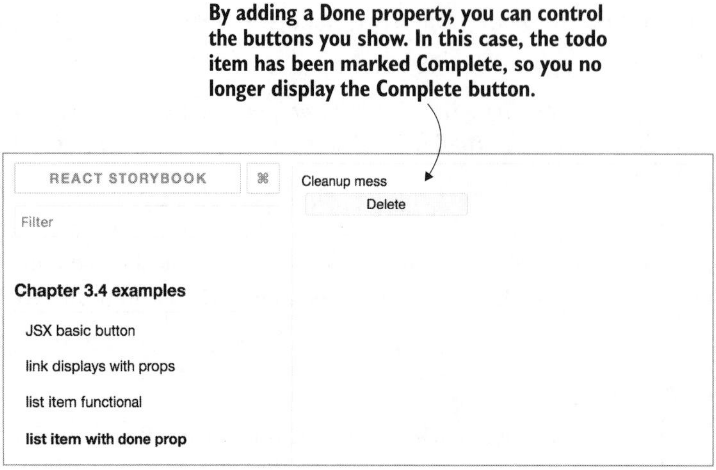
By adding a Done property, you can control the buttons you show. In this case, the todo item has been marked Complete, so you no longer display the Complete button.
REACT STORYBOOK
⌘
Filter
Chapter 3.4 examples
JSX basic button
link displays with props
list item functional
list item with done prop
Cleanup mess
Delete

Figure 3.12 The ListItem component has a property that indicates whether the item is done. When it's done, the Complete button no longer shows.

Instead, you'll add a check to see whether the List item being rendered has previously been completed. Listing 3.7 shows how to add a ternary expression to the code. Add the code shown in bold into the listItemFunctional.jsx file. Using a ternary expression, the component checks for the done property. If it's true, it doesn't render the Complete button and instead renders an empty string. If it's false, it renders the Complete button.

Listing 3.7 Make button optional—components/Chapter_3_4/listItemFunctional.jsx

```
const ListItemFunctional = (props) => {
  return (
    <div>
      //...other code
      {props.done ?
        "" :
        <Button key='Complete'
                clickHandler={this.complete}
```

```
                  label='Complete'></Button>}
    </div>
  )
}

export default ListItemFunctional;
```

To test the new property you've added, you can add a story with the ListItemFunctional component and the done property. The next listing shows how to update the story. Add this code to the Chapter_3_4.js story. After you've added it, you'll be able to see the component without the Complete button, as shown in figure 3.12.

Listing 3.8 Test the listItem done prop—components/stories/chapter_3_4.js

```
storiesOf('Chapter 3.4 examples', module)
  .add('JSX basic button', () => ())
  .add('link displays with props', () => ())
  .add('list item functional', () => ())
  .add('list item with done prop', () => (
    <ListItemFunctional completeCallback={actions.complete}
                        deleteCallback={actions.delete}
                        name="Cleanup mess"
                        done="true"/>
  ))
  .add('list container with list item', () =>());
```

Add a story with the add() function—pass in a title for the story and a function that returns the component you want to render.

Add done property—component checks for truthy value here, so you can set it to true.

From a logic standpoint, the change you made to the ListItemFunctional component is straightforward. If the todo list item is complete, don't show the Complete button. If it isn't complete, show the Complete button. But how do you do that is in JSX? It doesn't support `if` statements because it's just markup.

For low-complexity conditionals such as showing the Complete button, you can use a ternary statement. Remember, anything you put inside the {} will execute as JavaScript code.

```
props.done ? "" : <button>Complete</button>
```

The `done` property is a Boolean on the todo's data that's passed in via `props`. If it's true, it will render nothing, but if it's false, it'll show the button so the user is able to take the complete action on the todo.

Loops

Now that you have a todo item, you want to be able to display a list of multiple todo items. The List component is a pure component that iterates over an array of data that has been provided. It takes each object passed in and renders a child ListItem component. This List component is still a functional component because it has no state. It's purely responsible for rendering the items. The following listing shows the code you need to add to the list.jsx file in the Chapter_3_4 folder. Make sure to replace all the placeholder code.

Listing 3.9 List component—components/Chapter_3_4/list.jsx

```
import React from 'react';
import Item from './itemDone.jsx'

const List = (props) => {

let listItems = [];
    props.data.forEach((item)=>{
        listItems.push(
          <Item key={item.id} {...item} actions={props.actions}/>
         );
    });
  return <div>{listItems}</div>;
}
export default List;
```

Create array to push each child component into.

Data is passed in as an array, loop over each item in array.

Push each Item component into the listItems array; pass in all properties of item and all props.

As in the previous section, you can handle this looping logic before the JSX part of the render. The data that'll be passed into the List component is shown in the following listing. I've already included this for you in the stories file for this section.

Listing 3.10 Todo data—components/stories/chapter_3_4.js

```
[
  {
    name: "Finish the dishes",
    done: true,
    id: 0
  },
  {
    name: "Walk the dog",
    done: false,
    id: 1
  },
  {
    name: "Get a haircut",
    done: true,
    id: 2
  },
  {
    name: "Work on Chapter 3",
    done: false,
    id: 3
  }
]
```

This data has four todos. Two have already been marked as `done`. In the code example for the List component, you can see that given this data array, four list items will be created. They're pushed into an array that JSX is able to render.

At this point, the List component will work. But you'll need to add one more property to each ListItem to get this component finished. In React, when there are several components of the exact same type next to each other, you have to add a key value. The key must be unique. You need to modify the way you're creating items:

```
<ListItem key={item.id} {...item} {...props} />
```

Remember, this matters because React doesn't know which item changed in the list when updates are made. It knows that the list changed, but without the key React will have to re-create the entire list. With the key, React knows which items were updated and can do an intelligent update and render.

If you'd like to see the final code from the last few sections, you can switch to the react-components-complete branch (`git checkout react-components-complete`).

3.5 Interactive components: React state

Until now, you've made components that display things and components that lay out their children. But web apps require interactivity and state. In this section, you'll add interactivity to the Todo app by adding different lists of cards. That will also require the app to have some application state. If you want to follow along and build the components, you can switch to the react-state branch in the GitHub repo (`git checkout react-state`).

> **NOTE** You'll find the files for this section in components/todo and components/stories/todo.js.

To do this, you'll create the Tab component. This component communicates state changes to its parent component via a callback that's passed in as a property. Figure 3.13 shows the Tab components rendered above the list of todos. The app will display three lists: All, Current, and Done todos.

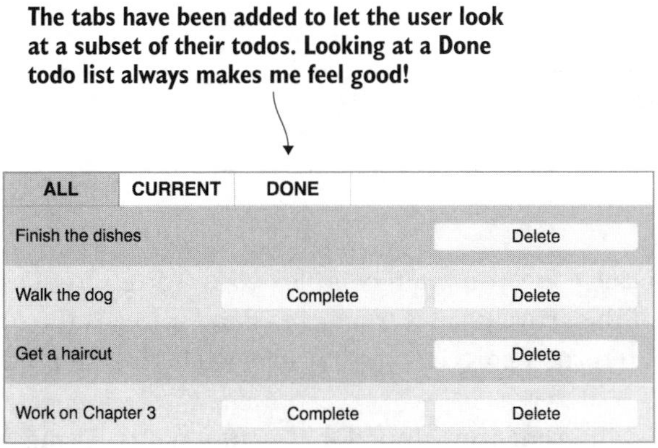
The tabs have been added to let the user look at a subset of their todos. Looking at a Done todo list always makes me feel good!
ALL
CURRENT
DONE
Finish the dishes
Delete
Walk the dog
Complete
Delete
Get a haircut
Delete
Work on Chapter 3
Complete
Delete

Figure 3.13 Adding tabs lets the app display different lists of todo items.

3.5.1 *Using classes*

The Tab components are going to be interactive and will need to have methods for handling clicks. For components that aren't pure functional components, React provides a class that can be extended. That gives you the benefit of access to several built-in React lifecycle methods and the other React component API methods such as `setState`. The following listing shows the code for the Tab component, which should be added to the tabs.jsx file in the todo folder.

Listing 3.11 Tab component complete—components/todo/tabs.jsx

```
import React from 'react';
import classnames from 'classnames';

   class Tabs extends React.Component {}

class Tab extends React.Component {
  constructor(props) {
    super(props);
    this.handleClick = this.handleClick.bind(this);
  }

  handleClick() {
    this.props.actions.updateTabView(this.props.index)
  }

  render() {
    const classes = classnames(
                                      {
                                         active: this.props.active
                                      },
                                      'tab'
                                   )

    return (
      <div className={classes}
        onClick={this.handleClick}>
        {this.props.name}
      </div>
    )
  }
}
```

- npm package lets you build complex class strings.
- Constructor method runs each time a component class instance is created.
- Call super and pass along params (props)—must be first thing that happens in constructor.
- Click handler method notifies app of change in active tab.
- Render method runs on each render, equivalent to functions created earlier for pure components.

As you can see, the npm package lets you build complex class strings. In this case, you want to add an active class if the active prop is true. `classnames` reads the object and list of strings passed in and returns a correctly spaced string. This is rendered into the `className` prop.

Writing a React class is different from functional components. Using ES6 JavaScript classes, you extend the React base class to make a new component:

```
class Todo extends React.Component {}
```

Then you can add the `constructor()` and `render()` methods. The constructor runs when the class instance is created. The render method is just like the functional methods you wrote to make the List and ListItem components. It returns the JSX of the component.

You can add any additional class functions or React lifecycle functions you might need. The Tab component adds a click handler called `handleClick`, which calls the action's callback with the index of the current tab.

NOTE The actions object holds Redux actions. For now, the implementation of these actions will be in your root component rather than Redux. In chapter 6, I'll show you how to connect to Redux actions.

To make the click handler function work, you need to add an event listener to the tab by adding an `onClick` attribute to the tab `div`. React handles all the underlying bindings and cleanup for you. Most events can be attached this way:

```
<div className="tab" onClick={this.handleClick}>
  {this.props.name}
</div>
```

Adding event listeners in React with classes has a gotcha. In ES6 classes, class functions aren't automatically bound to the `this` context. If you've been working with JavaScript for a while, this can be confusing at first, because in the prototype structure each function on a prototype is bound to the `this` context. In the ES6 class structure, each function ends up with the context of the caller (as opposed to the parent class).

When working with event listeners, an event listener's `this` context will be the event itself by default, rather than the class. Fixing this requires forcing the event listener to be bound to context of the class. You'll do this in the class `constructor` method:

```
constructor(props) {
  ...
  this.handleClick = this.handleClick.bind(this);
   }
```

After you've added the `bind` call to the constructor, the `this` context of your event handler will be the class, allowing you to call `this.props` or `this.state`. So the final Tab component will have a constructor, render, and click handler.

3.5.2 React state

So far, we've discussed components written as pure functions and stateless class-based components. React can also handle state inside components. Sometimes this might be application state. More often, this state ends up being user-interaction state. For example, is a modal hidden or displayed?

In the Todo app, the root component will manage the state. In later chapters, you'll use Redux to manage the application state. The following listing shows you the code for the todo root component, which you add to todo.jsx.

Listing 3.12 Todo component—components/todo/todo.jsx

```
import React from 'react';
import List from './list.jsx';
import Tabs from './tabs.jsx';
import AddItem from './addItem.jsx';

class Todo extends React.Component {

  constructor(props) {
    super(props);
    this.state = {
      tab: 0
    }
  }

  updateTabView(index) {
    this.setState({
      tab: index
    })
  }

  filterTodos() {
    return this.props.todos.filter((todo) => {
      if (this.props.activeTab == 0) {
        return true;
      } else if (this.props.activeTab == 1) {
        return !todo.done;
      } else {
        return todo.done;
      }
    });
  }

  render(){
    let actions = {updateTabView: updateTabView}
    return (
      <div className='todo-app'>
        <h1>ToDo App</h1>
        <Tabs {...this.props} actions={actions}/>
        <List {...this.props} data={this.filterTodos()} />
        <AddItem {...this.props} />
      </div>
    )
  }
}

export default Todo;
```

Method provides current list of todos to show based on the activeTab property. (annotation on `filterTodos()`)

Set updateTabView method as an action. (annotation on `let actions = ...`)

Pass in the calculated list of todos to List component. (annotation on `<List ...>`)

Pass in actions to the Tabs component so each tab can call back to this root component to update the state. (annotation on `<Tabs ...>`)

Each React class component has a state object that's accessible at `this.state`. You need to initialize this state object in the constructor:

```
constructor(props) {
    super(props);
    this.state = {tab: 0}
  }
```

After you've initialized the state in the constructor, state becomes *read-only*. React provides another method called `setState` for state updates (writes). If you want to update the `tab` value, you call `setState`:

```
updateTabView(index) {
  this.setState({tab: index});
   }
```

An important note about `setState`: it's *asynchronous*. The good news is, if you need to run code after you're sure that the state update has completed, you can use the hook that React provides:

```
updateTabView(index) {
  this.setState({tab: index}, () => {
   // do something after the state updates
  });
   }
```

You've now built most of the Todo app! You've also learned how to use all of React's core concepts:

- Creating components with JSX
- Pure components
- Properties
- Class components
- State

If you want to view the complete code presented in this chapter, check out the master branch. In the next chapter, you'll learn about React's component lifecycle and the hook functions available to handle more complex logic cases.

Summary

In this chapter, you learned how to get up and running with React. You walked through key pieces of the Todo app built with React. We covered all the React basics you need to understand before building an isomorphic app:

- React uses a declarative style mixed with functional concepts to provide a simple view interface.
- The virtual DOM powers React's ability to intelligently and quickly make updates.
- JSX is React's declarative template language. It uses an HTML-like syntax with the ability to execute JavaScript.
- React relies on `props` for communication between components.
- State is discouraged in React, but when needed it's a powerful tool for handling user interactions and managing application state.

4 Applying React

This chapter covers

- Configuring React Router for the browser
- Rendering the route contents in a consistent way by using `props.children`
- Building reusable components
- Using higher-order components to abstract common business logic
- Taking advantage of the React component lifecycle

In chapter 3, you learned the basics of building views with React. Now you'll build on those skills by exploring more-advanced concepts with React. This chapter will teach you what you need to know in order to build a production app with React.

You'll be working with the All Things Westies app described in chapter 1. This is the first of many chapters in which you'll be building this app. The code can be found at https://github.com/isomorphic-dev-js/complete-isomorphic-example.git. To start, you should be on branch chapter-4.1.1 (`git checkout chapter-4.1.1`).

The master branch for this repo contains the complete code from all the chapters in the book.

To run the app for this chapter, use these commands:

```
$ npm install
$ npm start
```

When the server is running, the app in this chapter will be loaded from http://localhost:3000/ (although there's nothing to see on the chapter-4.1.1 branch). It's not isomorphic because I want you to stay focused on the React concepts. As you build out this app in chapters 7 and 8, you'll turn the app into an isomorphic app.

The app is shown in figure 4.1. I've called out the component parts that need to be added to make this work.

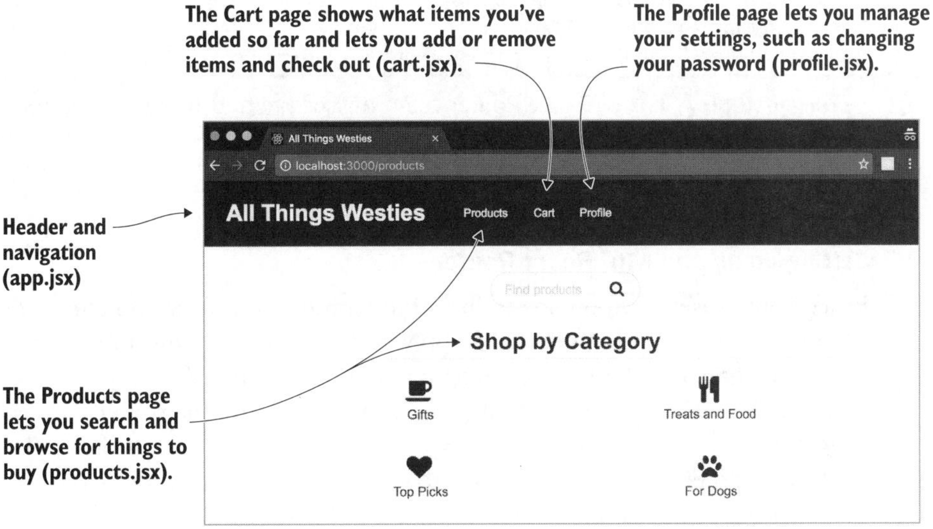
The Cart page shows what items you've added so far and lets you add or remove items and check out (cart.jsx).
The Profile page lets you manage your settings, such as changing your password (profile.jsx).
All Things Westies
localhost:3000/products
All Things Westies
Products
Cart
Profile
Header and navigation (app.jsx)
Find products
Shop by Category
Gifts
Treats and Food
Top Picks
For Dogs
The Products page lets you search and browse for things to buy (products.jsx).

Figure 4.1 The All Things Westies sample app that you'll begin building in this chapter. You'll build out the various parts of this app in later chapters.

There are three main routes (and a home route, /): /products, /cart, and /profile. In the next section, you'll set up the routing.

4.1 React Router

To build a web application, you usually need a router. *Routers* provide a mapping between the URL-based route and the view that the route should load. Because React is the view library, it doesn't handle application routing on its own. That's where React Router comes into play.

React Router has become the community choice for routing in React apps. It even has support for server-side routing, making it a great choice for isomorphic apps (covered in chapter 7). React Router makes creating your routes straightforward because it uses JSX to let you declare routes. React Router is a React component that handles your routing logic.

> **React Router versions**
>
> This app and the rest of the book use React Router 3 (v3.0.5). Since I started writing this book, a newer version (v4) has come out. The latest version is a complete rewrite of the way React Router works. It's more in line with how React works, but it requires a new way of thinking about how the router interacts with an isomorphic app.
>
> I've provided a version of the app with explanation in three appendices (A–C). You'll find examples related to this chapter in appendix A. I explain how to get started with React Router 4 and the major changes with the removal of the React Router lifecycle.
>
> The good news is the React Router team has committed to supporting v3 for the indefinite future (because of the breaking nature of v4). But I do recommend you explore v4 if you're starting a new project.

4.1.1 Setting up an app with React Router

React Router uses components to introduce routing into your app and to define the child routes. Before you initiate the app with the router, you must first define a set of routes that'll be used. You'll set them up in a sharedRoutes.jsx file.

In this first section, you'll add the App component with the router. This will let you easily support the server-rendering use case you'll build later in the book. The following listing shows you the code to add to sharedRoutes.jsx. Remember, if you want to follow along, you should be on branch chapter-4.1.1.

Listing 4.1 App routes—src/shared/sharedRoutes.jsx

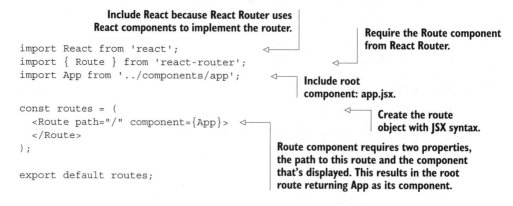

```
import React from 'react';
import { Route } from 'react-router';
import App from '../components/app';

const routes = (
  <Route path="/" component={App}>
  </Route>
);

export default routes;
```

- **Include React because React Router uses React components to implement the router.** (`import React from 'react';`)
- **Require the Route component from React Router.** (`import { Route } from 'react-router';`)
- **Include root component: app.jsx.** (`import App from '../components/app';`)
- **Create the route object with JSX syntax.** (`const routes = (`)
- **Route component requires two properties, the path to this route and the component that's displayed. This results in the root route returning App as its component.** (`<Route path="/" component={App}>`)

I've provided the skeleton of the App component for you so you don't need to add this code. The following listing shows the App component.

Listing 4.2 App component—src/components/app.jsx

```
import React from 'react';

const App = () => {
  return (
    <div>
      <div className="ui fixed inverted menu">
        <h1 className="header item">All Things Westies</h1>
        <a to="/products" className="item">Products</a>
        <a to="/cart" className="item">Cart</a>
        <a to="/profile" className="item">Profile</a>
      </div>
      <div className="ui main text container">
        Content Placeholder
      </div>
    </div>
  );
};

export default App;
```

Title of app

Root navigation links—each will be added to the sharedRoutes file in the next section.

Each route's contents will render here—for now, there is placeholder text.

Next, you'll set up your app to use React Router. The following listing shows you how to set up the main.jsx file.

Listing 4.3 Render the app with React Router—src/main.jsx

```
import React from 'react';
import ReactDOM from 'react-dom';
import {
  browserHistory,
  Router
} from 'react-router';
import sharedRoutes from './shared/sharedRoutes';

ReactDOM.render(
  <Router
    routes={sharedRoutes}
    history={browserHistory}
  />,
  document.getElementById('react-content')
);
```

Include your React and ReactDOM dependencies.

Include the Router component and the browserHistory module from React Router.

Include the sharedRoutes file you created.

Render the React app into the DOM by declaring the Router component as your root component.

Router takes in the routes you included from sharedRoutes.

Router component needs to know which implementation of history it should use—here use browser history module so the app can use the built-in browser history API.

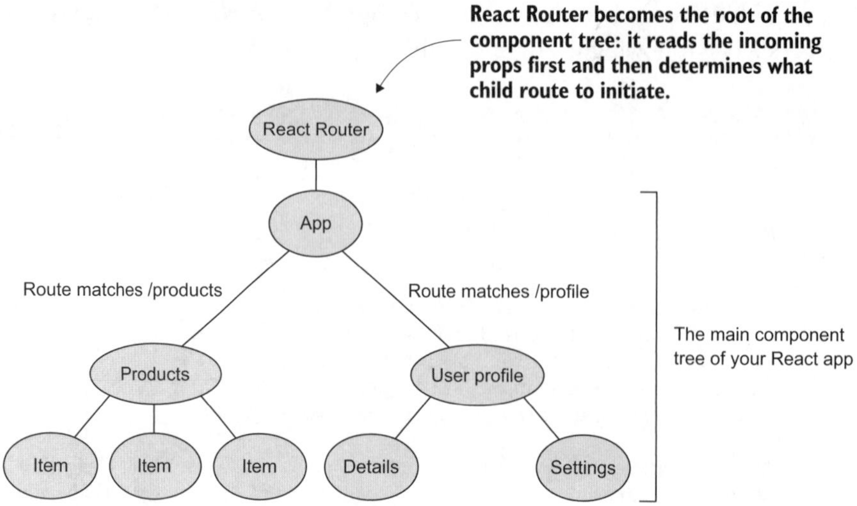
React Router becomes the root of the component tree: it reads the incoming props first and then determines what child route to initiate.
React Router
App
Route matches /products
Route matches /profile
The main component tree of your React app
Products
User profile
Item
Item
Item
Details
Settings

Figure 4.2 Example component tree with React Router as the root element

Instead of rendering a root component into the DOM, React Router ends up being your root component. Another way to think of it is as the top component in your component tree (see figure 4.2).

Under the hood, the router is using the browser history object. It hooks into this object to use push state and other browser-routing APIs.

Additionally, React Router allows you to pass in this history object. That way, it doesn't make any assumptions about which environment it runs in. On the browser, you pass in a different history object than on the server. That's part of what makes React Router good for isomorphic apps. Passing in the history object is also a more testable pattern.

4.1.2 Adding child routes

To make the rest of the app work, add the child routes the user will use to navigate between the views in the app. This requires two additional steps: creating child routes and setting up app.jsx to render any child. The following listing shows how to add the new routes to the sharedRoutes file. If you want to follow along, the base code for this section is in branch chapter-4.1.2 (`git checkout chapter-4.1.2`).

Listing 4.4 Adding child routes—src/shared/sharedRoutes.jsx

```
//... other import statements
import Cart from '../components/cart';
import Products from '../components/products';
import Profile from '../components/profile';
```

Include the component for each route.

```
const routes = (
  <Route path="/" component={App}>
    <Route path="/cart" component={Cart} />
    <Route path="/products" component={Products} />
    <Route path="/profile" component={Profile} />
  </Route>
);

export default routes;
```

Create child routes by nesting them inside the App route.

Each of the child routes will be combined with App. React Router will know the appropriate child component that should be made available to App to be rendered.

React: rendering any children

The next step in getting the child routes working is to set up the App component to display any arbitrary child. The App component doesn't need to know which child it's rendering—only that it needs to render a child. You decouple the implementation of the child and parent. This creates a reusable pattern in which the same child can be used in multiple views, or vice versa. Figure 4.3 shows the React Router and child route relationship.

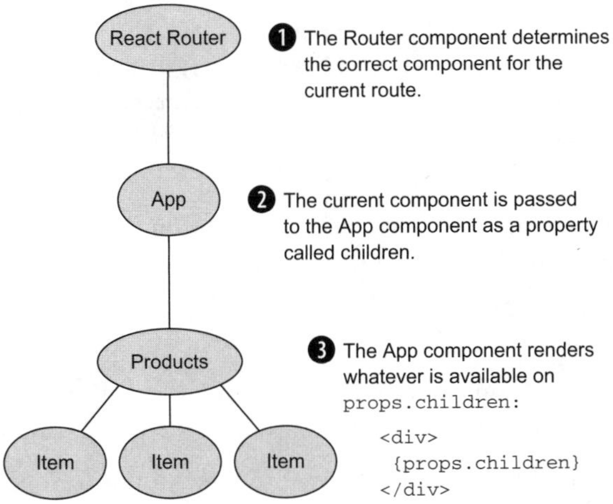
React Router
App
Products
Item
Item
Item
1 The Router component determines the correct component for the current route.
2 The current component is passed to the App component as a property called children.
3 The App component renders whatever is available on props.children:
<div>
{props.children}
</div>

Figure 4.3 Using `props.children` to render components at runtime

You can pass in children by nesting React components:

```
<MyComponent>
  <ChildComponent />
</MyComponent>
```

Then inside the `render` function of `MyComponent` you reference the child on the `props` object:

```
render() {
  return <div>{props.children}</div>
}
```

NOTE React Router handles passing down the children component by assigning props via JavaScript and using the lower-level React APIs such as `createElement`. You don't need to worry about this, but if you're interested in exploring further, check out https://github.com/ReactTraining/react-router/blob/v3/docs/API.md#routercontext.

This pattern allows the child component to be determined dynamically at runtime. The following listing shows how to update the App component to do this. Add the code from the listing to the app.jsx component code that already exists.

Listing 4.5 Rendering any child—src/components/app.jsx

```
const App = (props) => {
  return (
    <div>
      <div className="ui fixed inverted menu">
        ...
      </div>
      <div className="ui main text container">
        {props.children}
      </div>
    </div>
  );
};

App.propTypes = {
  children: PropTypes.element
};
```

- App component renders the children property (`{props.children}`)
- Setting propTypes on the component (`App.propTypes = {`)
- Prop children is a React element—the propTypes object describes this information. (`children: PropTypes.element`)

Setting `propTypes` on components provides documentation and is considered best practice. It's an object that describes the expected properties, including whether they're required.

ROUTER PROPERTIES

Because the Router wraps the App component, it passes down several router objects as `props`. Many of these objects are required in child components, but I'll focus on three:

- `location`—This mirrors the `window.location` object, built from the history you passed in to the router. It contains properties such as query and pathname that you can use in components.
- `params`—This object contains all the dynamic parameters on the route. If you had a route such as /products/treats that matched a route such as /products/:category, this object would contain a property called category: `{ category: treats }`.
- `router`—This object contains many methods for interacting with the router and history, including lower-level APIs. Most commonly, I find the need to use the `push()` method to navigate around an app from JavaScript.

In the next section, you'll use the Link component, which takes advantage of the lower-level router and history APIs so you don't have to.

4.1.3 Routing from components: Link

React Router goes one step further and provides a React component for you to use when you want to trigger navigation. That way, you don't need to worry about what's going on under the hood.

The Link component renders an `<a>` tag. To use the Link component, you include it in your component and then render it with the properties it needs. If you want to follow along with this section and get the code so far, switch to the branch called chapter-4.1.3 (`git checkout chapter-4.1.3`). The following listing shows you how to update the header to use the Link component instead of standard links in app.jsx.

Listing 4.6 Using the Link component—src/components/app.jsx

```
import React from 'react';
import { Link } from 'react-router';          <-- Include the Link component
                                                  from React Router
const App = (props) => {
  return (
    <div>
      <div className="ui fixed inverted menu">
        <h1 className="header item">All Things Westies</h1>
        <Link to="/products" className="item">Products</Link>
        <Link to="/cart" className="item">Cart</Link>
        <Link to="/profile" className="item">Profile</Link>
      </div>                                    Convert <a> tags
      <div className="ui main text container">  to <Link> tags
        {props.children}
      </div>
    </div>
  );
};
```

Note that instead of an `href` property, the Link component requires a `to` property. After adding the Link components, your app will properly route between views.

The React Router library has one more important part that you'll want to know about for building production apps: how to hook into the router lifecycle.

4.1.4 Understanding the router lifecycle

React Router provides hooks into its lifecycle to allow you to add logic between routes. A common use case for lifecycle hooks is adding page-view tracking analytics to your application so you know how many views each route gets.

> **NOTE** If you're using React Router 4, check out appendix A to see how to move this code into the React lifecycle and how to handle the concepts discussed in this section.

Imagine if you tried to add this logic into your components. You'd end up with the tracking logic in every top-level component (Cart, Products, Profile). Or you'd end up trying to detect changes based on properties in the App component. Both methods are undesirable and leave a lot of room for error.

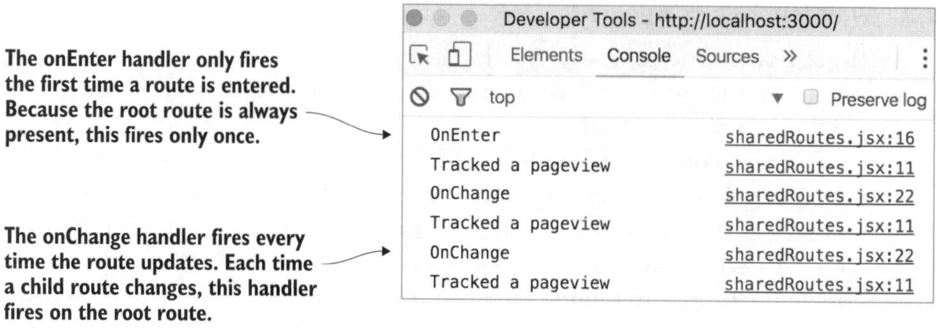
The onEnter handler only fires the first time a route is entered. Because the root route is always present, this fires only once.
The onChange handler fires every time the route updates. Each time a child route changes, this handler fires on the root route.
Developer Tools - http://localhost:3000/
Elements
Console
Sources
top
Preserve log
OnEnter sharedRoutes.jsx:16
Tracked a pageview sharedRoutes.jsx:11
OnChange sharedRoutes.jsx:22
Tracked a pageview sharedRoutes.jsx:11
OnChange sharedRoutes.jsx:22
Tracked a pageview sharedRoutes.jsx:11

Figure 4.4 The `onEnter` handler fires only once for the root route, but the `onChange` handler fires on every subsequent route change.

Instead, you want to use the `onChange` and `onEnter` lifecycle events for React Router. (A third lifecycle hook, `onLeave`, isn't covered here.) Figure 4.4 shows the order in which these handlers fire.

For each route, `onEnter` is fired when the app goes to the route from a different route. Because / is the root route, it can be entered only once. The `onChange` handler is fired each time a child route changes. For the root route, this happens on each route action after the first. The following listing shows how to implement these handlers in the sharedRoutes.jsx file. If you're following along and want to see the code from the previous sections, you can find it on branch chapter-4.1.4 (`git checkout chapter-4.1.4`).

Listing 4.7 Using `onChange` in the router—src/shared/searchRoutes.jsx

```
const trackPageView = () => {
  console.log('Tracked a pageview');
};

const onEnter = () => {
  console.log('OnEnter');
  trackPageView();
};

const onChange = () => {
  console.log('OnChange');
  trackPageView();
};

const routes = (
  <Route path="/" component={App} onEnter={onEnter} onChange={onChange}>
    <Route path="/cart" component={Cart} />
    <Route path="/products" component={Products} />
    <Route path="/profile" component={Profile} />
  </Route>
);
```

- Reusable function for tracking page views (in the real world, you'd call your analytics tool)
- Handler for onEnter—logs OnEnter
- Handler for onChange—logs OnChange
- Each Route can have an onEnter and/or onChange property.

Next, you'll explore React's component lifecycle, which is a completely different set of lifecycle functions specific to React. The lifecycle functions give you greater control over when things happen in your app.

4.2 Component lifecycle

A site that has user accounts requires a login. Certain parts of the site will always be locked down so you can view them only if you're logged in. For example, with the All Things Westies app, users who want to view their settings page to update their password or view past orders will need to log in.

This use case is the opposite of the analytics use case in the preceding section. Instead of doing something on every route, you want to check for logged-in status only on certain routes. You could do that on the routes, if you'd like, with `onChange` or `onEnter` handlers. But you can also put this logic inside the appropriate React component. For this example, we'll use the component lifecycle.

React provides several hooks into the lifecycle of components. The render function, which you've already used, is part of this lifecycle. The lifecycle of a component can be broken into three parts (illustrated in figure 4.5):

1. *Mounting events*—Happen when a React element (instance of a component class) is attached to a DOM node. This is where you'd handle the check for being logged in.
2. *Updating events*—Happen when React element is updating either as a result of new values of its properties or state. If you had a timer in your component, you'd manage it in these functions.
3. *Unmounting events*—Happen when React element is detached from the DOM. If you had a timer in your component, you'd clean it up here.[1]

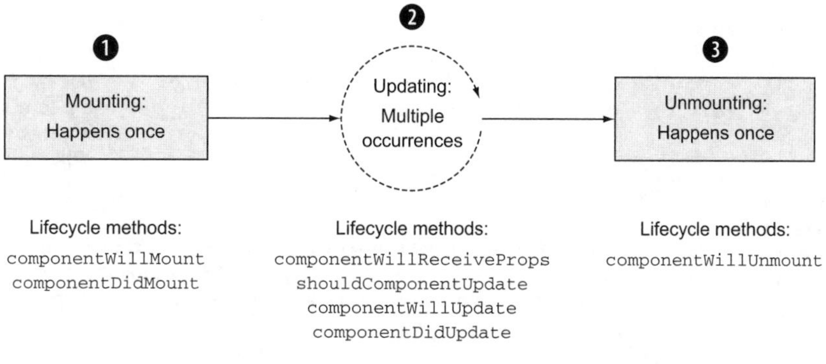
1
2
3
Mounting:
Happens once
Updating:
Multiple
occurrences
Unmounting:
Happens once
Lifecycle methods:
componentWillMount
componentDidMount
Lifecycle methods:
componentWillReceiveProps
shouldComponentUpdate
componentWillUpdate
componentDidUpdate
Lifecycle methods:
componentWillUnmount

Figure 4.5 The React lifecycle consists of three types of lifecycle events. Each has corresponding method hooks.

[1] React lifecycle list and illustration concept are from Azat Mardan's *React Quickly* (Manning, 2017, https://www.manning.com/books/react-quickly).

4.2.1 Hooking into mounting and updating to detect user's logged-in status

To detect whether the user is logged in, you'll take advantage of one of the React lifecycle functions. This function is fired before the component has *mounted* (been attached to the DOM). Listing 4.8 shows how to add the check to the user profile component inside `componentWillMount`. There's a placeholder for Profile, and you'll want to update it with this code. If you're following along and want to check out the code from the previous sections, switch to branch chapter 4.2.1 (`git checkout chapter-4.2.1`).

Listing 4.8 Using lifecycle events—src/components/profile.jsx

```
class Profile extends React.Component {

  componentWillMount() {
       if (!this.props.user) {
      this.props.router.push('/login');
    }
  }

  render() {}
}
```

- Check for a user property—if it doesn't exist, assume the user needs to log in. (`if (!this.props.user)`)
- Force user to route to log in using the router object. (`this.props.router.push('/login')`)

In profile.jsx, you added a reference to the router prop. But if you run the code now and load the /profile route, the app will throw an error because you haven't passed in the router object. To do that, you need to update app.jsx to pass props to its children. The following listing takes advantage of two React top-level API calls: `React.Children` and `React.cloneElement`.

Listing 4.9 Passing `props` to children—src/components/app.jsx

```
const App = (props) => {
  return (
    <div>
      <div className="ui fixed inverted menu"></div>
      <div className="ui main text container">
        {
          React.Children.map(
            props.children,
            (child) => {
              return React.cloneElement(
                child,
                { router: props.router }
              );
            }
          )
        }
      </div>
    </div>
  );
};
```

- Use the React.Children.map top-level API method to iterate over the current children property. (`React.Children.map(`)
- The map function takes in props.children as its first argument. (`props.children,`)
- The second argument is a callback function that gets called for each child. (`(child) => {`)
- Use the React.cloneElement top-level API to copy the current child and pass in additional props. (`return React.cloneElement(`)

FIRST RENDER CYCLE

In an isomorphic app, the first render cycle is the most important. That's where you'll use lifecycle events to control what environment the code runs in. For example, some third-party libraries aren't loadable or usable on the server because they rely on the `window` object. Or you might want to add custom scroll behavior on the window event. You'll need to control this by hooking into the various lifecycle methods available on the first render.

The first render lifecycle is made up of three functions (`render` and two mounting events):

- `componentWillMount()`—Happens before the render and before the component is mounted on the DOM
- `render()`—Renders the component
- `componentDidMount()`—Happens after the render and after the component is mounted on the DOM

For the isomorphic use case, it's important to note some differences between `componentWillMount` and `componentDidMount`. Although both methods run exactly once on the browser, `componentWillMount` runs on the server, whereas `componentDidMount` never runs on the server. In the previous example, you wouldn't want to run the user logged-in check in `componentWillMount` because the check would also run on the server. Instead, you'd put the check in `componentDidMount`, guaranteeing that it happens only in the browser.

`componentDidMount` never runs on the server because React never attaches any components to the DOM on the server. Instead, React's `renderToString` (used on the server in place of `render`) results in a string representation of the DOM. In the next section, you'll use `componentDidMount` to add a timer for a modal—something you want to do only in the browser.

4.2.2 Adding timers

Imagine that you want to add a countdown timer to the Products page. This timer launches a tooltip modal after a set amount of time. Figure 4.6 shows what this looks like. Timers are asynchronous and break the normal flow of user event-driven React

This message displays after 10 seconds—as a prompt to get the user to take an action. The timer is added in componentDidMount.

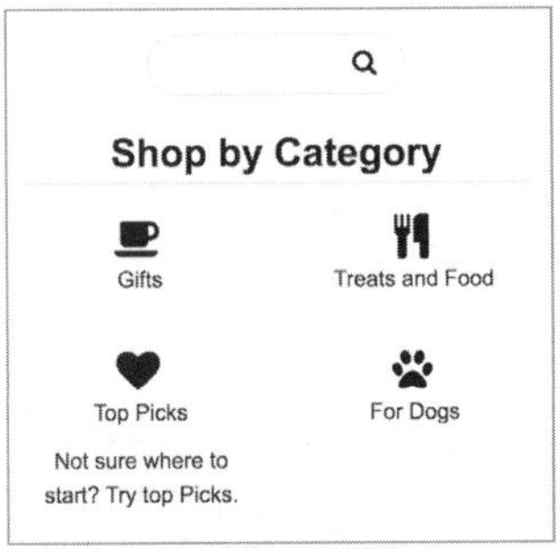

Shop by Category
Gifts
Treats and Food
Top Picks
For Dogs
Not sure where to start? Try top Picks.

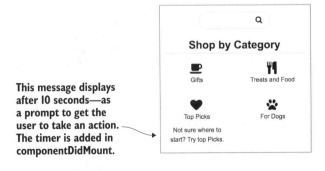

Figure 4.6 The tooltip that shows as a user prompt

updates. But React provides several lifecycle methods that can be used to handle timers within the lifecycle of a React component.

To add a timer to your component, you need to kick it off after the component has mounted. Additionally, you'll need to handle the cleanup of the timer when the component unmounts or when certain other actions happen. To check out the base code for this section, switch to branch chapter 4.2.2 (`git checkout chapter-4.2.2`). The following listing shows how to add the timer code to products.jsx. The base component already exists, so update the code in bold.

Listing 4.10 Adding the timer—src/components/products.jsx

```
import React from 'react';

class Products extends React.Component {
  constructor(props) {
    super(props);
    this.state = {
      showToolTip: false,
      searchQuery: ''
    };
    this.updateSearchQuery = this.updateSearchQuery.bind(this);
  }

  componentDidMount() {
    setTimeout(() => {
      this.setState({
        showToolTip: true
      });
    }, 10000);
  }

  updateSearchQuery() {
    this.setState({
      searchQuery: this.search.value
    });
  }

  render() {
    const toolTip = (
      <div className="tooltip ui inverted">
        Not sure where to start? Try top Picks.
      </div>
    );
    return (
      <div className="products">
        <div className="ui search">
          <div className="ui item input">
            <input
              className="prompt"
              type="text"
              value={this.state.searchQuery}
              ref={(input) => { this.search = input; }}
              onChange={this.updateSearchQuery}
```

- **In componentDidMount, trigger the timer—the setTimeout callback sets the component state after 10 seconds.**
- **Change handler for search input, sets state of searchQuery.**
- **Search is set by taking the value from the input element that's been saved to this.search in the ref callback.**
- **The div displays the toolTip (declaring it as a variable makes the ternary statement more readable). It shows only when showToolTip is true (after the timer has triggered).**
- **The value for input is tied to state so input uses the component state as its source of truth.**

```
          />
          <i className="search icon" />
        </div>
        <div className="results" />
      </div>
      <h1 className="ui dividing header">Shop by Category</h1>
      <div className="ui doubling four column grid">
        <div className="column segment secondary"></div>
        <div className="column segment secondary"></div>
        <div className="column segment secondary">
          <i className="heart icon" />
          <div className="category-title">Top Picks</div>
          { this.state.showToolTip ? toolTip : ''}
        </div>
        <div className="column segment secondary"></div>
      </div>
    </div>
  );
 }
}

export default Products;
```

The div displays the toolTip (declaring it as a variable makes the ternary statement more readable). It shows only when showToolTip is true (after the timer has triggered).

The tooltip shows up at this point (it's set to show after 10 seconds). But let's imagine you want to show the tooltip only if the user has never interacted with the page. In that case, you need a way to clear the tooltip when the user has interacted. Technically, you could do that in the `onChange` handler for search, but for illustrative purposes, you'll add this in `componentWillUpdate`. The following listing shows how to do that.

Listing 4.11 Clearing the timer on user interaction—src/components/products.jsx

```
class Products extends React.Component {
 componentDidMount() {
   this.clearTimer = setTimeout(() => {
     this.setState({
       showToolTip: true
     });
   }, 10000);
 }

 componentWillUpdate(nextProps, nextState) {
   if (nextState.searchQuery.length > 0) {
     clearTimeout(this.clearTimer);
   }
   console.log('cWU');
 }
 updateSearchQuery() {}
}
```

Capture return value of setTimeout so timer can be cleared.

When component receives new state, check state for presence of search query.

Clear timer.

Log shows that the componentWillUpdate method fires each time a letter is typed into the search box (with abbreviation cWU).

If you restart the app and interact with the Products page before the 10-second timer is finished, you'll notice that the tooltip never appears.

UPDATE LIFECYCLE

The update lifecycle methods are made up of several update methods and the `render` method, which you can see in the listing. With the exception of the `render` method, these methods never run on the server (so the accessing window and document are safe):

- `componentWillReceiveProps(nextProps)`—Happens when the component is about to receive properties (runs only when an update happens in a parent component)
- `shouldComponentUpdate(nextProps, nextState) -> bool`—Allows you to optimize the number of render cycles by determining when the component needs to update
- `componentWillUpdate(nextProps, nextState)`—Happens right before the component renders
- `render()`—Renders the component
- `componentDidUpdate(prevProps, prevState)`—Happens right after the component renders[2]

TIP Remember, the mounting lifecycle will always run before any of these methods.

UNMOUNTING EVENT

One final improvement you need to make to the timer is to make sure it gets cleaned up if the user navigates away from the Products page before the timer finishes running. If you don't do that, you'll see a React error in the console after 10 seconds. The error explains that the code being run is trying to reference a component that's no longer mounted in the DOM. This happened because you navigated away from the component the timer was in without turning off the timer. Figure 4.7 is a screenshot of the error.

```
OnEnter                                                    sharedRoutes.jsx:16
Tracked a pageview                                         sharedRoutes.jsx:11
OnChange                                                   sharedRoutes.jsx:22
Tracked a pageview                                         sharedRoutes.jsx:11
▶ Warning: setState(...): Can only update a mounted        warning.js:36
  or mounting component. This usually means you called setState()
  on an unmounted component. This is a no-op. Please check the
  code for the Products component.
```

Figure 4.7 If a component is unmounted, but listeners or timers aren't cleaned up, they'll end up with a reference to a null component.

[2] Update lifecycle based on Azat Mardan's *React Quickly* (Manning, 2017).

The following listing shows how to add the time-out cleanup to your `componentWillUnmount` lifecycle function.

Listing 4.12 Cleaning up the timer—src/components/products.jsx

```
class Products extends React.Component {

  componentWillUpdate(nextProps, nextState) {}

  componentWillUnmount() {
    clearTimeout(this.clearTimer);        <-- Clear timer on unmount.
  }

  updateSearchQuery() {}
}
```

There's only one unmount event: `componentWillUnmount()`. You can take advantage of this event to clean up any manually attached event listeners and shut down any timers you may have running. This method runs only in the browser. To see all the code for the chapter, you can check out branch chapter-4-complete (`git checkout chapter-4-complete`).

Now that you understand the React lifecycle, let's explore component architecture patterns that can help you build great React apps.

4.3 Component patterns

You can compose React components in user interfaces in two well-defined ways:

- Higher-order components
- Presentation and container components

In the All Things Westies app, it's beneficial to create reusable parts for the view and business logic. This has long-term maintainability benefits for developers and makes your code easier to reason about.

In some cases, you add reusability by creating a component that takes in another component and extends its functionality—a decorator. This happens in Redux when you wrap a view component with the Connect component. In other cases, you split your components into two types: components that focus on business logic and components that focus on what the app looks like. For example, the Products component focuses on the business logic of the view.

4.3.1 Higher-order components

When building a modular, component-driven UI, you end up having a lot of components that need the same kind of data fetching or that have the same view with different data fetching. For example, you may have many views that use user data in some way. Or you may have many views that use a List component but with different data sets. In these cases, you want a way to pull out the data-fetching and manipulation logic, making it separate from the component that displays the data.

Even though you haven't added any data fetching to the All Things Westies app yet, you'll eventually need to do that. The products view will need to know about the products available for sale. Imagine you wanted to make a component that knew how to fetch all the products. It'd look something like this:

```
const ProductsDataFetcher = (Component) => {
  ... // fetches the products data
  ... // ensures data is compatible with the products component
  return <Component data={this.state.data} />
}
```

The most important part of this example function is that you pass in the component (the Products component in this example) to the `ProductsDataFetcher` function. In this case, the higher-order component (HOC) function knows how to get the product data and will then pass that data into the component (Figure 4.8). This abstracts away any state or logic from the Products View component, leaving it to focus on the UI concerns.

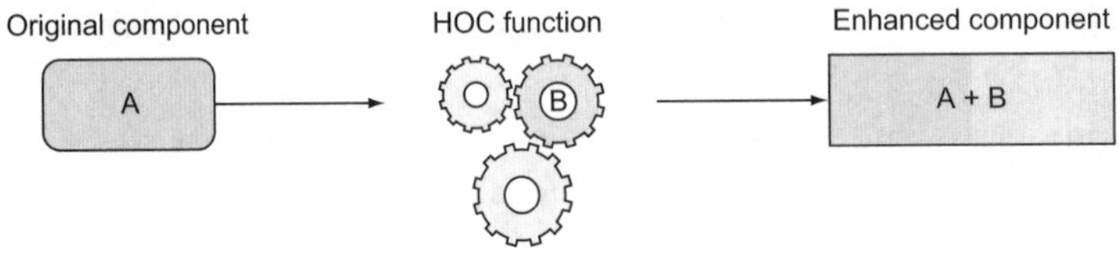
Original component
A
HOC function
B
Enhanced component
A + B

Figure 4.8 Higher-order functions take a function and return a new function with additional functionality. (Reproduced from Azat Mardan's *React Quickly*, Manning, 2017.

If you have a component and then pass it into the higher-order component, you'll end up with the original component plus additional functionality. In React, this almost always results in offloading some sort of state management to the parent HOC. In the `ListDataFetcher` example, the HOC knows about the app state and fetching the data. That allows the List component to be a presentation component that's highly reusable.

4.3.2 Component types: presentation and container

It's possible to categorize React components into two distinct buckets: presenters and containers. By following this binary type pattern, you can maximize your code reuse and minimize unnecessary code coupling and complexity.

Earlier in this chapter, you built the Products page of the All Things Westies app. This has a component called Products that holds onto the state for its part of the application. Later in the book, it'll also be responsible for managing data fetching via Redux. These responsibilities make it a container component.

On the other hand, the Item and App components are presentation components. Both contain display elements and rely on properties to determine their functionality. Presentation components determine how the app looks.

Table 4.1 lists the value of container and presentation components.

Table 4.1 Attributes of component types

Container	Presentation
Contains state	Limited state (for user interactions), ideally implemented as a functional component
Responsible for how the app works	Responsible for how the app looks
Children: container and presentation components	Children: container and presentation components
Connect to rest of application (for example, Redux)	No dependencies on model or controller portions of the app (for example, Redux)

Container components abstract state away from their children. They also handle layout and are generally responsible for the *how* of the application. Some higher-order components have this as their main purpose. They listen for data changes and then pass that state down as properties. Redux provides a higher-order component that helps with this (see chapter 6).

Presentation components contain only state related to user interactions. Whenever possible, they should be implemented as pure components. They're concerned with what the application looks like.

One important note is that containers can have other containers and presentation components as children. Conversely, presentation components can have both containers and presentation components as children. These two types of component nesting should be kept flexible to maximize code composition. That may feel strange at first, but keeping the two component types clear will help you in the long run.

Summary

In this chapter, you learned how to set up and use React Router to have a complete single-page app experience. You also learned more about React by exploring the component lifecycle. Finally, you learned key patterns that are commonly used when building React apps.

- React Router uses React's concepts of components to compose routes into any React app.
- React Router abstracts the history object and provides utilities for linking.
- React Router has routing hooks that let you add advanced logic.
- React lifecycle methods are used as hooks into the render cycle.
- The initial render cycle can be used to trigger timers or lock down logged-in routes.
- Many component patterns are available for composing React components in reusable and maintainable ways.

5 Tools: webpack and Babel

This chapter covers

- Using webpack to load Node.js packages via npm in order to use them in browser code
- Compiling code with Babel using webpack loaders
- Loading CSS with webpack loaders
- Using webpack plugins to prepare your code for production
- Creating multiple configurations to manage builds for multiple environments

The JavaScript ecosystem provides many great libraries and tools to make writing applications faster and easier for developers. To take advantage of them, you need to have tooling in place that can compile, transform, and prepare your code for production. Enter webpack, a build tool that's entirely configuration driven.

I'm going to be completely honest with you: webpack isn't an intuitive tool. I found it frustrating to work with at first. But it's extremely powerful and worth learning. Webpack gives you the ability to include any JavaScript code in your build, even libraries that haven't been set up to run in the browser (for example, npm packages). It also can take care of many other build steps, including compiling your code with Babel and preparing your code for production. This chapter covers all the basics you need in order to have a good workflow in your isomorphic project.

NOTE If you ever want to start a React project with webpack set up for you, I recommend Create React App. This tool generates a base React app with webpack (https://github.com/facebookincubator/create-react-app). Note that it's not isomorphic!

5.1 Webpack overview

Imagine you're starting a new isomorphic React project. You want to build a calendar reminder app like the one in figure 5.1. This chapter is about the build tools—so this is just a signpost to help you make sure things are loading.

In this example, you've decided not to build a calendar from scratch. A lot of well-written React calendar packages are available on npm. To use these packages and build your own app on top of them, you need a build tool that will package your Java-Script modules in a way that the browser understands. (Also, this chapter is about the build tool, not making an app, so using a package will let you focus on learning webpack.)

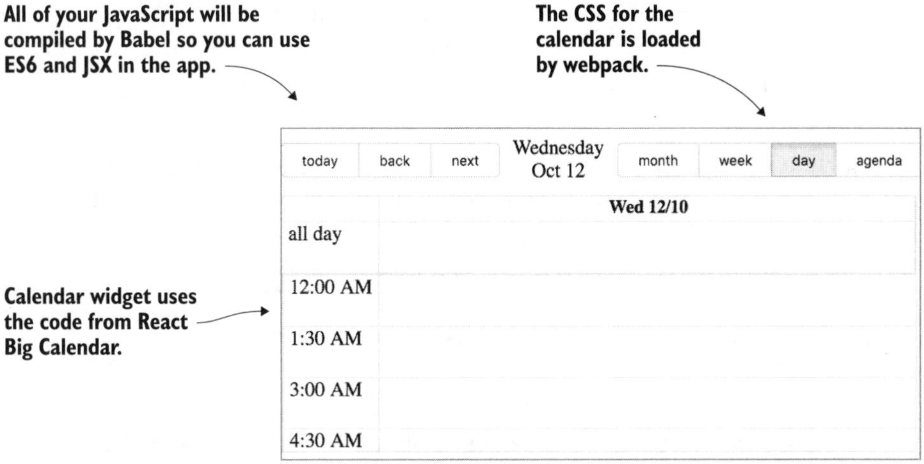
All of your JavaScript will be compiled by Babel so you can use ES6 and JSX in the app.
The CSS for the calendar is loaded by webpack.
Calendar widget uses the code from React Big Calendar.
today
back
next
Wednesday Oct 12
month
week
day
agenda
Wed 12/10
all day
12:00 AM
1:30 AM
3:00 AM
4:30 AM

Figure 5.1 The calendar reminder app you'll be setting up with webpack in this chapter

If you're wondering why you need to learn yet another build tool, give me a few minutes to convince you. Let's cover the app requirements to establish why a build tool is necessary. That way, you don't have to take my word for it. Table 5.1 gives an overview of the app requirements and the reasons you need webpack.

Table 5.1 An overview of the various app requirements that make a build tool necessary

Requirement	Webpack required	Reason
Calendar widget (react-big-calendar)	Yes	Import from npm package. In particular, this is something that can't be achieved through tools such as Gulp and Grunt or npm build scripts.
ES6	Yes	Requires compilation to work in all browsers. This could be achieved with other tools, but webpack loaders make it straightforward.
Load CSS	Optional	Optimize development flow by including in the webpack build. This can't be achieved with tools such as Gulp or Grunt.
Environment-specific code	Yes	Webpack plugins allow you to inject custom variables. This can't be achieved with Gulp or Grunt.

Additionally, there are many other reasons a build tool is required for the app. You want to use ES6 to write the latest JavaScript code, but cross-browser support for ES6 is mixed. To allow you to use all the latest language features, you need to compile your code.

Finally, in order to load CSS, you need webpack loaders. You also need webpack plugins to inject variables into code. Remember, all the code will run in the server and the browser! (If this reminder is starting to feel repetitive, that's great—you're on your way to thinking in isomorphic terms.)

RUNNING THE CODE

All code for this chapter is located on GitHub at https://github.com/isomorphic-dev-js/chapter5-webpack-babel. After you've checked out the code with Git, you need to do an npm install:

```
$ npm install
```

To run the complete example, run the following command:

```
$ npm run start
```

Then you can load the calendar example at http://localhost:3050. You'll use additional scripts and examples throughout the chapter. I'll explain them as needed.

Before we dive into the specifics of a webpack configuration, I'm going to show you how to set up your environment to work with webpack, including how to run the webpack command-line interface (CLI). The command-line tool will be useful for debugging issues and is great for working on small projects. Later in the chapter, you'll learn to use webpack via JSON configuration.

To use webpack, you need to install it (I've already set up the repo with webpack). I recommend doing this on a per project basis rather than installing it globally so you can use the version of webpack appropriate to each project.

After webpack is installed, you can use the webpack CLI to generate your first webpack bundle. The syntax is shown next.

DEFINITION A *bundle* is the file outputted by the webpack transformation pipeline. You can name a bundle anything you want.

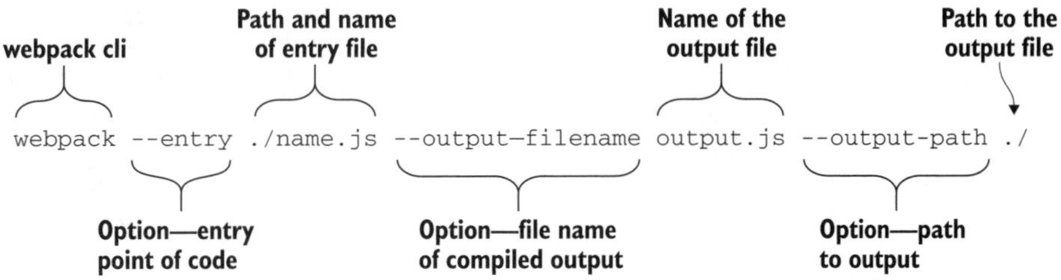
webpack cli
Path and name of entry file
Name of the output file
Path to the output file
webpack --entry ./name.js --output–filename output.js --output-path ./
Option—entry point of code
Option—file name of compiled output
Option—path to output

To run this command in the repo, put this command into your terminal:

```
$ node_modules/.bin/webpack --entry ./src/entry.js --output-filename
     output.js --output-path ./
```

After running this command, you'll notice a new file in the root of the project code directory called output.js, shown in listing 5.1. This file contains your compiled code from entry.js and any dependencies. First take a look at the entry.js file contents (written in ES5—later in the chapter, you'll add Babel to compile ES6). This code is already provided in the repo.

Listing 5.1 Entry.js contents—src/entry.js

```
var path = require('path');

console.log("path to root", path.resolve('../'));
```

Path included as dependency—require() is used instead of import because this code isn't being compiled by Babel. (var path = require('path');)

Log the path to the root folder using path.resolve with the relative path (console.log(...))

The compiled version of this code is nearly 400 lines of code, some of which is shown in the next listing. That's because webpack collects all the referenced files (the node module path, in this case) and includes them in the bundled output.

Listing 5.2 Compiled webpack output, partial view—output.js

```
/* ...additional file contents */
/******/  // Load entry module and return exports, and additional
/******/polyfills/webpack code
/* WEBPACK VAR INJECTION */}.call(
/***/ exports,
```

```
/***/__webpack_require__(1)))

/***/ }),
/* 4 */
/***/ (function(module, exports, __webpack_require__) {

"use strict";


module.exports = __webpack_require__(31);


/***/ }),
/* 5 */
/***/ (function(module, exports, __webpack_require__) {
/* additional file contents... */
```

Webpack wraps modules (your code, any included npm libraries) in JavaScript closures, which allows webpack to control, and rewrite import statements.

The require statement for path compiles into a custom webpack require statement. The path module is located by number key.

Human-readable comments indicating the number of each module are added to the final output (helps with debugging).

The bundled code includes additional functions that are part of the webpack library. This includes a browser-friendly polyfill of the Node.js process object, which allows you to safely include many npm modules that were originally written for Node.js.

There are some exceptions to this. For example, the Node.js file system (fs) module isn't safe for isomorphic use. If an npm package relies on the fs module, you shouldn't use it for browser code. Now that you've seen how to use the command line to bundle your code, take a look at figure 5.2. It shows how webpack takes your code and creates a bundled output.

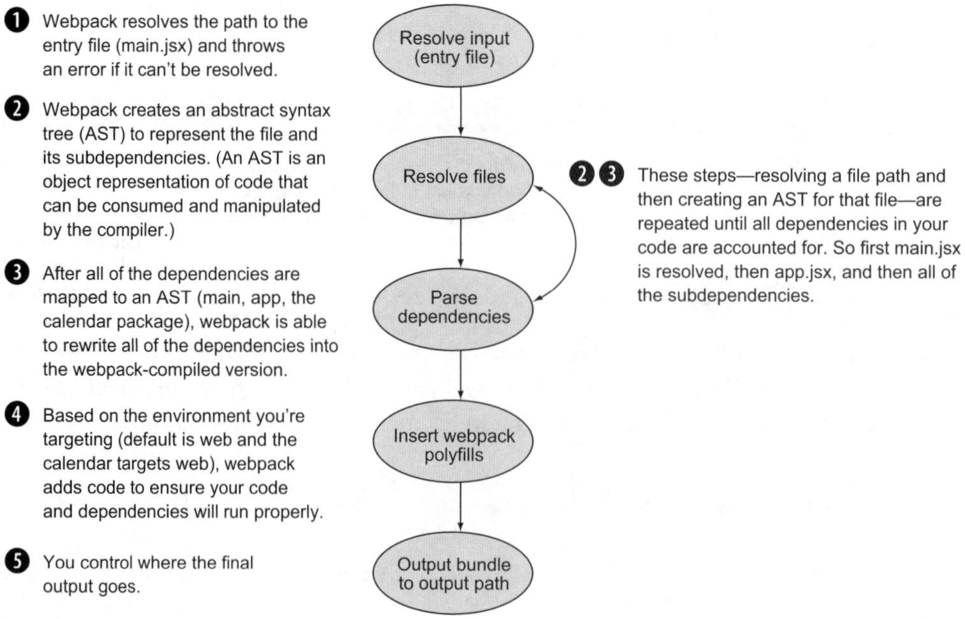
1 Webpack resolves the path to the entry file (main.jsx) and throws an error if it can't be resolved.
2 Webpack creates an abstract syntax tree (AST) to represent the file and its subdependencies. (An AST is an object representation of code that can be consumed and manipulated by the compiler.)
3 After all of the dependencies are mapped to an AST (main, app, the calendar package), webpack is able to rewrite all of the dependencies into the webpack-compiled version.
4 Based on the environment you're targeting (default is web and the calendar targets web), webpack adds code to ensure your code and dependencies will run properly.
5 You control where the final output goes.
Resolve input (entry file)
Resolve files
Parse dependencies
Insert webpack polyfills
Output bundle to output path
2 3 These steps—resolving a file path and then creating an AST for that file—are repeated until all dependencies in your code are accounted for. So first main.jsx is resolved, then app.jsx, and then all of the subdependencies.

Figure 5.2 The webpack compiler flow

DEBUGGING WEBPACK

Sometimes webpack will fail to compile. You have two helpful command-line options for debugging. The first option, `--debug`, shows errors in the command line. The second option, `--display-error-details`, provides an additional level of detail about any errors that occur.

Webpack can also be debugged using `node --inspect`. This loads a debugging tool with which you can see Node.js code in the Chrome DevTools. Then you can use breakpoints to debug. For more `--inspect` resources, see https://nodejs.org/en/docs/inspector/.

Now that you've seen how to use webpack and explored the parts of a webpack bundle, you'll learn how to use webpack loaders to compile your code.

5.2 Babel overview

Babel is a tool for compiling JavaScript. It takes code that isn't yet supported in all JavaScript environments and compiles it into something understandable by browsers. If you want to use the latest and greatest parts of the JavaScript spec (ES6, ES7, or sometimes also referred to as ES2015, ES2016, and so forth), you must use a compiler. It should be noted that the latest versions of Node.js now support most (but not quite all) of the JavaScript spec. But in the browser, support is varied and rolls out more slowly.

In the preceding section, you learned that webpack is a tool that brings together many loaders and plugins to create a single bundled code file. Babel is a library that does a single job: it compiles JavaScript. Babel is one of many loaders you can use with webpack.

5.2.1 Getting started with Babel

Babel compiles to code that can be understood by any browser running ES5 JavaScript. The generated output is human readable, as you can see in the following listing, and includes Babel-injected code that helps convert ES6 syntax into something understood by older JavaScript engines.

Listing 5.3 Babel sample output

```
'use strict';

var _createClass = function () {/*implementation code*/}();

var _react = require('react');

var _react2 = _interopRequireDefault(_react);

function _interopRequireDefault(obj) {
  /*implementation code*/
}
```

- `_createClass`: Babel-injected function that converts ES6 class into ES5
- `require('react')`: All import statements converted to requires
- `_react2`: Each import statement converts to two requires: one the standard ES5 require, the other using a special function to ensure the export default feature of ES6 works properly.
- `_interopRequireDefault`: Babel-injected function that checks for the default export

```
var Link = function Link(props) {
  return _react2.default.createElement(
    'a',
    { href: props.link },
    props.children
  );
};

var Button = function (_React$Component) {
  _{/*implementation code*/}
}

_createClass(Button, [{
    key: 'render',
    value: function render() {{/*implementation code*/}
  }]);

  return Button;
}(_react2.default.Component);
```

ES6-style functions converted to function() {} syntax

Button written as a class in ES6, so here it's wrapped by Babel _createClass helper function.

The compiled code in listing 5.3 is based on the ES6 code in listing 5.4. Notice that the base code is much simpler and doesn't include many of the helper functions that Babel adds to help run your code in JavaScript environments that don't yet support ES6.

Listing 5.4 ES6 code to compile—src/compile-me.js

```
import React from 'react';
import classnames from 'classnames';

const Link = (props) => {
  return (<a href={this.props.link}>
          {this.props.children}
        </a>)
}

class Button extends React.Component {
  constructor(props) {
    super(props);
  }

  render() {
    let classes = 'button';
    if (this.props.classname) {
      classes = classnames(classes, this.props.classnames);
    }
    return (
      <Button
        className={classnames}
        onClick={this.props.clickHandler}>
        {this.props.children}
      </Button>
    );
  }
}
```

Currently, import statements need to be compiled for all environments (node and browsers).

ES6 function syntax with scope of parent rather than caller

A class declaration

The let variable (or in other cases, const)

Babel compiler also compiles the JSX.

5.2.2 The Babel CLI

Babel can be used on its own as a command-line tool. To get started and understand how this tool works, you'll use the Babel CLI to process the ES6 from listing 5.3:

```
$ ./node_modules/.bin/babel src/compile-me.jsx
```

Babel takes the input (the code in src/compile-me.js), parses it, transforms it, and then generates a version of the code that's compatible with standard browser and Node.js environments. Figure 5.3 shows this compile flow. You'll notice that this flow is similar to webpack's flow.

The command in this section outputs the result to the command line. Later, you'll use Babel to compile the code as part of the webpack build.

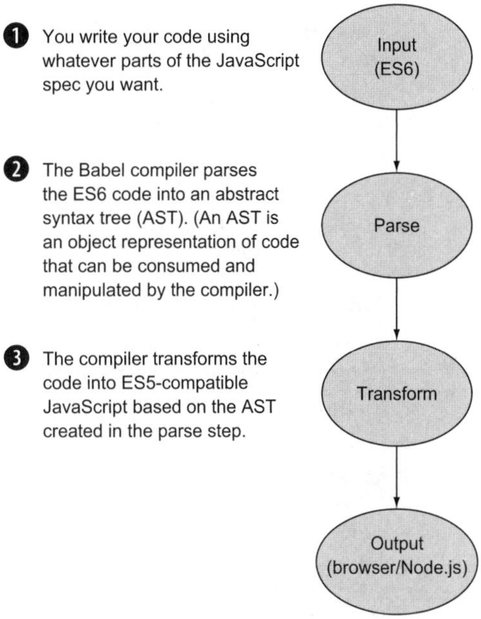

1 You write your code using whatever parts of the JavaScript spec you want.
2 The Babel compiler parses the ES6 code into an abstract syntax tree (AST). (An AST is an object representation of code that can be consumed and manipulated by the compiler.)
3 The compiler transforms the code into ES5-compatible JavaScript based on the AST created in the parse step.
Input (ES6)
Parse
Transform
Output (browser/Node.js)

Figure 5.3 How the Babel compiler transforms ES6 into browser- and Node.js-compatible code

BABEL PLUGINS AND PRESETS

Out of the box, Babel doesn't know what rules to use to compile your code. But you can use plugins that tell Babel what to do. Conveniently, these plugins are often grouped into *presets*. Presets and plugins need to be installed from npm. If you wanted to use the Babel React preset, you'd install the following:

```
$ npm install babel-preset-react
```

If you're working with the provided code, all the presets you need for this chapter are already installed. After you've installed all the Babel presets you want to use, you can reference them in the .babelrc file, provided in the repo and shown in the following listing.

Listing 5.5 .babelrc configuration file—.babelrc

```
{
  "presets": ["es2015", "react"]
}
```

Tell Babel what presets to use when compiling (you can list multiple presets in an array).

These presets tell Babel to compile everything to ES2015 and properly process JSX. Next we'll look at the Calendar App code.

5.3 The app code

Throughout the rest of this chapter, when you run webpack, you'll be compiling the Calendar App code. Two files make up this example: src/app.jsx and src/main.jsx.

The entry point file for the webpack builds is main.jsx. The following listing shows the code that's provided in the repo.

Listing 5.6 Entry file—src/main.jsx

```
import React from 'react';
import ReactDOM from 'react-dom';
import App from './app';

ReactDOM.render(
  <App></App>,
  document.getElementById('attach-react')
);
```

- Import dependencies including React and App component
- Attach the root component (App) to the DOM.

The entry point file includes a single component called App from src/app.jsx. Shown in the next listing, this component includes npm packages and renders the React Big Calendar component. It also includes the CSS for the calendar. We'll talk more about including the CSS in this format when you learn about webpack loaders.

Listing 5.7 App component—src/app.jsx

```
import React, { Component } from 'react';
import BigCalendar from 'react-big-calendar';
import moment from 'moment';
require('react-big-calendar/lib/css/
➥ react-big-calendar');

BigCalendar.momentLocalizer(moment);

class App extends Component {
  render() {
    return (
      <div className="calendar-app">
        <BigCalendar
          events={[]}
          startAccessor='startDate'
          endAccessor='endDate'
          timeslots={3}>
        </BigCalendar>
      </div>
    )
  }
}

export default App;
```

- Import all dependencies including moment (react-big-calendar requires a date library).
- Require the CSS that comes with react-big-calendar.
- Initialize the Calendar component.
- Create the App component.
- Render Big Calendar with the required props.

These files are simple but will allow you to learn webpack without the example getting in the way. They require Babel to compile the ES6 features (`import`, `class`) and the JSX. You also need to load the CSS properly. The next section shows how to configure webpack from a JavaScript file and introduces using loaders.

5.4 Webpack config with loaders

Earlier in the chapter, you bundled your code with webpack via the command line. But webpack is also configurable with a JavaScript configuration file. This file is called webpack.config.js by convention. (You can use any name you want in your own projects.)

The config file is loaded by the `webpack` command. By default, the command will look for a file called webpack.config.js. To load the default config, run the following command in Terminal:

```
$ ./node_modules/.bin/webpack
```

This loads the configuration file, compiles your code, and outputs a bundle file that can then be loaded in the browser. The most basic configuration file includes an entry point and output information (if you ever find yourself needing a simple configuration like this one, you can also stick to the command-line options introduced at the beginning of the chapter), as shown in the following listing.

Listing 5.8 webpack.config.js

```
var path = require('path');

module.exports = {
  entry: path.resolve(__dirname + '/src/main.js'),
  output: {
    path: path.resolve(__dirname + '/'),
    filename: 'webpack-bundle.js'
  }
}
```

- Entry point uses Node.js path module to resolve path relative to current directory (helpful for continuous integration tools).
- Declare output object.
- Use path module to resolve path to output (in this case, root directory).
- Declare filename of output.

Next, you'll add in webpack loaders to compile your ES6 and CSS.

5.4.1 Configuring the Babel loader

To use Babel within webpack, you need two things. First, you still need the .babelrc file you saw earlier in the chapter. This tells Babel what presets to compile with (React and ES6). Second, you need to declare Babel as a loader in the webpack configuration. Listing 5.9 shows the code for the loader.

> **TIP** Pay close attention to the shape of the configuration object—otherwise, your build will fail silently. This will be followed by a series of apocalyptic events and a sudden dislike for all build tools. In all seriousness, if your webpack build is failing silently, check that you put all your properties in the right place. You can use the `--debug` and `--progress` options to help you debug (more info at https://webpack.js.org/api/cli/#debug-options).

Listing 5.9 Adding Babel loader webpack.config.js

```
var path = require('path');

module.exports = {
  entry: path.resolve(__dirname + '/src/main.js'),
  output: {
    path: path.resolve(__dirname + '/'),
    filename: 'webpack-bundle.js'
  },
  module: {                          <- Add module object.
    rules: [                         <- Array of all loaders to use (called rules)
      {
        test: /\.(js|jsx)$/,         <- Regular expression that determines what files
                                        should be processed by this loader—for Babel,
                                        we want js and jsx files.
        exclude: /node_modules/,     <- You can tell the loader to ignore files,
                                        Node.js packages are already compiled, so
                                        you don't need to process them again.
        loader: "babel-loader"       <- Declare which loader should be
                                        used for this loader configuration.
      }
    ]
  }
}
```

Loaders are applied during the resolver step of the webpack compile process. Figure 5.4 shows how this fits into the overall webpack flow. Notice that this will happen many times, as each dependency may pass through one or many loaders.

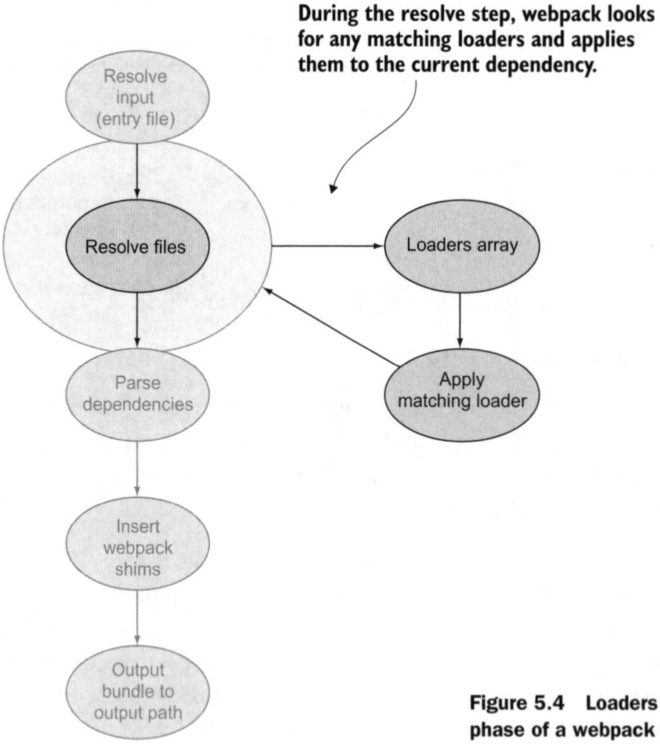
During the resolve step, webpack looks for any matching loaders and applies them to the current dependency.
Resolve input (entry file)
Resolve files
Loaders array
Apply matching loader
Parse dependencies
Insert webpack shims
Output bundle to output path

Figure 5.4 Loaders are applied during the resolver phase of a webpack compile.

USING CUSTOM EXTENSIONS

Often when writing JSX and ES6, it's nice to be able to declare your files with an extension other than .js. This indicates to other developers (and in some cases, to your IDE) that the file is of a specific syntax type.

It can also be convenient to not have to write an extension on your `import` statements. This can be a requirement for some testing setups to work properly. In webpack, to cover these uses cases, you add the `resolve` property and declare an array of extensions to use. See the following listing.

Listing 5.10 Extension list webpack.config.js

```
module.exports = {
  entry: path.resolve(__dirname + '/src/main.js'),
  output: {},
  module: {},
  resolve: {                                  // Add resolve object.
    extensions: ['.js', '.jsx', '.css']       // Declare array of extensions—for calendar example, you need .js, .jsx, and .css.
  }
}
```

5.4.2 Configuring the CSS loader

Webpack can pack almost anything into your JavaScript bundle, including your CSS. This is awesome for development, but for many production use cases you'll still want to load your CSS and other assets separately (don't worry, webpack can do that too!). See the next listing.

Listing 5.11 Including CSS with webpack—webpack.config.js

```
module.exports = {
  ...
  module: {
    rules: [
      {
        test: /\.(js|jsx)$/,
        exclude: /node_modules/,
        loader: "babel-loader"
      },
      {
        test:/\.css/,              // For this loader you need to process only CSS files, so regular expression looks for .css.
        loaders: ['style-loader', 'css-loader']   // This loader uses two webpack loaders, style-loader and CSS-loader—note the key has changed from loader to loaders because list is declared as array of strings.
      }
    ]
  }
}
```

This code adds two loaders. The CSS loader takes any `import` and `url()` references and interprets them as `require`. The style loader includes the styles in the bundle so your CSS is available in the browser.

By including the CSS, you can take advantage of the component style of writing your CSS. To do this, you create a set of styles for each component and namespace them. Then you don't have to worry about overwriting common class names such as `.button` or `.active`.

Additionally, I've found this modular CSS to be easier to reason about for large development teams, though there are trade-offs. One major trade-off is you tend to end up with less DRY (don't repeat yourself) CSS. But this can be combatted with shared global classes or mixins if you're using PostCSS or other compiled CSS options (LESS, SASS, and so forth).

ADDITIONAL LOADERS

Many more loaders can be used with webpack. You can load all kinds of files, including JSON, HTML, and image assets. You can also preprocess your preferred CSS using LESS/SASS/PostCSS.

You can also use loaders for linting. For example, if you want to use ESLint in your project, there's a webpack loader for it (the example introduced in chapter 4 uses ESLint). There are loaders for almost anything you can think of doing in a web app project!

For a list of webpack loaders, check out https://webpack.js.org/loaders/.

5.5 Bundling for dev and production

So far, you've used only a single configuration file for your development environment. But for a real-world app, you need to prepare your webpack configuration files for multiple environments.

For simplicity, you'll set up two environment-specific configuration files called dev.config.js and prod.config.js. Because these files are just JavaScript, you can create a base file, called base.config.js. All these files will live in the config folder.

The base file is identical to the webpack.config.js file you've already created in this chapter. The other two files require it and then extend the configuration. First you'll add a webpack plugin to dev.config.js.

5.5.1 Using webpack plugins

A webpack plugin is an additional code module that you can include in the plugins array of your webpack configuration. The webpack library ships with several built-in plugins. Many plugins can also be found on npm, and you even can write your own plugin.

For the dev config, you need the html-webpack-plugin. This plugin autogenerates an HTML file that loads the bundled JavaScript. This is set up in the dev.config.js file, as shown in the following listing.

Listing 5.12 Add a plugin—config/dev.config.js

```
var baseConfig = require('./base.config.js');                  <-- Require base configuration object.
var HtmlWebpackPlugin = require('html-webpack-plugin');        <-- Include html-webpack-plugin that will autogenerate a HTML file.
```

```
module.exports = Object.assign(baseConfig, {
  output: {
    filename: 'dev-bundle.js'
  },
  plugins: [
    new HtmlWebpackPlugin({
      title: "Calendar App Dev",
      filename: 'bundle.html'
    })
  ]
})
```

Use Object.assign to merge environment-specific configuration onto baseConfig; keys from this configuration will override base configuration.

Declare environment-specific filename.

Declare plugins array.

Create new instance of HtmlWebpackPlugin.

Title property sets <title> tag in HTML template.

Output filename for generated HTML.

To use this code, run the following command:

```
$ npm run dev
```

Then you can navigate to http://localhost:3050/bundle.html and see the dev bundle.

Plugins can hook into a variety of webpack compiler steps. They can add code at the beginning of the compile step, during the optimization step, during the emit files stage, and at many other phases of the webpack compiler.

The HTML webpack plugin does most of its work during the emit step because its main job is to create a file. The emit step is where the files are created based on all the previous compilation steps.

5.5.2 *Creating globals*

You can also use plugins to define environment variables. Webpack ships with a plugin called definePlugin that allows you to inject variables into your webpack module, as shown in listing 5.13. You can then access these variables in code:

```
console.log("current environment: ", __ENV__);
```

During the compile step, webpack converts the variable to the injected value. In this case, the code in the bundle will look like this:

```
console.log("current environment: ", ("dev"));
```

Listing 5.13 Inject globals—config/dev.config.js

```
var webpack = require('webpack');

var injectEnvironment = new webpack.DefinePlugin({
  __ENV__: JSON.stringify("dev")
});

module.exports = Object.assign(baseConfig, {
  output: {},
  plugins: [
    ...,
    injectEnvironment
  ]
})
```

Require webpack because DefinePlugin is included with webpack.

Create new instance of DefinePlugin.

Inject any number of variables here—in this case, set environment value.

Load plugin in plugin array.

One gotcha with DefinePlugin is that for strings, it's important to use JSON.stringify. If you just assign a string (`__ENV__: "dev"`), then in the bundled version you'll get the following output:

```
console.log("current environment: ", (dev));
```

That will throw a `ReferenceError` in your browser because it'll read `dev` as a JavaScript variable.

5.5.3 Working with sourcemaps

One of the drawbacks of developing with webpack is that the bundled code isn't human readable and no longer resembles the source code. Fortunately for debugging, webpack provides the ability to enable sourcemaps. Without sourcemaps, it's difficult to match code errors up to your file structure.

With sourcemaps enabled, webpack generates additional code (sometimes inline and sometimes in a separate file) that maps the generated code back to the original file structure. That's helpful when debugging, because tools such as Chrome DevTools will allow you to inspect the original code rather than the compiled code. Figure 5.5 shows how Chrome DevTools loads the original file.

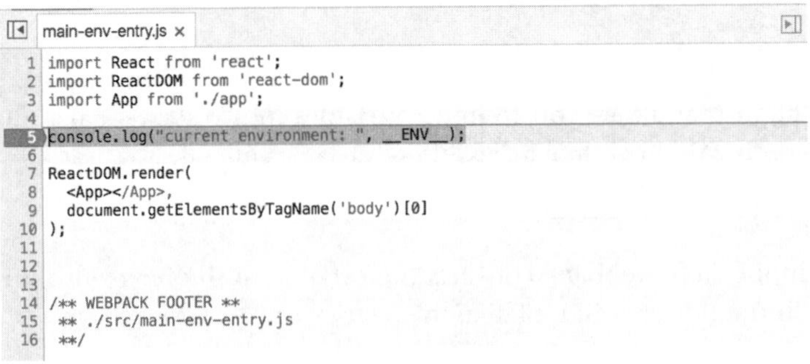
main-env-entry.js ×
import React from 'react';
import ReactDOM from 'react-dom';
import App from './app';
console.log("current environment: ", __ENV__);
ReactDOM.render(
<App></App>,
document.getElementsByTagName('body')[0]
);
/** WEBPACK FOOTER **
** ./src/main-env-entry.js
**/

Figure 5.5 Chrome DevTools uses the generated sourcemaps to link the compiled code to the source file.

Enabling sourcemaps is straightforward, as shown in listing 5.14. You add the `devtool` property to your webpack configuration to enable sourcemaps from the webpack configuration file. According to the webpack docs, you can use this sourcemap option for production. For bigger projects, this can have performance impacts, so tread carefully.

Listing 5.14 Adding sourcemaps—config/dev.config.js

```
module.exports = Object.assign(baseConfig, {
  output: {},
  devtool: 'source-map',
  plugins: []
})
```

Several valid sourcemap options are available for webpack. Each one makes a trade-off between performance and developer readability. The option in dev.config.js outputs a separate map file and loads the full original source. But it's on the slower side. If you need to adjust your sourcemap options, I recommend checking out webpack's documentation for sourcemaps at https://webpack.js.org/configuration/devtool/.

Next we'll use webpack plugins to create a production-ready configuration.

5.5.4 Preparing the build for production

To prepare a production build, you need to do a few things:

- Make the bundle as small as possible: add plugins for uglifying and deduping your code
- Inject production environment variables
- Output to a different output bundle

The goal is to end up with a non-human-readable, minified file with the smallest footprint possible. It should look something like figure 5.6.

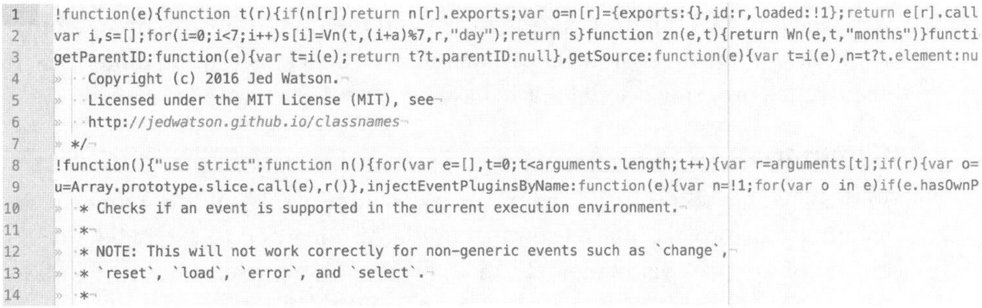

```
!function(e){function t(r){if(n[r])return n[r].exports;var o=n[r]={exports:{},id:r,loaded:!1};return e[r].call
var i,s=[];for(i=0;i<7;i++)s[i]=Vn(t,(i+a)%7,r,"day");return s}function zn(e,t){return Wn(e,t,"months")}functi
getParentID:function(e){var t=i(e);return t?t.parentID:null},getSource:function(e){var t=i(e),n=t?t.element:nu
    Copyright (c) 2016 Jed Watson.
    Licensed under the MIT License (MIT), see
    http://jedwatson.github.io/classnames
  */
!function(){"use strict";function n(){for(var e=[],t=0;t<arguments.length;t++){var r=arguments[t];if(r){var o=
u=Array.prototype.slice.call(e),r()},injectEventPluginsByName:function(e){var n=!1;for(var o in e)if(e.hasOwnP
   * Checks if an event is supported in the current execution environment.
   *
   * NOTE: This will not work correctly for non-generic events such as `change`,
   * `reset`, `load`, `error`, and `select`.
   *
```

Figure 5.6 Production output compiled with additional webpack plugins

In order to end up with production output, you will use some additional plugins to prepare the code. The following listing shows how to create a webpack configuration file that is ready for production.

Listing 5.15 Production build—config/prod.config.js

```
var baseConfig = require('./base.config.js');
var webpack = require('webpack');
var HtmlWebpackPlugin = require('html-webpack-plugin');

var injectEnvironment = new webpack.DefinePlugin({
  __ENV__: JSON.stringify("prod")            <-- Inject prod environment variable.
});
```

```
module.exports = Object.assign(baseConfig, {
  output: {
    filename: 'prod-bundle.js'
  },
  plugins: [
    new webpack.optimize.UglifyJsPlugin({
        compress: {
            warnings: false,
            drop_console: true
        }
    }),
    new HtmlWebpackPlugin({
      title: "Calendar App",
      filename: 'prod-bundle.html'
    })
    injectEnvironment
  ]
});
```

Change bundle name for current environment.

Uglify your code—this both compresses and uglifies the code.

Change filename of outputted HTML file.

Plugins have many use cases and can help you with everything from configuration to uglifying your output. For this reason, several plugins ship with webpack that can help you prepare your build for production. In addition to the plugins shown in the preceding listing, you can read about other webpack plugins on the webpack site (https://webpack.js.org/configuration/plugins/) and the npm site (www.npmjs.com/search?q=webpack+plugin). As of the latest version of webpack, deduping module includes and occurrence ordering are default behaviors.

Summary

In this chapter, you learned that webpack is a powerful build tool that can be used to compile your project into a browser bundle. You learned to use Babel on its own and as part of webpack via loaders. Both of these tools are useful in many JavaScript contexts and make great additions to your personal toolkit.

- With webpack, you can compile your JavaScript code, including npm modules.
- With the Babel compiler you can use the latest features of JavaScript and still run your code in all browsers and Node.js environments.
- Loaders are add-on modules for webpack that allow you to use additional tools such as Babel to bundle your code.
- CSS can be loaded and compiled via webpack using loaders.
- Plugins are powerful add-ons for the webpack compiler that give you access to many additional features, including preparing your build for production and automatically generating HTML wrappers for your webpack code.

6 Redux

This chapter covers

- Managing your application state with Redux
- Implementing Redux as an architecture pattern
- Managing your application state with actions
- Enforcing immutability with reducers
- Applying middleware for debugging and asynchronous calls
- Using Redux with React

Redux is a library that provides an architecture for writing your business logic. With React apps, you can handle much of your application state within your root components. But as your application grows, you end up with a complex set of callbacks that need to be passed down to all the children in order to manage application state updates. Redux provides an alternative for storing your application state by doing the following:

- Dictating a clear line of communication between your view and your business logic

- Allowing your view to subscribe to the application state so it can update each time the state updates
- Enforcing an immutable application state

DEFINITION Immutable objects are read-only. To update an immutable object, you need to clone it. When you change an object in JavaScript, it affects all references to that object. This means mutable changes can have unintended side effects. By enforcing immutability in your store, you prevent this from happening in your app.

6.1 Introduction to Redux

Redux dictates a single-directional flow of writing application state updates into a single root store. The store can be a simple or a complex JavaScript object depending on your app's requirements. Redux handles wiring updates into the store. It also handles any subscribers to the store and notifies them of updates to the store object.

DEFINITION The Redux store is a *singleton* (only one instance per app) object that holds all your application state. The store can be passed into your view in order to display and update your app.

Redux can be hooked up to any view, but it works especially well with React. React's top-down flow of props and state through nested components work well with Redux's single-direction state update flow.

NOTE React state isn't the same as Redux application state! React state is localized to each component in your app. It can be updated and affected within the React lifecycle. It should be used infrequently but is often needed in components that handle user input and sometimes in container components. Chapter 3 explains React state in more detail.

6.1.1 Getting started with notifications example app

The code for this chapter can be found at https://github.com/isomorphic-dev-js/chapter6-redux. All the code is provided on the master branch, or you can follow along and build it yourself. To run the app:

```
$ npm install
$ npm start
```

Then the app will be running at http://localhost:3000.

You'll be building a notifications app that displays messages in three states (Error, Warning, or Success). The idea is that the app receives updates from various paging apps, continuous integration build tools, and other systems (think GitHub, TravisCI, CircleCI, VictorOps, PagerDuty, and so forth). It then displays the notifications in the appropriate shelf. The app also has a settings panel that can be updated and a debug panel that lets you dispatch notifications for testing. Figure 6.1 shows the running application.

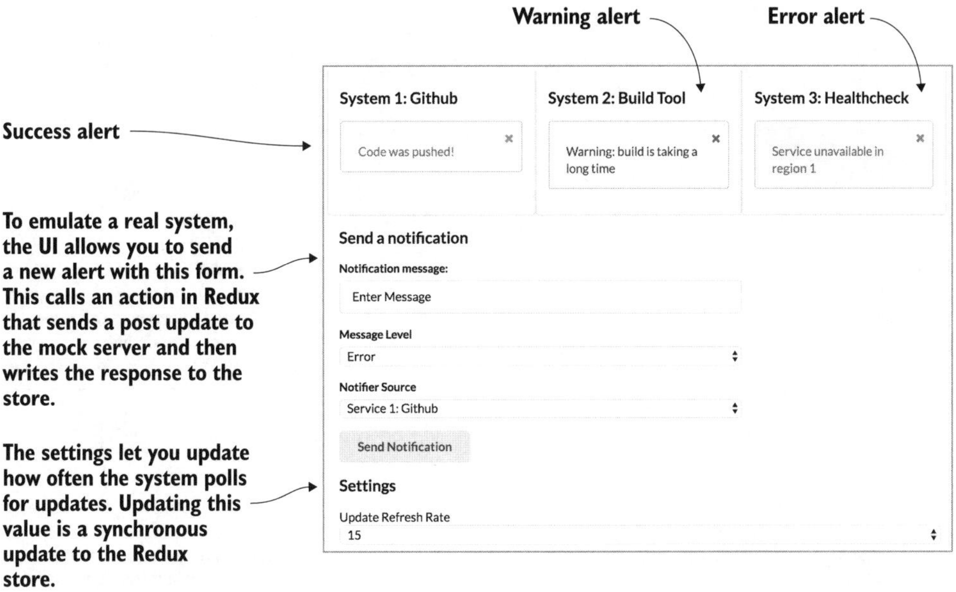
Warning alert
Error alert
Success alert
To emulate a real system, the UI allows you to send a new alert with this form. This calls an action in Redux that sends a post update to the mock server and then writes the response to the store.
The settings let you update how often the system polls for updates. Updating this value is a synchronous update to the Redux store.
System 1: Github
System 2: Build Tool
System 3: Healthcheck
Code was pushed!
Warning: build is taking a long time
Service unavailable in region 1
Send a notification
Notification message:
Enter Message
Message Level
Error
Notifier Source
Service 1: Github
Send Notification
Settings
Update Refresh Rate
15

Figure 6.1 Notifications update app—send and receive notifications

The code has some React components and webpack already set up. I'm not going to spend much time on these topics so you can stay focused on learning Redux. If you want to review React, you can review chapters 3 and 4. For webpack, review chapter 5.

Also note that there's an in-memory object on the Node server that backs up the simple CRUD (create, read, update, delete) service for this project. If you were to build this in the real world, you'd want to explore using a WebSocket connection and connect a database. The "Send a notification" section of the interface allows you to emulate the app receiving alerts from services without having to hook it up to any real inputs.

6.1.2 Redux overview

In the first part of this chapter, we'll walk through all the pieces of Redux that are required to get updates flowing in your application. Figure 6.2 reviews Redux's single-direction update flow in the context of the notifications app and introduces you to the three main parts of Redux:

- *Actions*—Implement business logic, things like updating settings or adding new notifications to the list
- *Reducers*—Write state changes triggered by actions to the store
- *Store*—Current application state, holds the notification array and the values of any settings for the app

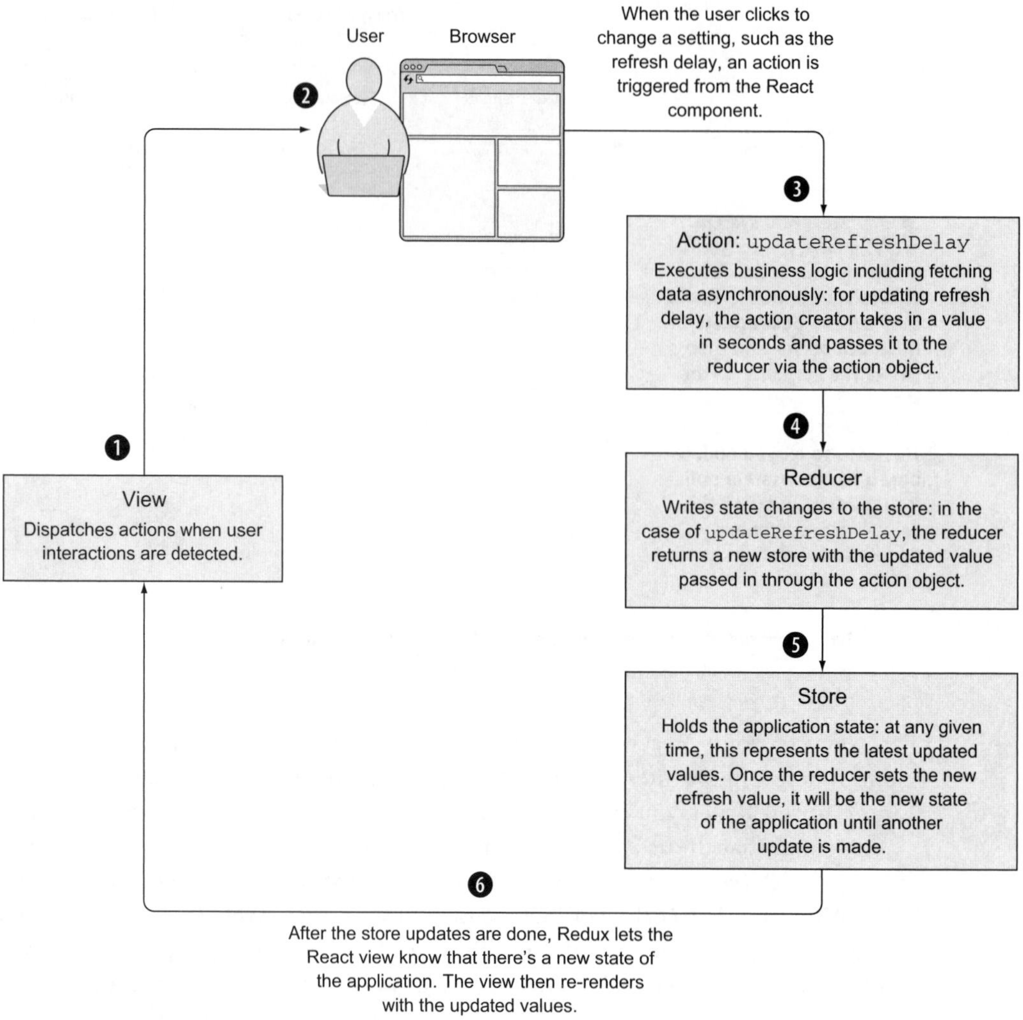

User
Browser
When the user clicks to change a setting, such as the refresh delay, an action is triggered from the React component.
Action: updateRefreshDelay
Executes business logic including fetching data asynchronously: for updating refresh delay, the action creator takes in a value in seconds and passes it to the reducer via the action object.
Reducer
Writes state changes to the store: in the case of updateRefreshDelay, the reducer returns a new store with the updated value passed in through the action object.
Store
Holds the application state: at any given time, this represents the latest updated values. Once the reducer sets the new refresh value, it will be the new state of the application until another update is made.
View
Dispatches actions when user interactions are detected.
After the store updates are done, Redux lets the React view know that there's a new state of the application. The view then re-renders with the updated values.

Figure 6.2 Redux single-direction flow from view

CONNECTING REACT AND REDUX

In the second part of this chapter, you'll learn how to use the React Redux library to connect your React view to your Redux application state. This includes using a top-level component provided by the library called Provider that takes in the store and makes it available to another component called connect. The connect component is a higher-order component that wraps some components in your application. These wrapped components are then able to receive store updates in the form of properties. The connect component has React state, so your other components don't need to have React state! Figure 6.3 illustrates how these pieces fit into your application structure.

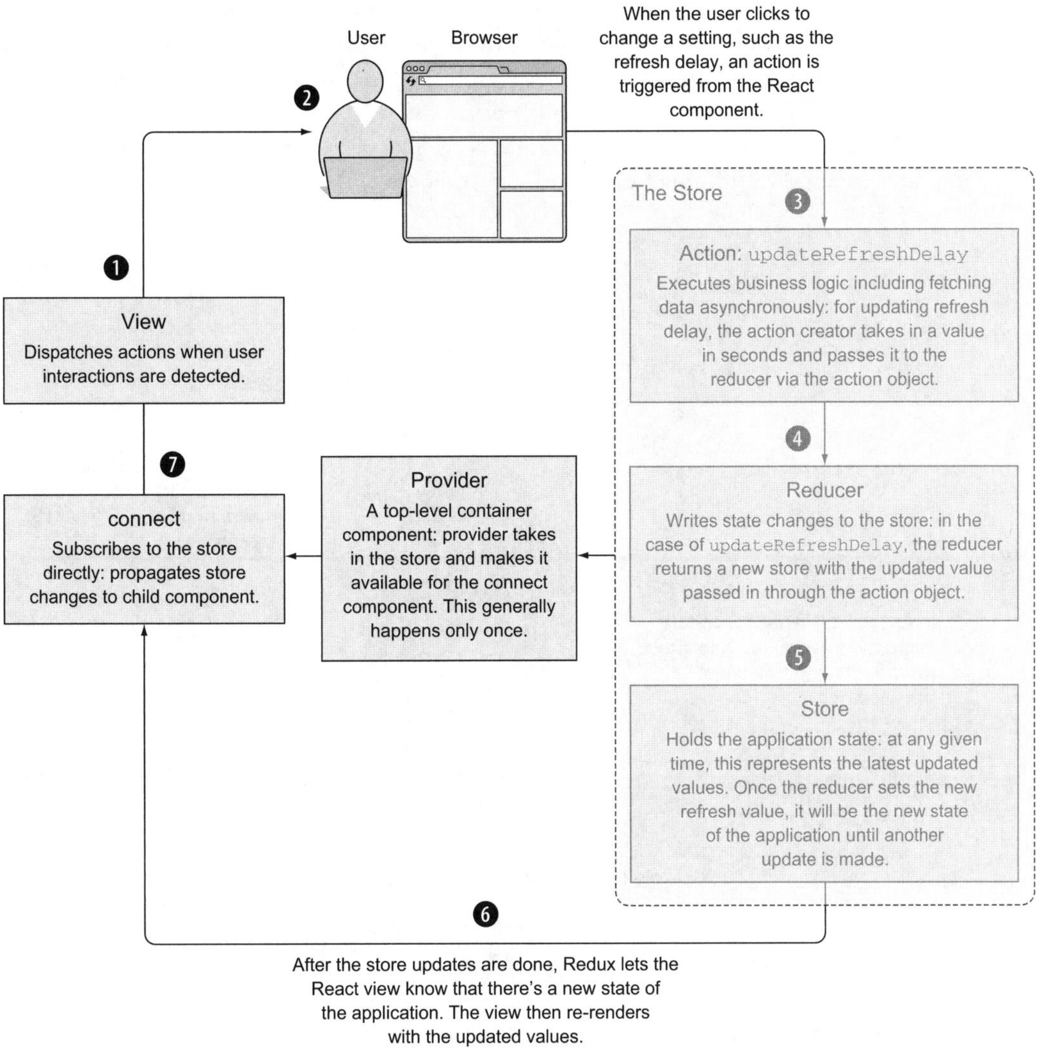
User
Browser
When the user clicks to change a setting, such as the refresh delay, an action is triggered from the React component.
The Store
Action: updateRefreshDelay
Executes business logic including fetching data asynchronously: for updating refresh delay, the action creator takes in a value in seconds and passes it to the reducer via the action object.
View
Dispatches actions when user interactions are detected.
Reducer
Writes state changes to the store: in the case of updateRefreshDelay, the reducer returns a new store with the updated value passed in through the action object.
Provider
A top-level container component: provider takes in the store and makes it available for the connect component. This generally happens only once.
connect
Subscribes to the store directly: propagates store changes to child component.
Store
Holds the application state: at any given time, this represents the latest updated values. Once the reducer sets the new refresh value, it will be the new state of the application until another update is made.
After the store updates are done, Redux lets the React view know that there's a new state of the application. The view then re-renders with the updated values.

Figure 6.3 Using React Redux's Provider and connect components to hook up the React view with the application state

6.2 *Redux as an architecture pattern*

Often, when building web applications, you use a Model-View-Controller (MVC) pattern. Many common frameworks use this pattern. In this case, there's a view, the HTML of the application, a model that's some sort of representation of application state, and a controller that's the interface that the user interacts with. The business logic is also handled by the controller.

Frameworks such as Angular 1 and Ember each have their own implementations of MVC but historically have used two-way binding to handle the View-Controller part of the framework. The flow of Angular 1 differs from the traditional MVC in that the view is really a View-Controller (always the same as a container component, as we discussed in chapter 3). But the framework still tries to follow an MVC pattern. This leads to confusing flows and hard-to-debug code.

Let's walk through what this would look like if we applied it to the app you're going to build in this chapter. Figure 6.4 shows how the application flow works in this case.

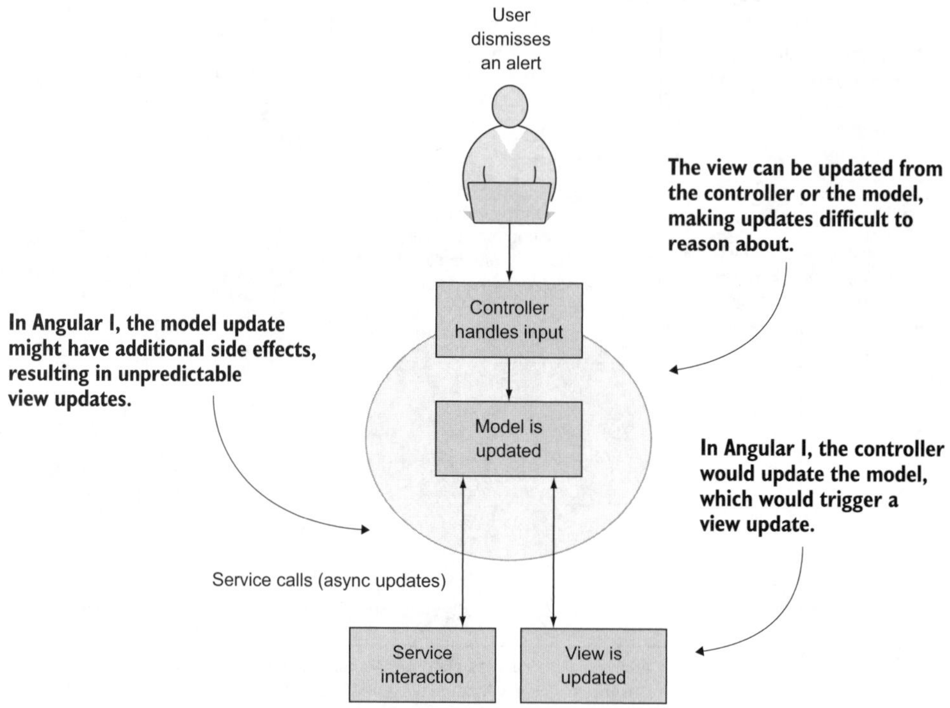
User dismisses an alert
The view can be updated from the controller or the model, making updates difficult to reason about.
Controller handles input
In Angular I, the model update might have additional side effects, resulting in unpredictable view updates.
Model is updated
In Angular I, the controller would update the model, which would trigger a view update.
Service calls (async updates)
Service interaction
View is updated

Figure 6.4 Model-View-Controller (MVC) flow in Angular 1

Redux's implementation has some overlap with MVC. I like to think of it as an evolution of MVC that works better for UI-based apps (as opposed to services/CRUD apps). There are a few major differences:

- Redux insists on a single-directional data flow resulting in easier-to-follow code and no side effects.
- There are no controllers. Rather, the views are also the controllers—called *view-controllers*. In this case, the View-Controller is React. This fits into the browser model well, where the view is rendered by the HTML and where user events are handled by the DOM.

- In Redux, there's always only one single root store, which represents the application state. That simplifies much of the logic, because views need to subscribe only to the root store and then pay attention to the specific subtrees they're interested in.

Redux flow relies on the store to dispatch actions. The `dispatch` function is a hook into the root store that allows you to trigger actions on the store. Sometimes you'll be triggering synchronous updates to the store and sometimes you'll be triggering an asynchronous call that will eventually update the store. Additionally, views are able to subscribe to the store and be notified when an update is complete. Figure 6.5 illustrates this flow.

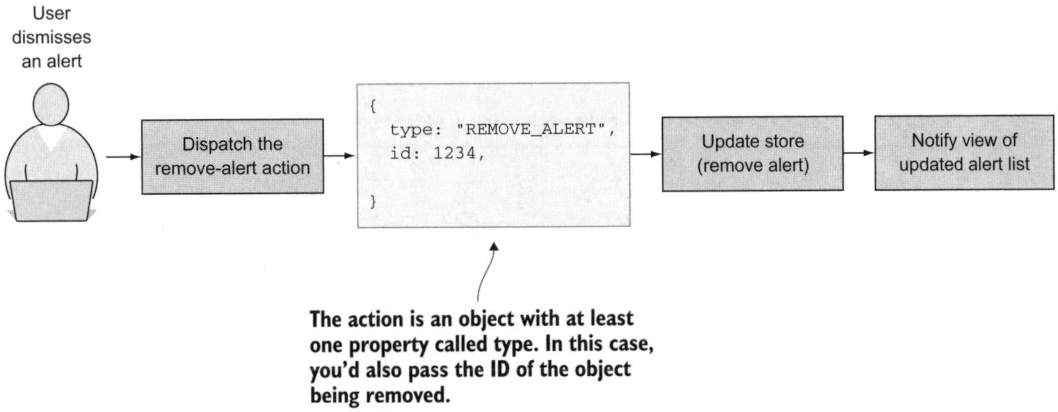
User dismisses an alert
Dispatch the remove-alert action
{
type: "REMOVE_ALERT",
id: 1234,
}
Update store (remove alert)
Notify view of updated alert list
The action is an object with at least one property called type. In this case, you'd also pass the ID of the object being removed.

Figure 6.5 Redux flow when initiated by a user action

Redux implementation (the part of the code you'll write) is made up of the store, the actions, and the reducers. The store holds your application state. The actions take care of your business logic. The reducers are called to update the store.

> **DEFINITION** The *store* in Redux is the model of your application. It holds the current state of your application. I'll use *store* and *state* interchangeably to talk about the model in Redux.

To recap, Redux provides a concrete pattern for managing your application's state that's easy to use as a developer. It also makes reasoning about and debugging your application straightforward.

6.3 Managing application state

The primary job of Redux is to allow your state (or model) and the view to communicate. This is achieved by allowing the view to subscribe to state updates and trigger updates on the state. Figure 6.6 shows this flow in the context of the sample app.

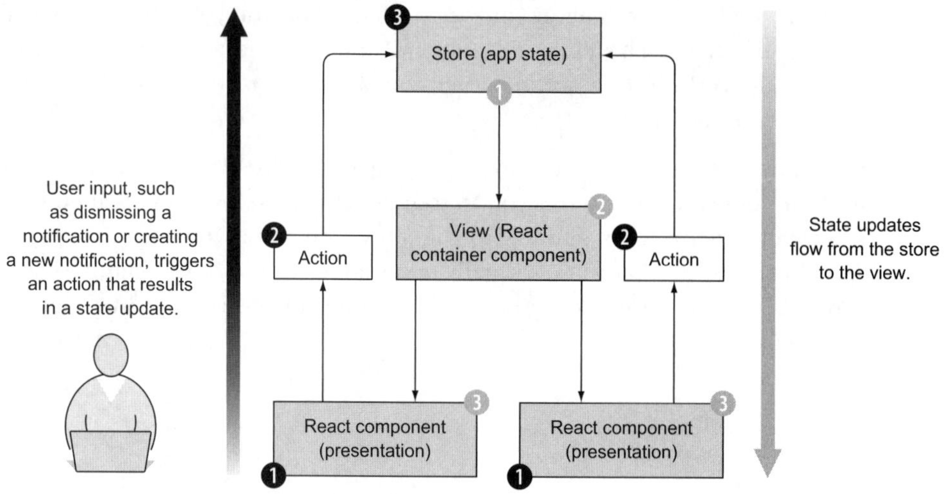
Store (app state)
User input, such as dismissing a notification or creating a new notification, triggers an action that results in a state update.
Action
View (React container component)
Action
State updates flow from the store to the view.
React component (presentation)
React component (presentation)

Figure 6.6 The flow of information between the view and Redux

Redux state can be a plain JavaScript object. The store (which contains the state object) has several methods that can be called on it. Here are the ones I'll cover:

- `dispatch(action)`—Triggers an update on the store (step 1 in figure 6.6).
- `getState()`—Returns the current store object (listing 6.1 shows what this looks like)
- `subscribe()`—Listens to changes on the store (step 2 in figure 6.6)

After actions are dispatched to the store, the state will match the code in the following listing.

Listing 6.1 An example store object (application state)

```
{
  notifications: {                 <-- Inside root store, you can set up
    all: [                         <-- substores—this app has stores
      {                                for notifications and settings.
        serviceId: 1,
        messageType: "success",        The all array holds active
        message: "Code was pushed!"    notifications for your app.
      },
      {
        serviceId: 3,
        messageType: "error",
        message: "Service unavailable in region 1"
      },
      {
        serviceId: 2,
        messageType: "warning",
```

```
        message: "Warning: build is taking a long time"
      }
    ]
  }
  settings: {
    refresh: 30
  }
}
```

The refresh property lets the user set the rate of long polling for updates.

Inside root store, you can set up substores—this app has stores for notifications and settings.

Redux provides a way to initialize the state (store). It manages the flow of updates to the store and notifies subscribers (the view). To configure the store in your app, you need to create your reducers and then initialize the store with them. The following listing shows how this works; you can find this code in src/init-redux.es6 in the repo.

Listing 6.2 Initialize Redux—src/init-redux.es6

```
import { createStore, combineReducers } from 'redux';
import notifications from './notifications-reducer';
import settings from './settings-reducer';

export default function (){
  const reducer = combineReducers({
    notifications,
    settings
     });
  return createStore(reducer)
}
```

Import helper methods from Redux.

Import app reducers.

Export function that can be called from other modules (makes it reusable so it can be called from browser and server in isomorphic app).

Call combineReducers helper method from Redux; builds map of reducers from multiple reducers.

Call createStore, pass in combined reducers—here you'll have store.notifications and store.settings.

If you aren't using Redux with React (later in the chapter you'll learn how to use redux-react to wire the two libraries together), you need to subscribe to store updates manually. The `subscribe` function works like a standard JavaScript event handler. You pass in a function that gets called every time a store update occurs. But the store doesn't pass its state to the update handler function; instead, you call `getState()` to access the current state. The following listing shows an example of this code, which you can find in main.jsx.

Listing 6.3 Subscribe to store, without React Redux—src/main.jsx

```
const store = initRedux();

store.subscribe(() => {
  console.log("Store updated", store.getState());
  // do something here
});
```

Initialize store (see listing 6.2).

Call the subscribe() method on the store and pass in a function to handle updates.

Log the current state of the store by calling getState().

Next you'll write a reducer and learn about maintaining immutability in Redux.

6.3.1 Reducers: updating the state

Reducers have a special name, but when broken down, they're pure functions. Each reducer takes in the store and an action and returns a new, modified store. Figure 6.7 shows the functional nature of a reducer function.

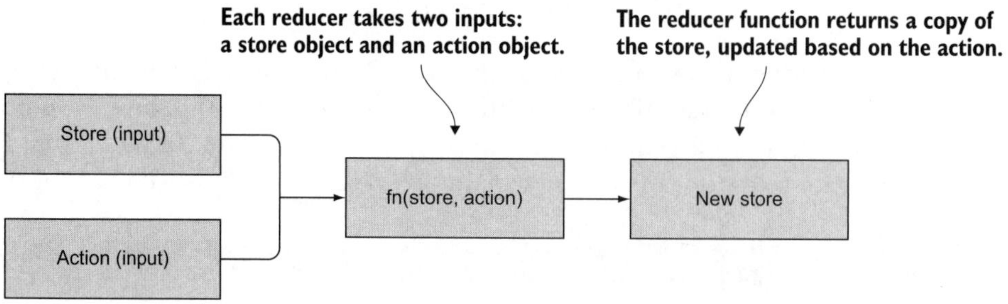
Each reducer takes two inputs: a store object and an action object.
The reducer function returns a copy of the store, updated based on the action.
Store (input)
Action (input)
fn(store, action)
New store

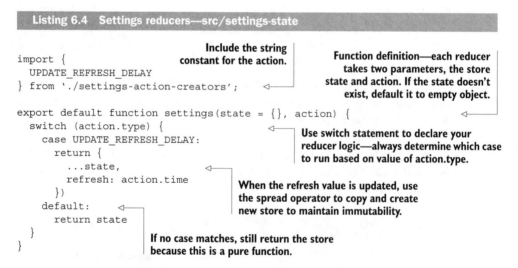

Figure 6.7 The input and output flow of a pure reducer function

The reducers in the notifications application are the wiring between the actions and the store. They're the only part of your code that should ever write updates to the store. Any other code that writes to the store is an antipattern. The following listing shows the reducer function for settings.

Listing 6.4 Settings reducers—src/settings-state

```
import {
  UPDATE_REFRESH_DELAY
} from './settings-action-creators';

export default function settings(state = {}, action) {
  switch (action.type) {
    case UPDATE_REFRESH_DELAY:
      return {
        ...state,
        refresh: action.time
      })
    default:
      return state
  }
}
```

- Include the string constant for the action.
- Function definition—each reducer takes two parameters, the store state and action. If the state doesn't exist, default it to empty object.
- Use switch statement to declare your reducer logic—always determine which case to run based on value of action.type.
- When the refresh value is updated, use the spread operator to copy and create new store to maintain immutability.
- If no case matches, still return the store because this is a pure function.

There are two important points to understand about reducers:

- *Reducers must always be pure functions*—They take in values, use those values to create a new store, and then return a store.
- *Reducers must enforce the immutable nature of the store*—The store received by the function must be cloned if it needs to be updated.

Both concepts prevent unintended side effects. The next sections explain pure functions and immutability.

PURE FUNCTIONS

One of the most important parts of writing reducers is making sure the function stays pure (no side effects). *Pure* functions take in arguments that are used to calculate the return value—they don't use any state or do work on state. Code without side effects has many benefits, including being more testable and easier to understand and preventing hard-to-debug issues. Let's take a look at an example of a function with side effects and then compare it to a pure function. The following listing shows the difference between a pure and not pure function.

Listing 6.5 Pure function example

```
// side effect
let result;
function add(a, b) {
  result = a + b;
}

add(1, 2);
console.log(result); // logs 3

// functional - no side effects
function add(a, b) {
  return a + b;
}

console.log(add(1,2); // logs 3
```

Function doesn't return anything, but updates the value of result.

When add is called in this case, you can log the result to see what happened (global state).

In this function, result of add is returned.

This time log result of calling add function—there's no state.

ENFORCING THE IMMUTABLE STORE

Another way to keep your code easy to understand and debug is to make sure the app state (or the store) is always immutable. The risk of not enforcing immutability is that you end up with issues that are difficult to track down and caused by changes in other parts of your code. By creating a new object each time, you ensure that other code won't accidentally change the whole app state.

You need to pay attention to a few things in order to enforce immutability in your store. Let's start with how to make sure your objects stay immutable, as shown in the following listing.

Listing 6.6 Mutating vs. immutable object

```
// mutation: bad
function addNotification(item, key, state) {
  return state[key] = item;
}

//immutable: good
function addNotification(item, key, state) {
```

Function declaration that takes three params: item, key, and state

In the bad example, item is inserted directly into the state object, then the state is returned.

```
  return {
    ...state,
    key: item
  }
}
```

In the good example, the object is cloned using spread operator, which takes state that was passed in and creates the object with its keys. Then the new copied object is returned.

Here, you can see that the immutable way of returning the store object involves the JavaScript function spread operator. You create a new object by spreading the old object and then adding any new or updated keys. The new keys will overwrite the old. But if you have a deeply nested object, you need to build the full object here or use a helper library to manage deeply nested keys.

Similarly, arrays need to be kept immutable. With arrays, pushing directly into the array is a mutation, so it's necessary to create a new array instead. The following listing demonstrates the wrong and the right way to do this.

Listing 6.7 Immutable arrays

```
// bad: mutating the original array
function addItem(item) {
  return itemsArray.push(item)
}

// good: creating a new array
function addItem(item) {
  return [...itemsArray, item]
}
```

Pushes item into array, returns original array—this is a mutation.

Shows immutable way: return brand-new array with items from original array and new item; uses spread operator to push items into an array.

6.3.2 Actions: triggering state updates

Actions are the only way to trigger an update to your application state in a Redux application. This is important to ensure that your app enforces the single-direction flow. (It's technically possible to update the store directly, but you should *never* do that). Only reducers triggered by actions should update the state.

Because actions are synchronous by default, any update that needs to be made can happen quickly. In fact, the dispatcher itself is completely synchronous. By default, Redux supports only synchronous actions. (Later in this chapter, you'll learn to use middleware with Redux in order to allow asynchronous actions.)

TIP You can't dispatch an action from a reducer. That breaks the single-directional flow of Redux and could lead to unwanted side effects. Don't worry, Redux won't let you do it, but it's important to avoid thinking about updates in that way.

The simplest action is an object with one property called `type`:

```
{ type: 'UPDATE' }
```

Actions will often be objects that contain data to be updated in the store in addition to the `type` property. Because most actions in your application will be reused by more than one view, it's recommended to create reusable functions called *action creators* that return the action you want to dispatch.

Action creator files are also a good place to define your string constants for actions. This reduces errors by ensuring that the action creator dispatches the same action type value the reducer is looking for. This can also lead to gains in developer speed in some IDEs if you have static type checking or similar features enabled.

You can see these two concepts in the next listing. This code can be found in the repo as well. The listing shows an action for updating the time interval for the long polling functionality of the app.

Listing 6.8 Synchronous actions—src/settings-action-creators.es6

```
export const UPDATE_REFRESH_DELAY
➥ = 'UPDATE_REFRESH_DELAY';

export function updateRefreshDelay(time) {
  return {
    type: UPDATE_REFRESH_DELAY,
    time: time
  }
}
```

- Setting type value to a constant reduces errors
- Action creator function declaration takes one parameter called time.
- Returned action has two properties—type property is required and its value is always a string.
- The time property is added to the action so that the value can be used by the view when it updates—each action will have different data properties.

You can use the `const` in the first line from the reducer to ensure that the action creator and the reducer point at the same value. To dispatch this update to the store, all you have to do is call `dispatch` on `store` and pass in the action. Because you're using an action creator, you call the action creator and pass the result into `dispatch`:

```
store.dispatch(updateRefreshDelay(5));
```

The reducer will then be triggered, and the store will be updated.

Next, you'll learn how to set up Redux with middleware so you can include additional functionality such as making asynchronous calls.

6.4 Applying middleware to Redux

Redux includes a helper method that lets you extend the default functionality of the dispatcher. For every middleware you apply to the dispatcher, it adds a function to the chain of calls that will happen before the final default dispatch behavior. Here's a simplified example of what that looks like:

```
middleware1(dispatchedAction).middleware2(dispatchedAction).middleware3(dispa
    tchedAction).dispatch(dispatchedAction)
```

This allows you to add functionality for debugging and making asynchronous calls. First, let's look at how you add debugging.

6.4.1 *Middleware basics: debugging*

It's possible to add improved debugging with middleware. One example of this is the Redux Logger library. This library helps you see the state changes clearly in the console. Figure 6.8 shows sample action logs.

```
▼ action @ 01:16:53.198 FETCH_NOTIFICATIONS
    prev state ▶Object {notifications: Object, settings: Object}
    action ▶Object {type: "FETCH_NOTIFICATIONS", notifications: Object}
    next state ▶Object {notifications: Object, settings: Object}
```

Figure 6.8 Redux Logger console output

You add middleware when you instantiate your store. The following listing shows how to do that. The code can also be found in the repo.

Listing 6.9 Setting up middleware—src/init-redux.es6

```
export default function () {
  const reducer = combineReducers({…});
  let middleware = [logger];
  return compose(
    applyMiddleware(...middleware)
  )(createStore)(reducer);
}
```

Create middleware array so you can pass an arbitrary number of middleware and easily control the order.

Call compose and pass in the store so the middleware will be applied to store.

Call applyMiddleware on middleware array to set up middleware properly.

When you run the app, you'll see the logging in the console; this is helpful for debugging.

6.4.2 *Handling asynchronous actions*

Earlier in the chapter, you dispatched actions by writing functions that return an action object. As stated previously, we call those functions action creators. *Asynchronous action creators* apply the same principles, but instead of immediately returning the object, they wait for something to happen (for example, a network call to complete) and then return the action object.

To do that, you need access to the `dispatch` object inside your action creator function. This requires another middleware library, called Redux Thunk. To use the middleware, you need to add it to the middleware array in init-redux.es6 (refer to listing 6.9). It's already in the code in the repo.

Then to take advantage of this middleware, you write an action creator that looks like this:

```
export const UPDATE_ACTION = 'UPDATE_ACTION';

export function actionCreator() {
```

```
    return dispatch => {
      return dispatch({
          type: UPDATE_ACTION
        })
    }
}
```

By adding the Thunk middleware, you can now access the `dispatch` function on the store inside your action creator (all the middleware does is provide the `dispatch` parameter to your returned function). Note that you also need to export your action creator and the corresponding `const` for the action. This is identical to earlier in the chapter, when you created a synchronous action creator.

In the notifications app, you need three asynchronous actions: adding a notification, fetching the notifications, and deleting a notification. The following listing shows the Fetch Notifications action creator. The code can be found in the repo along with other action creators.

Listing 6.10 Asynchronous action creators—src/action-creators.es6

```
import request from 'isomorphic-fetch';

export const FETCH_NOTIFICATIONS
➥ = 'FETCH_NOTIFICATIONS';

export function fetchNotifications() {
  return dispatch => {
    let headers = new Headers({
      "Content-Type": "application/json",
    });
    return fetch(
        'http://localhost:3000/notifications',
        { headers: headers }
      )
      .then((response)=>{
        return response.json().then(data => {
          return dispatch({
            type: FETCH_NOTIFICATIONS,
            notifications: data
          })
        })
      })
  }
}
```

Use isomorphic fetch so both server and browser can handle the fetch call.

Const for action type

The action creator returns a function instead of an object. Thunk middleware calls this function and injects the dispatch method from store.

Create headers to talk to the API.

Call fetch with URL and options.

Promise handler

Get JSON out of the response—because this is also a promise, add second promise handler.

After you have data, dispatch the action.

Now that you've seen how the Redux reducers and actions work, let's go over how to hook up React and Redux.

6.5 Using Redux with React components

In a React app, the actions are typically dispatched from components. To have access to the store in a component, you need to wire up your React components to Redux. I recommend using the react-redux library, which is provided by the author of Redux as the official bindings for React. It implements all the code necessary to subscribe to and receive updates from the Redux store.

There are two distinct parts to this. One is a top-level root component called Provider. The other is a higher-order component (HOC) called connect.

6.5.1 Wrapping your app with provider

First, you need to pass the store into your app. You want to pass it down as a React prop. Remember, React components have a property called `props`. The `props` object is created by passing down values from the parent React component to its children. This object is immutable and can be changed only from the parent component.

Because you also want to be able to subscribe to the store, you should use the Provider component that comes with React Redux. This React component acts as the root of your application and makes the store available to the connect HOC. The following listing shows how to do this.

Listing 6.11 Connecting Redux to React —src/main.jsx

```
import React from 'react';
import ReactDOM from 'react-dom';
import App from './components/app.jsx';
import { Provider } from 'react-redux';
import initRedux from './init-redux.es6';
require('./style.css');

const initialState = window.__INITIAL_STATE;
const store = initRedux(initialState);

store.subscribe(() => {
  console.log("Store updated", store.getState());
  // if not using React, do something here
});

ReactDOM.render(
  <Provider store={store}><App /></Provider>,
  document.getElementById('react-content')
);
```

The component takes in the store and properly passes it to its children.

Render the App component inside Provider so it'll have access to store and pass in store to Provider component.

Now you have access to the store in your components. But you need to do a couple more things to completely connect your app to Redux.

6.5.2 Subscribing to the store from React

The second part of getting store updates is wrapping your container components in the connect HOC. This component handles subscribing to the store for you. It holds all the React state that's necessary to pass down properties to its child component.

The connect HOC also provides helper methods that make it easier to map the store to properties and easier to call actions from the view. Wrapping a component with connect and then exporting it for use in your app looks like this:

```
export default connect(mapStateToProps, mapDispatchToProps)(Component);
```

The functions mapStateToProps and mapDispatchToProps are the two helper callbacks that connect runs. The first one, mapStateToProps, is run every time an update occurs to the store. Inside of it, you'll define what items from the store should be mapped to React props. The following listing shows this in action.

Listing 6.12 Connect React to Redux—src/components/app.jsx

```
class App extends React.Component {

  componentDidMount() {}

  getSystemNotifications(id) {
    let items = [];
    if (this.props.all) {                                      ◁ Component accesses notifications directly on props.
      this.props.all.forEach((item, index)=>{                  ◁ Using notifications array, you build an array of notification items.
        if (item.serviceId == id) {
          let classes = classnames("ui", "message", item.messageType);
          items.push(
            <div className={classes} key={index}>
              <i
                className="close icon"
                onClick={
                  this.dismiss.bind(this, index)
                }>
              </i>
              <p>
                {item.message}
              </p>
            </div>
          )
        }
      })
    }
    return items;
  }

  render() {}
}

function mapStateToProps(state) {                  ◁ The function tells connect to pull specific keys out of the store and put them directly on props.
  let { all } = state.notifications;               Pull out relevant items (notifications and refresh); refresh is required by the child component.
  let { refresh } = state.settings;
  return {                                         ◁ Return just the keys the component needs instead of the whole store.
    all,
    refresh
  }
}

function mapDispatchToProps(dispatch) {}

export default connect(
                  mapStateToProps,
                  mapDispatchToProps
                )(App)                             ◁ Pass mapStateToProps into the connect function; it will be called during render cycle.
```

With `mapDispatchToProps`, you're making actions available to be dispatched directly from the component's properties. Normally, you'd need to fully write out `dispatch(actionCreator())` every time you wanted to initiate an action. This helper method lets you use JavaScript's `bind` to automatically dispatch actions when they're called from the view. The following listing shows how this works. Note that React Redux provides another helper method to automate the bind code.

Listing 6.13 Connect React to Redux—src/components/app.jsx

```
import React from 'react';
import { connect } from 'react-redux';
import { bindActionCreators } from 'redux';
import * as actionCreators from '../action-creators';
import * as settingsActionCreators
➥ from '../settings-action-creators';

import CreateNotification from './create-notification';
import Settings from './settings';
import classnames from 'classnames';

let intervalId;

class App extends React.Component {
  //...component implementation code

  componentDidMount() {
    intervalId = setInterval(() => {
      this.props.notificationActions.
      ➥ fetchNotifications();
    }, this.props.refresh * 1000);
  }
}

function mapDispatchToProps(dispatch) {
  return {
    notificationActions:
    ➥ bindActionCreators(actionCreators, dispatch),
    settingsActions:
    ➥ bindActionCreators(settingsActionCreators, dispatch)
  }
}

export default connect(null, mapDispatchToProps)(App)
```

- **Connect is the higher-order function provided by React Redux. It subscribes to the store and passes the updated store down as props into the connected component.** (points to `import { connect } from 'react-redux';`)
- **Import action creators so you can call actions in your component.** (points to the action-creator imports)
- **bindActionCreators is a helper method that takes in an action or an object with actions and creates a function that, when called, dispatches the requested action.** (points to `import { bindActionCreators } from 'redux';` and the two `bindActionCreators(...)` calls)
- **Call the fetchNotifications action on a regular interval; actions are passed down as props by connect.** (points to `fetchNotifications();`)
- **Function passed into connect so connect component can pass down bound actions as properties—prevents having to call dispatch every time you want to call an action.** (points to `function mapDispatchToProps(dispatch) {`)
- **Call connect, passing in mapDispatchToProps and then passing in the component you want to connect to Redux** (points to `export default connect(null, mapDispatchToProps)(App)`)

After you've wired up your container component (App) to connect it to Redux, all you have to do is pass the properties into the children. Then the child components can see any state you mapped to `props` and call any actions you've bound to `dispatch`.

Summary

In this chapter, you learned how Redux works, including how to implement unidirectional data flow, maintain an immutable store, and connect React with Redux.

- Redux implements an architecture pattern that's an evolution of the traditional MVC pattern.
- The single-directional flow of Redux, where the view dispatches actions and subscribes to store updates, makes reasoning about the system simpler for developers.
- The store, or state, of your application is a single root object that holds all the information for your view.
- Reducers are pure functions that make changes to the store. They never mutate the store and instead use immutable patterns to make updates to the store.
- Actions are used to trigger updates to the store.
- Middleware allows debugging tools and asynchronous actions to be used in Redux.
- Connecting React and Redux requires additional functionality provided by the React Redux library, which includes a higher-order component that subscribes to the store for its child component.

Part 3

Isomorphic architecture

Now that you've seen how isomorphic architecture works and what foundational skills are needed to build a React application, it's time to dive into the nitty-gritty of isomorphic apps. This part covers a wide range of topics while focusing on getting you ready to build a production-ready isomorphic application. It takes the concepts introduced in chapter 2 and examines each piece of the flow in detail. It also covers several advanced topics, including testing, real-world app challenges, user sessions, and caching.

The first two chapters in this section cover isomorphic architecture basics. In chapter 7, you'll learn to use Express and how to use React and React Router on the server to enable server-rendered app routes. In chapter 8, you'll see how to hand off the server-rendered page to the browser in a seamless way.

The next three chapters cover the advanced topics. In chapter 9, you'll learn how to think about testing in the context of an application that behaves as both a server-rendered page and a single-page application. In chapter 10, you'll learn how to handle cases such as code that can run only in the browser because it uses the `window` object and how to avoid duplicating your error-handling code. Finally, in chapter 11, you'll get your app ready for production. You'll learn performance best practices, caching strategies, and how to handle user sessions in an isomorphic app.

7 Building the server

This chapter covers

- Setting up Node.js with Express
- Writing Express middleware
- Using React Router on the server to handle view routing
- Rendering React on the server with the `renderToString` function
- Fetching data on the server using Redux
- Implementing a static method on your components to handle data fetching

This chapter is all about the code that needs to happen on the server. I'll cover server-specific topics including using Express and using your component and routing code on the server. For example, you'll learn how to declare the actions of your application in a way that allows the server to fetch them automatically on every page render.

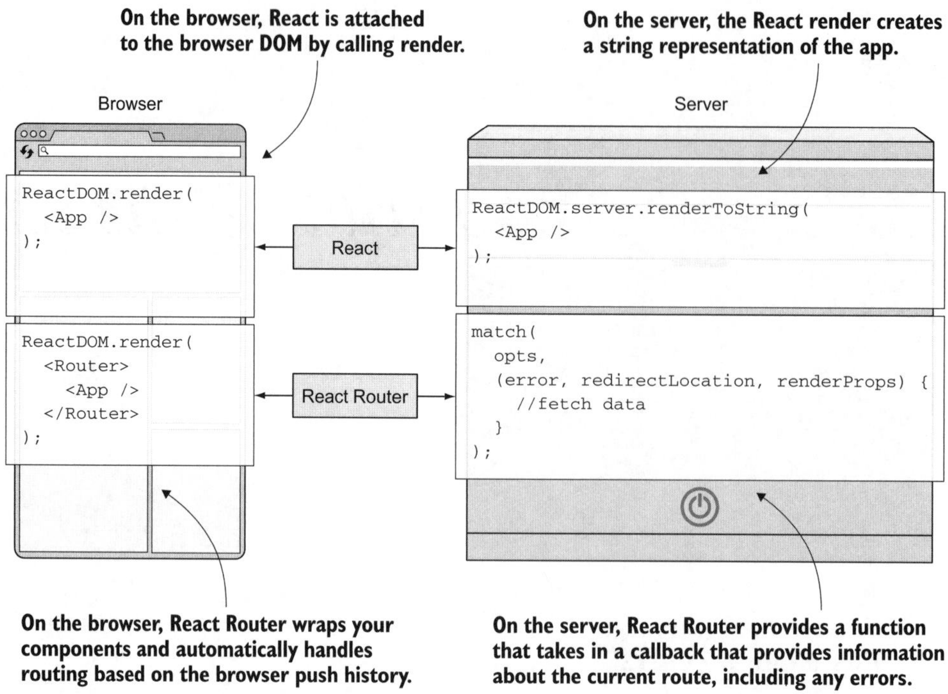
On the browser, React is attached to the browser DOM by calling render.
On the server, the React render creates a string representation of the app.
Browser
Server
ReactDOM.render(<App />);
React
ReactDOM.server.renderToString(<App />);
ReactDOM.render(<Router> <App /> </Router>);
React Router
match(opts, (error, redirectLocation, renderProps) { //fetch data });
On the browser, React Router wraps your components and automatically handles routing based on the browser push history.
On the server, React Router provides a function that takes in a callback that provides information about the current route, including any errors.

Figure 7.1 The main differences between server and browser code for React and React Router

Yes, you read that correctly: you're going to run your React, React Router, and Redux code on the server. React and React Router each provides server-specific APIs to make this work. Redux needs only minor changes—mostly you'll call actions from the server. Figure 7.1 illustrates how this works.

To get the code shown in figure 7.1 working, you need to do the following things:

- Set up app routing with Express
- Handle specific routes (for example, the cart and products routes) with React Router using the `match` function
- Render your React components on the server using `renderToString`
- Fetch the data for your components on the server
- Respond to requests with the rendered app

These pieces make up the server-rendered part of an isomorphic application. That includes everything from the initial user request for your app to sending a rendered response to the browser.

RENDERTOSTRING VS. RENDER

Let's go over the differences between the `render` and `renderToString` methods so you can better understand why we treat the render on the server as different from the browser render. Table 7.1 describes the output and use case for each method.

Table 7.1 Comparing `render` and `renderToString`

	Output	Runs once?	Environment
`render`	JavaScript representation of your components	No. Runs every time there's an update.	Browser
`renderToString`	A string of DOM elements	Yes. Doesn't hold any state.	Server

Figure 7.2 shows the part of the isomorphic application flow that this chapter covers. The app you'll build in this chapter is the All Things Westies app that you started

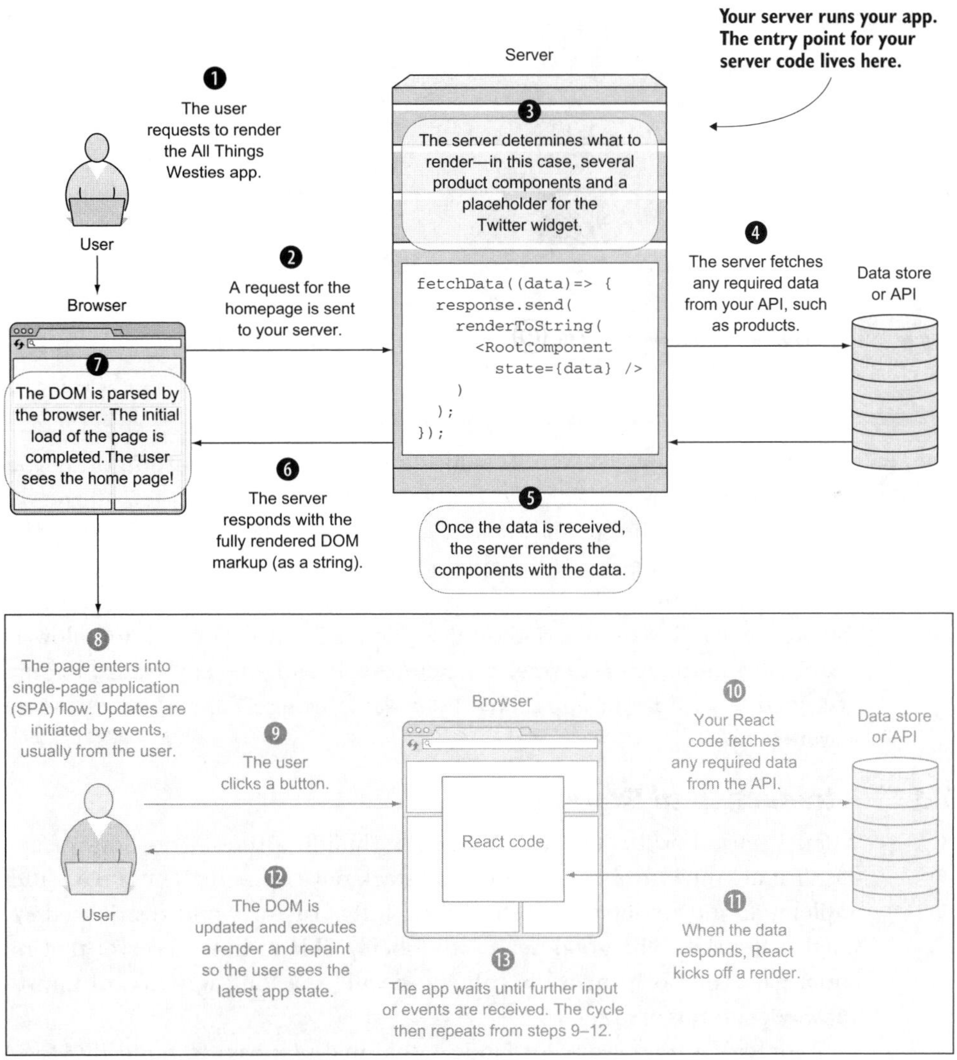

Your server runs your app. The entry point for your server code lives here.
Server
1 The user requests to render the All Things Westies app.
User
Browser
2 A request for the homepage is sent to your server.
3 The server determines what to render—in this case, several product components and a placeholder for the Twitter widget.
fetchData((data)=> {
response.send(
renderToString(
<RootComponent
state={data} />
)
);
});
4 The server fetches any required data from your API, such as products.
Data store or API
7 The DOM is parsed by the browser. The initial load of the page is completed.The user sees the home page!
6 The server responds with the fully rendered DOM markup (as a string).
5 Once the data is received, the server renders the components with the data.
8 The page enters into single-page application (SPA) flow. Updates are initiated by events, usually from the user.
Browser
10 Your React code fetches any required data from the API.
Data store or API
9 The user clicks a button.
React code
User
12 The DOM is updated and executes a render and repaint so the user sees the latest app state.
11 When the data responds, React kicks off a render.
13 The app waits until further input or events are received. The cycle then repeats from steps 9–12.

Figure 7.2 Isomorphic app flow—server render only

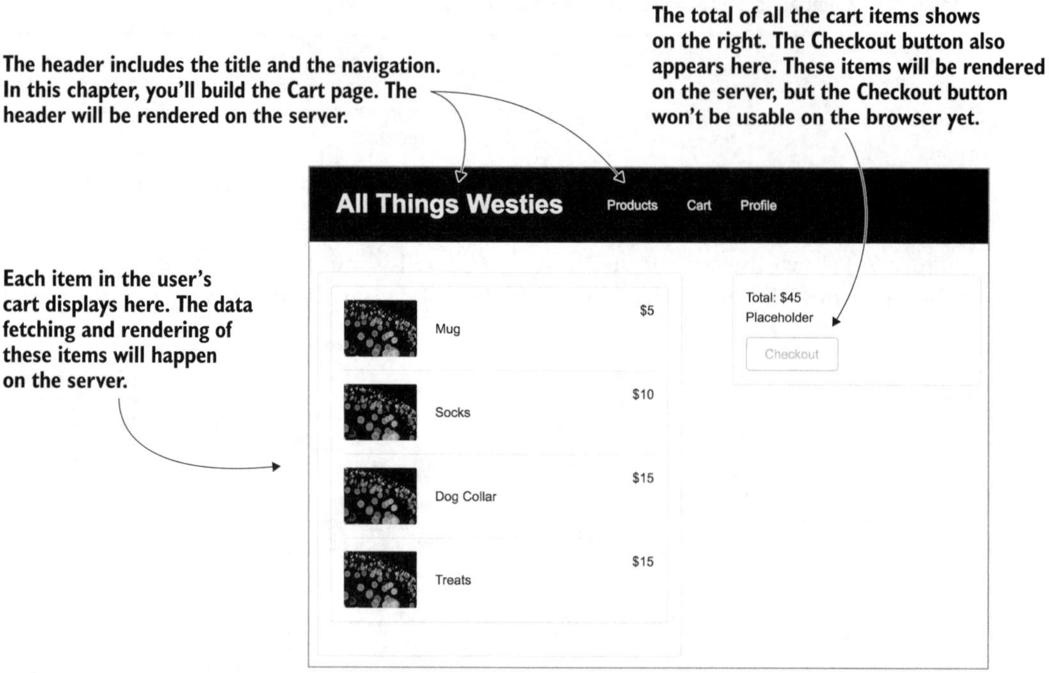
The header includes the title and the navigation. In this chapter, you'll build the Cart page. The header will be rendered on the server.
The total of all the cart items shows on the right. The Checkout button also appears here. These items will be rendered on the server, but the Checkout button won't be usable on the browser yet.
Each item in the user's cart displays here. The data fetching and rendering of these items will happen on the server.
All Things Westies
Products
Cart
Profile
Mug
$5
Socks
$10
Dog Collar
$15
Treats
$15
Total: $45
Placeholder
Checkout

Figure 7.3 The portion of the app you'll build and render on the server in this chapter

working on in chapter 4. You'll build the server-rendered portion of the cart but not any of the browser-specific code or interactions. In this chapter, all the data will be mocked out from the server. Figure 7.3 shows what this app looks like after it's built out. (You'll build the rest of the app in later chapters.)

You can find the code for this app at http://mng.bz/8gV8. After you've pulled this code down, you'll want to switch to the chapter-7-express branch to follow along (`git checkout chapter-7-express`). Before you add the `renderToString` call, you first need to set up your app server. Let's walk through Express basics and get the app server set up.

7.1 Introduction to Express

When I started as a client app developer (building the UI portions of apps), there wasn't much need to be able to do full-stack development. These days, the ability to implement and understand web servers, infrastructure, and distributed systems is a sought-after skill. The good news is that being able to build a server that renders the initial page load of your isomorphic app will go a long way toward improving your knowledge in this area.

Express is a framework for Node.js that makes it easy to build REST APIs and to implement view rendering. In the All Things Westies app, Express handles the incoming requests to the Node.js server—for example, when the user wants to go to the Products page, the first place the request gets handled is by the Express app routing. Part of building an isomorphic app with JavaScript is handling initial requests to your web server; the server handles routing, fetching data, and rendering the page. The fully rendered page is then sent in the response to the browser.

7.1.1 Setting up the server entry point

First, you need to get a basic server up and running. You want to use the command line to start your server and get it running on port 3000, as shown in figure 7.4. I've already supplied the root entry point files for you (server.js and app.es6).

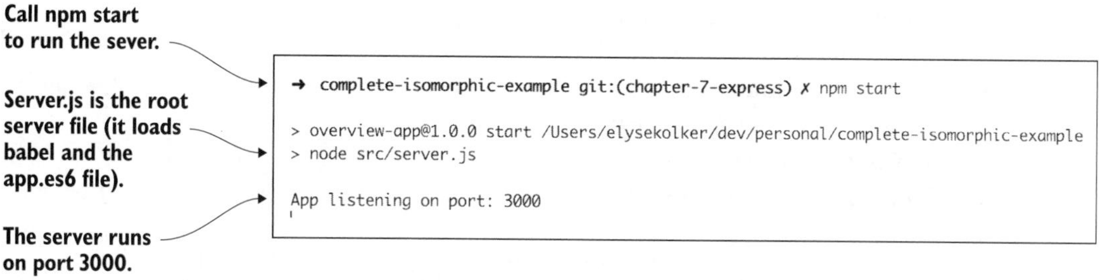
Call npm start to run the sever.
Server.js is the root server file (it loads babel and the app.es6 file).
The server runs on port 3000.
➜ complete-isomorphic-example git:(chapter-7-express) ✗ npm start
> overview-app@1.0.0 start /Users/elysekolker/dev/personal/complete-isomorphic-example
> node src/server.js
App listening on port: 3000

Figure 7.4 Starting the Node.js server

In the current branch, Express is already in package.json. To use it with your Node.js application, you need to install it with npm. This will install all the packages needed for this section:

```
$ npm install
$ npm start
```

When you navigate to localhost:3000, you'll see an error, as in figure 7.5.

The following listing shows the server entry file that's already provided for you in the base code on the chapter-7-express branch.

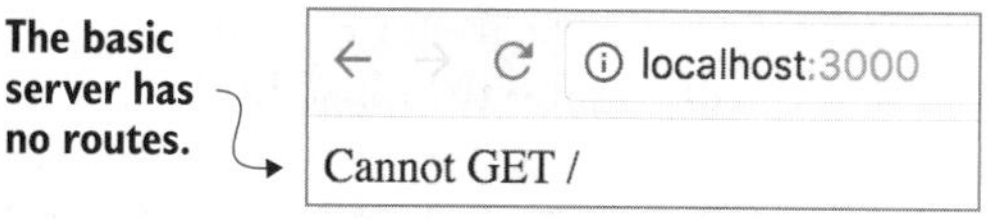
The basic server has no routes.
localhost:3000
Cannot GET /

Figure 7.5 Without route handling, the server throws an error.

Listing 7.1 Server entry—src/app.es6

```
import express from 'express';

const app = express();

// other code - routes for data endpoints
```

Include Express framework in project.

Initialize Express and assign it to app.

```
app.listen(3000, () => {
  console.log('App listening on port: 3000');
});
```

Call listen on app and set port to 3000—you can do anything in the callback, the console.log statement lets the user know which port the server is running on.

Now that you've seen the initial setup of the server code, you'll add routing with Express.

7.1.2 Setting up routing with Express

The Express router handles all incoming requests to the application and decides what to do with each request. For example, if you want to have a route such as /test that returns text and a 200 response, you need to add code that handles this route to the app.es6 file. Figure 7.6 shows the expected output. Because you haven't added route handling, this won't work right now. Eventually, this route handling will allow you to render app routes with React.

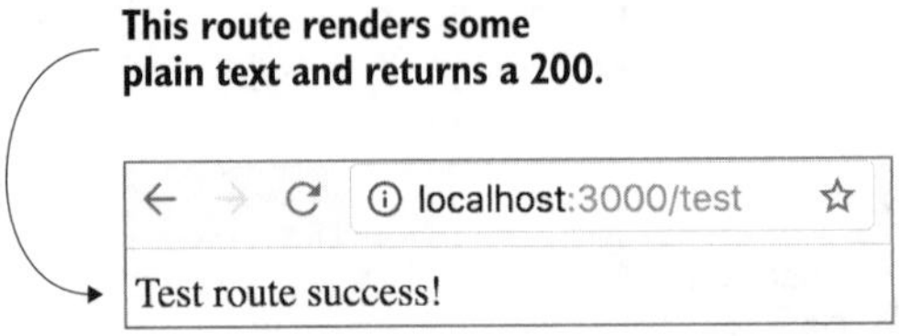
This route renders some plain text and returns a 200.
localhost:3000/test
Test route success!

Figure 7.6 Routing to the test route with Express

> **NOTE** In Express, every incoming request is represented by a request object. This object holds information about the URL, cookies, and other HTTP information such as any headers that were sent.

You can set up specific routes for any type of HTTP verb (`GET`, `POST`, `PUT`, `OPTIONS`, `DELETE`). For the main portion of the app, you'll need to implement only `GET` requests to respond to user requests for individual web app pages. Listing 7.2 shows how to add a route handler for a `GET` request to the /test route. You'll add the code in the listing to app.es6.

> **NOTE** Express creates a response object for every incoming request. This object holds information that will be sent back to the browser such as headers, cookies, status code, and response body. It also has helper functions for setting the response body and status code.

Listing 7.2 Add a route—src/app.es6

```
app.get('/api/blog', (req, res) => {});

app.get('/test', (req, res) => {
  res.send('Test route success!');
});

app.listen(3000, () => {});
```

get function takes in route (/test) and a callback.

Callback must respond to the response (or the request will hang indefinitely).

Here you're sending a simple string back to the browser indicating that the route exists. The response is sent with the `send()` method, which is found on the response object.

REGULAR EXPRESSIONS IN ROUTES

In addition to hardcoding full string paths such as /test, Express supports regular expressions as routes. This is helpful for building an app with React Router because you want to hand off the route handling to React Router instead of having individual Express routes. If you wanted the Express app to know about routes such as /cart and /products, you'd have to have duplicate logic in place in both Express and React Router. Figure 7.7 illustrates the differences.

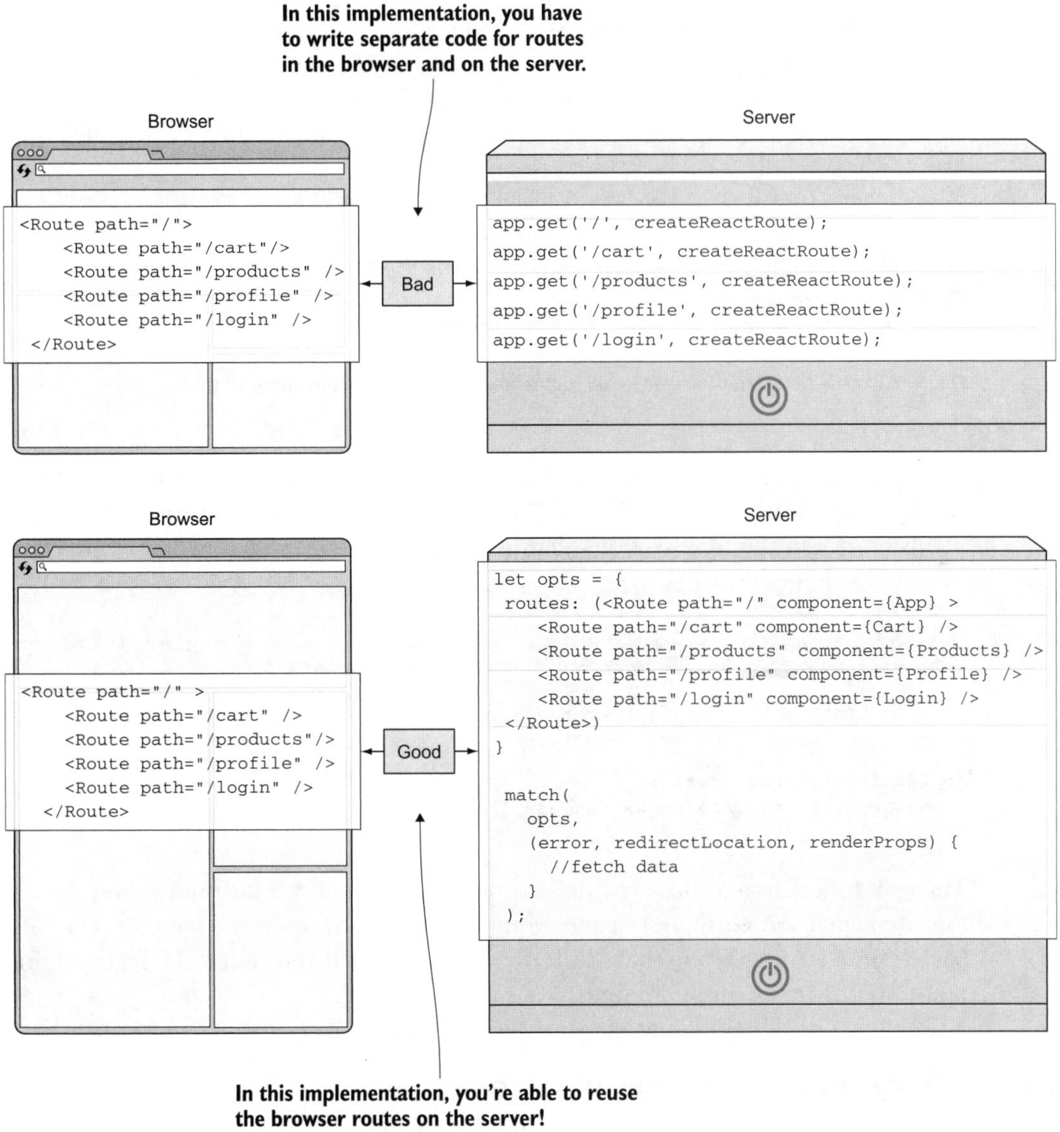
In this implementation, you have to write separate code for routes in the browser and on the server.
Browser
Server
<Route path="/">
<Route path="/cart"/>
<Route path="/products" />
<Route path="/profile" />
<Route path="/login" />
</Route>
Bad
app.get('/', createReactRoute);
app.get('/cart', createReactRoute);
app.get('/products', createReactRoute);
app.get('/profile', createReactRoute);
app.get('/login', createReactRoute);
Browser
Server
<Route path="/" >
<Route path="/cart" />
<Route path="/products"/>
<Route path="/profile" />
<Route path="/login" />
</Route>
Good
let opts = {
routes: (<Route path="/" component={App} >
<Route path="/cart" component={Cart} />
<Route path="/products" component={Products} />
<Route path="/profile" component={Profile} />
<Route path="/login" component={Login} />
</Route>)
}
match(
opts,
(error, redirectLocation, renderProps) {
//fetch data
}
);
In this implementation, you're able to reuse the browser routes on the server!

Figure 7.7 Efficiency versus lots of code duplication makes server routing with React Router the best choice.

If you re-create the routes in Express (the bad option in figure 7.7)

- You have code duplication and no single source of truth for routes.
- You need to somehow provide the same React Router interface to these routes so that your app render on the server ends up matching your app render in the browser. *This is a lot of work!*

By reusing React Router and taking advantage of its built-in server functions, you save time and you don't have to worry about your initial app state on the server being different from the initial app state on the browser.

You want to do this in an isomorphic application because it lets you reuse more of your code by using the routes from React Router. That lets you use the same routes in both environments. Figure 7.8 shows how typing in an arbitrary route will print that route with a success message. This route won't work until you add the code from listing 7.3.

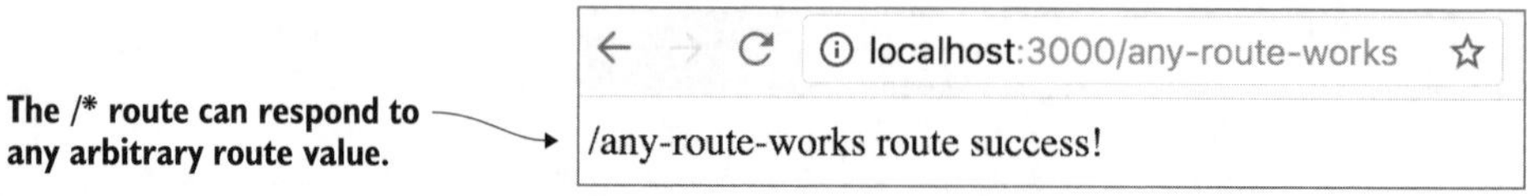
localhost:3000/any-route-works
The /* route can respond to any arbitrary route value.
/any-route-works route success!

Figure 7.8 The GET route handler for all routes allows you to pass any route to the server.

Listing 7.3 shows how to set up a global route handler in your app.js file. The global route handler will always come last. It'll call a middleware function (renderView.jsx—see listing 7.4 in the next section) that uses React Router's match logic to figure out which view to render.

Listing 7.3 Add a route to handle any view—src/app.es6

```
// all other routes go before the global handler
app.get('/test', (req, res) => {...});

app.get('/*', (req, res) => {
  res.send(`${req.url} route success!`);
});
```

The `get` function takes in a regular expression. * will match all routes—any routes that are matched before the /* route won't be handled by this route handler. The callback responds with a string that prints the current URL. If you restart the server at this point, you'll see the output in figure 7.8.

Next you'll add middleware to your route handlers.

7.2 Adding middleware for view rendering

So far, you've set up routes that are terminated in a single function that takes in the request and responds to it with the response object. Next, you want to implement a middleware function that checks for a route match with one of the app views (for example, /cart). Express can chain multiple functions together to handle complex business logic. These individual functions are called *middleware.* (If you're thinking this sounds a lot like Redux middleware, it is!)

Because we've decided to let React Router handle all the view routing, you'll use the same sharedRoutes file you created in chapter 4. You can review the code in shared/sharedRoutes.jsx. There are four routes inside a root route (and an `IndexRoute` to make sure something renders on the root route):

```
<Route path="/" component={App} >
  <IndexRoute component={Products} />
  <Route path="/cart" component={Cart} />
  <Route path="/products" component={Products} />
  <Route path="/profile" component={Profile} />
  <Route path="/login" component={Login} />
</Route>
```

NOTE If you're using React Router 4, check out appendix A for an overview of setting up the routes.

After you've configured the React Router routes, it's time to write your first Express middleware, which will call the `match` function and determine whether the requested route exists in your app.

7.2.1 *Using match to handle routing*

The `renderView` middleware handles route matching. It uses a function called `match` that's provided by React Router. After you've added it, you'll be able to navigate to each route you created in sharedRoutes. Figure 7.9 shows sample output of navigating to localhost:3000/cart after you add the code from listings 7.4 and 7.5.

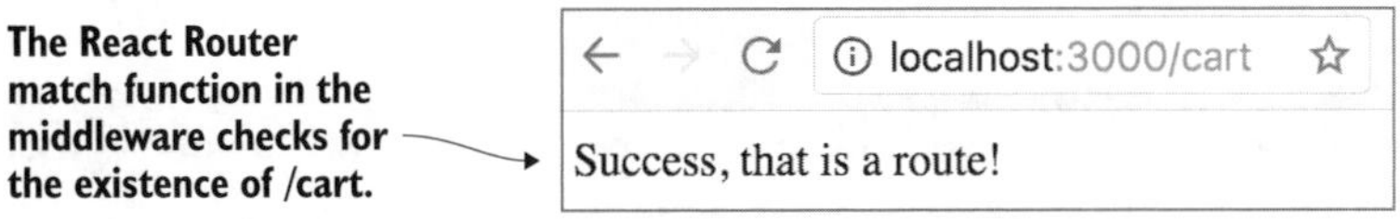
The React Router match function in the middleware checks for the existence of /cart.
localhost:3000/cart
Success, that is a route!

Figure 7.9 The middleware allows routing on the server to respond correctly based on the React Router shared routes.

NOTE If you're using React Router 4, check out appendix B for an overview of how to handle the routes on the server.

To get the middleware hooked up to the `/*` (all) route handler you set up in the previous section, you'll replace the request handler function with the `renderView` middleware function. The following listing shows the basic route-matching logic of the middleware.

Listing 7.4 Route-matching middleware—src/middleware/renderView.jsx

```
import { match } from 'react-router';                      // Include match function from React Router.
import routes from '../shared/sharedRoutes';               // Include the routes from shared routes.

export default function renderView(req, res) {             // Middleware function takes in several parameters.
  const matchOpts = {
    routes,
    location: req.url
  };                                                        // Configure the match function options. The object requires your shared routes as well as the location being requested (the URL from the request).
  const handleMatchResult = (
                          error,
                          redirectLocation,
                          renderProps
                        ) => {                              // This callback will be called from the match function after it determines what to do with the current route.
    if (!error && !redirectLocation && renderProps) {       // Check to make sure there isn't an error or redirect.
      res.send('Success, that is a route!');
    }
  };

  match(matchOpts, handleMatchResult);                      // Call match function with options and callback.
}
```

Multiple callbacks are used in the listing. The request and response objects are passed to each middleware function. The next parameter is a callback function used to pass to the next middleware in the chain. The other callback for React Router has three parameters: an `error` object, a redirect location, and `renderProps`, which represents the components to be rendered if the route is valid.

After you have the middleware set up, you also need to use it in app.es6. The following listing shows how to import and apply the middleware by passing it in as a callback to the route handler. Update app.es6 with the code from the listing.

Listing 7.5 Using `renderView` middleware for the catchall route—src/app.es6

```
  import renderViewMiddleware from './middleware/renderView';   // Import your renderView middleware.

app.get('/*', renderViewMiddleware);   // Replace inline anonymous route handler (you pass middleware function into the route handler).
```

Figure 7.10 shows how a request enters your app via Express, gets routed by the /* router in Express, and then passes through various middleware functions that handle React Router routes such as /cart or errors. Each middleware function has the option to either terminate the request (successfully or with an HTTP error response code) or call the next callback. Calling `next` passes the request to the next middleware function in the chain.

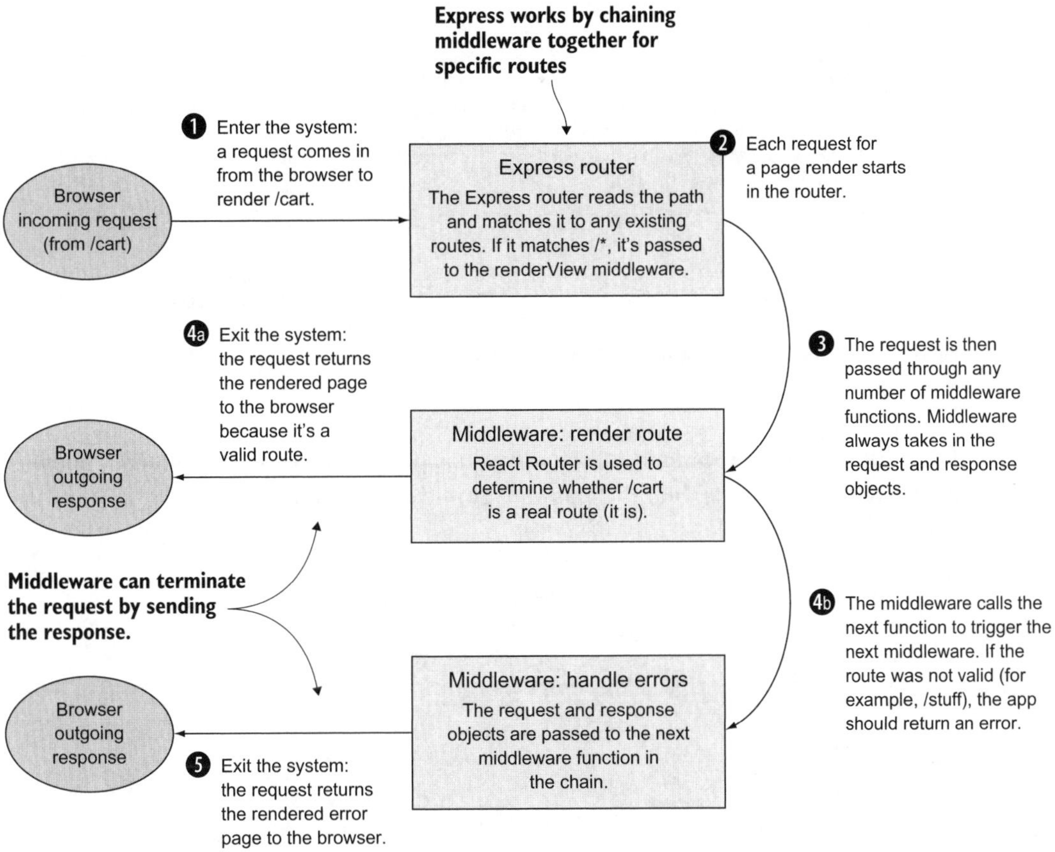
Express works by chaining middleware together for specific routes
1 Enter the system: a request comes in from the browser to render /cart.
Browser incoming request (from /cart)
Express router
The Express router reads the path and matches it to any existing routes. If it matches /*, it's passed to the renderView middleware.
2 Each request for a page render starts in the router.
4a Exit the system: the request returns the rendered page to the browser because it's a valid route.
3 The request is then passed through any number of middleware functions. Middleware always takes in the request and response objects.
Browser outgoing response
Middleware: render route
React Router is used to determine whether /cart is a real route (it is).
Middleware can terminate the request by sending the response.
4b The middleware calls the next function to trigger the next middleware. If the route was not valid (for example, /stuff), the app should return an error.
Middleware: handle errors
The request and response objects are passed to the next middleware function in the chain.
Browser outgoing response
5 Exit the system: the request returns the rendered error page to the browser.

Figure 7.10 The flow of a request through the Express router and associated middleware that use React Router to check for the presence of a valid route

This section covered how to use Express middleware alongside React Router on the server to determine the existence of app routes. Next, you'll render the components on the server.

7.2.2 Rendering components on the server

Phew! You've reached the critical juncture—the climax of the story, so to speak. (I saw you roll your eyes.) This section covers the core of getting your components rendered on the server. The goal is to end up with a string representation of the DOM that can be sent as the response to the browser (figure 7.11).

Ensure standards compliance **The HTML wrapper**

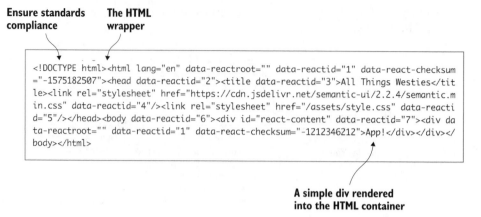

```
<!DOCTYPE html><html lang="en" data-reactroot="" data-reactid="1" data-react-checksum
="-1575182507"><head data-reactid="2"><title data-reactid="3">All Things Westies</tit
le><link rel="stylesheet" href="https://cdn.jsdelivr.net/semantic-ui/2.2.4/semantic.m
in.css" data-reactid="4"/><link rel="stylesheet" href="/assets/style.css" data-reacti
d="5"/></head><body data-reactid="6"><div id="react-content" data-reactid="7"><div da
ta-reactroot="" data-reactid="1" data-react-checksum="-1212346212">App!</div></div></
body></html>
```

A simple div rendered into the HTML container

Figure 7.11 Rendered output for the HTML in string form

Rendering your components on the server has two parts. Let's imagine what happens when the user requests the /cart route. Figure 7.12 shows this flow.

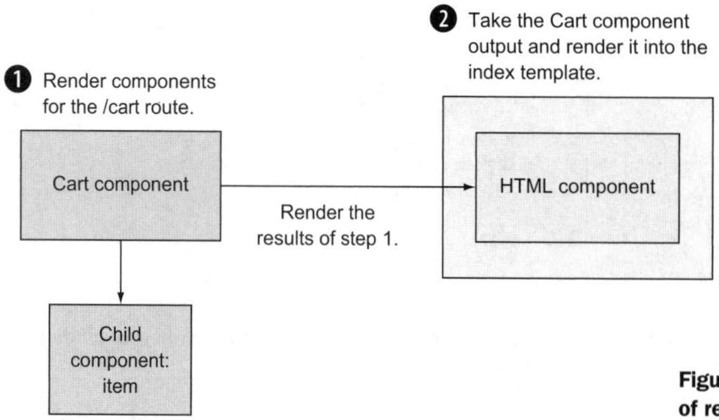

❶ Render components for the /cart route.
❷ Take the Cart component output and render it into the index template.
Cart component
Render the results of step 1.
HTML component
Child component: item

Figure 7.12 The two-step process of rendering a valid HTML route

Here are the steps:

1. Each view request must render the React tree based on the route matched with React Router. For /cart, this includes the App component, Cart component, and Item component. You saw the App component in chapter 4, and we'll go over the other components in this chapter.
2. The final request must contain a complete HTML page with head and body tags. Your core App components don't include this markup. Instead, you need to create an HTML.jsx component that handles the wrapper markup. Think of this as your index.html file.

These two steps require you to render twice on the server. (This method has alternatives, but they all require additional templating languages and setup. If you want to explore one of these other options, either EJS or Pug work nicely with Node.js.) The first React app I worked on used Pug. Although there's nothing wrong with this approach, it presents challenges. For one, you need to be up-to-date on yet another library. Also, it doesn't play as nicely with some of the cool tools available for your workflow such as the Webpack Dev Server.

BUILDING YOUR INDEX COMPONENT

First, let's render a basic HTML page so you have a container to put your components into. If you've been following along, you can continue in the current branch. If you've gotten lost or want to skip to the next checkpoint, you can change branches to the chapter-7-rendering branch (`git checkout chapter-7-rendering`). The following listing shows the React component that represents your root HTML container. Add this code to html.jsx.

Listing 7.6 HTML container —src/components/html.jsx

```
import React from 'react';
import PropTypes from 'prop-types';

const HTML = (props) => {
  return (
    <html lang="en">
      <head>
        <title>All Things Westies</title>
        <link
          rel="stylesheet"
          href="https://cdn.jsdelivr.net/semantic-ui/2.2.2/semantic.min.css"
        />
        <link rel="stylesheet" href="/assets/style.css" />
      </head>
      <body>
        <div
          id="react-content"
          dangerouslySetInnerHTML={{ __html: props.
     renderedToStringComponents }}
        />
      </body>
    </html>
  );
};

HTML.propTypes = {
  renderedToStringComponents: PropTypes.string
};

export default HTML;
```

Will be rendered only on the server, will never have state and can be a pure (stateless) component represented by a function.

Build basic HTML structure with <html>, <head>, and <body> tags.

Include Semantic UI CSS library.

Where rendered React component markup for the current route will go

Add prop type string to indicate rendered components will be provided as string.

The rendered React component markup will be passed in as a string. Because you're injecting HTML, you must use `dangerouslySetInnerHTML` to insert the DOM elements. The most important piece of this React component is that it takes in the rendered HTML that makes up the rest of the component tree. In the next section, you'll render the main component tree into the html.jsx component.

Remember that components are always rendered only once on the server, so only the first React lifecycle is triggered. Components that are used only on the server (such as html.jsx) can be stateless if they don't rely on `componentWillUpdate`.

> **dangerouslySetInnerHTML**
>
> The `dangerouslySetInnerHTML` property is provided by React to allow you to inject HTML into React components. Generally speaking, you *shouldn't* use this property. But sometimes you need to. Every rule has exceptions!
>
> What's really happening when you set this attribute? Under the hood, React is setting the `innerHTML` property. But setting `innerHTML` is a security risk. It can expose you to cross-site scripting (XSS) attacks.
>
> React considers using `dangerouslySetInnerHTML` a best practice because it reminds you that you don't want to be setting `innerHTML` most of the time. For more information, see http://mng.bz/69Ne.

7.2.3 *Using renderToString to create the view*

The next step is rendering output into the HTML container from listing 7.6. In the following listing, you can see how to call `renderToString` twice to get your main content rendered into an HTML page. Update the `renderView` middleware with this code.

Listing 7.7 Render HTML output in the middleware—src/middleware/renderView.jsx

```
import React from 'react';                                  // Include React because of JSX in middleware (this is why it's a .jsx file).
import { renderToString } from 'react-dom/server';          // Import renderToString function from React DOM library.
import { match} from 'react-router';
import routes from '../shared/sharedRoutes';
import HTML from '../components/html';                      // Include the HTML component.

export default function renderView(req, res, next) {
  const matchOpts = {
    routes,
    location: req.url
  };
  const handleMatchResult = (error, redirectLocation, renderProps) => {
    if (!error && !redirectLocation && renderProps) {
      const app = renderToString(<div>App!</div>);           // Call renderToString on placeholder <div>.
      const html = renderToString(
       <HTML renderedToStringComponents ={app} />           // Call renderToString on HTML component, inject rendered app content into component.
      );
```

```
      res.send(`<!DOCTYPE html>${html}`);        Send composed string back on
    } else {                                     response, append DOCTYPE tag
      next();                                    to make markup valid.
    }
  };
  match(matchOpts, handleMatchResult);
}
```

Calling `renderToString` on the placeholder `<div>` creates the page content that will be inserted in the HTML component.

In the next section, you'll replace this with the App component.

RENDERING COMPONENTS

The final step is to completely render a route inside the middleware. This requires the following:

- Dynamically rendering app.jsx and a child component based on the route (for example, the cart and all its children)
- Taking the string output from the render and passing it into html.jsx as a property

You already built the App component in chapter 4. It's in src/components/app.jsx. You now need to add the Cart component.

The Cart component renders the items in a user's cart and displays the total cost. It also has a Checkout button. For now, this component has placeholder text (the linter will complain, but you'll fix this soon). In the next section, you'll add Redux and data fetching, and the cart will dynamically render the items you pass into it. You already have a cart.jsx from chapter 4. Replace the existing code with the following listing.

Listing 7.8 Cart component—src/components/cart.jsx

```
import React, { Component } from 'react';

class Cart extends Component {
  render() {
    return (                                            Container for
      <div className="cart main ui segment">            rendering
        <div className="ui segment divided items">      cart items
          Items will go here.
        </div>
        <div className="ui right rail">
          <div className="ui segment">                  Render total number
            <span>Total: </span><span>$10</span>        of items in cart.
            <div></div>
            <button                                     Checkout
              className="ui positive basic button">     button
              Checkout
            </button>
          </div>
        </div>
      </div>
```

```
      );
    }
  }
  export default Cart;
```

Now that you have the components for the /cart route, you still need to render them on the server. Listing 7.9 shows you how to take the middleware code and update it to work with dynamic routes.

> **NOTE** If you're using React Router 4, check out appendix B for an overview of how to handle the routes on the server.

Listing 7.9 Render—src/middleware/renderView.jsx

```
import React from 'react';
import { renderToString } from 'react-dom/server';
import { match, RouterContext } from 'react-router';
import routes from '../shared/sharedRoutes';
import HTML from '../components/html';

export default function renderView(req, res, next) {
  const matchOpts = {
    routes,
    location: req.url
  };
  const handleMatchResult = (
      error,
      redirectLocation,
      renderProps
    ) => {
    if (!error && !redirectLocation && renderProps) {
      const app = renderToString(
        <RouterContext
          routes={routes}
          {...renderProps}
        />
      );
      const html = renderToString(<HTML renderedToStringComponents={app} />);
      console.log(`<!DOCTYPE html>${html}`);
      res.send(`<!DOCTYPE html>${html}`);
    } else {
      next();
    }
  };

  match(matchOpts, handleMatchResult);
}
```

RouterContext is a React Router component used to properly render your component tree on the server.

Pass in shared routes to RouterContext so the location is properly initialized and matches the browser render.

Calculated by the match function from React Router, passed into RouterContext, which knows how to pull out the correct component to render.

The key takeaway is to use the `renderProps` value (passed into your callback from React Router). This lets the Router know which component to render. It's also how you make the routing consistent on both the server and the browser.

So far, you've learned how to take advantage of React's `renderToString` to render your components on the server. But you also need to be able to fetch the data that populates your components on the server. In the next section, you'll hook up Redux and add a static method called `prefetchActions` to your React components to indicate what actions need to be called for an individual component to be rendered properly at runtime.

7.3 Adding Redux

As you add Redux to the app, you'll be rendering the fetched data into the view, as in figure 7.13.

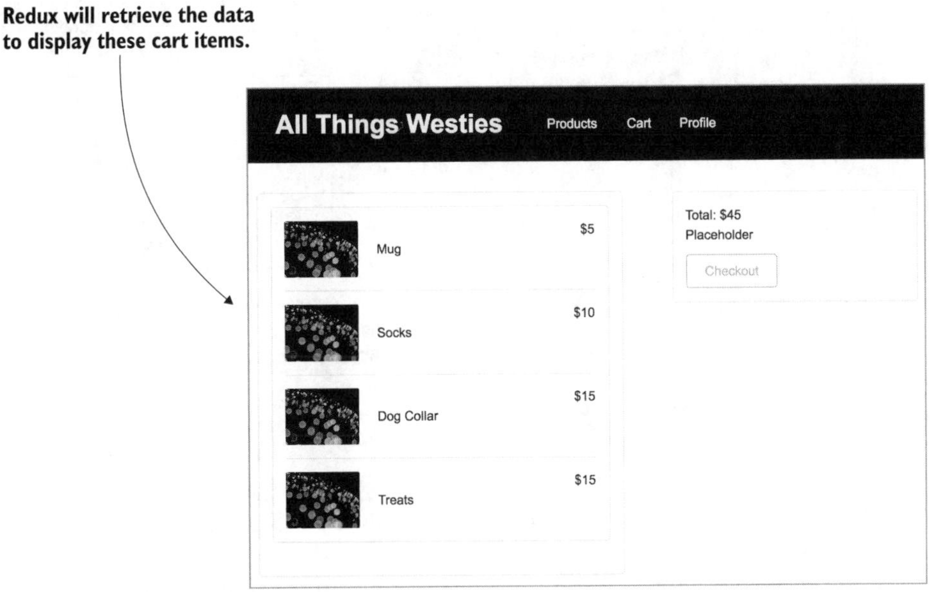
Redux will retrieve the data to display these cart items.
All Things Westies
Products
Cart
Profile
$5
Mug
$10
Socks
$15
Dog Collar
$15
Treats
Total: $45
Placeholder
Checkout

Figure 7.13 The data fetched by Redux on the server will be rendered into the list view in the cart.

One of the trickiest parts of building web apps (or any data-driven, user-facing app) is handling asynchronous code. It's kind of like when I'm cooking breakfast and my premade breakfast sausages say they'll take 6–8 minutes to make. Does that mean I should start my eggs 4 minutes after starting to cook the sausages, or 8 minutes? My eggs will cook much faster than the sausages, but I want everything to be ready at the same time.

Similarly, when using Redux on the server, you need your data to be ready before you render your view, or the view created on the server and the view created after the browser code runs won't always match. You need to guarantee that the data needed by

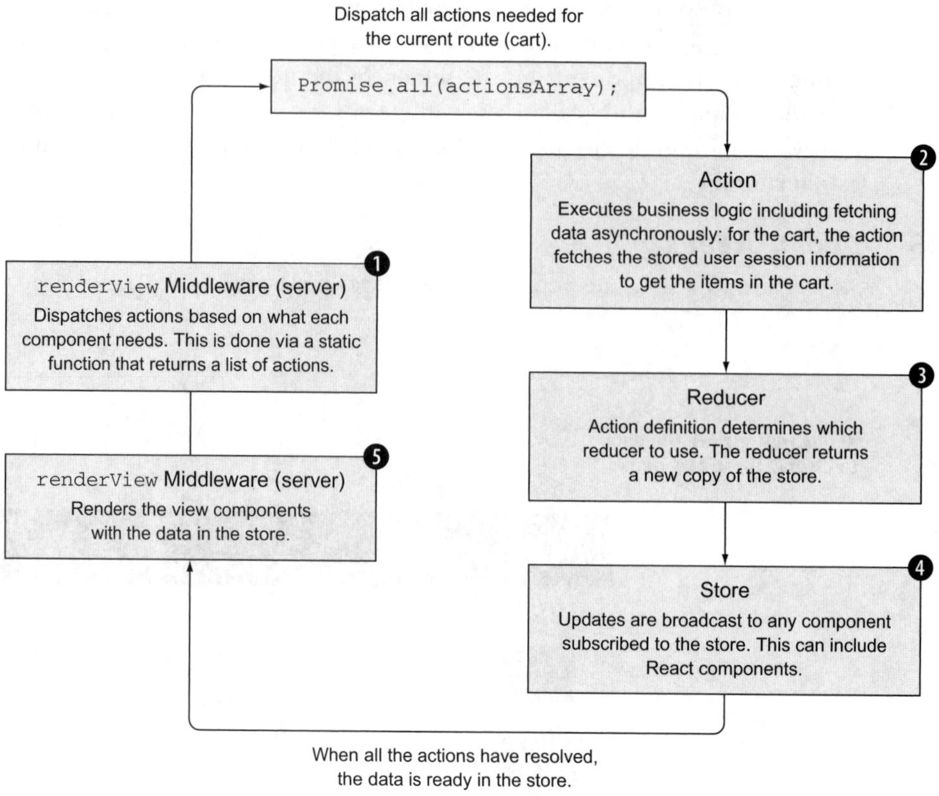
Dispatch all actions needed for the current route (cart).
Promise.all(actionsArray);
Action
Executes business logic including fetching data asynchronously: for the cart, the action fetches the stored user session information to get the items in the cart.
renderView Middleware (server)
Dispatches actions based on what each component needs. This is done via a static function that returns a list of actions.
Reducer
Action definition determines which reducer to use. The reducer returns a new copy of the store.
renderView Middleware (server)
Renders the view components with the data in the store.
Store
Updates are broadcast to any component subscribed to the store. This can include React components.
When all the actions have resolved, the data is ready in the store.

Figure 7.14 The Redux flow on the server

the view is available before you begin to render the view. Figure 7.14 shows the flow of Redux on the server.

You'll take several steps to make sure you can fetch all the necessary data for the Cart component (the same process can be applied to other parts of the app):

- Create cart actions and reducers to fetch the cart data
- Use the `renderView` middleware to call actions
- Use a static method on your Cart component to allow the middleware to know what actions it needs to call
- Display the fetched data in the Cart component

7.3.1 Setting up the cart actions and reducers

The All Things Westies app has the concept of user sessions and being logged out or logged in. Therefore, the app can track items in the user's cart and then persist this data so the user can come back later and finish the transaction. (You could also use cookies or local storage to do this.)

In this section, you're going to assume that the user has previously put items in the cart and has come back directly to the cart to finish shopping. You'll be working with the cart route (http://localhost:3000/cart).

First you need to initialize Redux on the server. The following listing shows the Redux configuration that you need to add to init-redux.es6. If you've been following along, you can add this code, or you can switch to chapter-7-adding-redux (`git checkout chapter-7-adding-redux`).

Listing 7.10 Initialize the Redux store—src/shared/init-redux.es6

```
import {
  createStore,
  combineReducers,
  applyMiddleware,
  compose } from 'redux';
import thunkMiddleware from 'redux-thunk';
import loggerMiddleware from 'redux-logger';
import cart from './cart-reducer.es6';

export default function (initialStore = {}) {
  const reducer = combineReducers({
     cart
  });
  const middleware = [
                      thunkMiddleware,
                      loggerMiddleware
                    ];
  return compose(
      applyMiddleware(...middleware)
    )(createStore)(reducer, initialStore);
}
```

- Import all functions needed from Redux.
- Import Thunk middleware so you can use asynchronous actions.
- Import logger middleware to help with debugging—on the server, it'll log in terminal.
- Import cart reducer.
- Create the root reducer, which will eventually have other subreducers for user, product, and blog data.
- Set up the middleware.
- Compose the middleware and reducers to create new store.

You also need to create the action you'll be calling to fetch the cart data. The cart needs to know what items are currently in the user's cart. You add this code in the cart-action-creators.es6 file, shown in the following listing.

Listing 7.11 Cart actions—src/shared/cart-action-creators.es6

```
import fetch from 'isomorphic-fetch';

export const GET_CART_ITEMS = 'GET_CART_ITEMS';

export function getCartItems() {
  return (dispatch) => {
    return fetch('http://localhost:3000/api/user/cart',
      {
        method: 'GET'
      }
    ).then((response) => {
      return response.json().then((data) => {
```

- String constant for the action
- On the server, the getCartItems action will be called from the renderView middleware.
- Use fetch API to get cart data from the Node.js server.
- On a success response, read JSON from the response.

```
          return dispatch({
            type: GET_CART_ITEMS,
            data: data.items
          });
        });
      })
    };
}
```

Take parsed JSON; return action object.

In that last line, the `type` is the string constant, and the `data` is the items array from the JSON. Listing 7.12 shows what this data looks like.

For the All Things Westies app, all the data will be handled on your Node.js server. Everything is mocked out in JSON files. The cart data is shown in the following listing. It's already provided for you in the branch.

Listing 7.12 Mock cart data—data/cart.json

```
{
  "items": [
    {
      "name": "Mug",
      "price": 5,
      "thumbnail":
➥ http://localhost:3000/assets/cart-item-placeholder.jpg
    },
    {
      "name": "Socks",
      "price": 10,
      "thumbnail":
➥ http://localhost:3000/assets/cart-item-placeholder.jpg
    },
    {
      "name": "Dog Collar",
      "price": 15
    },
    {
      "name": "Treats",
      "price": 15,
      "thumbnail":
➥ http://localhost:3000/assets/cart-item-placeholder.jpg
    }
  ]
}
```

JSON returns object with an array of cart items.

Each item has a name that's a string.

Each item has a price that's a number.

Each item has a thumbnail that's a string with an image URL.

After the cart data is fetched from the server by the `getCartItems` action, your cart reducer will put the data in the Redux store. Listing 7.13 shows the code required to set up the cart reducer. Remember that the job of the reducer is to take in the current store and an action. It then uses the action to update the store and return a new state of the app. Add the code from the listing to the cart reducer.

Listing 7.13 Cart reducers—src/shared/cart-reducer.es6

```
import {
  GET_CART_ITEMS
} from './cart-action-creators.es6';

export default function cart(state = {}, action) {
  switch (action.type) {
    case GET_CART_ITEMS:
      return {
        ...state,
        items: action.data
      };
    default:
      return state;
  }
}
```

- Use an action string constant to ensure consistency.
- Read the type from the action passed into reducer to see if you should handle the action in this reducer.
- Write data from the action into current state.

Good job! You've created all the pieces of Redux (setup, action, and reducer) needed to fetch the route data in the `renderView` middleware. Next, you'll implement the data-fetching logic so you can see the data loaded into the view.

7.3.2 Using Redux in renderView middleware

Now you need to include the store in your `renderView` middleware. The following listing shows how to add this in.

Listing 7.14 Adding the Redux store to your middleware—src/middleware/renderView.jsx

```
import initRedux from '../shared/init-redux.es6';

export default function renderView(req, res, next) {
  const matchOpts = {...};
  const handleMatchResult = (error, redirectLocation, renderProps) => {
    if (!error && !redirectLocation && renderProps) {
      const store = initRedux();
      // ... more code
    }
  }
  // ... more code
}
```

- Include initialization code in middleware.
- Call initialization function and store it on a const variable called store.

After you have the store in the middleware, you can dispatch actions on the server. But you want to be smart and dispatch only the actions for the current route. To do that, you need to extend your React components to be able to declare your actions on a per-route basis.

SETTING UP INITIAL ACTIONS

There are a couple of valid ways to declare the data needs for a route. You can store this information with the route declaration or you can put the data declaration on the components. I'm going to show you how to put the data declaration on the components. The Cart component knows which action creator functions need to be called to fetch the appropriate data for the cart view. Later, the `renderView` middleware will use these function references and call them to get the JSON data responses needed to populate the store.

With React Router, you can easily access any component you've declared in a route component. By declaring the data needs on the components that are in your shared routes, you can compose a list of actions from multiple components in the middleware. The next listing shows how the Cart component declares its action needs. In this case, it needs the data fetched by the `getCartItems` action. To indicate that, it stores a reference to the action creator function. The `renderView` middleware will call this action.

Listing 7.15 Declaring initial actions—components/cart.jsx

```
import { getCartItems } from '../shared/cart-action-creators.es6';

class Cart extends Component {

  static prefetchActions() {
    return [
      getCartItems
    ];
  }
  render(){
    return {
      <div className="cart main ui segment">...</div>
    }
  }
}
```

Declare static function.

Return array so you can list multiple action creators (actions hold business logic of how to fetch data and update app state).

List action creators needed for component (don't call them here, just pass them as function references).

Remember that static functions aren't part of the class instance. They don't have access to any specifics of the component instance such as properties or state. Any context for a static function needs to be passed in from the caller. In this case, you don't need any context.

> **Static functions**
>
> *Static functions* live on the React class or any JavaScript class. These functions can be called without instantiating an instance of the class.
>
> Why would you want to use a static function? Usually, they're used to provide a utility. In an isomorphic application, you can use static functions to define the data calls that a React component needs to be rendered.

7.3.3 Adding data prefetching via middleware

Now that your Cart component is declaring its own data needs by defining the actions that need to be called for it be rendered properly, you can use the middleware to fetch the data before you render the components. The first thing you need to add is code that collects all the actions from the components on `renderProps`. The following listing shows you what to add to get this working.

Listing 7.16 Calling all initial actions on components—src/middleware/renderView.jsx

```
export default function renderView(req, res, next) {
  const matchOpts = {...};
  const handleMatchResult = (error, redirectLocation, renderProps) => {

    if (!error && !redirectLocation && renderProps) {
      const store = initRedux();
      let actions = renderProps.components.map(
        component) => {
        if (component) {
          if (component.displayName &&
            component.displayName.toLowerCase().indexOf('connect') > -1
          ) {
            if (component.WrappedComponent.prefetchActions) {
              return component.
                WrappedComponent.prefetchActions();
            }
          } else if (component.prefetchActions) {
            return component.prefetchActions();
          }
        }
        return [];
      });
    actions = actions.reduce((flat, toFlatten) => {
      return flat.concat(toFlatten);
    }, []);
  };
  match(matchOpts, handleMatchResult);
}
```

Run map on each component returned by renderProps.

Check if component is wrapped by looking for 'connect' (check for and call prefetchActions on WrappedComponent property).

Call prefetchActions on component if function exists, should always return array.

map function will create an array of arrays—reduce it so you can concat them into one array.

This code enables the server to know what actions to call for the route. Remember, you can call `prefetchActions` only on components that are known to React Router.

The actions array is now a list of action creators that can be called. Next you'll set them up to dispatch and then use `Promise.all` to wait until all your initial actions complete before rendering the React components. Remember, you're calling only the actions required for the current route. The following listing shows how to add the asynchronous code handling so that you wait to render the components until you have all the data needed for the route.

Listing 7.17 Calling all initial actions on components—src/middleware/renderView.jsx

```
import { Provider } from 'react-redux';

export default function renderView(req, res, next) {
  const matchOpts = {...};
  const handleMatchResult = (error, redirectLocation, renderProps) => {
```

Import Provider component from React Redux (to create components with Redux on the server).

```
      if (!error && renderProps) {
        const store = initRedux();

        let actions = renderProps.components.map((component) => {...});
        actions = actions.reduce((flat, toFlatten) => {...}, []);

        const promises = actions.map((initialAction) => {
          return store.dispatch(initialAction());
        });
        Promise.all(promises).then(() => {
          const app = renderToString(
            <Provider store={store}>
              <RouterContext routes={routes} {...renderProps} />
            </Provider>
          );
          const html = renderToString(<HTML html={app} />);
          return res.status(200).send(`<!DOCTYPE html>${html}`);
        });
      }
    }
    match(matchOpts, handleMatchResult);
  }
```

Call store.dispatch on each action creator.

Call Promise.all on your actions—after they've resolved, you can render components.

Wrap React Router component inside Provider.

After you wrap the React Router component inside Provider, you pass the store into Provider. The store will now be updated with all the data fetched and updated by your actions.

DISPLAYING DATA IN THE CART

Because the app is now fetching the data for the route, you can make your Cart component update with the dynamic data. The following listing shows the additional logic in your Cart component that displays each cart item.

Listing 7.18 Complete Cart component—components/cart.jsx

```
import React, { Component } from 'react';
import PropTypes from 'prop-types';
import { bindActionCreators } from 'redux';
import { connect } from 'react-redux';
import { getCartItems } from '../shared/cart-action-creators.es6';
import Item from './item';

class Cart extends Component {

  static prefetchActions() {}

  constructor(props) {
    super(props);
    this.proceedToCheckout = this.proceedToCheckout.bind(this);
  }

  getTotal() {
    let total = 0;
    const items = this.props.items;
```

```
    if (items) {
      total = items.reduce((prev, current) => {
        return prev + current.price;
      }, total);
    }
    return total;
  }

  proceedToCheckout() {
    console.log('clicked checkout button', this.props);
  }

  renderItems() {
    const components = [];
    const items = this.props.items;
    if (this.props.items) {
      this.props.items.forEach((item, index) => {
        components.push(<Item key={index} {...item} />);
      });
    }
    return items;
  }

  render() {
    return (
      <div className="cart main ui segment">
        <div className="ui segment divided items">
          {this.renderItems()}
        </div>
        <div className="ui right rail">
          <div className="ui segment">
            <span>Total: </span><span>${this.getTotal()}</span>
            <button
              onClick={this.proceedToCheckout}
              className="ui positive basic button"
            >
                Checkout
            </button>
          </div>
        </div>
      </div>
    );
  }
}

Cart.propTypes = {
  items: PropTypes.arrayOf(
    PropTypes.shape({
      name: PropTypes.string.isRequired,
      price: PropTypes.number.isRequired,
      thumbnail: PropTypes.string.isRequired
    })
  )
};
```

Calculate total based on cart items on prop, use reduce to return sum of all prices.

Placeholder click handler for button (you won't see console.log output because you haven't hooked up the browser code).

Render cart items with the Item component, create new Item for each item in items array.

```
function mapStateToProps(state) {
  const { items } = state.cart;
  return {
    items
  };
}

function mapDispatchToProps(dispatch) {
  return {
    cartActions: bindActionCreators([getCartItems], dispatch)
  };
}

export default connect(
                       mapStateToProps,
                       mapDispatchToProps
                     )(Cart);
```

Hook up cart to Redux so it can get cart items on props.

Restart the app. Then if you navigate to /cart, you'll see each item fully rendered. But the Checkout button doesn't work! You won't see any console output when you click it because you haven't rehydrated the React tree in the browser. Chapter 8 will teach you how to make the server/browser handoff and get the browser-specific code working.

Summary

In this chapter, you learned how to implement server-side rendering. You wrote Express middleware that handles the routing and rendering for your app. And you learned how to use Redux on the server and prefetch your data to create the Cart component on the server.

- Express can be used to render your views.
- You can use React Router on the server so you don't have to duplicate your routing code.
- You create and use custom Express middleware to determine the route you're on and render the components for the current route.
- React provides a method called `renderToString` that allows you to return a string including the markup from your route.
- Instead of letting the normal app flow fetch your data, you prefetch the data needed for your components.

8 Isomorphic view rendering

This chapter covers

- Creating an entry point for the browser code that renders your React components
- Serializing the data so the browser code can start up (bootstrap) with the state from the server
- Deserializing the data in the browser to hydrate your code
- Including information from the original server request in your serialized data to maintain a consistent state between the browser and the server
- Transitioning to a single-page application (SPA) experience to handle user interactions in the browser

Throughout this chapter, you'll build the browser portion of the isomorphic view render. You're focusing on the lower half of the image in figure 8.1. You've seen this figure many times, but I'm revisiting it here to give context to this chapter.

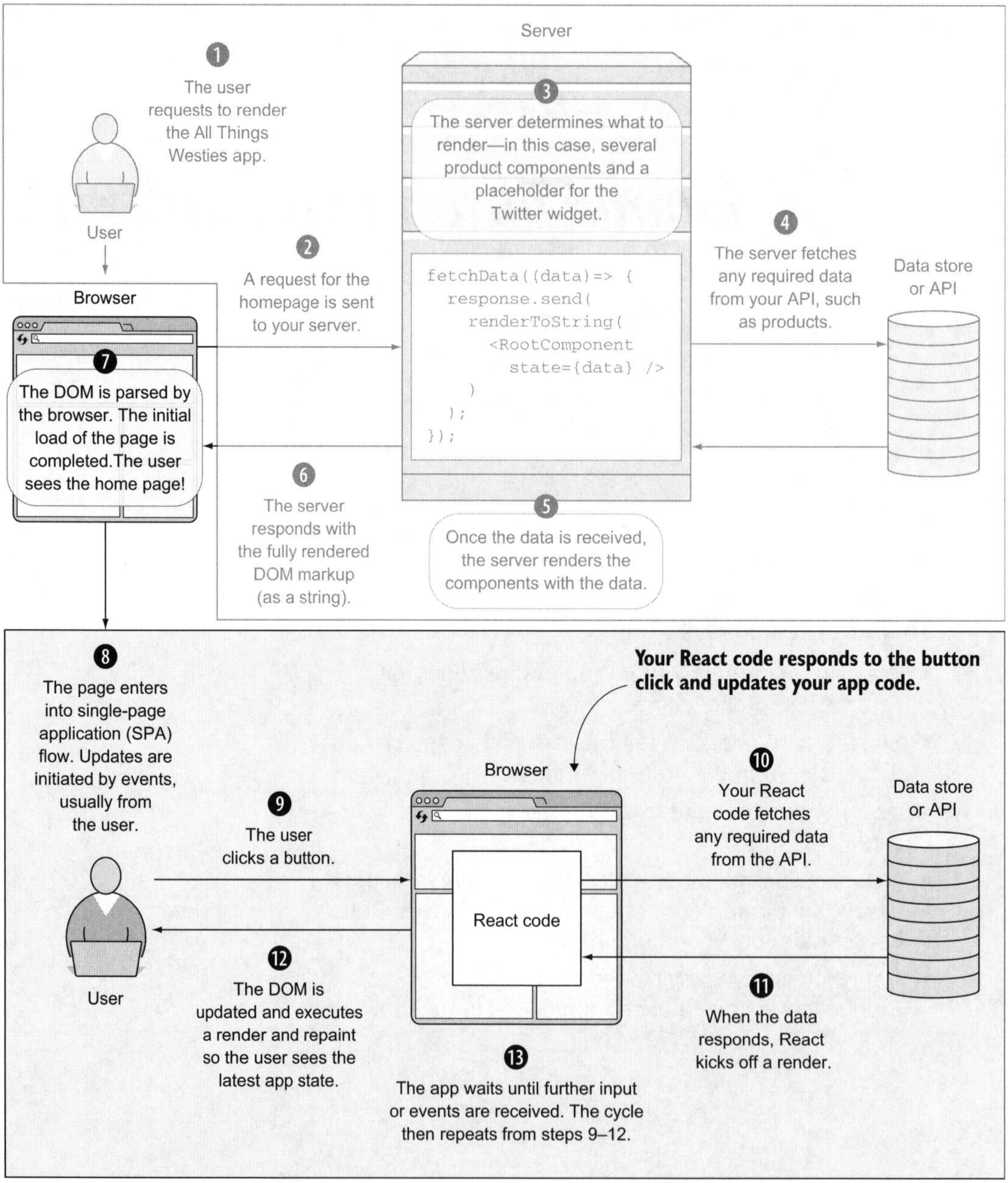
Server
1
The user requests to render the All Things Westies app.
User
3
The server determines what to render—in this case, several product components and a placeholder for the Twitter widget.
Browser
2
A request for the homepage is sent to your server.
fetchData((data)=> {
response.send(
renderToString(
<RootComponent
state={data} />
)
);
});
4
The server fetches any required data from your API, such as products.
Data store or API
7
The DOM is parsed by the browser. The initial load of the page is completed.The user sees the home page!
6
The server responds with the fully rendered DOM markup (as a string).
5
Once the data is received, the server renders the components with the data.
8
The page enters into single-page application (SPA) flow. Updates are initiated by events, usually from the user.
Your React code responds to the button click and updates your app code.
Browser
10
Your React code fetches any required data from the API.
Data store or API
9
The user clicks a button.
React code
User
12
The DOM is updated and executes a render and repaint so the user sees the latest app state.
11
When the data responds, React kicks off a render.
13
The app waits until further input or events are received. The cycle then repeats from steps 9–12.

Figure 8.1 This chapter focuses on the lower half of the flow, everything that happens after the server render (the browser render and the SPA logic).

All the code for this chapter is in the same GitHub repo that's used in chapter 7, which can be found at http://mng.bz/8gV8. After you've pulled down this code, switch to chapter-8.1.1 (`git checkout chapter-8.1.1`), which has the code for the first section of the chapter. Each branch provided in a section includes the skeleton code needed from previous sections, but not what will be added in that specific section. The next section's code will contain the complete code from previous sections. Each time you need to switch branches, I'll let you know.

Remember that you need to run the `start` command each time you want to build the code (and after you make any changes):

```
$ npm start
```

The app runs at http://localhost:3000 in your browser.

8.1 Setting up the browser entry point

The first thing you need to do to render your code in the browser is to set up your browser entry point. This is called main.jsx. It'll be where you bootstrap (initialize) your React code in the browser. Your main.jsx entry point will end up being responsible for several things, including the following:

- Deserializing the server state
- Initializing Redux with the current state
- Setting up React Router
- Rendering React components in the browser

8.1.1 Referencing the browser code

To get the browser code loading, you need to make sure to reference it from your HTML. It needs to be included as a script in the page, at the end of the body. That ensures it doesn't block page loading and rendering. Because the page was already rendered once on the server, your user won't know the script hasn't loaded yet!

The code in the branch (chapter-8.1.1) already includes the webpack configuration. When you run `npm start`, the browser code is created by webpack and is available to use in the app. Open the html.jsx file and use the code from the following listing to add a reference to the bundled browser file. Note that in production, you'd want to make this URL configurable to wherever your static asset files will live.

Listing 8.1 Adding your browser source code—src/components/html.jsx

```
<body>
  <div
    id="react-content"
    dangerouslySetInnerHTML={{ __html: props.html }}
  />
  <script
    type="application/javascript"
    src="browser.js"
  />
</body>
```

Insert a script tag that points to your JavaScript bundle.

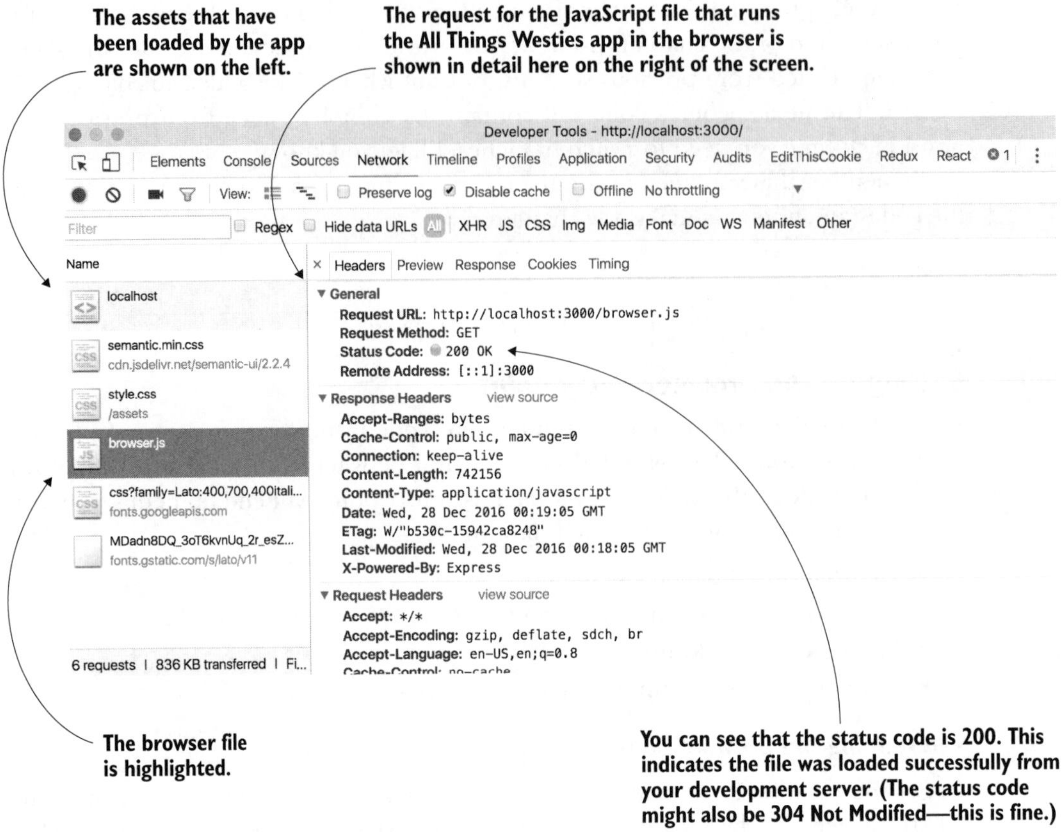
The assets that have been loaded by the app are shown on the left.
The request for the JavaScript file that runs the All Things Westies app in the browser is shown in detail here on the right of the screen.
Developer Tools - http://localhost:3000/
Elements Console Sources Network Timeline Profiles Application Security Audits EditThisCookie Redux React
View: Preserve log Disable cache Offline No throttling
Filter Regex Hide data URLs All XHR JS CSS Img Media Font Doc WS Manifest Other
Name
localhost
semantic.min.css
cdn.jsdelivr.net/semantic-ui/2.2.4
style.css
/assets
browser.js
css?family=Lato:400,700,400itali...
fonts.googleapis.com
MDadn8DQ_3oT6kvnUq_2r_esZ...
fonts.gstatic.com/s/lato/v11
6 requests | 836 KB transferred | Fi...
Headers Preview Response Cookies Timing
General
Request URL: http://localhost:3000/browser.js
Request Method: GET
Status Code: 200 OK
Remote Address: [::1]:3000
Response Headers view source
Accept-Ranges: bytes
Cache-Control: public, max-age=0
Connection: keep-alive
Content-Length: 742156
Content-Type: application/javascript
Date: Wed, 28 Dec 2016 00:19:05 GMT
ETag: W/"b530c-15942ca8248"
Last-Modified: Wed, 28 Dec 2016 00:18:05 GMT
X-Powered-By: Express
Request Headers view source
Accept: */*
Accept-Encoding: gzip, deflate, sdch, br
Accept-Language: en-US,en;q=0.8
The browser file is highlighted.
You can see that the status code is 200. This indicates the file was loaded successfully from your development server. (The status code might also be 304 Not Modified—this is fine.)

Figure 8.2 Using the Network tab of Chrome Developer Tools to confirm that your JavaScript code is loading in the browser

After you've done this, restart the server. To check whether the browser.js file is properly loading, use the Network tab in Chrome DevTools to see if it loaded. Figure 8.2 shows what to look for.

You should also try adding a `console.log` statement or setting a breakpoint to verify that your script is loading. After you get this working, you're ready to render your React components in the browser.

8.1.2 *Rendering React in the browser*

This section covers how to render React in the browser. We already covered this in chapter 3, when you learned all about using React. I'm going to revisit the core implementation details here. Also, I'll demonstrate why this step is necessary.

Let's start with the /cart route because it's already built out from chapter 7. In case you don't remember, figure 8.3 shows what it looked like by the end of chapter 7.

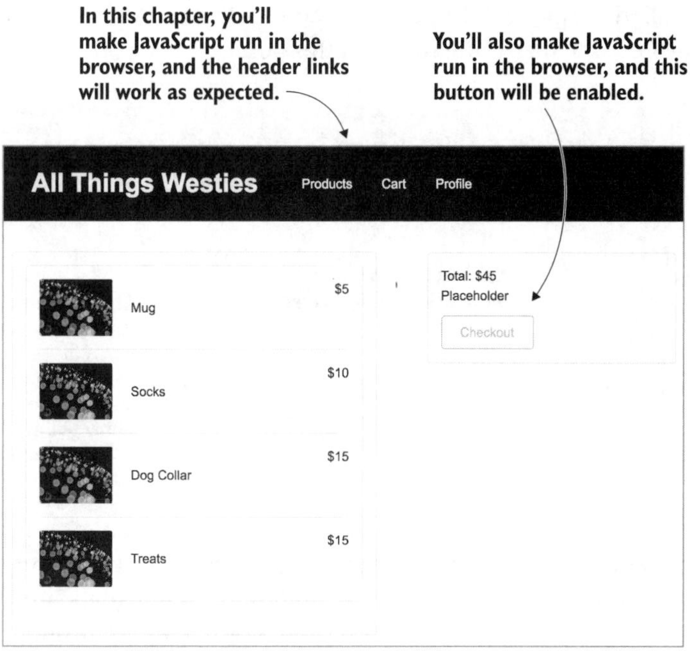
In this chapter, you'll make JavaScript run in the browser, and the header links will work as expected.
You'll also make JavaScript run in the browser, and this button will be enabled.
All Things Westies
Products
Cart
Profile
Mug
$5
Socks
$10
Dog Collar
$15
Treats
$15
Total: $45
Placeholder
Checkout

Figure 8.3 The Cart page of your application before rendering in the browser or adding SPA functionality

So far, you've made this render only on the server. Some things don't yet work, such as the Checkout button, which has a button handler with additional logic. The first step to getting that hooked up in the browser is to call `ReactDOM.render` in the browser. You're going to add a simple render call that displays a Browser Render message after the browser code is executed and rendered. Figure 8.4 shows what this looks like.

To get this output, you need to set up main.jsx with React and then call `render`. Listing 8.2 shows your entry point file rendering a simple `div` with a message. Add the code from the listing to main.jsx. If you need to catch up, all the code up to this point

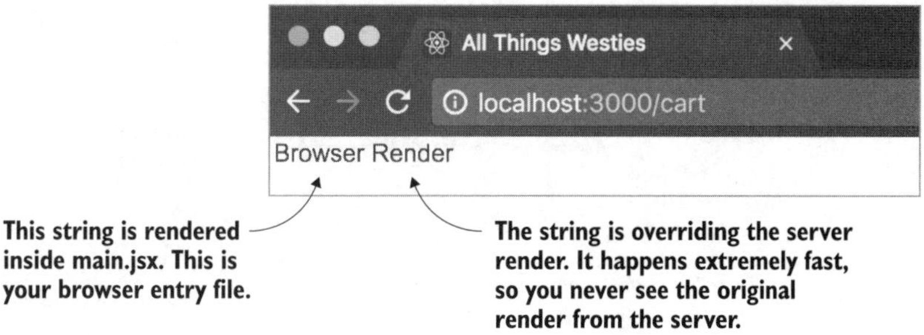
All Things Westies
localhost:3000/cart
Browser Render
This string is rendered inside main.jsx. This is your browser entry file.
The string is overriding the server render. It happens extremely fast, so you never see the original render from the server.

Figure 8.4 The expected output after you render a simple `div` and message in the browser

is on the branch called chapter-8.1.2 (`git checkout chapter-8.1.2`). Or you can keep working on your code that you have up to this point.

Listing 8.2 Rendering an HTML element in the browser—src/main.jsx

```
import React from 'react';
import ReactDOM from 'react-dom';

function init() {
  ReactDOM.render(
    <div>
      Browser Render
    </div>,
    document.getElementById('react-content'));
}

init();
```

- You must include React and React DOM to call render in this file.
- Call render function with a simple div element.
- Create an init function so you can add asynchronous code to your entry point.
- Pass in the DOM element; React will render your div into.

The obvious problem with this code is that your application has disappeared! That's not what you want to happen. Open your developer tools and select the Sources tab to set a breakpoint in your main.jsx file. (Use Cmd-P and search for main.jsx—then you'll be able to set the breakpoint.) Figure 8.5 shows what your Chrome DevTools will look like after setting the breakpoint.

Now that you've set the breakpoint, refresh your browser. The code execution will pause on your breakpoint. Look at your app in the main browser window. It'll look correct, with the cart route rendered (as in figure 8.3). If your app is loading but you notice a React error in the console output, don't worry about it for now (something like "React attempted to reuse markup in a container"). I'll explain that later in the chapter.

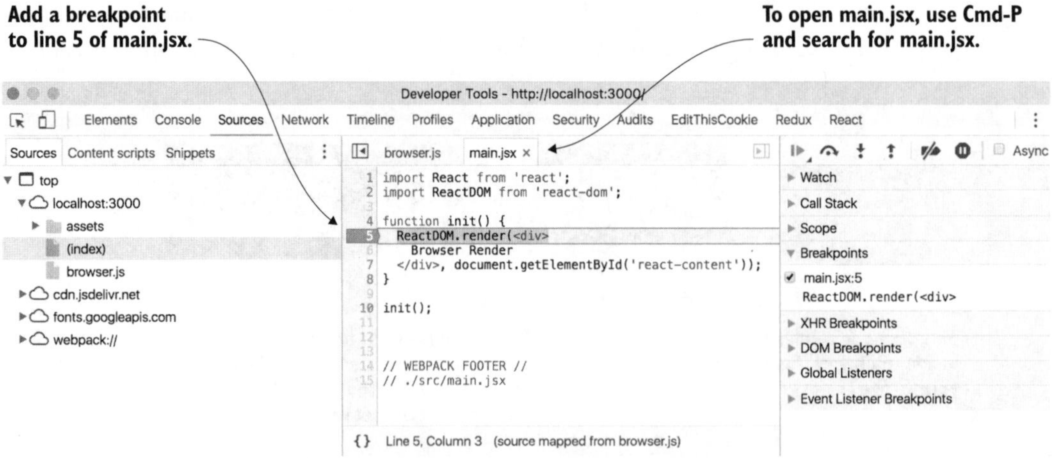

Add a breakpoint to line 5 of main.jsx.
To open main.jsx, use Cmd-P and search for main.jsx.
Developer Tools - http://localhost:3000/
Elements Console Sources Network Timeline Profiles Application Security Audits EditThisCookie Redux React
Sources Content scripts Snippets
top
localhost:3000
assets
(index)
browser.js
cdn.jsdelivr.net
fonts.googleapis.com
webpack://
browser.js main.jsx
import React from 'react';
import ReactDOM from 'react-dom';
function init() {
ReactDOM.render(
Browser Render
, document.getElementById('react-content'));
}
init();
// WEBPACK FOOTER //
// ./src/main.jsx
Line 5, Column 3 (source mapped from browser.js)
Async
Watch
Call Stack
Scope
Breakpoints
main.jsx:5
ReactDOM.render(
XHR Breakpoints
DOM Breakpoints
Global Listeners
Event Listener Breakpoints

Figure 8.5 Set a breakpoint on line 5 of main.jsx in the Sources tab of Chrome Developer Tools. This lets you view the browser output before the browser JavaScript runs.

Compare the DOM markup from the two states to see what's going on before and after the browser render. Figure 8.6 shows the markup before and after the browser render call is made.

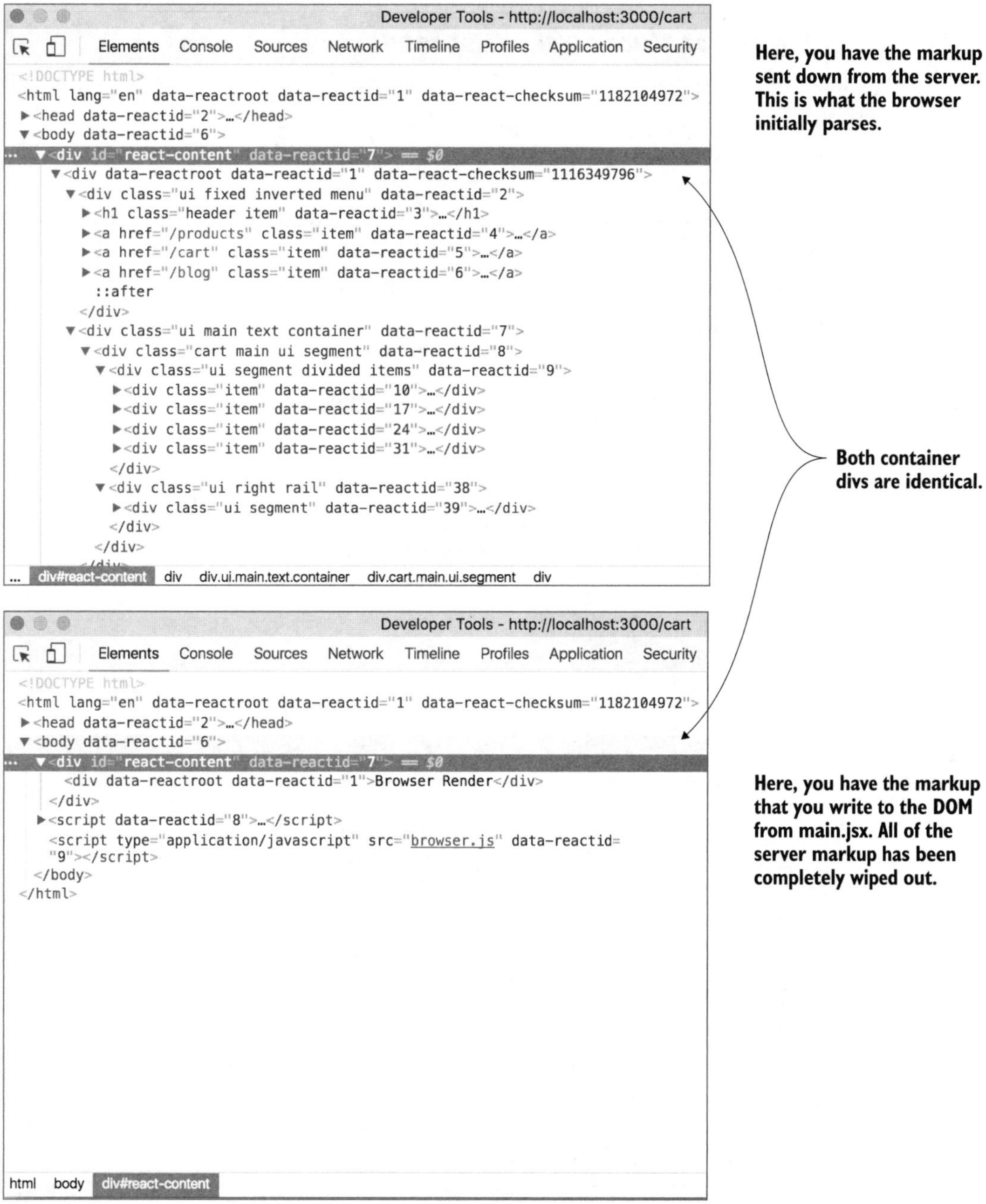
Developer Tools - http://localhost:3000/cart
Elements Console Sources Network Timeline Profiles Application Security
<!DOCTYPE html>
<html lang="en" data-reactroot data-reactid="1" data-react-checksum="1182104972">
<head data-reactid="2">…</head>
<body data-reactid="6">
<div id="react-content" data-reactid="7"> == $0
<div data-reactroot data-reactid="1" data-react-checksum="1116349796">
<div class="ui fixed inverted menu" data-reactid="2">
<h1 class="header item" data-reactid="3">…</h1>
<a href="/products" class="item" data-reactid="4">…</a>
<a href="/cart" class="item" data-reactid="5">…</a>
<a href="/blog" class="item" data-reactid="6">…</a>
::after
</div>
<div class="ui main text container" data-reactid="7">
<div class="cart main ui segment" data-reactid="8">
<div class="ui segment divided items" data-reactid="9">
<div class="item" data-reactid="10">…</div>
<div class="item" data-reactid="17">…</div>
<div class="item" data-reactid="24">…</div>
<div class="item" data-reactid="31">…</div>
</div>
<div class="ui right rail" data-reactid="38">
<div class="ui segment" data-reactid="39">…</div>
</div>
</div>
… div#react-content div div.ui.main.text.container div.cart.main.ui.segment div
Here, you have the markup sent down from the server. This is what the browser initially parses.
Both container divs are identical.
Developer Tools - http://localhost:3000/cart
Elements Console Sources Network Timeline Profiles Application Security
<!DOCTYPE html>
<html lang="en" data-reactroot data-reactid="1" data-react-checksum="1182104972">
<head data-reactid="2">…</head>
<body data-reactid="6">
<div id="react-content" data-reactid="7"> == $0
<div data-reactroot data-reactid="1">Browser Render</div>
</div>
<script data-reactid="8">…</script>
<script type="application/javascript" src="browser.js" data-reactid="9"></script>
</body>
</html>
html body div#react-content
Here, you have the markup that you write to the DOM from main.jsx. All of the server markup has been completely wiped out.

Figure 8.6 Comparing the DOM from the server render with the DOM from the `div` rendered in main.jsx

In this section, you've set up the browser code to run and added a simple React render to the browser. This illustrates the interaction between the server render and the initial browser render. In the next section, we'll walk through using the server state in the browser.

8.2 Matching server state on the first render

To make the app isomorphic, you need to re-create the state from the server. Follow these steps:

1. Serialize the state of the app on the server and send it down in the stringified DOM markup.
2. Deserialize the state on the browser so it's a consumable JSON object.
3. Initialize Redux with the app state (JSON object).
4. Pass the initialized Redux store into your React components.

Figure 8.7 shows this flow in the context of the All Things Westies app.

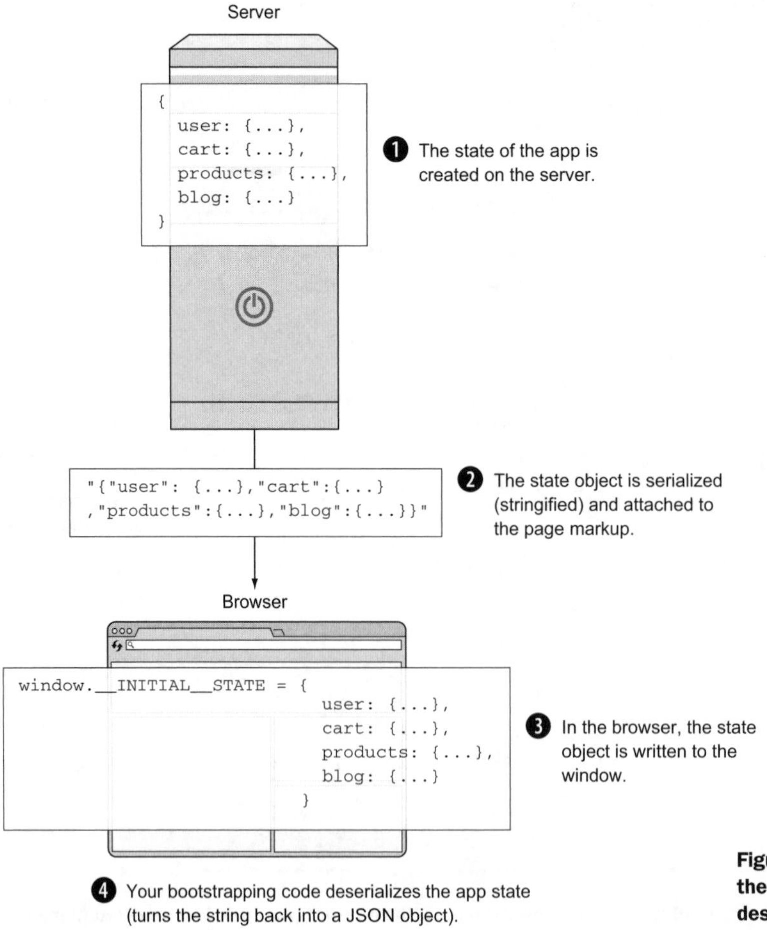
Server
{
user: {...},
cart: {...},
products: {...},
blog: {...}
}
1 The state of the app is created on the server.
"{"user": {...},"cart":{...}
,"products":{...},"blog":{...}}"
2 The state object is serialized (stringified) and attached to the page markup.
Browser
window.__INITIAL__STATE = {
user: {...},
cart: {...},
products: {...},
blog: {...}
}
3 In the browser, the state object is written to the window.
4 Your bootstrapping code deserializes the app state (turns the string back into a JSON object).

Figure 8.7 The flow of the state serialization/ deserialization

It's important to remember that the state created on the server needs to *exactly* match the state used to bootstrap your React code on the browser. That ensures that there's no need to update the browser DOM during the initial load of the page.

First, let's set up the data on the server—both serializing it and then sending it down to the browser to be consumed.

8.2.1 Serializing the data on the server

In this section, you'll update the code in renderView.jsx (created in chapter 7). The first step is to capture and serialize the current app state.

> **DEFINITION** *Serialization* is the act of taking data (often JSON in JavaScript) and converting it to a format that can be sent between environments. In this case, you send it from the server to the browser via a network request.

By the end of this section, you'll be able to access your server state in the console because you'll be putting the server state on the `window` object. Figure 8.8 shows this output in Chrome Developer Tools.

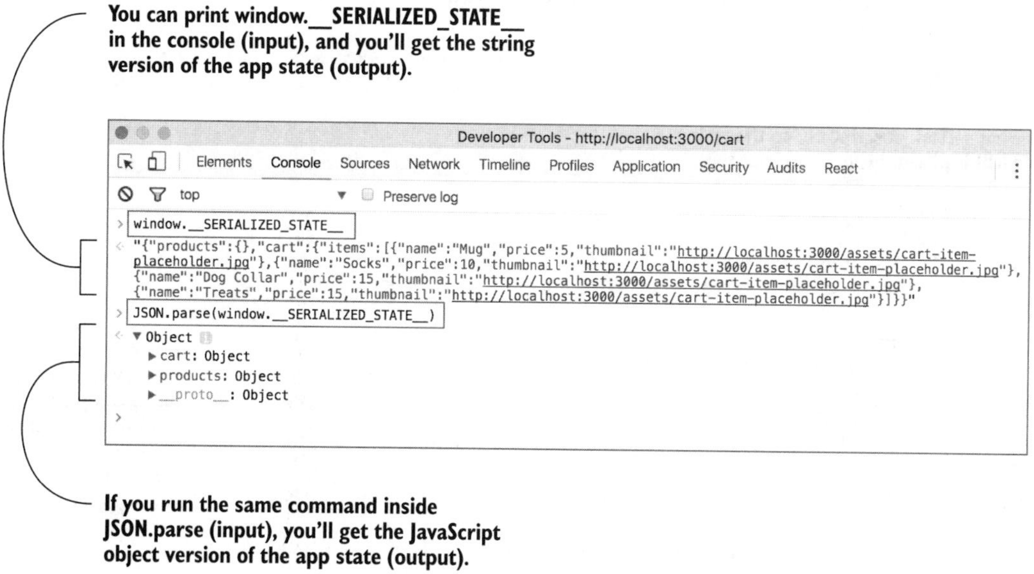
You can print window.__SERIALIZED_STATE__ in the console (input), and you'll get the string version of the app state (output).
Developer Tools - http://localhost:3000/cart
Elements
Console
Sources
Network
Timeline
Profiles
Application
Security
Audits
React
top
Preserve log
window.__SERIALIZED_STATE__
"{"products":{},"cart":{"items":[{"name":"Mug","price":5,"thumbnail":"http://localhost:3000/assets/cart-item-placeholder.jpg"},{"name":"Socks","price":10,"thumbnail":"http://localhost:3000/assets/cart-item-placeholder.jpg"},{"name":"Dog Collar","price":15,"thumbnail":"http://localhost:3000/assets/cart-item-placeholder.jpg"},{"name":"Treats","price":15,"thumbnail":"http://localhost:3000/assets/cart-item-placeholder.jpg"}]}}"
JSON.parse(window.__SERIALIZED_STATE__)
Object
cart: Object
products: Object
__proto__: Object
If you run the same command inside JSON.parse (input), you'll get the JavaScript object version of the app state (output).

Figure 8.8 The serialized state in the browser

You can switch to the chapter-8.2.1 branch to get the base code for this section (`git checkout chapter-8.2.1`), or keep following along with the code you've added so far. The branch has all the code listings so far. The following listing walks you through how to get and serialize your app's current state in your `renderView` middleware. Add this new code to the `renderView` middleware.

Listing 8.3 Capture and serialize current app state—src/middleware/renderView.jsx

```
Promise.all(promises).then(() => {
  const serverState = store.getState();
  const stringifiedServerState
  ➥ = JSON.stringify(serverState);
  const app = renderToString(
    <Provider store={store}>
      <RouterContext routes={routes} {...renderProps} />
    </Provider>
  );
  const html = renderToString(
    <HTML
      html={app}
      serverState={stringifiedServerState}
    />
  );
  return res.send(`<!DOCTYPE html>${html}`);
```

Get current state of the Redux store—getState() is a helper method that returns the store.

Serialize the state by creating a string from the JSON.

Pass the serialized state into the HTML component as a serverState prop.

Now that you've created the string representation of the current app state, you need to set it in the DOM markup. You do that using `dangerouslySetInnerHTML` and a script tag. The following listing shows the code to add to html.jsx.

Listing 8.4 Set the serialized state in the DOM—src/components/html.jsx

Set innerHTML of script tag so the string of JSON is placed inside the script tag.

```
<body>
  <div
    id="react-content"
    dangerouslySetInnerHTML={{ __html: props.html }}
  />
  <script
    dangerouslySetInnerHTML={{
      __html: `
        window.__SERIALIZED_STATE__ =
        ➥ = JSON.stringify(${props.serverState})
      `
    }}
  />
  <script type="application/javascript" src="browser.js" />
</body>
```

Assign stringified server state.

Should be placed at end of body (so it isn't render blocking) but before main JavaScript executes—browser.js depends on the state being available on the window object.

Set state on the __SERIALIZED_STATE__ property of window.

Upon restarting the server, you'll be able to see your app state stringified and printed in the browser console (as in figure 8.8) by running the following:

```
window.__SERIALIZED_STATE__
```

Although it's cool that you can now see your state in the browser, this isn't useful. In the next two sections, we'll walk through how to take this state and use it with Redux and your React components.

8.2.2 Deserializing the data in the browser

If this sounds complicated and scary, don't fear! It's simple. In fact, it's easier than serializing the state in the first place. The goal is to take the stringified data that the server sends down and get it into a state that the app can work with. You take a string input and turn it back into a JavaScript object.

> **DEFINITION** *Deserialization* is the act of taking serialized data and converting it to a format that's usable by the current environment. In this case, you take a string and convert it to a JavaScript object.

The following listing shows the code you need to add to main.jsx to get the state off the window object. Parse the `window.__SERIALIZED_STATE__` value and save it to a variable.

Listing 8.5 Getting the state in the browser—src/main.jsx

```
import React from 'react';
import ReactDOM from 'react-dom';

const initialState
  = JSON.parse(window.__SERIALIZED_STATE__);
console.log(initialState);
```

Parse string into an usable object. (annotates the `JSON.parse` line)

Add log statement to see that it worked in the console. (annotates the `console.log` line)

If you view the browser console, you'll see the state. That's all there is to deserializing the app state. Next, you'll take this state and inject it into Redux so your app starts up in the same state as on the server.

8.2.3 Hydrating the store

Now that you have the state deserialized, you need to initialize Redux with the state that was generated on the server. You don't need to add any new Redux code; everything you created in chapter 7 works perfectly here. The branch for this section is chapter-8.2.3 (`git checkout`).

> **NOTE** If you're using React Router 4, check out appendix A for an overview of setting up the routes and related router code. The appendix shows the main.jsx setup code compared to the Router code in listing 8.6 in this chapter.

All you need to do in main.jsx is initialize Redux with the correct state. The following listing shows you how to pass in the state to the init Redux function. You should update main.jsx with this code (replacing the placeholder code from the previous sections).

Listing 8.6 Setting up Redux and the component tree—src/main.jsx

```
import React from 'react';
import ReactDOM from 'react-dom';
import { Provider } from 'react-redux';
import { browserHistory, Router } from 'react-router';
import initRedux from './shared/init-redux.es6';
import sharedRoutes from './shared/sharedRoutes';

const initialState = JSON.parse(window.__SERIALIZED_STATE__);
console.log(initialState);

const store = initRedux(initialState);

function init() {
  ReactDOM.render(
    <Provider store={store}>
      <Router
        routes={sharedRoutes}
        history={browserHistory}
      />
    </Provider>,
   document.getElementById('react-content'));
}

init();
```

- Include Redux bootstrapping code.
- Include the Provider component from React Redux so components have access to the store as needed.
- Include the Router component from React Router, which configures Routes from sharedRoutes, and include the correct history for the browser environment.
- Include sharedRoutes.
- Create Redux store based on deserialized state.
- Pass store into the Provider component as a prop.
- Pass sharedRoutes and browserHistory into Router as props.

Main.jsx imports initRedux from initRedux.jsx. The code in the initRedux.jsx module takes in the state and creates the store. That's how you hydrate the store. You added this code in chapter 7. It's shown here as a reminder, but it's already in the repo for you in src/shared/init-redux.es6:

```
export default function (initialStore = {}) {
  const reducer = combineReducers({
    products,
    cart
  });
  const middleware = [thunkMiddleware, loggerMiddleware];
  return compose(
      applyMiddleware(...middleware)
    )(createStore)(reducer, initialStore);
}
```

Notice that the `initialStore` param that's passed into the function is used in the `createStore` function to initialize the Redux store. Because this happens before your components are created, the first render of your components ends up using the state from the server.

With the state from the server, React is able to calculate that the initial virtual DOM matches the DOM attached to the root container provided to the render function. It knows that making any browser DOM updates is unnecessary.

Now that you've successfully rendered the view in the browser, let's explore potential gotchas around the details of the first render in the browser. Note that up to this point, you've only set up the code that handles the initial render. Later in the chapter, you'll add support for getting data when routing in the browser.

8.3 Performing the first load

At this point, it should be clear how to get your app loading in the browser. It's also important to understand what happens during the initial render in the browser, because it's different from what happens later as the user interacts with the app.

8.3.1 The React lifecycle on the first load

This section walks you through the first render of React in the browser. React begins to bootstrap in your main.jsx file when you call `ReactDOM.render`. Each component that's being initiated goes through the following steps:

1. The constructor is called.
2. `componentWillMount` is triggered.
3. The render method is called.
4. `componentDidMount` is called.

Remember that this starts with the root components, which all come from third-party libraries (React Redux and React Router). It then moves on to the components that React Router calculates need to be loaded for the current route. Then any of their child components are rendered.

INITIAL RENDER DIFFERENCES

It's important to understand that `componentWillMount` is called on the first load for every component on both the server and the browser! Any code you have in it needs to be truly isomorphic. For example, if you were to add the following code to src/components/app.jsx, your server would break and be unable to load any routes:

```
componentWillMount() {
  window.test = true;
}
```

That's because your server can't find a global variable called `window`. The `window` object doesn't exist in Node.js. If you put this code into any of the methods that run during the first render (`constructor`, `componentWillMount`, or `render`), it'll break on the server.

Conversely, `componentDidMount`, which runs after the first render is complete, is called only in the browser. This distinction becomes powerful when you need to update a component after reaching the browser but you don't want to break the isomorphic render.

8.3.2 Isomorphic render errors

You may have noticed a big red warning in the console early in this chapter. Figure 8.9 shows what that looks like.

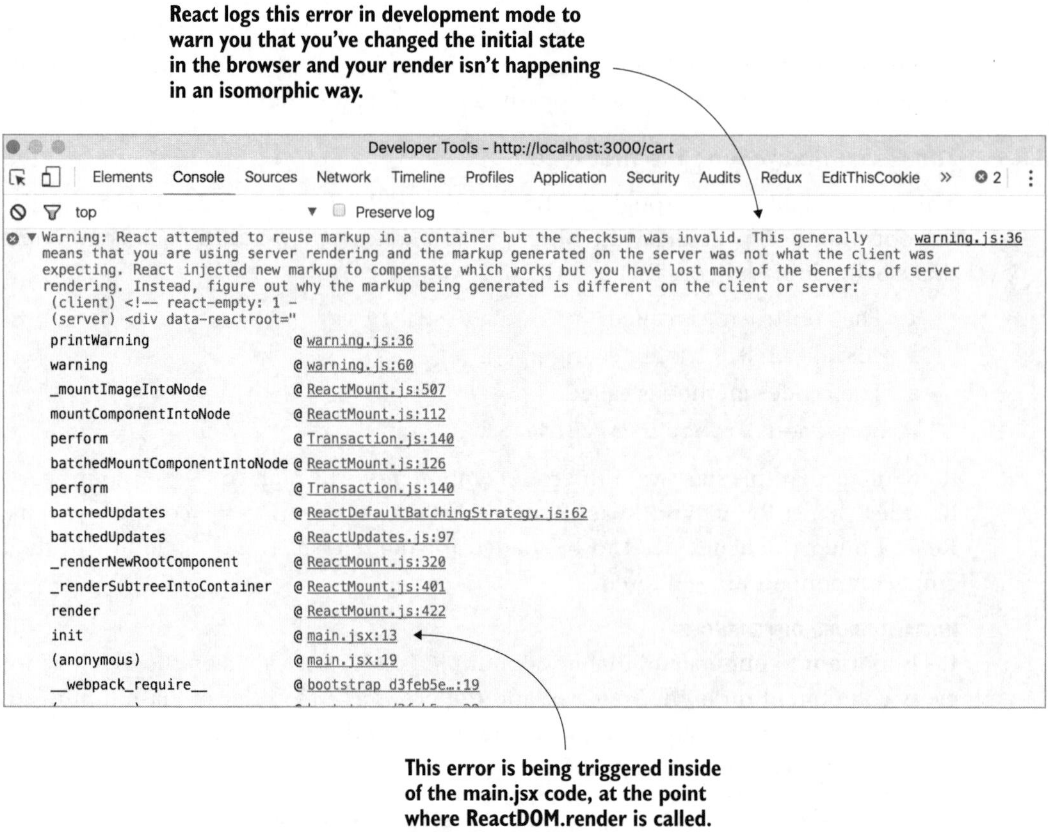
React logs this error in development mode to warn you that you've changed the initial state in the browser and your render isn't happening in an isomorphic way.
Developer Tools - http://localhost:3000/cart
Elements Console Sources Network Timeline Profiles Application Security Audits Redux EditThisCookie » 2
top
Preserve log
Warning: React attempted to reuse markup in a container but the checksum was invalid. This generally means that you are using server rendering and the markup generated on the server was not what the client was expecting. React injected new markup to compensate which works but you have lost many of the benefits of server rendering. Instead, figure out why the markup being generated is different on the client or server:
warning.js:36
(client) <!-- react-empty: 1 -
(server) <div data-reactroot="
printWarning @ warning.js:36
warning @ warning.js:60
_mountImageIntoNode @ ReactMount.js:507
mountComponentIntoNode @ ReactMount.js:112
perform @ Transaction.js:140
batchedMountComponentIntoNode @ ReactMount.js:126
perform @ Transaction.js:140
batchedUpdates @ ReactDefaultBatchingStrategy.js:62
batchedUpdates @ ReactUpdates.js:97
_renderNewRootComponent @ ReactMount.js:320
_renderSubtreeIntoContainer @ ReactMount.js:401
render @ ReactMount.js:422
init @ main.jsx:13
(anonymous) @ main.jsx:19
__webpack_require__ @ bootstrap d3feb5e…:19
This error is being triggered inside of the main.jsx code, at the point where ReactDOM.render is called.

Figure 8.9 The isomorphic warning log that React issues when it's detected an isomorphic render that isn't truly isomorphic. This happens when the virtual DOM from the initial render cycle and the browser DOM don't match.

This isn't a fun error. (To be fair, errors aren't usually fun.) It sounds hard to debug the first time you read it: "the checksum was invalid"—what the bleep does that mean?

It means React rendered the component tree in the browser, compared it to the DOM that already exists, and found it to be different. But React is smart and knows that if there are already children inside the DOM element that you told it to render into, this is an isomorphic render. The two DOMs should match on the first render. But something broke, and they didn't match!

THE EXPERIMENT THAT BROKE THE RENDER

At work, we often run a/b tests to experiment with various design and UX implementations to find out what works best to meet our goals with the product. One day we went to test our Login button. We wanted to find out whether we should call it "Login" or "Signup." Even though the team is experienced in working with an isomorphic app, the experiment still ended up being run inside `componentWillMount` of our header component, and the isomorphic render warning started getting thrown.

Adding to our problems, another update was made to the code (around the same time) that changed the app state inside `componentWillMount`. It turns out that React will display this warning only for the first instance it runs into, which meant that when we fixed the first problem, we uncovered the second problem.

It's surprisingly easy to get into this situation. One small change in the browser to the app state anytime in the first render (inside your `constructor`, `componentWillMount`, or `render`) can cause the error. The most common reason I've seen for getting into this situation is changing state based on cookies.

> **WARNING** *Cookies* are global state that lives outside your app code. They're a powerful and important tool for web app development. But they can complicate your initial app state. You either should account for the cookies on the server, or make sure to deal with them at the correct time in the browser. Chapter 10 covers this in more depth.

The reason you should care about this warning is that you lose all the positive benefits of your isomorphic render. You still have the good perceived performance—the UI and content is shown right away—but it can take a noticeably long time for the page to become usable, causing frustration for your user.

This is where `componentDidMount` becomes a powerful tool in your application. The next section explores how to use it to avoid isomorphic render errors.

8.3.3 Using componentDidMount to prevent isomorphic load errors

Let's say you wanted to save a user preference in the cookies. A common use case is whether to show a site-wide dismissible banner. This is beneficial to the user because it allows for global, easily accessible state in the browser. But you must be vigilant about when to check for these cookies to prevent isomorphic errors.

> **NOTE** This example and solution assume you don't want to read cookies on the server. In some apps, it may be more practical to read the cookies on the server and start with the correct app state in the server. We'll walk through these trade-offs in more depth in chapter 10.

In this example, you'll add a banner that informs users of a semi-annual sale. The rules for showing the banner are: show it to a user if they've never seen it before, and continue showing it until they dismiss it. You track whether they've seen it by writing a cookie in the browser. Figure 8.10 shows what you want this to look like.

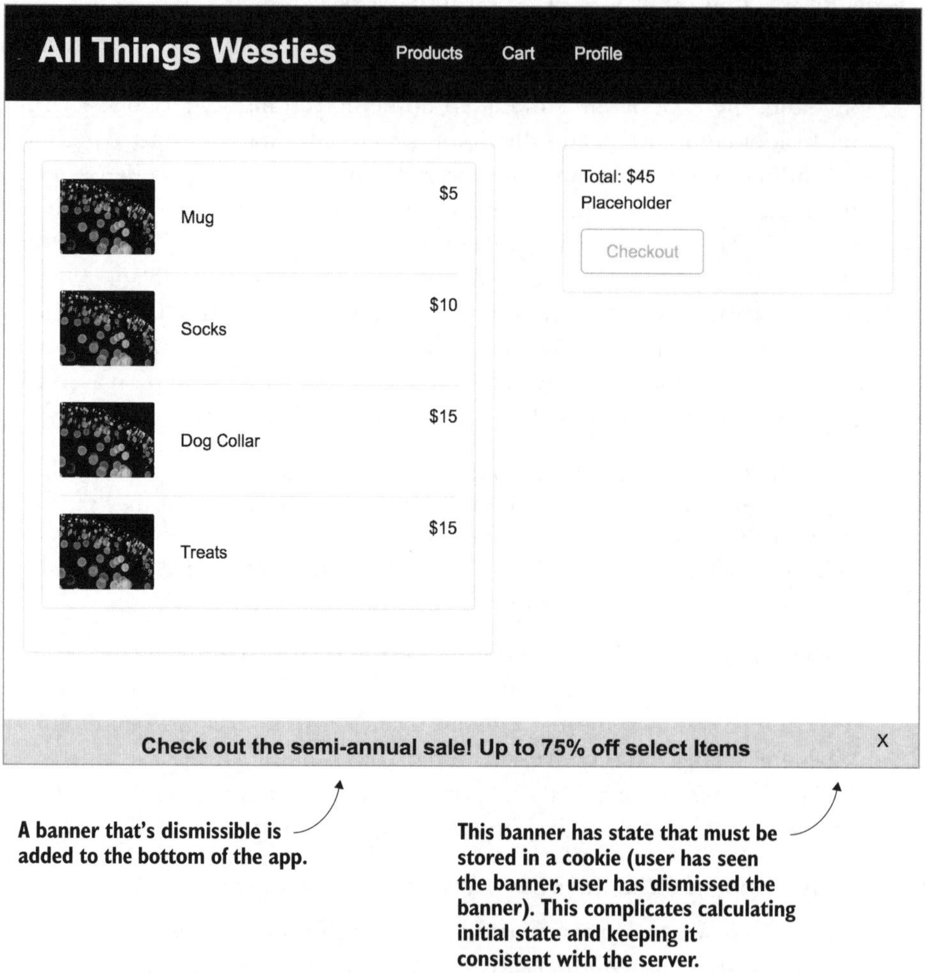
All Things Westies
Products
Cart
Profile
Mug
$5
Socks
$10
Dog Collar
$15
Treats
$15
Total: $45
Placeholder
Checkout
Check out the semi-annual sale! Up to 75% off select Items
X
A banner that's dismissible is added to the bottom of the app.
This banner has state that must be stored in a cookie (user has seen the banner, user has dismissed the banner). This complicates calculating initial state and keeping it consistent with the server.

Figure 8.10 Adding a banner to the bottom of the page

Now you need to add a banner. If you want to check out the base code, switch to branch 8.3.3 (`git checkout chapter-8.3.3`), which has all the code added in this chapter so far and already has this banner component created for you (writing this component isn't important to understanding this concept, but I've provided it for you in the following listing so you have some context).

Listing 8.7 Banner component—src/components/banner.jsx

```
class Banner extends React.Component {

  handleDismissBanner() {
    // will do something
  }

  render() {
    return (
      <div className=="banner" }>
        <div className="dismiss">
          <button
            className="btn-reset"
            onClick={this.handleDismissBanner}
          >
            X
          </button>
        </div>
        <div className="content">
          {this.props.children}
        </div>
      </div>
    );
  }
}
```

Click handler placeholder for the dismiss button.

Dismiss button lives here.

onClick handler references the handleDismissBanner function.

Parent component sets children for banner (making it more reusable).

Additionally, the following code has been added after the header in src/components/app.jsx (~line 13):

```
<Banner show>
  <h3>Check out the semi-annual sale! Up to 75% off select Items</h3>
</Banner>
```

Now you need to add the code that decides whether to show this banner when the page loads. That involves checking a cookie and then telling the banner to be visible or stay hidden. The following listing shows how to update banner.jsx to make this work.

Listing 8.8 Showing the banner component—src/components/banner.jsx

```
class Banner extends React.Component {

  constructor(props) {
    super(props);
    this.state = {
      show: false
    };
    this.handleDismissBanner = this.handleDismissBanner.bind(this);
  }

  componentDidMount() {
    const cookies = document.cookie;
    const hideBanner = cookies.match('showBanner=false');
    if (!hideBanner) {
      this.setState({
```

Create initial state in constructor—to match the server, banner should be hidden by default.

Get cookies, see if user has previously dismissed the banner—if not, set state to show banner (will trigger re-render).

```
        show: true
      });
    }
  }

  handleDismissBanner() {
    document.cookie = 'showBanner=false';
    this.setState({
      show: false
    });
  }

  render() {
    const bannerClasses = classnames(
                             { show: this.state.show },
                             'banner'
                           );
    return (
      <div className={bannerClasses}>
        <div className="dismiss">
          <button
            className="btn-reset"
            onClick={this.handleDismissBanner}
          >
            X
          </button>
        </div>
        <div className="content">
          {this.props.children}
        </div>
      </div>
    );
  }
}
```

When user dismisses the browser, write cookie to page and set state to hidden.

Use state to generate banner classes.

Using state to generate banner classes will add a class called show when the banner is visible. The CSS for this class changes the display to block so the component becomes visible.

Generally, you don't want to set state in componentDidMount. But in this case, the isomorphic render makes it the best place to update the state, because we want to ensure that the first render matches the server state. Be careful setting state in this function—you can easily get into a situation where you cause unnecessary re-renders of your component.

8.4 Adding single-page app interactions

Congrats, you've made it! Your app loads and renders from the server and successfully renders in the browser. Sadly, it still doesn't do anything in the browser because you haven't told it to do anything. Let's make the app load data in the browser when routing between routes.

8.4.1 Browser routing: data fetching

The routes you've set up will make the routes at the top of the page work. But if you navigate first to the root or to /products and then click Cart, you'll find that the cart loads without any items. That's because you haven't set up the SPA portion of the app to fetch any data. Figure 8.11 shows what this looks like.

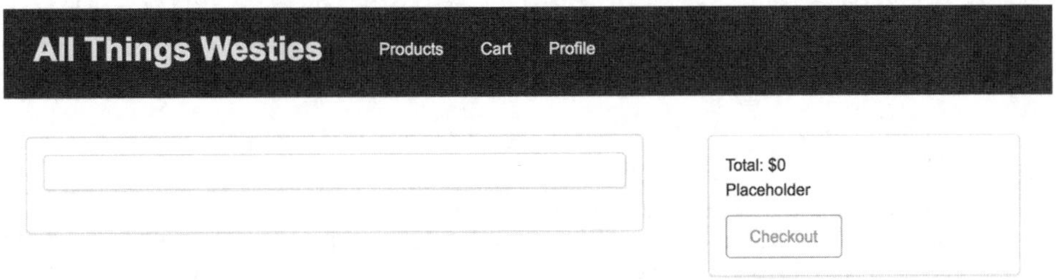
All Things Westies
Products
Cart
Profile
Total: $0
Placeholder
Checkout

Figure 8.11 Loading the cart from the Products page results in an empty state.

To get the app fetching data in the browser, you'll take advantage of the `prefetchActions` static function to fetch the data on each route. React Router provides callbacks for various portions of its own lifecycle. There's an `onChange` callback that can be configured. The function provided will be called before each route is rendered, giving you the opportunity to fetch any data from your API that's needed for the route.

> **NOTE** If you're using React Router 4, check out appendix A for an overview of setting up the routes and related router code. It also shows how to prefetch the data on the browser and handle route changes in the React lifecycle instead of the React Router lifecycle.

If you want to check out the base code, switch to branch 8.4.1 (`git checkout chapter-8.4.1`). The following listing shows the code to add to sharedRoutes.jsx.

Listing 8.9 Fetching data in the browser—src/shared/sharedRoutes.jsx

```
let beforeRouteRender =
➥ (dispatch, prevState, nextState) => {
  const { routes } = nextState;
};
```

- Declare onChange handler, which takes in the dispatch function from Redux and parameters provided from React Router, prevState, and nextState.
- Pull routes array from nextState so you can iterate over the components and get the actions from prefetchActions

```
export const routes = (onChange = () => {}) => {
  return (
    <Route
      path="/"
      component={App}
      onChange={onChange}
    >
      <Route path="/cart" component={Cart} />
      <Route path="/products" component={Products} />
      <Route path="/product/detail/:id" component={Detail} />
      <Route path="/profile" component={Profile} />
    </Route>
  );
};
```

Create a routes function that returns the routes, letting you pass in the onChange handler.

Assign onChange handler to top-level route—all changes between children routes will trigger this handler.

```
const createSharedRoutes = ({ dispatch }) => {
  beforeRouteRender = beforeRouteRender.bind(this, dispatch);
  return routes(beforeRouteRender);
};

export default createSharedRoutes;
```

Bind dispatch to onChange handler.

Returns routes function with onChange handler passed in.

Default export of module is now a function, requires Redux store passed in.

Passing in the `onChange` handler is necessary because you need to bind `dispatch` to it in the browser. This function is exported so the server code can call it. A couple of things are important here. First, you need to add the `onChange` handler only to the top-level route. That's because `onChange` fires whenever a subroute changes. When the user changes between cart or products, it'll be fired. This also means it won't fire on the initial render. That would be unnecessary because the data is already available from the server state.

The most complicated piece of this logic is getting the `prefetchActions` array from the components. This is where the `routes` variable from `nextState` is important. The `routes` variable is an array of objects. Each route has a component listed on it. From this, it's possible to collect all the actions that need to be called for the route. The following listing shows the last piece of code you need in order to make all this work. Add the code to sharedRoutes.jsx. You'll notice it's similar to the code in renderView.jsx.

Listing 8.10 Call `prefetchActions` on route change—src/shared/sharedRoutes.jsx

```
let beforeRouteRender = (dispatch, prevState, nextState) => {
  const { routes } = nextState;

  routes.map((route) => {
    const { component } = route;
    if (component) {
      if (component.displayName &&
        component.displayName
```

Use map to iterate over each route in the array (root app route and whatever route was requested).

Grab the component from route.

```
➥ .toLowerCase().indexOf('connect') > -1
    ) {
      if (component.WrappedComponent
      ➥ .prefetchActions) {
        return component.WrappedComponent.prefetchActions ();
      }
    } else if (component.prefetchActions) {
      return component. prefetchActions();
    }
  }
  return [];
}).reduce((flat, toFlatten) => {
  return flat.concat(toFlatten);
}, []).map((initialAction) => {
  return dispatch(initialAction());
});
};
```

Check if component is HOC connect component—if so, grab subproperty of component.

If component has WrappedComponent property, call prefetchActions.

Take results of map, which can be a nested array of arrays, and reduce them to single array.

Use map to iterate over the final flattened array; on each item call dispatch with the action.

You may notice that the structure of `sharedRoutes` has changed quite a bit. That's because you need access to the `dispatch` method from Redux to trigger actions. In both main.jsx and renderView.jsx, you need to update the way you're accessing the shared routes. The following listing shows the change that needs to be made in main.jsx.

Listing 8.11 Updating Main to call sharedRoutes—src/main.jsx

```
function init() {
  ReactDOM.render(
    <Provider store={store}>
      <Router routes={sharedRoutes(store)} history={browserHistory} />
    </Provider>, document.getElementById('react-content'));
}
```

Instead of directly plugging in the routes, the default export is now a function. Here you call the function, passing in the store so that `sharedRoutes` can pass `dispatch` into the `onChange` handler.

The change to the `renderView` middleware is similar to the change in main.jsx. But you have to first change the import because on the server you don't need to do the `onChange` logic—it'll never fire. The following listing demonstrates what needs to change.

Listing 8.12 Updating `renderView` to use routes—src/middleware/renderView.jsx

```
...additional code
import { match, RouterContext } from 'react-router';
import { routes } from '../shared/sharedRoutes';
import initRedux from '../shared/init-redux.es6';
import HTML from '../components/html';
```

Include routes instead of the default export—the server doesn't need to initialize the onChange handler because it'll never be called on the server.

```
export default function renderView(req, res, next) {
  const matchOpts = {
    routes: routes(),          <-- Call the routes function
    location: req.url              to get the shared routes.
  };
  ...additional code
}
```

With everything configured to load data on the server, you should see the cart populated. Additionally, if you view the Network tab, you'll see the cart data being fetched from the server. This will be shown only if you load the app via /products first and then select Cart from the navigation. Figure 8.12 shows what you're looking for.

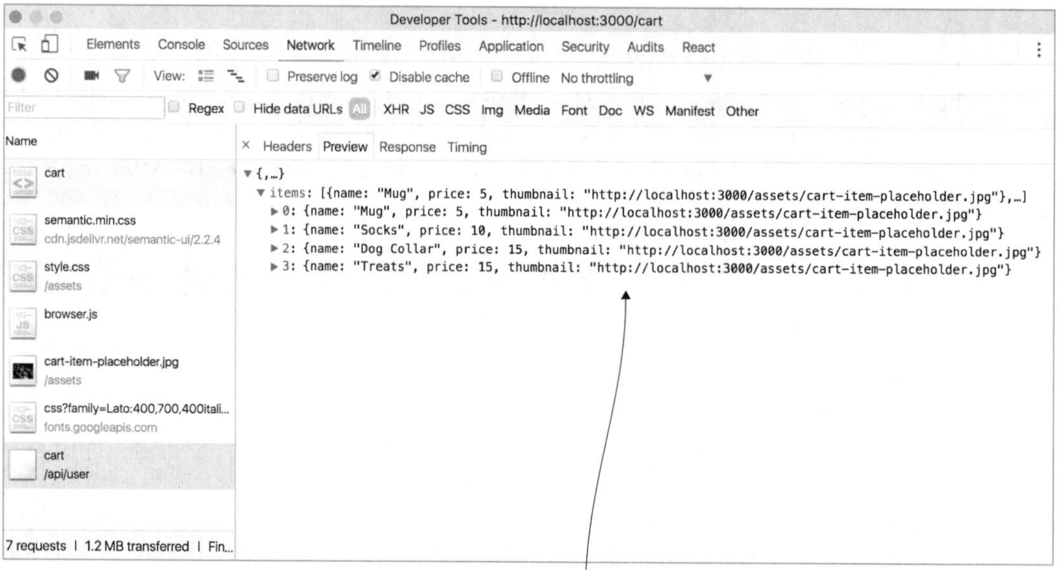
Developer Tools - http://localhost:3000/cart
Elements Console Sources Network Timeline Profiles Application Security Audits React
View: Preserve log Disable cache Offline No throttling
Filter Regex Hide data URLs All XHR JS CSS Img Media Font Doc WS Manifest Other
Name
Headers Preview Response Timing
cart
semantic.min.css
cdn.jsdelivr.net/semantic-ui/2.2.4
style.css
/assets
browser.js
cart-item-placeholder.jpg
/assets
css?family=Lato:400,700,400itali...
fonts.googleapis.com
cart
/api/user
7 requests | 1.2 MB transferred | Fin...
▼{,…}
▼items: [{name: "Mug", price: 5, thumbnail: "http://localhost:3000/assets/cart-item-placeholder.jpg"},…]
▶0: {name: "Mug", price: 5, thumbnail: "http://localhost:3000/assets/cart-item-placeholder.jpg"}
▶1: {name: "Socks", price: 10, thumbnail: "http://localhost:3000/assets/cart-item-placeholder.jpg"}
▶2: {name: "Dog Collar", price: 15, thumbnail: "http://localhost:3000/assets/cart-item-placeholder.jpg"}
▶3: {name: "Treats", price: 15, thumbnail: "http://localhost:3000/assets/cart-item-placeholder.jpg"}
The data returned from the API call to get the cart info

Figure 8.12 Now that the browser fetches data, you see the XHR call in the Network tab of the Chrome Developer Tools.

Now that you've built out the browser portion of the code, you can review the complete code for this chapter on branch chapter-8-complete (`git checkout chapter-8-complete`).

Summary

In this chapter, you learned how to build the browser portion of an isomorphic app. You added a browser entry-point file called main.jsx and handled the initialization logic required to make the app start in the browser in the same state that it was rendered on the server.

- The initial server state is added to the DOM as a string and sent down as part of the server-rendered page.
- The browser entry point handles deserializing the server-created state, initializing Redux, and rendering the React component tree into the DOM.
- The server attaches the state of the app to the DOM as a string.
- The browser reads the string into an object that can be passed into Redux.
- Redux can be initialized with a base state, which is the deserialized state from the server.
- React's component lifecycle can make or break an isomorphic render. It's important to make updates to the app state at the correct point in the lifecycle.
- The browser code also needs to handle data fetching for the single-page application portion of the app.

9 Testing and debugging

This chapter covers

- Creating a test environment that reflects the complexities of an isomorphic app
- Using Enzyme to create unit tests for your React components
- Using React Developer Tools to debug in the browser
- Using Redux Dev Tools to debug in the browser

Have you ever worked in a code base that has lots of tests, but the tests break randomly, require constant updating, and never prevent you from creating regression errors? This situation is surprisingly easy to create when you have more than two developers working on a code base. Having a solid testing strategy and understanding where to draw the line between unit tests and integration tests is important for any app. But isomorphic apps have an additional level of complexity that needs to be thought through: is this a test for code that runs on the server, in the browser, or in both environments?

The first part of this chapter explores how to think about testing an isomorphic app. You'll learn to test React with Enzyme and how to test your components in multiple environments. The second part of the chapter covers debugging tools that can help with real-world development.

The code for this chapter can be found in the complete-isomorphic-example repo on GitHub:

```
$ git clone https://github.com/isomorphic-dev-js/complete-isomorphic-
    example.git
```

Each section has base code provided in a branch. The first branch you'll use is chapter-9.1.1:

```
$ git checkout chapter-9.1.1
$ npm install
$ npm start
```

9.1 Testing: React components

The goal of the first half of this chapter is to walk you through how to approach testing when you have code that can run in multiple environments. Doing that requires the following:

- Having the right tools to run tests in both the server and browser environments
- Knowing when code should be tested in a specific environment (for example, you don't need to test Express middleware in the browser)

There are many categories of tests, including unit tests, integration tests, contract tests, end-to-end tests, and so on. Whenever possible, you want to match your real-word development builds with the way you build your test. You also want to run unit tests for your code in a way that allows for browser and server verification.

I've already set up much of the unit-testing environment for you. We'll be using Mocha as the test library and Karma as our test runner (so that debugging the browser tests is straightforward). If you're new to unit testing or need a refresher, I highly recommend *The Art of Unit Testing* by Roy Osherove (Manning, 2013). This book was my introduction to unit testing and is an invaluable resource. To see documentation on Karma, visit https://karma-runner.github.io/1.0/index.html. You can learn more about Mocha at https://mochajs.org.

If you'd like to see how I set up the unit-testing configuration for this chapter, you'll find the config file in karma.conf.js (located in the root directory) and the script in package.json under test:browser. The tests are set up with Karma (test-runner), Mocha (test library), and Chai (assertion library). The Karma test configuration uses webpack with the same config you use for development to bundle the tests. The code under test is compiled the same way that the app code is compiled. By the end of this section, you'll have test output in the terminal that looks something like figure 9.1.

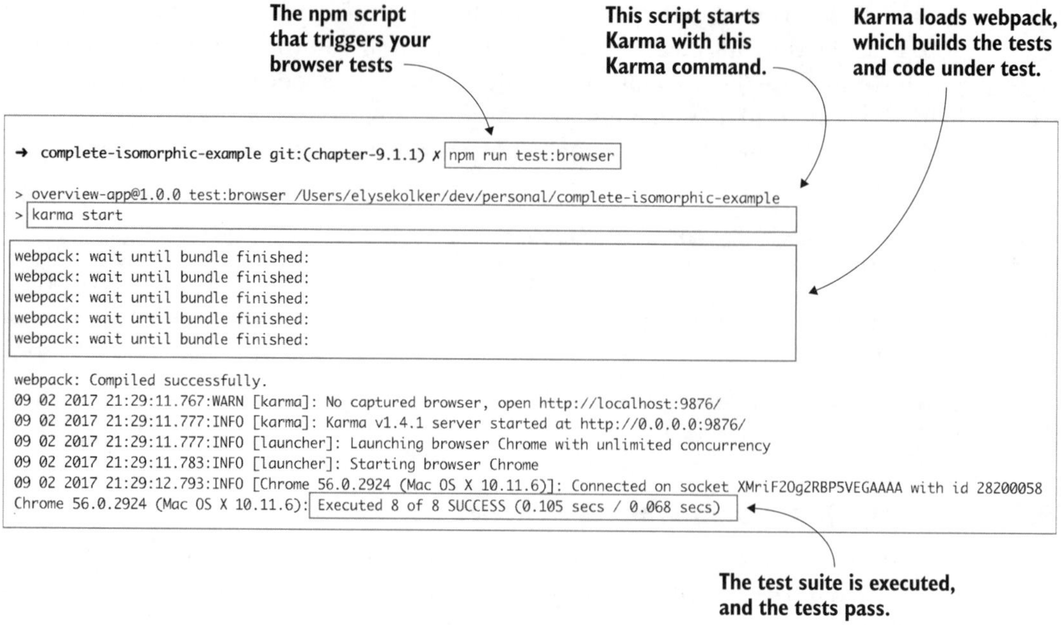
The npm script that triggers your browser tests
This script starts Karma with this Karma command.
Karma loads webpack, which builds the tests and code under test.
→ complete-isomorphic-example git:(chapter-9.1.1) ✗ npm run test:browser
> overview-app@1.0.0 test:browser /Users/elysekolker/dev/personal/complete-isomorphic-example
> karma start
webpack: wait until bundle finished:
webpack: wait until bundle finished:
webpack: wait until bundle finished:
webpack: wait until bundle finished:
webpack: wait until bundle finished:
webpack: Compiled successfully.
09 02 2017 21:29:11.767:WARN [karma]: No captured browser, open http://localhost:9876/
09 02 2017 21:29:11.777:INFO [karma]: Karma v1.4.1 server started at http://0.0.0.0:9876/
09 02 2017 21:29:11.777:INFO [launcher]: Launching browser Chrome with unlimited concurrency
09 02 2017 21:29:11.783:INFO [launcher]: Starting browser Chrome
09 02 2017 21:29:12.793:INFO [Chrome 56.0.2924 (Mac OS X 10.11.6)]: Connected on socket XMriF20g2RBP5VEGAAAA with id 28200058
Chrome 56.0.2924 (Mac OS X 10.11.6): Executed 8 of 8 SUCCESS (0.105 secs / 0.068 secs)
The test suite is executed, and the tests pass.

Figure 9.1 The browser test output when all the tests are passing

To run the tests for this section, run the following:

```
$ npm run test:browser
```

For now, there are no tests, so you'll see "Executed 0 out of 0" in the terminal. Notice that a new instance of Google Chrome is also opened, as shown in figure 9.2.

Try clicking the Debug button. It opens a new tab. You can use this tab to open the Chrome DevTools and debug your tests as you'd debug your application when you get stuck.

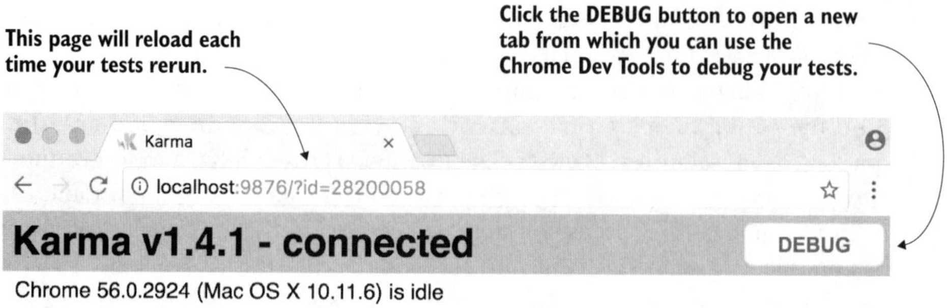
This page will reload each time your tests rerun.
Click the DEBUG button to open a new tab from which you can use the Chrome Dev Tools to debug your tests.
Karma
localhost:9876/?id=28200058
Karma v1.4.1 - connected
DEBUG
Chrome 56.0.2924 (Mac OS X 10.11.6) is idle

Figure 9.2 Karma launches Google Chrome for you so that your test runs in a real browser environment.

Now let's learn how to use Enzyme to write your first React test.

> **Testing alternatives: Jest**
>
> Another good testing library is Jest. Documentation can be found at https://facebook.github.io/jest/docs/en/getting-started.html. Jest is a testing framework built by Facebook that provides everything you need with zero configuration. In the world of testing, that's a nice change!
>
> By default, Jest ships with Jasmine and its own mocking utilities. It's also fast out of the box, which saves you time locally and when running tests on a continuous integration server.
>
> You'll have trade-offs when using Jest with a webpack-configured project. You'll probably have to do some extra setup (so, not exactly zero configuration). The docs provide a helpful guide: https://facebook.github.io/jest/docs/en/webpack.html #content.
>
> Additionally, you're no longer running your tests in the context of a browser. Karma even lets you run your tests in multiple browsers. But you may not find this important for your project, and Karma is much slower than Jest. If you value the speed and easy configuration more, I recommend trying Jest.

9.1.1 *Using Enzyme to test components*

A library called Enzyme has become popular for testing React components (https://github.com/airbnb/enzyme). It provides an API that makes writing test assertions against your view components straightforward.

The simplest form of unit test you can write with Enzyme renders a shallow version of the component you're testing. Any child components won't be rendered. That's important because it allows you to test a single component without reaching down into child components. This makes your tests true unit tests, which results in less-brittle, cleaner tests.

The first test you'll add is for the App component. App has multiple children, including the Link component from React Router, which we aren't interested in testing. The following listing shows how to use shallow rendering to do basic assertions on a component. Add the code from the listing to a new test file test/components/app.spec.jsx.

Listing 9.1 Rendering with `shallow`—test/components/app.spec.jsx

Include expect from Chai to write assertions—you can subsitute a preferred assertion style.

Include React—you'll use JSX to shallow load the App component.

Include shallow function from Enzyme, which loads the component without loading its child components (loads only one level of the React tree).

```
import React from 'react';
import { expect } from 'chai';
import { shallow } from 'enzyme';
```

```
import { Link } from 'react-router';
import App from '../../src/components/app';

describe('App Component', () => {
  let wrappedComponent;

  beforeEach(() => {
    wrappedComponent = shallow(<App />);
  });

  afterEach(() => {
    wrappedComponent = null;
  });

  it('Uses Link Components', () => {
    expect(
          wrappedComponent.find(Link).length
        ).to.eq(3);
  });

  it('Links to /products, /cart and /profile pages', () => {
    expect(
          wrappedComponent.find({
                                  to: '/products'
                                }).length
        ).to.eq(1);
    expect(
          wrappedComponent.find({
                                  to: '/cart'
                                }).length
          ).to.eq(1);
    expect(
          wrappedComponent.find({
                                  to: '/profile'
                                }).length
          ).to.eq(1);
  });
});
```

App component is loaded via the shallow function, returns wrapped component that gives you methods you can use to interact with and assert against the component under test.

Take advantage of Mocha's beforeEach and afterEach, which execute once before and after each test.

Enzyme supports using React component references to check for existence within a component—here you're checking for the presence of a Link component.

Demonstrates another type of selector you can use with Enzyme, here asserting that an element with attribute "to" exists, with each assertion looking for a specific route.

ENZYME SELECTORS

The two tests you just added show two of the three possible ways you can apply Enzyme selectors to find elements within the rendered tree:

- Component selectors (takes a React component reference)
- Attribute selectors (takes an object)

There's a third selector type: CSS selectors. They work like JQuery selectors: to find an element by ID, you look for `#id`. To find a component by class, you look for `.class` or `.multiple.class`.

Let's look at one more example that uses the class selector to find the element that contains the unit under test. In this example, you're adding tests for the Item component—a presentation component whose only job is to display properties passed in. In listing 9.2, you can see how to use Enzyme to assert that the expected parts of the Item component are rendered correctly. Notice that you're adding only tests that assert on the parts of the markup that are changed by the properties that are passed in. This reduces the brittleness of your tests. Asserting directly on the markup means your unit tests are subject to change because a class changed. Add the code in the listing to a new file called test/components/item.spec.jsx.

Listing 9.2 Testing a presentation component—test/components/item.spec.jsx

```
import { expect } from 'chai';
import { shallow } from 'enzyme';
import React from 'react';
import Item from '../../src/components/item';

describe('Item Component', () => {
  let testComponent;
  let props;

  beforeEach(() => {
    props = {
      thumbnail: 'http://image.png',
      name: 'Test Name',
      price: 10
    };
    testComponent = shallow(<Item {...props} />);
  });

  afterEach(() => {
    testComponent = null;
    props = null;
  });

  it('Displays a thumbnail sbased on its props', () => {
    expect(
            testComponent.find({
                                    src: props.thumbnail
                                  }).length
           ).to.eq(1);
  });

  it('Displays a name based on its props', () => {
    expect(
            testComponent.find(
                                    '.middle.aligned.content'
                                  ).text()
          ).to.eq(props.name);
  });

  it('Displays a price based on its props', () => {
    expect(
            testComponent.find(
                                    '.right.aligned.content'
                                  ).text()
          ).to.eq(`$${props.price}`);
  });
});
```

For this test, provide a mocked props object.

Test asserts that the thumbnail gets assigned to the src property.

Test asserts the name gets put in the correct element; text() returns inner contents of a HTML tag.

Test asserts the price gets placed in the component correctly.

The double dollar sign looks weird because of the string interpolation. The first $ is the literal one displayed in the view. The other is for the variable in the string.

Keep in mind that you want to use selectors for your tests that are unlikely to change frequently. You can't always predict that, but putting some thought into it ahead of time can reduce test refactoring.

Now that you understand the basics of using Enzyme to unit test your React components, let's look at how to write a test that validates user interaction with a component.

9.1.2 *Testing user actions*

Testing with shallow rendering also lets you test user interactions. In this section, you'll add a test to the Cart component to see whether a button click properly triggers a route update. Note that to do this test, I've added a route for /cart/payment to `sharedRoutes` and updated the Checkout button in `cart` to navigate to this route:

```
proceedToCheckout() {
  this.props.router.push('/cart/payment');
}
```

You can see this added code if you switch to the chapter-9.1.2 branch (`git checkout chapter-9.1.2`). If you're following along, you need to update `proceedToCheckout` for the test in listing 9.4 to pass.

You also need to make another update to the Cart component. Currently, the component is wrapped with Connect and then exported, making it extremely difficult to test. It also means you're testing a composed component instead of the Cart component in isolation. The following listing shows you how to update the Cart component to export the nonwrapped version for testing.

Listing 9.3 Add a second export to the Cart component—src/components/cart.jsx

```
export class CartComponent extends Component {
  //component implementation
}

CartComponent.propTypes = {}

export default connect(
  mapStateToProps,
  mapDispatchToProps
)(CartComponent);
```

- **Add an export to the class definition and update the component name (allows for future named exports).** (points to `export class CartComponent extends Component {`)
- **Update all references to Cart.** (points to `CartComponent.propTypes = {}`)
- **Update all references to Cart—note you still export a connect wrapped component.** (points to `)(CartComponent);`)

Listing 9.4 shows how to test that the Cart component properly calls the History component to navigate to the checkout section. The test imports the named export

`CartComponent` instead of the default wrapped component. Add this code to a new file called test/components/cart.spec.jsx.

Listing 9.4 Testing user interactions—test/components/cart.spec.jsx

```
import { expect } from 'chai';
import { shallow } from 'enzyme';
import React from 'react';
import sinon from 'sinon';
import { CartComponent } from '../../src/components/cart';

describe('Cart Component', () => {
  let testComponent;
  let props;

  beforeEach(() => {
    props = {
      items: [
        {
          thumbnail: 'http://image.png',
          name: 'Test Name',
          price: 10
        }
      ],
      router: {
        push: sinon.spy()
      }
    };
    testComponent = shallow(<CartComponent {...props} />);
  });

  afterEach(() => {
    testComponent = null;
    props = null;
  });

  it('When checkout is clicked, the router push method is triggered', () => {
    testComponent.find('.button').simulate('click');
    expect(props.router.push.called).to.be.true;
    expect(
            props.router.push.calledWith('/cart/payment')
         ).to.be.true;
  });
});
```

- **To run the test, you need an additional dependency; with Sinon you create mock functions that track whether they were called during a test.** (points to `import sinon from 'sinon';`)
- **Use sinon.spy() to mock out the router.push() function called in the proceedToCheckout() function in cart.jsx.** (points to `push: sinon.spy()`)
- **Use the simulate() method to generate a click on the Checkout button.** (points to `testComponent.find('.button').simulate('click');`)
- **Use the called property of the sinon spy to assert that the router.push() method was called by your component.** (points to `expect(props.router.push.called).to.be.true;`)
- **Use the calledWith property of sinon spy to assert the proper route was passed in.** (points to `).to.be.true;`)

The listing uses Sinon to create function mocks. To learn more about Sinon, visit their docs at http://sinonjs.org. The listing also uses Enzyme to test the event. One thing to note about `simulate` is that it doesn't propagate the mock events—you must find the element on which you have the event listener to trigger the listener. That applies to all components loaded via Enzyme, even ones that use `mount`. In the next section, you'll learn about writing integration tests with `mount`.

9.1.3 Testing nested components

Enzyme provides a second way to test your components, called `mount`. This fully renders your component along with all its children. It's most useful for integration tests, where you're testing bigger portions of an application. I don't recommend using it for unit tests, as `mount` makes your tests more brittle. A change in a subcomponent will break the tests for any parent components that are using `mount` to test.

Listing 9.5 shows how to add an integration test that loads the entire React tree, including React Router. This allows you to assert on the complete React tree, including all child components. The code up to this point is in chapter-9.1.3 (`git checkout chapter-9.1.3`). Add the code in the listing to the app specification. Note that this is a different app.spec.jsx that lives in the integration folder.

> **NOTE** If you're using React Router 4, check out appendix A for an overview of setting up the routes and related router code. The following listing shows the main.jsx code that also applies to test setup.

Listing 9.5 Rendering with `mount`—test/integration/app.spec.jsx

```
import React from 'react';
import {
  Router,
  createMemoryHistory
} from 'react-router';
import { expect } from 'chai';
import { mount } from 'enzyme';
import { routes } from '../../src/shared/sharedRoutes';

describe('App Component', () => {
  it('Uses Link Components', () => {
    const renderedComponent = mount(
      <Router
        routes={routes()}
        history={createMemoryHistory('/products')}
      />
    );
    expect(
            renderedComponent.find(
                                      '.search'
                                    ).length
          ).to.be.above(1);
  });
});
```

- Include dependencies to render React Router.
- Instead of browser history use createMemoryHistory, it lets you declare an initial route for router (without having to navigate in the browser).
- Assert that search is loaded, which lives only on the product page.

The test in the previous example is trivial. In a real integration test, you'd want to test something more complex, such as searching in the search box. Before moving on, here are some additional methods you can use to write more-complex test cases.

ADVANCED ENZYME API METHODS

Enzyme has many additional methods that can be called on your shallow or mounted React components. Here's a list of some of the most useful ones:

- `setProps`—Use this method to pass in updated properties to a loaded component. Useful for testing logic that happens in React lifecycle methods.
- `setState`—Use this method to change the state of a loaded component. It lets you test complex cases, such as the search input in products.jsx.
- `debug`—Useful for seeing the rendered HTML of the component at any point in time. Useful for debugging.
- `unmount`—Test any code that happens in your `componentWillUnmount`.

9.2 Testing: thinking isomorphically

With an isomorphic app, it isn't enough to write unit tests that run in the browser. The goal of your tests should be to run your code in all the environments it'll be run in.

Any code in your app that runs on the server should be tested with Mocha in the terminal. Any code that runs in the browser should be tested in a browser environment with Karma. But code that runs *only* in the server or *only* in the browser doesn't need to be tested in the opposite environment. Table 9.1 illustrates this with the types of code that run in the All Things Westies app.

Table 9.1 In an isomorphic app, it's important to test code in all environments

	Server tests	Browser tests
Components	Yes	Yes
Shared folder code	Yes	Yes
Middleware	Yes	No
Server entry code	Yes	No
Browser entry code	No	Yes

9.2.1 Testing React components on the server

The great thing about Enzyme is that the `shallow` function doesn't require a real DOM. You can run these tests with Karma and with Mocha in the terminal. But if you want to more accurately test your components in the way they'll be used on the server, you can add an additional server-only test. (You can switch to the chapter-9.2.1 branch if you want to start this section with all the code so far.)

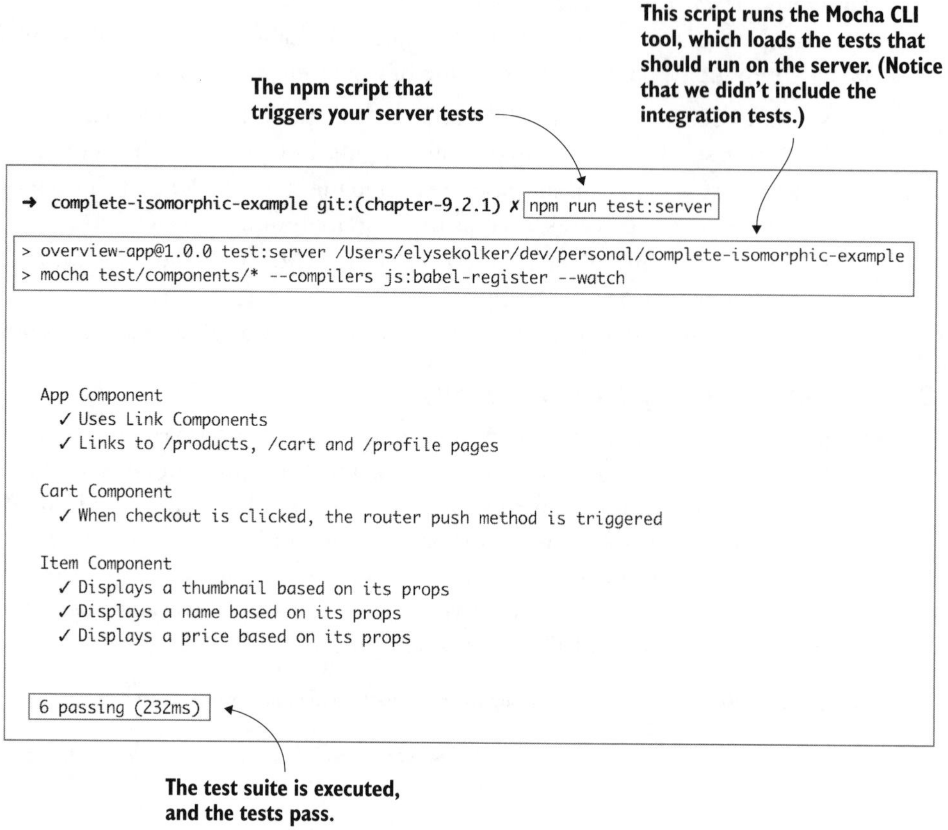
This script runs the Mocha CLI tool, which loads the tests that should run on the server. (Notice that we didn't include the integration tests.)
The npm script that triggers your server tests
➜ complete-isomorphic-example git:(chapter-9.2.1) ✗ npm run test:server
> overview-app@1.0.0 test:server /Users/elysekolker/dev/personal/complete-isomorphic-example
> mocha test/components/* --compilers js:babel-register --watch
App Component
✓ Uses Link Components
✓ Links to /products, /cart and /profile pages
Cart Component
✓ When checkout is clicked, the router push method is triggered
Item Component
✓ Displays a thumbnail based on its props
✓ Displays a name based on its props
✓ Displays a price based on its props
6 passing (232ms)
The test suite is executed, and the tests pass.

Figure 9.3 The server test output

Figure 9.3 shows the output of the server tests. The server tests are already running several of the tests you wrote previously. The only test that isn't running is the integration test, because that relies on having a browser environment.

Run the server tests with this command, which uses the Mocha CLI:

```
$ npm run test:server
```

To understand why running your tests on the server adds value, look at figure 9.4. It shows the server test failing because of a reference to browser environment code.

To try this yourself, add a reference to the `window` object in the Item component's render function, like this:

```
window.test = true;
```

When you run this code in your tests, it'll fail. If you try to run the app, you won't be able to navigate directly to localhost:3000/cart. Testing on the server prevents nasty environment-specific bugs.

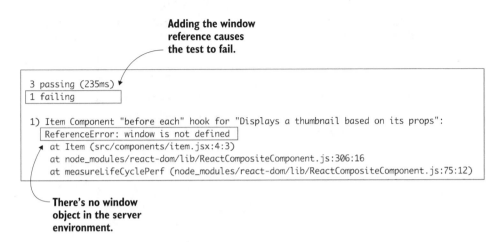

Adding the window reference causes the test to fail.

```
3 passing (235ms)
1 failing

1) Item Component "before each" hook for "Displays a thumbnail based on its props":
   ReferenceError: window is not defined
    at Item (src/components/item.jsx:4:3)
    at node_modules/react-dom/lib/ReactCompositeComponent.js:306:16
    at measureLifeCyclePerf (node_modules/react-dom/lib/ReactCompositeComponent.js:75:12)
```

There's no window object in the server environment.

Figure 9.4 Your tests will break if references are added that require a browser environment.

One of the benefits of tests is that as new people join to work on a project, the tests prevent them from causing problems for things they're unaware of. This type of server test helps because it takes some time for new team members to get used to thinking isomorphically.

9.2.2 *Testing all the things*

Depending on your project and the size of your team or organization, you may do some end-to-end or feature-automated testing with a tool like Selenium. Or you may have manual QA testers who look for bugs in your product. Or maybe your developers do the manual testing.

In all these cases, it's important to account for the multiple ways of getting to each part of your app:

- The initial page load from the server
- Navigating in your app via single-page application (SPA) flow

Although that may seem obvious to you at this point in the book, it's not an easy concept for those who don't work on an isomorphic app to grasp. To do manual QA, you have to run many test cases twice. Think about testing the cart in this app. Because the app assumes the user session is saved, you need to test loading the cart directly off the server and test navigating to the cart from another part of the app.

To illustrate this point, figure 9.5 shows the network output of the Cart page when you first load it from the server, compared with the network output of the Cart when you load it from another part of the app (SPA flow).

In this section, you learned how to think about testing isomorphically. The next section will add debugging tools to your tool belt.

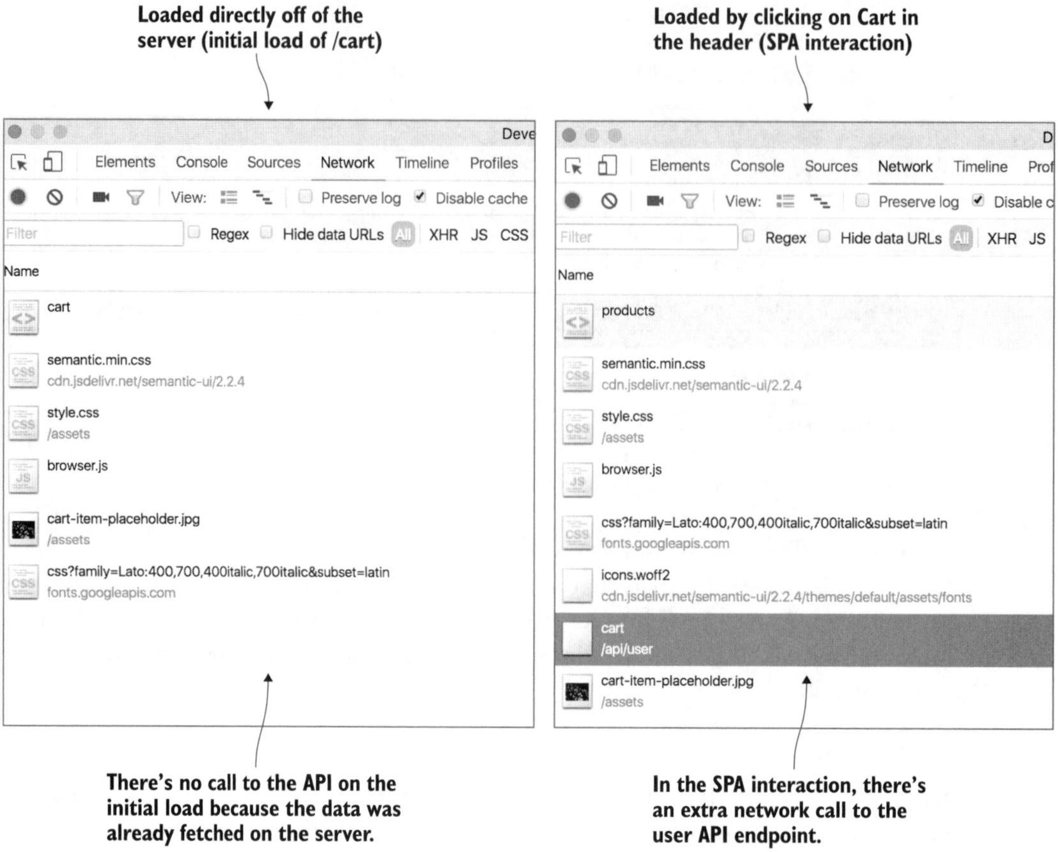
Loaded directly off of the server (initial load of /cart)
Loaded by clicking on Cart in the header (SPA interaction)
Elements Console Sources Network Timeline Profiles
Preserve log Disable cache
Regex Hide data URLs All XHR JS CSS
Name
cart
semantic.min.css
cdn.jsdelivr.net/semantic-ui/2.2.4
style.css
/assets
browser.js
cart-item-placeholder.jpg
/assets
css?family=Lato:400,700,400italic,700italic&subset=latin
fonts.googleapis.com
products
semantic.min.css
cdn.jsdelivr.net/semantic-ui/2.2.4
style.css
/assets
browser.js
css?family=Lato:400,700,400italic,700italic&subset=latin
fonts.googleapis.com
icons.woff2
cdn.jsdelivr.net/semantic-ui/2.2.4/themes/default/assets/fonts
cart
/api/user
cart-item-placeholder.jpg
/assets
There's no call to the API on the initial load because the data was already fetched on the server.
In the SPA interaction, there's an extra network call to the user API endpoint.

Figure 9.5 The differences between initial load and the SPA load require testing both use cases.

9.3 Using debugging tools

One of my favorite teaching moments with new developers or JavaScript newcomers is to show them how to use Chrome DevTools to improve their ability to troubleshoot and debug problems. Going from `console.log` statements littered throughout code to using breakpoints is often a mind-blowing moment for those who are new to troubleshooting and debugging. Breakpoints are useful because you can pause and inspect your code, stepping through the code to find problems. Chrome DevTools has several advanced options for breakpoints as well (find dev tips galore at https://umaar.com/dev-tips/28-dom-breakpoint-pane/).

I assume you have experience with the Chrome DevTools, but I want to walk you through two additional tools that can make your life much simpler when working with React and Redux. They're useful for debugging and manually testing your code:

- *React Chrome Extension*—Browser extension that shows you the React components in your markup and displays the properties and current state for each component

- *Redux Chrome Extension*—Browser extension that shows you the Redux actions in your application and allows you to replay a sequence of actions

9.3.1 React Chrome Extension

The React Chrome Extension loads React Dev Tools and gives you direct insight into the React components in your running app. It lets you inspect the HTML structure and see how components are wrapped. It also shows you what properties and state are set on each component.

You install this extension from http://mng.bz/mt5P. After you've installed it, load the app and inspect it. Navigate to the React tab. Figure 9.6 shows what you should see.

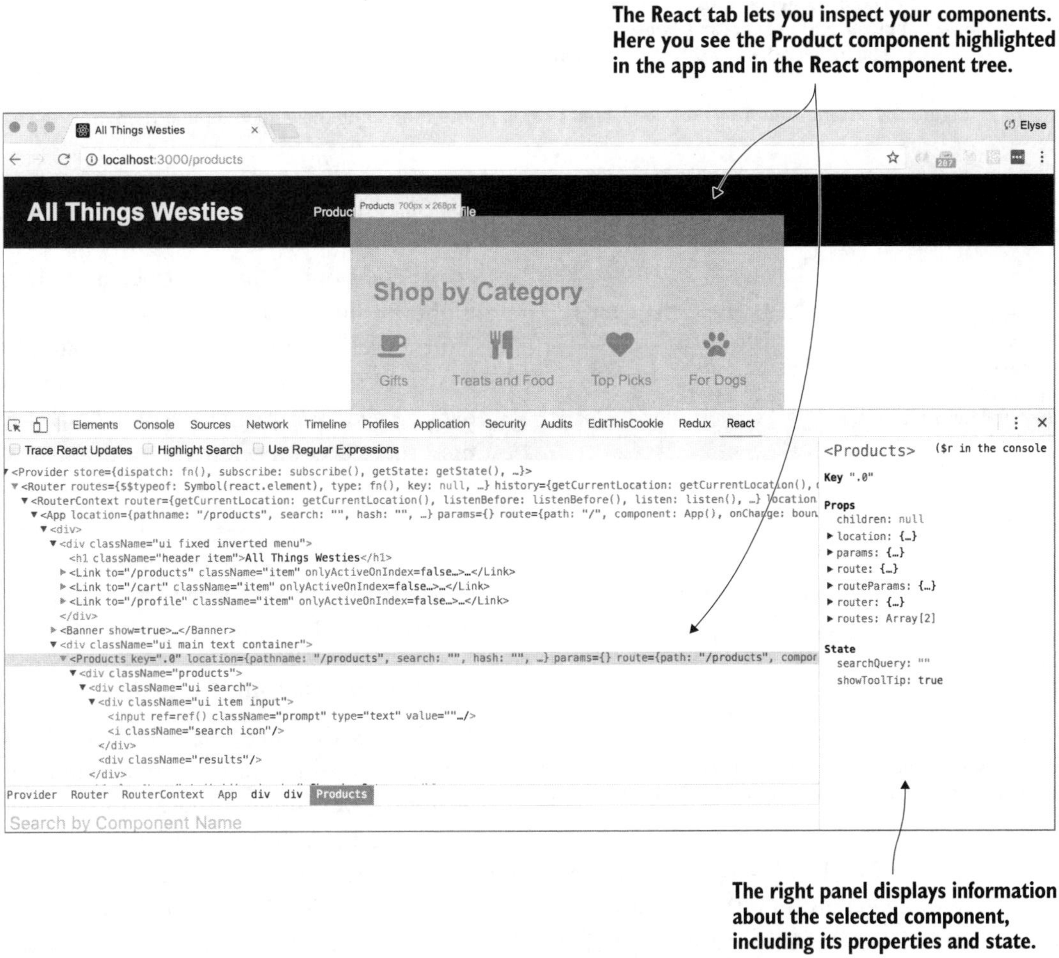
The React tab lets you inspect your components. Here you see the Product component highlighted in the app and in the React component tree.
All Things Westies
localhost:3000/products
Shop by Category
Gifts
Treats and Food
Top Picks
For Dogs
Elements Console Sources Network Timeline Profiles Application Security Audits EditThisCookie Redux React
Trace React Updates
Highlight Search
Use Regular Expressions
<Products> ($r in the console
Key ".0"
Props
State
searchQuery: ""
showToolTip: true
Provider Router RouterContext App div div Products
Search by Component Name
The right panel displays information about the selected component, including its properties and state.

Figure 9.6 The React Dev Tools tab open in Chrome DevTools

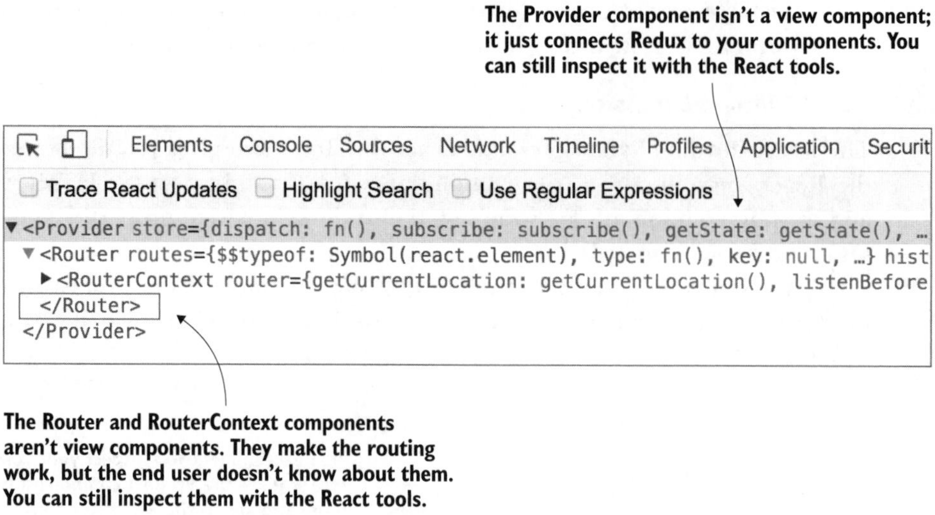
The Provider component isn't a view component; it just connects Redux to your components. You can still inspect it with the React tools.
Elements Console Sources Network Timeline Profiles Application Securit
Trace React Updates Highlight Search Use Regular Expressions
<Provider store={dispatch: fn(), subscribe: subscribe(), getState: getState(), …
<Router routes={$$typeof: Symbol(react.element), type: fn(), key: null, …} hist
<RouterContext router={getCurrentLocation: getCurrentLocation(), listenBefore
</Router>
</Provider>
The Router and RouterContext components aren't view components. They make the routing work, but the end user doesn't know about them. You can still inspect them with the React tools.

Figure 9.7 React Dev Tools let you inspect components that don't show up in regular HTML.

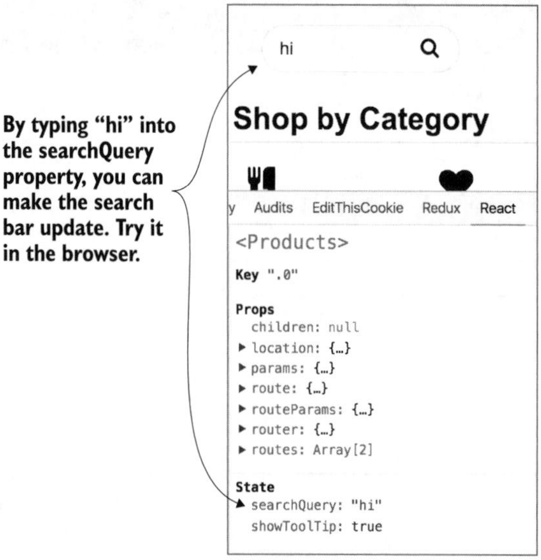
By typing "hi" into the searchQuery property, you can make the search bar update. Try it in the browser.
hi
Shop by Category
Audits EditThisCookie Redux React
<Products>
Key ".0"
Props
children: null
location: {…}
params: {…}
route: {…}
routeParams: {…}
router: {…}
routes: Array[2]
State
searchQuery: "hi"
showToolTip: true

Figure 9.8 Inspecting the state and props for the Products component. You can manipulate the state from this panel.

You can do many things with React Dev Tools. One useful tool is the ability to see every component in the tree, including higher-order components (figure 9.7).

Another useful feature is the ability to see properties and state. Figure 9.8 shows how to view the properties and state for the Products component.

Try changing the state property for `searchQuery`. Notice that it updates in the search box when you change it. This ability to override state live in the app is helpful for debugging.

9.3.2 Redux Chrome Extension

The Redux Chrome Extension provides a nearly zero-configuration implementation of Redux Dev Tools. Install it in Chrome by visiting http://mng.bz/NEBG.

Redux Dev Tools is an npm package that you can include in your project, but installing the extension is the fastest way to get up and running. You'll find all the documentation for the Redux Dev Tools Extension at the GitHub repo https://github.com/zalmoxisus/redux-devtools-extension. Figure 9.9 shows what Redux Dev Tools looks like running with your app.

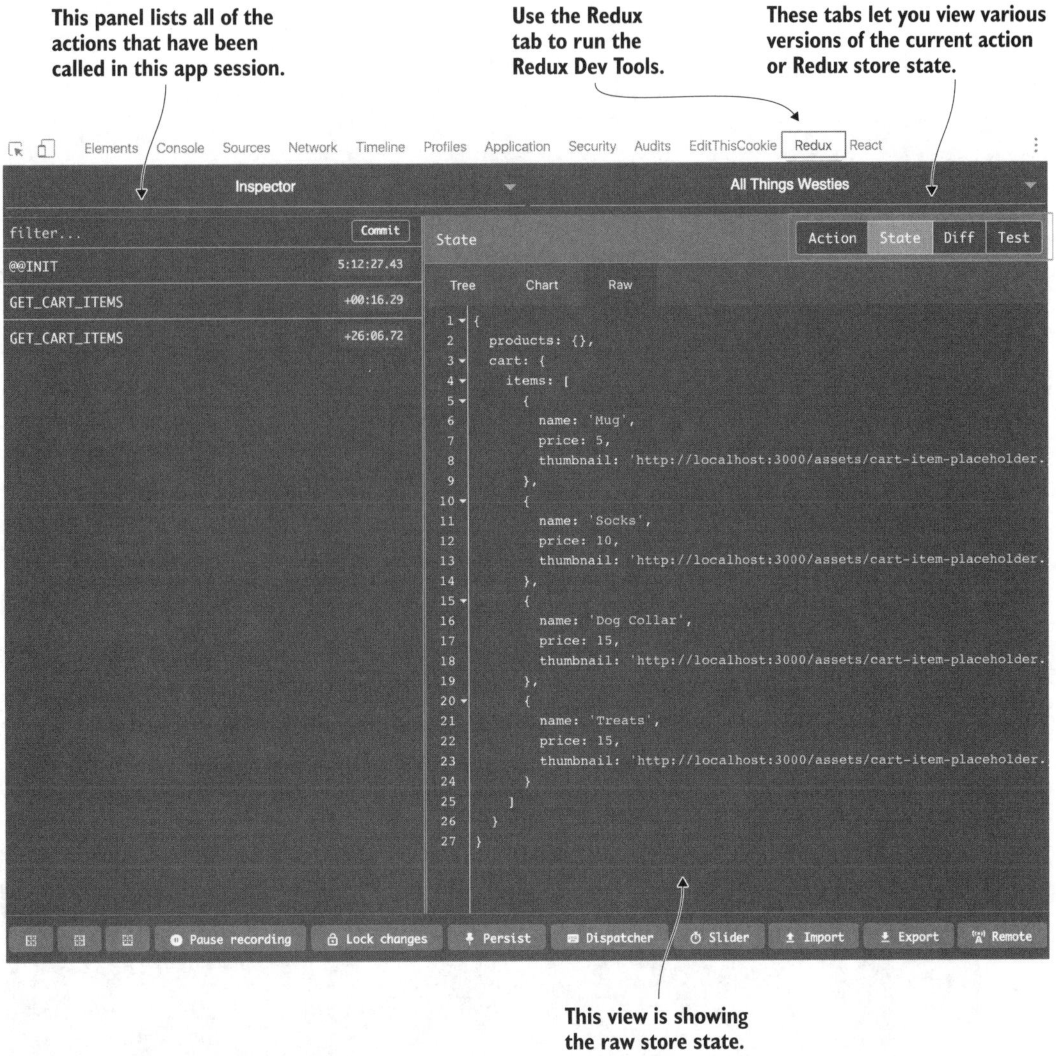
This panel lists all of the actions that have been called in this app session.
Use the Redux tab to run the Redux Dev Tools.
These tabs let you view various versions of the current action or Redux store state.
Elements
Console
Sources
Network
Timeline
Profiles
Application
Security
Audits
EditThisCookie
Redux
React
Inspector
All Things Westies
filter...
Commit
@@INIT 5:12:27.43
GET_CART_ITEMS +00:16.29
GET_CART_ITEMS +26:06.72
State
Action
State
Diff
Test
Tree
Chart
Raw
Pause recording
Lock changes
Persist
Dispatcher
Slider
Import
Export
Remote
This view is showing the raw store state.

Figure 9.9 Redux Dev Tools inside Chrome DevTools

To get Redux Dev Tools to see the Redux store in your app, you must update the `compose` function that's used by the initialize Redux code. The following listing shows how to do this. You use this code to replace the old `compose` call in `initRedux`.

Listing 9.6 Enable Redux Dev Tools—src/shared/initRedux.es6

```
import {
  createStore,
  combineReducers,
  applyMiddleware,
```

```
  compose } from 'redux';
import thunkMiddleware from 'redux-thunk';
import loggerMiddleware from 'redux-logger';
import products from './products-reducer.es6';
import cart from './cart-reducer.es6';

export default function (initialStore = {}) {
  const reducer = combineReducers({
    products,
    cart
  });
  const middleware = [thunkMiddleware, loggerMiddleware];
  let newCompose;
  if (typeof window !== 'undefined') {
    newCompose =
    ➥ window.__REDUX_DEVTOOLS_EXTENSION_COMPOSE__;
  }
  const composeEnhancers = newCompose || compose;
  return composeEnhancers(
      applyMiddleware(...middleware)
    )(createStore)(reducer, initialStore);
}
```

Updated compose function lives on window, but will break server—check for presence of window.

Grab compose function from window object.

If developer doesn't have Redux Dev Tools installed, fall back to base compose.

Use new compose function to set up Redux.

Now that you've enabled the Redux tools, let's walk through some of its features. Figure 9.10 shows how to use some of the testing features of Redux Dev Tools.

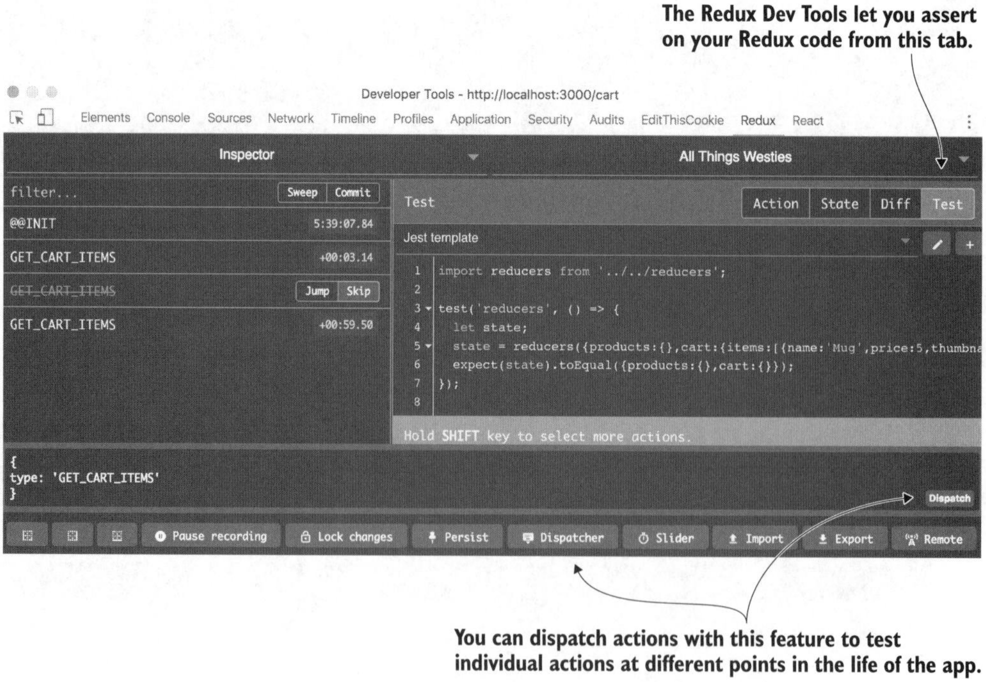
The Redux Dev Tools let you assert on your Redux code from this tab.
Developer Tools - http://localhost:3000/cart
Elements Console Sources Network Timeline Profiles Application Security Audits EditThisCookie Redux React
Inspector
All Things Westies
Sweep Commit
@@INIT
GET_CART_ITEMS
GET_CART_ITEMS
GET_CART_ITEMS
Jump Skip
Test
Action State Diff Test
Jest template
import reducers from '../../reducers';
test('reducers', () => {
let state;
expect(state).toEqual({products:{},cart:{}});
});
Hold SHIFT key to select more actions.
type: 'GET_CART_ITEMS'
Dispatch
Pause recording
Lock changes
Persist
Dispatcher
Slider
Import
Export
Remote
You can dispatch actions with this feature to test individual actions at different points in the life of the app.

Figure 9.10 Using the testing features of Redux Dev Tools

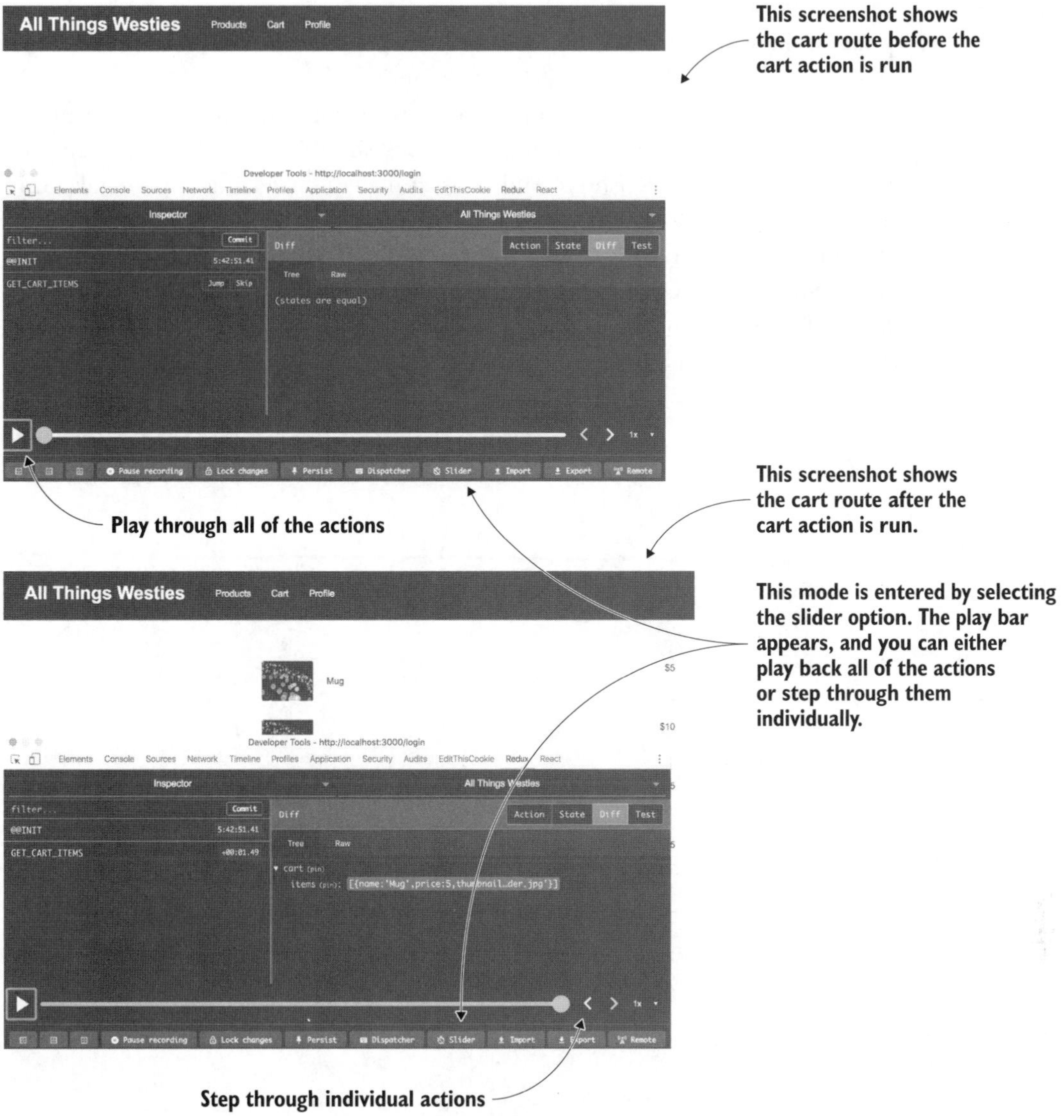
All Things Westies
Products
Cart
Profile
This screenshot shows the cart route before the cart action is run
Developer Tools - http://localhost:3000/login
Inspector
All Things Westies
Diff
Action
State
Test
@@INIT
GET_CART_ITEMS
(states are equal)
Play through all of the actions
This screenshot shows the cart route after the cart action is run.
This mode is entered by selecting the slider option. The play bar appears, and you can either play back all of the actions or step through them individually.
Mug
$5
$10
Step through individual actions

Figure 9.11 Using the playback feature of Redux Dev Tools

Finally, one of the coolest features of this debugging tool is the ability to replay actions. Figure 9.11 shows how to walk through the various states of the cart route.

Summary

In this chapter, you learned how to improve your developer workflow with React-specific testing and debugging tools for both the browser and the server. Now you can improve your speed of React and isomorphic development!

- Enzyme is a library for testing React components. It provides a way to test components in isolation via `shallow` and a way to write integration tests with `mount`.
- Testing an isomorphic app requires thinking through where the code will run and how that translates to testing. Unit tests should test code in the environment(s) it will run in. End-to-end tests and manual testing should take into account the initial load versus the SPA experience.
- React Dev Tools can be used via a Chrome extension and makes inspecting your React components easier. It also allows you to manipulate state in real time.
- Redux Dev Tools can be used via a Chrome extension. It lets you walk through your actions and clearly see the store update over time.

10 Handling server/browser differences

This chapter covers

- Isolating environment-specific code
- Enabling routes that are used on only the browser or the server
- Using static methods to add headers and page metadata to each app route
- Implementing consistent usage of a user agent between the server and the browser

This chapter and the next cover a variety of topics that will help you deal with real-world cases that I've run into when building isomorphic apps. As you embark on building a production-ready app, you'll often run into use cases that need special handling within the context of this type of architecture. Table 10.1 lists examples of these kinds of situations.

Table 10.1 Common problems and solutions within an isomorphic app

Problem	Solution	Server	Browser
Initialization code that can run only in the browser.	Use an environment Boolean flag.		✓
Define SEO metatags so they're rendered on the server.	Use a static function on top-level route components.	✓	
Progressive enhancement: feature detection is different between the browser and the server.	Feature-detect only on the browser.		✓
Progressive enhancement: if user agent detection is required, how do you create a single source of truth?	Use the server user agent and store it in a standard way in the app store.	✓	
Error handling duplication—both the server and the browser have logic to handle 404 states.	Save user-facing errors in a standard format that makes determining when to show a 404 easy.	✓	✓

All the code for this chapter can be found in the same shared GitHub repository as previous chapters: http://mng.bz/8gV8. We'll continue to use the branch system to step through the examples in this chapter. As usual, you can install and run the code:

```
$ npm install
$ npm start
```

Let's explore how to gate your code based on the browser or the server environment.

10.1 Isolate browser-specific code

Every web app I've ever built has a dependency on the `window` or `document` object. Sometimes it's to support a social widget, and other times it's a specific library I want to use (for example, analytics or bug tracking). But this poses a problem in an isomorphic app: how do you continue to use this kind of code without breaking your app on the server?

Imagine you have a reusable module for your analytics code. Your analytics doesn't need to run on the server because it's focused purely on user interactions with the page. But you want to ensure that six months from now, you or another developer doesn't accidentally run this code on the server. Figure 10.1 shows the state of the code in the branch for this section, chapter-10.1 (`git checkout chapter-10.1`).

In this section, you'll fix this error by wrapping the analytics module in code that prevents it from running on the server. This requires a couple of steps (figure 10.2 shows the end result):

1. Add environment variables (via webpack for the browser code).
2. Wrap the references to `window` in checks for the browser environment.

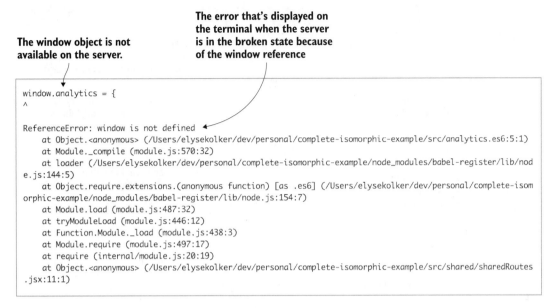

The window object is not available on the server.

The error that's displayed on the terminal when the server is in the broken state because of the window reference

```
window.analytics = {
^

ReferenceError: window is not defined
    at Object.<anonymous> (/Users/elysekolker/dev/personal/complete-isomorphic-example/src/analytics.es6:5:1)
    at Module._compile (module.js:570:32)
    at loader (/Users/elysekolker/dev/personal/complete-isomorphic-example/node_modules/babel-register/lib/nod
e.js:144:5)
    at Object.require.extensions.(anonymous function) [as .es6] (/Users/elysekolker/dev/personal/complete-isom
orphic-example/node_modules/babel-register/lib/node.js:154:7)
    at Module.load (module.js:487:32)
    at tryModuleLoad (module.js:446:12)
    at Function.Module._load (module.js:438:3)
    at Module.require (module.js:497:17)
    at require (internal/module.js:20:19)
    at Object.<anonymous> (/Users/elysekolker/dev/personal/complete-isomorphic-example/src/shared/sharedRoutes
.jsx:11:1)
```

Figure 10.1 The console output without preventing the analytics module from running on the server

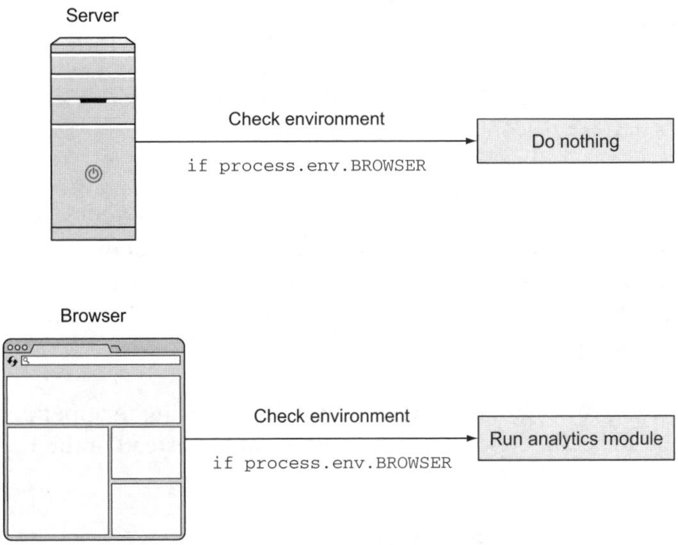

Server
Check environment
if process.env.BROWSER
Do nothing
Browser
Check environment
if process.env.BROWSER
Run analytics module

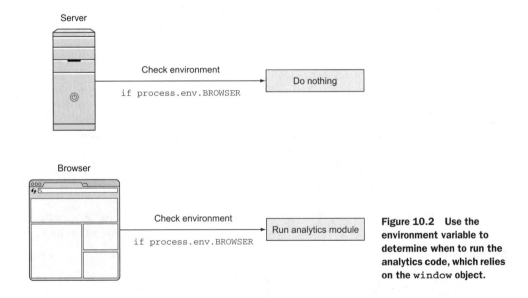

Figure 10.2 Use the environment variable to determine when to run the analytics code, which relies on the `window` object.

This analytics module is shown in listing 10.1. I've already created the base code of the analytics module for you. I've also created a mock endpoint on the Node.js server that responds with a 200 when you hit the endpoint. But if you run the code in this branch as is, you'll notice it's broken!

Listing 10.1 Analytics module—src/analytics.es6

```
import fetch from 'isomorphic-fetch';

window.analytics = {
  send: (opts) => {
    const headers = new window.fetch.Headers({
      'Content-Type': 'application/json'
    });

    fetch({
      url: 'http://localhost:3000/analytics',
      method: 'POST',
      headers,
      data: opts
    })
    .then((res) => {
      console.log('analytics result', res);
    })
    .catch((err) => {
      console.log('analytics err', err);
    });
  }
};

const getAnalytics = () => {
  return window.analytics;
};

export const sendData = (opts) => {
  getAnalytics().send(opts);
};
```

- Here, analytics library is a mock object added for you to the window object (in a real app, you'd import your library).
- Mock analytics library has one method, send, which takes in an options object.
- Send makes a POST request to the Node.js server (in a real app, the endpoint would be your analytics service).
- In this mock example, results and errors are being logged.
- Analytics module implements a getter method for the analytics object.
- Analytics module implements a sendData method, which calls send on the mock analytics object.

`sendData` is the public method that will be called from view modules. The code is broken because it's being called from shared routes, which are run on both the server and the browser. Because the server doesn't have a `window` object, the code breaks the app. Listing 10.2 shows the `sharedRoutes` code that's calling the analytics module. I've already provided this for you.

NOTE If you're using React Router 4, check out the first listing in appendix C for how to use the React lifecycle to handle this example, instead of the React Router lifecycle.

Listing 10.2 Calling the analytics code—src/shared/sharedRoutes.jsx

```
import { sendData } from '../analytics.es6';

let beforeRouteRender = (dispatch, prevState, nextState) => {
  const { routes } = nextState;
  routes.map((route) => {}).reduce((flat, toFlatten) => {
    }, []).map((initialAction) => {});
```

- Import the sendData function from the analytics module.

```
  sendData({
    path: nextState.location.pathname,
    type: 'navigation'
  });
};
```

Call sendData to track each location update.

To make this module work, you'll create environment-specific Boolean flags for detecting whether the code is running in the server or in the browser. Creating environment flags in Node.js is already built into the system. But to create the browser environment flag, you'll need to take advantage of webpack's plugin system.

10.1.1 Creating the environment variable for the server

On the server, providing an environment flag is done the same way you set the `NODE_ENV` variable. You pass in a `SERVER` value before starting the server. The following listing shows how to add this to the package.json start script.

Listing 10.3 Server startup script—package.json

```
"scripts": {
    ...
    "start":
      "NODE_ENV=development SERVER=TRUE node src/server.js",
    ...
  },
```

Add an environment variable to the start script.

After you've added this variable, you'll set up webpack to provide the `BROWSER` environment value.

10.1.2 Creating the environment variable for the browser

In chapter 5, I showed you how to create a custom webpack plugin to set the stage environment variable. This allowed you to indicate a production versus developer build. To create the `BROWSER` and `SERVER` variables in webpack, you follow the same pattern. The following listing indicates the code you need to add to the webpack configuration to create the environment variable for use in your browser code.

Listing 10.4 Adding the webpack plugin

```
const webpack = require("webpack");

const injectVariables = new webpack.DefinePlugin({
  process: {
    env: {
      NODE_ENV: JSON.stringify("development"),
      BROWSER: JSON.stringify("true"),
      SERVER: JSON.stringify("false")
    }
  }
});
```

Import webpack to call DefinePlugin.

Re-create the process.env object structure.

Add environment variables into the object, include BROWSER and SERVER.

```
module.exports = {
  //...other properties
  resolve: {},
  plugins: [
    injectVariables
  ]
};
```

Include plugins array in the options and add injectVariables to the array.

In the first line, you need to use `require` instead of the `import` statement because this file isn't being compiled by Babel. The final step is to use the `BROWSER` variable in the analytics module.

10.1.3 Using the variables

Now that the `BROWSER` and `SERVER` variables exist in the appropriate environments, you can use the `BROWSER` variable to wrap your analytics implementation code. Add the code in the following listing into the analytics module.

Listing 10.5 Checking for environment—src/analytics.es6

```
if (process.env.BROWSER) {
  window.analytics = {};
}

const getAnalytics = () => {
  if (process.env.BROWSER) {
    return window.analytics;
  }
  return false;
};
```

Add a check for process.env.BROWSER around the analytics mock object.

Add a check around any code that accesses the window object.

Now you can run the code without anything breaking! Try it for yourself.

Next let's discuss how this strategy can be expanded to feature flagging based on environment.

ENVIRONMENT-AWARE ROUTES

Other common use cases exist for changing code based on the environment. Another common reason you'd need to know the environment is to control which app routes are available. For example, maybe you need to create an internal access route—something that only a small number of people need access to. That might be an admin page or testing route. Conversely, you may want to have certain pages that aren't directly accessible from the server, maybe for privacy reasons or because you don't want the route to be accessible directly from the server.

To do that, you use the same check for `process.env.BROWSER` that you added to the analytics module. In this case, you'd add the check in the sharedRoutes.jsx component.

Another common use case occurs when you're developing a new feature and you want to make the route available only for testing in your development and staging environments. You can also add a check for the `NODE_ENV` value. This lets you determine whether a route should be shown only in development/staging or also in production. The following listing shows how to add this code to the sharedRoutes file.

NOTE If you're using React Router 4, check out the second listing in appendix C to see how to add a dynamic route.

Listing 10.6 Enabling routes—src/shared/sharedRoutes.jsx

```
let developmentRoute =
    process.env.NODE_ENV !== 'production' ?
        <Route path="/dev-test" component={App} />
        : null;

export const routes = (onChange = () => {}) => {
  return (
    <Route path="/" component={App} onChange={onChange}>
      ...other routes
      {developmentRoute}
    </Route>
  );
```

Add a variable that will hold the Route component.

Render route.

In the first lines, if the environment is production, the value will be null—otherwise, it'll be the route. To test that this code is working, change the `NODE_ENV` variable in your webpack config to `production`. The route will then be found on the server but won't exist on the browser, so it'll return a blank screen:

```
const injectVariables = new webpack.DefinePlugin({
  process: {
    env: {
      NODE_ENV: JSON.stringify("production"),
      BROWSER: JSON.stringify('true'),
      SERVER: JSON.stringify('false')
    }
  }
});
```

Or you can change the value in the start script to be `production` on the server. This will result in a "Cannot GET /dev-test" error from the server:

```
"scripts": {
    ...
    "start": "NODE_ENV=production SERVER=TRUE node src/server.js",
    ...
  },
```

Don't forget to change these values back when you're finished.

10.2 SEO and sharing

When building a public site, whether it's content-based or e-commerce as in the example, search engine optimization (SEO) is an important factor. Good SEO leads to

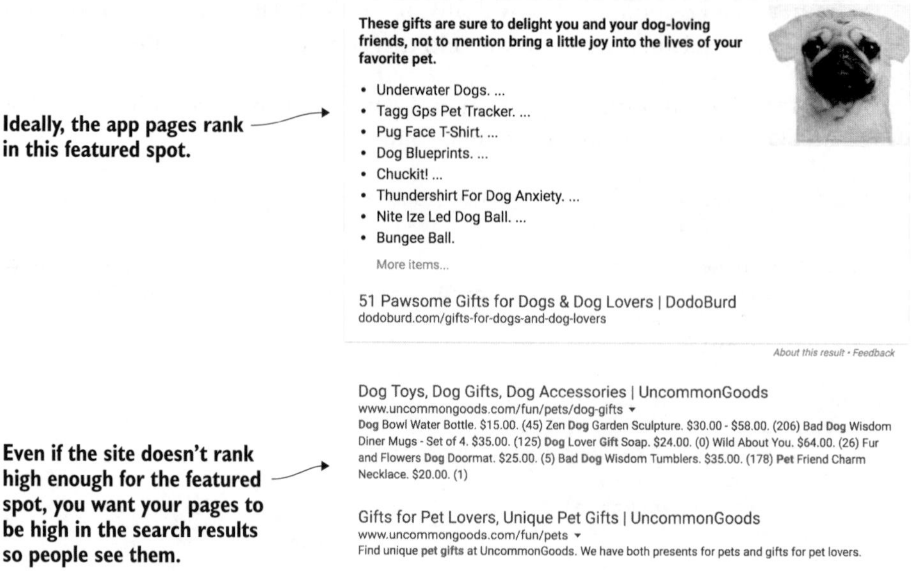
Ideally, the app pages rank in this featured spot.
These gifts are sure to delight you and your dog-loving friends, not to mention bring a little joy into the lives of your favorite pet.
• Underwater Dogs. ...
• Tagg Gps Pet Tracker. ...
• Pug Face T-Shirt. ...
• Dog Blueprints. ...
• Chuckit! ...
• Thundershirt For Dog Anxiety. ...
• Nite Ize Led Dog Ball. ...
• Bungee Ball.
More items...
51 Pawsome Gifts for Dogs & Dog Lovers | DodoBurd
dodoburd.com/gifts-for-dogs-and-dog-lovers
About this result • Feedback
Even if the site doesn't rank high enough for the featured spot, you want your pages to be high in the search results so people see them.
Dog Toys, Dog Gifts, Dog Accessories | UncommonGoods
www.uncommongoods.com/fun/pets/dog-gifts
Dog Bowl Water Bottle. $15.00. (45) Zen Dog Garden Sculpture. $30.00 - $58.00. (206) Bad Dog Wisdom Diner Mugs - Set of 4. $35.00. (125) Dog Lover Gift Soap. $24.00. (0) Wild About You. $64.00. (26) Fur and Flowers Dog Doormat. $25.00. (5) Bad Dog Wisdom Tumblers. $35.00. (178) Pet Friend Charm Necklace. $20.00. (1)
Gifts for Pet Lovers, Unique Pet Gifts | UncommonGoods
www.uncommongoods.com/fun/pets
Find unique pet gifts at UncommonGoods. We have both presents for pets and gifts for pet lovers.

Figure 10.3 Thoughtful SEO implementation leads to high rankings or featured rankings in Google search.

higher rankings in search engines, which in turn leads to more users for your web app. One of the reasons to build an isomorphic site is to make supporting good SEO easy.

In technical terms, this translates into adding SEO metatags and other metadata specifically for search engines to see when they crawl the app. Figure 10.3 shows an example of a featured page and a high-ranking page in Google search results.

But much of this metadata gets inserted in the head of the HTML page, making it difficult to implement alongside a React component. (Remember, React renders into a specific tag in the body of your HTML—it has no awareness of the rest of the HTML.) I'm going to walk you through using static functions and code specific to the server to handle this use case. I've used this method successfully. After you set it up the first time in an app, continuing to use the logic is straightforward.

You're going to work on a portion of the site you haven't touched yet: the product detail pages. Ideally, you want your products to rank high in Google searches so that more people come to the site and make purchases. Figure 10.4 shows what the detail page looks like to the user. The code you'll be adding is not directly for user consumption but for Googlebot and sharebots (for example, Facebook or Twitter—both sites hit your page directly to determine what content should be shared based on metatags).

I've already provided the Product Detail component for you. You'll want to switch to branch chapter-10.2 (`git checkout chapter-10.2`). Listing 10.7 shows the Product Detail component as it exists when you check out the code (if you're following along, you'll need to add this code yourself).

SEO tags tell Google what information on the page is important for providing good search results.

All Things Westies
Products
Cart
Profile
Embossed Westie Mug
All white mug with a Westie's adorable face.
Price: 15
12oz
Add To Cart

Figure 10.4 The product detail page

Listing 10.7 Product Detail component—src/components/detail.jsx

```
import React from 'react';
import { bindActionCreators } from 'redux';
import { connect } from 'react-redux';
import cartActions
➥ from '../shared/cart-action-creators.es6';
import productActions
➥ from '../shared/products-action-creators.es6';

class Detail extends React.Component {

  static prefetchActions (params) {}

  constructor(props) {}

  addToCart() {}

  render() {
    return (
      <div className="ui card middle">
        <h2>{this.props.name}</h2>
        <img src={this.props.thumbnail} alt={this.props.description} />
        <p>{this.props.description}</p>
        <div>Price: <span>{this.props.price}</span></div>
        <div>{this.props.details}</div>
        <button onClick={this.addToCart}>Add To Cart</button>
      </div>
    );
  }
}
```

Include dependencies—this component is a container, so it's connected to Redux.

Implements prefetchActions to get the appropriate state for the detail route.

render function displays the data fetched in prefetchActions.

```
Detail.propTypes = {};

function mapStateToProps(state) {
  const { currentProduct } = state.products;
  return {
    ...currentProduct
  };
}

function mapDispatchToProps(dispatch) {
  return {
    cartActions: bindActionCreators(cartActions, dispatch)
  };
}

export default connect(mapStateToProps, mapDispatchToProps)(Detail);
```

Next, you'll add the necessary SEO metatags to the component.

10.2.1 Setting up metadata tags

There are many parts to implementing good SEO on the detail pages (microdata tags, proper page markup, and so forth). Most of these things are handled easily within React components. But the metadata tags that should go in the head of every page aren't part of a React component. Metadata tags go in the head, which is static after being rendered by the server. It doesn't change on each React render cycle.

To create the SEO metatags in the head, I recommend using a `static` function so that your components can optionally declare their SEO metadata needs. The following listing shows the code you need to add to the detail.jsx component so that you can later add the metatags to the head.

Listing 10.8 Add a `static` function for creating metatags—src/components/detail.jsx

```
class Detail extends React.Component {

  static createMetatags(params, store) {
    const tags = [];
    const item = store.products ? store.products.currentProduct : null;
    if (item) {
      tags.push({
        name: 'description',
        content: item.description
      });
      tags.push({
        property: 'og:description',
        content: item.description
      });
      tags.push({
        property: 'og:title',
        content: item.name
      });
      tags.push({
```

Define static function.

Set up an array to store each metatag.

Each metatag is represented by two keys—name and content or property and content—depending on the specific metatag.

```
        property: 'og:url',
        content: `http://localhost:3000/product/detail/${item.id}`
      });
      tags.push({
        property: 'og:image',
        content: item.thumbnail
      });
    }
    return tags;
  }
```

The `static` function takes in a `params` object (just like `prefetchActions`) and the store so that it can grab the current product.

10.2.2 Rendering metatags into the head on the server

On the server, you can take advantage of these `static` functions to generate the metatags into the html.jsx component that's rendered and returned to the browser. The following listing shows the code you need to add.

Listing 10.9 Render metatags as part of html.jsx—src/components/html.jsx

```
const HTML = (props) => {
  const metatagsArray = [];
  props.metatags.forEach((item) => {     <-- Loop through each item provided
    metatagsArray.push(                      in the metatags array and create a
      <meta {...item} />                     metatag with item's properties.
    );
  });

  return (
    <html lang="en">
      <head>
        <title>All Things Westies</title>
        {metatagsArray}                  <-- Add metatags HTML to the <head>.
        <link
```

Finally, you need to add the code to renderView.jsx that will pull the metatag arrays out of the individual components. This code is identical to the code you added in chapter 7 for `prefetchActions`. I've pulled the code from chapter 7 into a reusable function for you.

Listing 10.10 `flattenStaticFunction` code—src/middleware/renderView.jsx

```
                                   Reusable function declaration takes in
                                   renderProps and the store so it can
                                   pull out the appropriate information.
function flattenStaticFunction(renderProps, staticFnName, store = {},
    request) {                                                       <--
  let results = renderProps.components.map((component) => {
    if (component) {
```

```
      if (component.displayName &&
        component.displayName.toLowerCase().indexOf('connect') > -1
      ) {
        if (component.WrappedComponent[staticFnName]) {        <-
          return component
            ➥ .WrappedComponent[staticFnName](                  <-
            renderProps.params,
            store,
            request
          );
        }
      } else if (component[staticFnName]) {                     <-
        return component[staticFnName](                         <-
          renderProps.params,
          store,
          request                              <-
        );
      }
    }
    return [];
  });

  results = results.reduce((flat, toFlatten) => {
    return flat.concat(toFlatten);
  }, []);

  return results;
}
```

Use the staticFnName variable instead of hardcoding the prefetchActions function name.

Some of the static functions need information about the request such as the headers. It's passed in here to give access to that information.

The reuseable function also takes in a `staticFnName`. This is the reusable bit that will let you use this function for multiple types of `static` functions (`prefetchActions`, `seoTags`, and so on). Because this code already exists for you, all you need to do is add the code in the following listing to renderView.jsx.

Listing 10.11 Fetch metatags array—src/middleware/renderView.jsx

```
const seoTags = flattenStaticFunction(          <-
  renderProps,
  'createMetatags',
  serverState
);

const app = renderToString();

const html = renderToString(
  <HTML
    html={app}                                  <-
    serverState={stringifiedServerState}
    metatags={seoTags}
  />
);
```

Call flattenStaticFunction with React Router renderProps, the name of the function to call, and the current state of the store—returns metatags array.

Pass these tags into the HTML component so they can be used by the code added in listing 10.9.

Now that you've seen how to handle SEO and sharing metatags, let's look at handling the title on the browser and the server.

10.2.3 Handling the title

Titles are important for SEO and for a good user experience. The combination of title and favicon makes your tab or window in a browser distinct from all the others. Figure 10.5 shows what this looks like in the browser.

The title appears in the tab. This title should be set on the server for the initial render. On subsequent renders, the title will be updated by mutating the tag directly.

Collar - All Things Westies
localhost:3000/product/detail/collar

Figure 10.5 The title displayed in the browser

TITLE ON THE SERVER

Handling the title on the server is similar to handling the metadata on the server. Each top-level component should provide a `static` function that outputs the title. In addition, I suggest breaking out the title output from the function that takes in the server data so you can reuse some of your logic on the browser. Add the code in the following listing to the Detail component.

Listing 10.12 Create title `static` function—src/components/detail.jsx

```
class Detail extends React.Component {

  static createTitle(props) {
    return `${props.name} - All Things Westies`;
  }

  static getTitle(params, store) {
    const currentProduct = store.products && store.products.currentProduct;

    return Detail.createTitle(currentProduct);
  }

  static createMetatags(params, store) {}
  //...other code
}
```

Static function creates the title from props, an abstraction that'll make creating the title on the browser easier.

On the server, renderView middleware will call getTitle, which takes in the store and pulls out the currentProduct data.

After you have a component with the proper `static` function, you can set up the title on the server. In the `renderView` code, you add a call to get the title. The following listing shows the code you add to renderView.jsx.

Listing 10.13 Add title for the route—src/middleware/renderView.jsx

```
const title = flattenStaticFunction(
  renderProps,
  'getTitle',
```

```
    serverState
  );

  const app = renderToString();

  const html = renderToString(
    <HTML
      html={app}
      serverState={stringifiedServerState}
      metatags={seoTags}
      title={title}
    />
  );
```

The first lines call `flattenStaticFunction` with the React Router `renderProps`, the name of the function (`getTitle`), and the `serverState` so that the title details can be fetched. A string title is returned. At the end, you pass the title into the HTML component.

Finally, you need to change the title in html.jsx to use the passed-in prop. The following listing shows you what to add.

Listing 10.14 Render the title for the route—src/components/html.jsx

```
<head>
  <title
    dangerouslySetInnerHTML={{
      __html: props.title || 'All Things Westies'
    }}
  />
  {metatagsArray}
  // ...more code
</head>
```

Use `dangerouslySetInnerHTML` to output the title string. If you render the title directly into the tag, React will append a comment that will then show up in the browser. If you run the server and reload the detail page, the title will be based on the product title.

Next, let's look at updating the title in the browser.

TITLE ON THE BROWSER

Most metatags are needed on only the initial render to serve to Googlebot (and share-bots). But the title tag is user facing and should get updated on every route change. This creates a unique situation, where you need to update a part of the DOM that isn't controlled by React. The following listing shows you what to add.

Listing 10.15 Add title update code to Detail—src/components/detail.jsx

```
class Detail extends React.Component {
  // ...more code
  componentDidMount() {
```

```
    document.getElementsByTagName('title')[0].innerHTML =
    ➥ Detail.createTitle(this.props);
  }

  componentDidUpdate() {
    document.getElementsByTagName ('title')[0].innerHTML =
    ➥ Detail.createTitle(this.props);
  }
//...more code
}
```

Add a call to update the contents of the title tag in both componentDidUpdate and componentDidMount.

This kind of situation is rare, but when it occurs, using direct DOM access is fine. Just make sure to ask yourself, "Can I do this the React way?" before accessing the DOM.

To practice the techniques from this section, you can add metatags and titles to other top-level React components in the project. This strategy can be applied anytime you need to have server-generated information based on a top-level component (for example, generating route-specific headers).

10.3 Multiple sources of truth

When building isomorphic apps, you may run into cases where you can get the same information from the server and the browser. Common examples are user agent and locale, which are both sent as headers to the server but can also be accessed in the browser. How do you approach handling these situations?

Simple: pick a single source of truth. The first place your app runs code is the server, so if possible, use the server as the source of truth.

10.3.1 User agent best practices

I've worked with video for most of my career, and one of the challenges with video on the web is that it isn't standardized at all. For example, every browser supports a different set of video-encoding options. Safari (desktop and mobile) support different options than Chrome, Firefox, and Microsoft Edge. Although there are some built-in ways to handle this problem (with the `<video>` tag and feature detection via `canPlayType`), in custom high-performance video players, you often have to handle the differences on your own.

This is one of the few places I've run into building web apps that consistently requires user agent detection. Although user agent detection is best avoided, it's worth covering here in case you do run into a similar situation. I have two principles to follow when using user agent detection in an isomorphic app:

1. *Always use a single source of truth*—This means parsing the user agent on the server and passing it down to the browser.
2. *Use the broadest definition possible*—Rather than ask, "Is this an iPhone?" ask, "Is this a mobile device?" It's extremely rare to need to know a specific version of a device category or specific browser.

10.3.2 Parse the user agent

You need two things to parse out the user agent into a usable value for your application. First, you need to add an action and reducer. Second, you need to pass the `User-Agent` header information into that action on the server. You'll want to switch to branch chapter-10.3 (`git checkout chapter-10.3`), which has all the code from the previous sections.

Listing 10.16 shows the code you need to add to the project: a new action in a new action file called app-action-creators.es6. This action will take in the request headers and parse them into a usable object using a third-party library. I've picked ua-parser-js here, but you could use any library of your choice that's isomorphic (https://github.com/faisalman/ua-parser-js). Make sure to install this package if you're following along:

```
$ npm install ua-parser-js
```

Listing 10.16 User agent action—src/shared/app-action-creators.es6

```
import UAParser from 'ua-parser-js';

export const PARSE_USER_AGENT = 'PARSE_USER_AGENT';

export function parseUserAgent(requestHeaders) {
  const uaParser = new UAParser();
  let userAgentObject;
  if (requestHeaders && requestHeaders['User-Agent']) {
    const userAgent = requestHeaders['User-Agent'];
    uaParser.setUA(userAgent);
    userAgentObject = uaParser.getResult(userAgent);
  }
  return {
    userAgent: userAgentObject,
    type: PARSE_USER_AGENT
  };
}

export default {
  parseUserAgent
};
```

- Include the user agent parser library. (import UAParser)
- Construct new instance of user agent parser. (const uaParser)
- Make sure there are request headers and a user agent request header. (if statement)
- Pass current user agent string into parser. (setUA)
- Create the object that represents the user agent. (getResult)
- Return the action to the reducer. (return)

After you've created the action code, it's time to add the reducer. The following listing shows the code you need to add to a new file called app-reducer.es6.

Listing 10.17 User agent reducer—src/shared/app-reducer.es6

```
import {
  PARSE_USER_AGENT
} from './app-action-creators.es6';
```

```
export default function app(state = {}, action) {
  switch (action.type) {
    case PARSE_USER_AGENT:
      return {
        ...state,
        userAgent: action.userAgent ?
                      action.userAgent : state.userAgent
      };
    default:
      return state;
  }
}
```

Set userAgent from the action on the state (if user agent on action is undefined, use previous state).

Don't forget that in order to wire up Redux actions and reducers, you have to add the reducer to the init-redux file. The following listing shows you the code to add.

Listing 10.18 Importing the app reducer—src/shared/init-redux.es6

```
import app from './app-reducer.es6';

export default function (initialStore = {}) {
  const reducer = combineReducers({
    products,
    cart,
    app
  });
  //...more code
```

Include app reducer.

Add reducer to combineReducers statement.

Now that your Redux business logic is in place, you need to call this action from the view. Rather than add this action to every single top-level component, you can add it to the root component (App). Remember, this component is loaded by the topmost route in your app. The following listing shows the code to add to app.jsx.

Listing 10.19 Calling `parseUserAgent` from the view—src/components/app.jsx

```
import {
      parseUserAgent
   } '../shared/app-action-creators.es6';

class App extends React.Component {

  static prefetchActions(params, store, request) {
    return [
      parseUserAgent.bind(null, request.headers)
    ];
  }
```

Import the action from action creators file.

Return the action and bind request headers (on the browser, it'll be empty, on the server, you'll pass in the request object).

Finally, you need to add code to the middleware to pass in the request to the `prefetchActions` function. This will happen in the `flattenStaticFunction`. Listing 10.20 shows the code to add.

Listing 10.20 Pass request to `prefetchActions`—src/middleware/renderView.jsx

```
function flattenStaticFunction(
  renderProps, staticFnName, store = {}, request
) {
  let results = renderProps.components.map((component) => {
    if (component) {
      if (component.displayName &&
        component.displayName.toLowerCase().indexOf('connect') > -1
      ) {
        if (component.WrappedComponent[staticFnName]) {
          return component.WrappedComponent[staticFnName](
            renderProps.params,
            store,
            request
          );
        }
      } else if (component[staticFnName]) {
        return component[staticFnName](
          renderProps.params,
          store,
          request
        );
      }
    }
    return [];
  });

  results = results.reduce((flat, toFlatten) => {}, []);

  return results;
}

export default function renderView(req, res, next) {
  const matchOpts = {};
  const handleMatchResult = (error, redirectLocation, renderProps) => {
    if (!error && !redirectLocation && renderProps) {
      const store = initRedux();
      const actions = flattenStaticFunction(
        renderProps,
        'prefetchActions',
        null,
        req
      );
      //... more code
```

Annotations:
- **Make the request object a property passed into flattenStaticFunction.** (store = {}, request)
- **Pass request object into static function being called (functions that don't use it will ignore it because it's the last parameter).** (both `request` arguments)
- **This use case of flattenStaticFunction doesn't require the store state to work, pass null instead.** (null)
- **Make sure to pass req object into flattenStaticFunction when you call it for prefetchActions.** (req)

Now you have a user agent parsed into your app state that doesn't get overridden on the browser. Set a breakpoint in the browser to see how the user agent will be undefined in the reducer and not get overridden. Figure 10.6 shows setting a breakpoint in the app-reducer.es6 code and inspecting the action value to see how it isn't set at all on the browser.

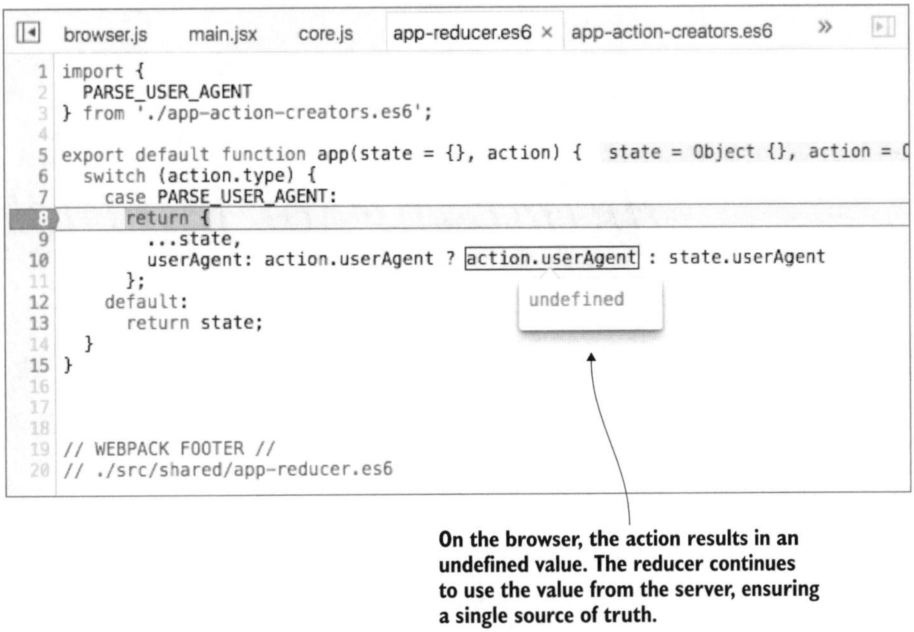
browser.js
main.jsx
core.js
app-reducer.es6
app-action-creators.es6
import {
PARSE_USER_AGENT
} from './app-action-creators.es6';
export default function app(state = {}, action) {
state = Object {}, action =
switch (action.type) {
case PARSE_USER_AGENT:
return {
...state,
userAgent: action.userAgent ? action.userAgent : state.userAgent
};
default:
return state;
}
}
// WEBPACK FOOTER //
// ./src/shared/app-reducer.es6
undefined
On the browser, the action results in an undefined value. The reducer continues to use the value from the server, ensuring a single source of truth.

Figure 10.6 Set a breakpoint in the app-reducer.es6 and inspect the `action.userAgent` value.

Summary

In this chapter, you learned to handle the environment-specific edge cases that come up in a real-world application. You also learned to handle errors properly.

- Handle browser- and server-only code using webpack to create the `process.env` object.
- Implement server and browser-specific routes as well as apply the same kind of logic to environment routes (development versus production).
- Determine SEO metadata tags and the page title on a per-route basis using static methods.
- Parse the user agent on the server and use it as the source of truth in the browser.

11 Optimizing for production

This chapter covers

- Optimizing performance for the browser
- Using streaming on Node.js to improve server performance
- Using caching to improve performance on the server
- Handling user sessions via cookies on the server and browser

Rather than doing a deep dive into any specific topic, this chapter covers a range of topics that will make your app perform better and improve your end-user experience. This includes React performance, Node.js performance, and various caching strategies. The last section of this chapter covers handling cookies in an isomorphic application and the trade-offs that this creates with some of the caching strategies.

This chapter continues to use the complete-isomorphic-example repo on GitHub. It can be found at http://mng.bz/8gV8. The first section uses the code on branch chapter-11.1 (`git checkout chapter-11.1`). You can find the completed code for the chapter on the chapter-11.complete branch (`git checkout chapter-11-complete`).

To run each branch, make sure to use the following:

```
$ npm install
$ npm start
```

11.1 Browser performance optimizations

As I've spent more time with React, I've discovered that although it's fast out of the box, in complex apps you'll run into performance problems. To keep your React web app performant, you need to keep performance in mind as your app grows and adds more-complex feature interactions. Two specific cases start to cause performance issues as your app grows:

- *The size of your JavaScript*—The next section covers using webpack chunking to reduce bundle size.
- *Unnecessary renders*—In section 11.1.2, we'll go over the basics of using `shouldComponentRender` to reduce unnecessary renders.

11.1.1 Webpack chunking

I've often experienced the following scenario when building an app of any kind: my app starts out small, and the JavaScript assets are small enough that they load quickly. Over time, I add features, get lazy about reviewing the size of included packages, and generally don't pay attention to bundle size. (Code base size management is especially difficult on larger teams.) Then one day I check the load time of the page and realize my JavaScript file has become too big! It's affecting the overall load time of the app. Cue freak-out moment!

Thankfully, webpack provides a way to solve this problem, by breaking the code into multiple bundles that can be loaded as they're needed. The next two diagrams walk you through this concept.

NOTE If you're using React Router 4, check out appendix C for information on code splitting with webpack.

Figure 11.1 demonstrates how the app is currently compiling. All the code is being pulled together into a single output file. This file is being referenced in html.jsx.

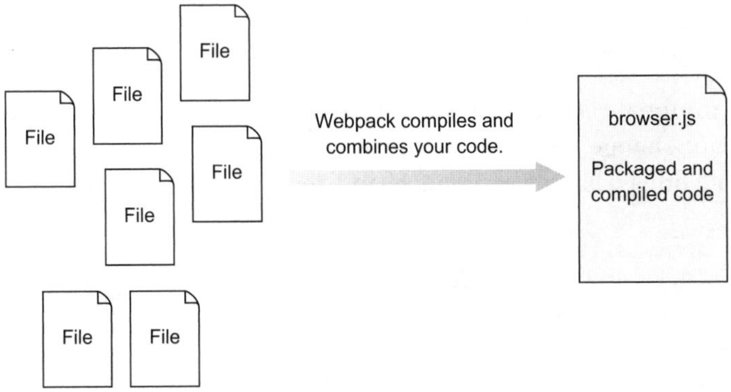
File
File
File
File
File
File
File
File
Webpack compiles and combines your code.
browser.js
Packaged and compiled code

Figure 11.1 The default behavior of webpack results in a single file that represents all your code.

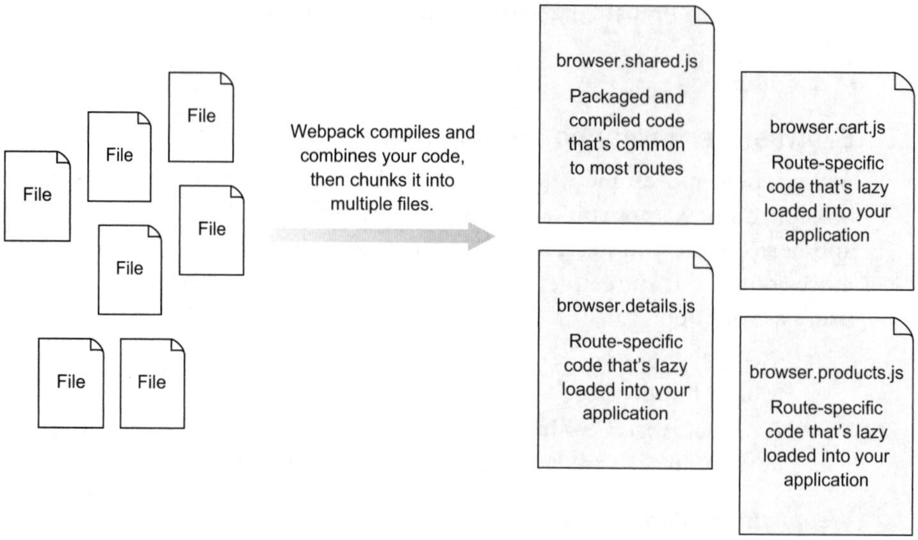
File
File
File
File
File
File
File
Webpack compiles and combines your code, then chunks it into multiple files.
browser.shared.js
Packaged and compiled code that's common to most routes
browser.cart.js
Route-specific code that's lazy loaded into your application
browser.details.js
Route-specific code that's lazy loaded into your application
browser.products.js
Route-specific code that's lazy loaded into your application

Figure 11.2 Using code splitting, webpack outputs multiple files that can be dynamically loaded. The specific files will vary by app.

Figure 11.2 shows what you'll implement in this section. The code is still combined in webpack's compilation step, but it's then split into multiple JavaScript files. This is configured by you in code (not in webpack configuration).

To make this happen in your code, you need to update the way you import the routes. This process has three steps:

1. Add Babel plugins that will handle dynamic import on the Node.js server and via the Babel loader in your webpack configuration.
2. Add dynamic import to `sharedRoutes`.
3. Enable chunks in webpack with `chunkFilename`.

Installing and adding the new Babel plugins is the first step. Run the following commands in your terminal:

```
$ npm install --save-dev babel-plugin-syntax-dynamic-import
$ npm install --save-dev babel-plugin-dynamic-import-node
```

Then you need to update .babelrc. Listing 11.1 shows the updates that are needed. This is a significant change from the old version because you need different plugins for webpack and Node.js. Later you'll make sure that webpack points at the webpack env config.

Listing 11.1 Add plugins to .babelrc

```
{
  "presets": ["es2015", "react"],
  "env": {                                    <-- Add an env config option.
```

```
    "webpack-env": {
      "plugins": [
        "syntax-dynamic-import"
      ]
    },
    "development": {
      "plugins": [
        "syntax-dynamic-import",
        "dynamic-import-node"
      ]
    }
  },
  "plugins": [
    "transform-es2015-destructuring",
    "transform-es2015-parameters",
    "transform-object-rest-spread"
  ]
}
```

Add two environments: development (the default) and webpack-env for webpack builds.

For webpack, add only the plugin that allows dynamic import syntax.

For node, both the syntax and implementation plugins are required.

The original plugins array is left intact. Env options are merged with any default options.

The main goal of the Babel config change is that it splits your Babel config into two versions, one for the server (development) and one for webpack (webpack-env).

Next, you have to add a dynamic import. Listing 11.2 shows how to create statements that tell webpack to create a code chunk. This replaces the `import` statements for components in `sharedRoutes`. For now, you'll apply this pattern to a single route: `cart`. But in production apps, I recommend you apply this based on your own traffic patterns (chunk your highest traffic routes separately from your low-traffic routes, or chunk admin or other authenticated pages separately from public ones). Additionally, this code could be abstracted and made reusable for a production use case—but for this example, it illustrates the changes in a clear, concise way.

Listing 11.2 Configure code chunking—src/shared/sharedRoutes.jsx

Remove the old import statement for the cart component. I've commented here to demonstrate it gets removed, but you can delete it.

```
// remove import Cart from '../components/cart';
<Route path="/" component={App} onChange={onChange}>
<IndexRoute component={Products} />
<Route
      path="cart"
     getComponent={(location, cb) => {
       import(
        /* webpackChunkName: "cart" */
        /* webpackMode: "lazy" */
        './../components/cart')
      .then((module) => {
        cb(null, module.default);
        onChange(null, {
          routes: [
            {component: module.default}
          ]
```

Use the getComponent prop.

Webpack reads these comments and uses them to determine how to handle the code chunk.

Use async import. You pass the path to the cart component into it.

Async import behaves like a Promise. Handle a success: take the loaded module and pass it to the React Router callback.

The component isn't yet loaded when onChange is called. By manually calling onChange, the data will still be loaded.

```
        });
      })
      .catch(error =>                                    <-- Add error handling.
        console.log('An error occurred while loading the component', error)
      );
    }}
  />
```

You'll notice that you both replaced the default import with a dynamic load and moved that dynamic load into React Router's `getComponent` property. The code will be lazy loaded (`webpackMode: lazy`); it won't be loaded until the user navigates to this route. This is advantageous because it prevents unnecessary loading of code for features that the user hasn't yet accessed.

Finally, it's useful to name your webpack chunks. This is configurable in the webpack configuration file. The following listing shows you how to add this property to your webpack config file.

Listing 11.3 Named webpack chunks—webpack.config.js

```
module.exports = {
  // ... other config options
  output: {
    path: __dirname + '/src/',
    filename: "browser.js",
    chunkFilename: "browser-[name].js"     <-- Add the chunkFilename option. Use [name] to indicate a dynamic naming of the compiled js file for each chunk.
  },
  module: {}
};
```

In the next section, we'll look at one way to improve React performance in situations where React's base performance isn't enough.

11.1.2 Should component render

As your app grows, you'll run into situations where your components are running through their render cycles unnecessarily (I've seen situations where re-renders get into the tens of seconds). If this is happening and causing a measurable impact on your application, use `shouldComponentRender` to limit the number of renders.

> **Performance measurement tools**
>
> Before making performance improvements, you should always profile your application. Record the performance metric you're measuring in the current version of your app. Then make any performance updates. Finally, measure the same performance metric to confirm that your changes had a positive impact.
>
> To get started profiling web apps, you should become an expert on the Chrome DevTools performance panels: http://mng.bz/a9wf.

The best way to implement `shouldComponentRender` without causing yourself later pain and headaches is to make sure your properties are being created with immutable patterns. In this application, this is already being handled in the Redux reducers. By creating immutable objects, the object references change, and a shallow comparison becomes enough to check whether two objects are different from one another. Listing 11.4 shows you how to do this in the context of a Detail Page component. Add the code from the listing to detail.jsx.

> **WARNING** Using `shouldComponentRender` can send you down a rabbit hole of despair. Use it sparingly and use it wisely. (You can end up with complex, large functions that are calculating whether to render. That's bad and should be avoided.)

Listing 11.4 Block renders, `shouldComponentRender`—src/components/detail.jsx

```
componentDidMount() {}

shouldComponentUpdate(nextProps) {
  if (this.props.name === nextProps.name &&
      this.props.description === nextProps.description &&
      this.props.details === nextProps.details &&
      this.props.price === nextProps.price &&
      this.props.thumbnail === nextProps.thumbnail) {
    return false;
  }
  return true;
}

componentDidUpdate() {}
```

- Check each property to make sure it hasn't changed.
- Return false if nothing has changed; this prevents the component from rendering.
- Return true if there have been changes; this allows the normal render to execute.

This will work for many situations but it's not without gotchas. One problem is this implementation requires you to write many checks based on the implementation details of the properties. You could abstract the concept of this code—comparing each property on `this.props/nextProps`—into a function that can be reused for many components. The online article "Performance Optimisations for React Applications" by Alex Reardon (http://mng.bz/QJk3) covers using `shouldComponentUpdate` with additional detail. It includes a sample implementation of an abstracted deep equals function that does only reference checks. Check out the code on GitHub (http://mng.bz/q7yU).

Finally, if you need `shouldComponentUpdate` to only do a shallow comparison on both the `props` object and the `state` object, you can use React Pure Component. This is a class provided by React. You can find the docs at https://reactjs.org/docs/react-api.html#react.purecomponent.

Unfortunately, a deeper dive into React performance optimizations is outside the context of this book. Fortunately, many other great resources are available on this topic! Here are some that will take you deeper:

- *React Perf Tools*—https://facebook.github.io/react/docs/perf.html. Use these tools to profile your application. Don't forget to run your app in production mode when you're doing performance testing! (These are being deprecated for React 16.)
- *React Performance Overview*—http://mng.bz/l5J8 and http://mng.bz/eWHH provide good places to start with React performance.
- *More on* `shouldComponentRender`—http://jamesknelson.com/should-i-use-shouldcomponentupdate/ goes in depth on why you should avoid using `shouldComponentRender`.

In the next section, we'll look at server-side performance improvements that can be used to have a positive impact on your Node.js application.

11.2 Server performance optimizations

In an isomorphic app, your server's performance is just as important as the browser performance. When we first started working with React at work, it greatly simplified building our pages for search bots. But we quickly realized that React's server render was slower than we'd have liked. Creating a fully rendered string output for many components takes time and is a process-blocking task on the server. This limits the number of requests per second that your server is able to handle.

In the rest of this section, and in the caching section, I'll discuss strategies you can use to improve your server performance times:

- Using streaming concepts to respond to requests sooner
- Adding connection pooling to manage multiple HTTP requests from the server

The first thing you'll add is the ability for your page response to be streamed to the browser. If you're following along and want to switch to this section's GitHub branch, check out chapter-11.2 (`git checkout chapter-11.2`).

11.2.1 Streaming React

If your main goal is to improve time to first byte and allow the DOM to start processing as soon as possible, streaming your rendered page response can be a good solution. Node.js streams are a way to represent large amounts of data and deliver it over time. Rather than wait for an entire HTML page to download, the page can be delivered in chunks over time (more info on streams at http://mng.bz/s91m).

By turning the server response into a stream, you improve the speed at which the browser can begin downloading and displaying the HTML. Listing 11.5 shows how to use the react-dom-stream library to render streams instead of strings. Add the code to renderView.jsx. You also need to run the following command before this code will work:

```
$ npm i --save react-dom-stream
```

You can find more information about this package at https://github.com/aickin/react-dom-stream. Note that it hasn't been fully upgraded to work with the latest

React, so you may not want to use it in production, but it illustrates the streaming concept well.

Listing 11.5 Set up streaming library—src/middleware/renderView.jsx

```
import React from 'react';
import {
  renderToString
} from 'react-dom-stream/server';
import { Provider } from 'react-redux';

const streamApp = renderToString(
  <Provider store={store}>
    <RouterContext routes={routes} {...renderProps} />
  </Provider>
);

const streamHTML = renderToString(
  <HTML
    html={streamApp}
    serverState={stringifiedServerState}
    metatags={seoTags}
    title={title}
  />
);

streamHTML.pipe(res, { end: false });
streamHTML.on('end', () => {
  res.end();
});
```

- Instead of importing the React version of renderToString, use the streaming library's version.
- The initial render of the app components gets converted to the creation of a stream. Rename the variable for better context.
- React DOM Stream supports nested streams in JSX. Now we pass the stream into HTML.jsx.
- Instead of responding to the request directly, the stream library pipes the render into the response.
- Add a listener for the end of the stream.
- Close the response.

11.2.2 Connection pooling

In addition to using React, we also use GraphQL at work. This enables us to gather data from many microservices. More importantly, it also allows us to request the data we need for our views rather than use REST APIs with predetermined responses. Think of it as a front end for your back-end REST services. You can learn more about GraphQL at http://graphql.org.

This is a powerful setup, but GraphQL makes a lot of network calls. We ran into an issue of network calls that were timing out. The services we were talking to didn't show any time-outs; they showed fast response times. After much investigation, the team figured out that we were making so many requests that the call stack was causing some of the requests to time out. The call stack became a block, and requests were timing out before they had a chance to receive any response.

This can also happen in your React isomorphic app. If a page of your app makes a lot of network calls for a specific view, you might run into this slow network request problem. One strategy to fix this is to enable connection pooling on your Node.js server.

The solution to this problem in Node.js is to create a permanent connection pool to reduce the cost of opening connections. A *connection pool* guarantees that there are always available socket connections in your Node.js app. This saves time when making a request, because opening a socket takes time (for additional info, see the blog post at www.madhur.co.in/blog/2016/09/05/nodejs-connection-pooling.html). The following listing shows how to add this option to the server.

Listing 11.6 Enable connection pooling—src/app.es6

```
import http from 'http';
import bodyParser from 'body-parser';
import renderViewMiddleware from './middleware/renderView';

http.Agent({
  keepAlive: true,
  keepAliveMsecs: 1500,
  maxFreeSockets: 1024
});
```

Import the http module.

Before the rest of the code on the server, setting the options for http.Agent.keepAlive: true tells the server to reuse connections. The other options can be adjusted to fit your use case.

You could also use GraphQL, which will greatly reduce the number of network calls you make. But that's a topic for another book.

NODE PERFORMANCE

This isn't a book about Node.js implementation and performance, but lots of good resources are available if you want to learn more about this topic. Here are some places to get started:

- *Tips from Nginx on optimizing Node.js apps*—www.nginx.com/blog/5-performance-tips-for-node-js-applications/
- *Best practices for using Express in production*—https://expressjs.com/en/advanced/best-practice-performance.html
- *Node profiling tools*—https://nodejs.org/en/docs/guides/simple-profiling/
- *Netflix deep dive into flame profiling Node apps*—https://medium.com/netflix-tech-blog/node-js-in-flames-ddd073803aa4

11.3 Caching

Another powerful server performance tool is caching. I've employed caching in different forms, including edge caching, in-memory caching, and saving views in a Redis (a NoSQL database) persisted cache. Each of these strategies has trade-offs, so it's important to understand what these are and then pick the right strategy for your use case. Table 11.1 lists caching options.

Table 11.1 Comparing caching options

	SEO	User sessions
In-memory	✓	✓
Persisted storage	✓	(Higher overhead, but possible)
Edge caching	✓	

11.3.1 Caching on the server: in-memory caching

The easiest (and most naïve) solution for caching involves saving components directly in memory. For simple apps, you can achieve this by using a basic LRU cache (size-limited) and stringifying your components after they're rendered. Figure 11.3 shows a

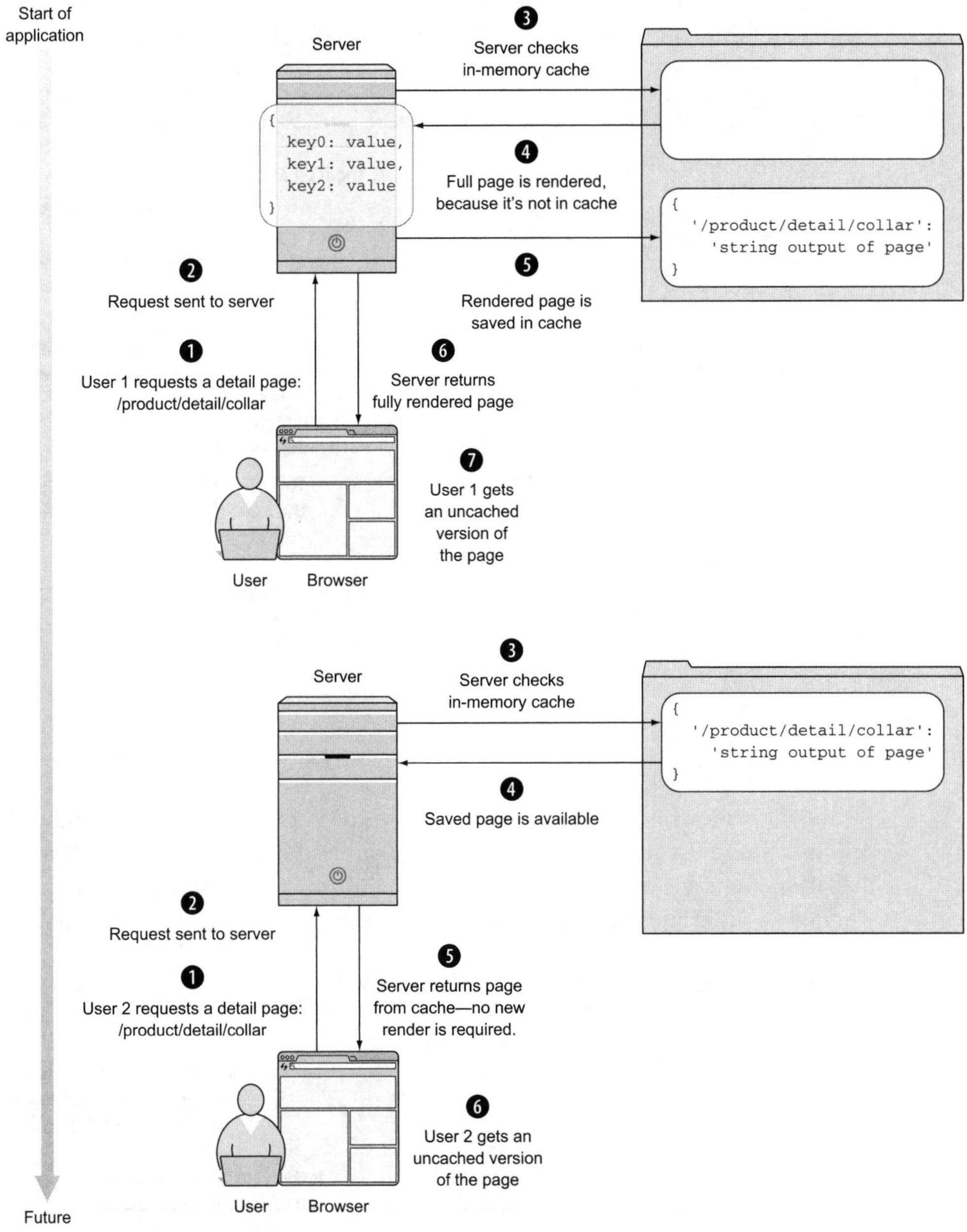

Start of application
Server
3 Server checks in-memory cache
{ key0: value, key1: value, key2: value }
4 Full page is rendered, because it's not in cache
{ '/product/detail/collar': 'string output of page' }
5 Rendered page is saved in cache
2 Request sent to server
1 User 1 requests a detail page: /product/detail/collar
6 Server returns fully rendered page
7 User 1 gets an uncached version of the page
User
Browser
Server
3 Server checks in-memory cache
{ '/product/detail/collar': 'string output of page' }
4 Saved page is available
2 Request sent to server
1 User 2 requests a detail page: /product/detail/collar
5 Server returns page from cache—no new render is required.
6 User 2 gets an uncached version of the page
User
Browser
Future

Figure 11.3 In-memory caching allows some requests to benefit from faster response times.

timeline of using an in-memory cache. The first user to load a page gets a fully rendered (and slower) version of the page. This is also saved in the in-memory cache. All subsequent users get the cached version, until that page gets pushed out of the cache because the cache filled up.

The following listing shows how to add a simple caching module (abstracting this code will make it easier to update caching strategies to match your future needs). You should add this code to the new cache.es6 file in the shared directory.

Listing 11.7 Add an LRU in memory cache—src/shared/cache.es6

```
import lru from 'lru-cache';

// maxAge is in ms
const cache = lru({
  maxAge: 300000,
  max: 500000000000,
  length: (n) => {
    // n = item passed in to be saved (value)
    return n.length * 100;
  }
});

export const set = (key, value) => {
  cache.set(key, value);
};

export const get = (key) => {
  return cache.get(key);
};

export default {
  get,
  set
};
```

Annotations:
- Import the lru cache.
- Create the lru cache.
- maxAge sets a time-based expiration for values stored in the cache.
- max is the total allowed length of all items in the cache.
- length is the individual max allowed length for each value added.
- This is a public set method that sets the key/value pair on the cache.
- This is a public get method that retrieves a value based on a key from the cache.

Listing 11.8 shows how to take advantage of the caching module in renderView.jsx. Add its code to the module. Note that I recommend using either the caching logic or the streaming logic, but not both at the same time. If you want to cache and stream, you need a different streaming implementation than the one shown in this chapter.

Listing 11.8 Save and fetch cached pages—src/middleware/renderView.jsx

```
import cache from '../shared/cache.es6';

//..other code

const cachedPage = cache.get(req.url);
if (cachedPage) {
  return res.send(cachedPage);
}
```

Annotations:
- Try to retrieve the value from the cache by using the cache module from listing 11.7.
- If the value exists, use it to respond to the request.

```
const store = initRedux();
//...more code
Promise.all(promises).then(() => {
  //...more code
  cache.set(req.url, `<!DOCTYPE html>${html}`);
  return res.send(`<!DOCTYPE html>${html}`);
})
```

If a full page render is required, save the rendered page before responding to the request.

This strategy will work, but it has some problems:

- This solution is simple, but what happens when the use cases get more complex? What happens as you start to add users? Or multiple languages? Or you have tens of thousands of pages? This methodology doesn't scale well to these use cases.
- Writing to memory is a blocking task in Node.js, which means that if you're trying to optimize for performance by using a cache, you're trading one problem for another.
- Finally, if you're using a distributed scaling strategy to run your servers (which is common these days), the cache applies to only a single box or container (if using Docker). In this case, your server instances can't share a common cache.

Next, we'll look at another strategy, caching with Redis, which will allow the caching to be done asynchronously and nonblocking. We'll also look at using a smarter caching implementation to cache individual components, which scales better for more-complex applications.

11.3.2 Caching on the server: persisted storage

The first isomorphic React app I worked on was written before Redux and React Router were stable community best-choice libraries, so we home-rolled a lot of the code. Combine this decision with React being slow on the server, and we needed a solution that would speed up server renders.

What we implemented was string storage of full pages in Redis. But storing full pages in Redis has significant trade-offs for larger sites. We had the potential for millions of entries to end up stored in Redis. Because full stringified HTML pages add up pretty fast, we were using quite a bit of space.

Thankfully, the community has come up with improvements on this idea since then. Walmart Labs put out a library called electrode-react-ssr-caching that's easy to use to cache your server-side renders. This library is powerful for a couple of reasons:

- It comes with a profiler that will tell you which components are most expensive on the server. That allows you to cache only the components you need to.
- It provides a way to template components so you can cache the rendered components and insert the properties later.

In the long run, because of the number of pages we serve and the percentage of them that are served with 100% public-facing content, we ended up moving to an edge-caching strategy. But your use case may benefit from the Walmart Labs approach.

11.3.3 CDN/edge strategies

Edge caching is the solution we currently use for our isomorphic React app at work. This is due to some business logic needing to expire content on demand (when things change at other points in the system, as in a CMS tool). Modern CDNs such as Fastly provide this capability out of the box and make it much easier to manage TTLs (time to live) and to force-expire web pages. Figure 11.4 illustrates how this works.

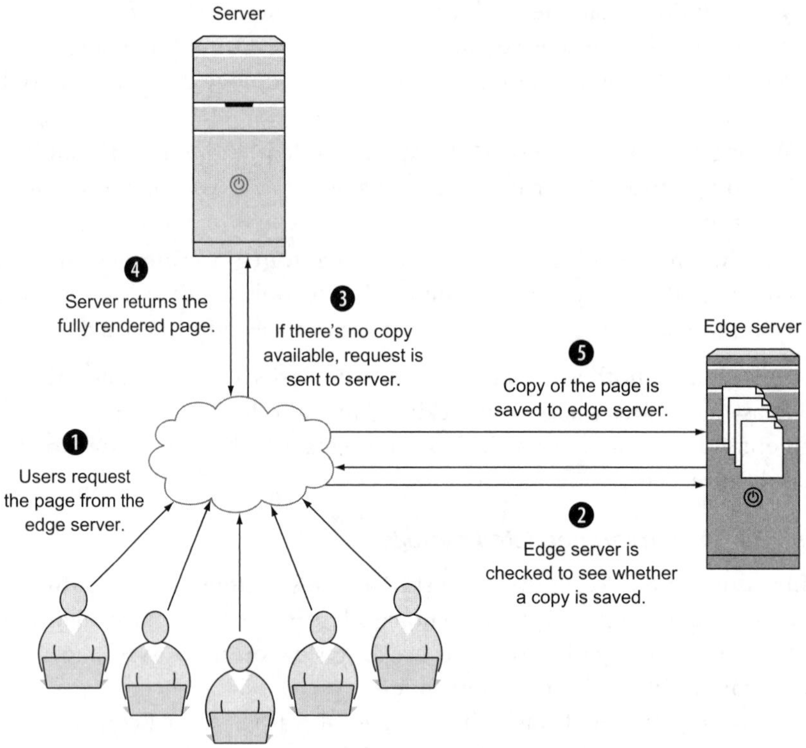
Server
4
Server returns the fully rendered page.
3
If there's no copy available, request is sent to server.
Edge server
5
Copy of the page is saved to edge server.
1
Users request the page from the edge server.
2
Edge server is checked to see whether a copy is saved.

Figure 11.4 Adding an edge server moves the caching in front of the server.

Showing you how to implement this is beyond the scope of this book. If you have public-facing content that drives SEO (e-commerce, video sites, blogs, and so forth), you'll definitely want a CDN in your stack.

One caveat with this approach is that it complicates user session management. The next section explores user sessions and covers the trade-offs with various caching strategies.

11.4 User session management

Modern web applications use cookies in the browser almost without exception. Even if your main product isn't directly using cookies, any ads, tracking, or other third-party tools that you use on your site will take advantage of cookies. Cookies let the web app know that the same person has come back over time. Figure 11.5 illustrates how this works.

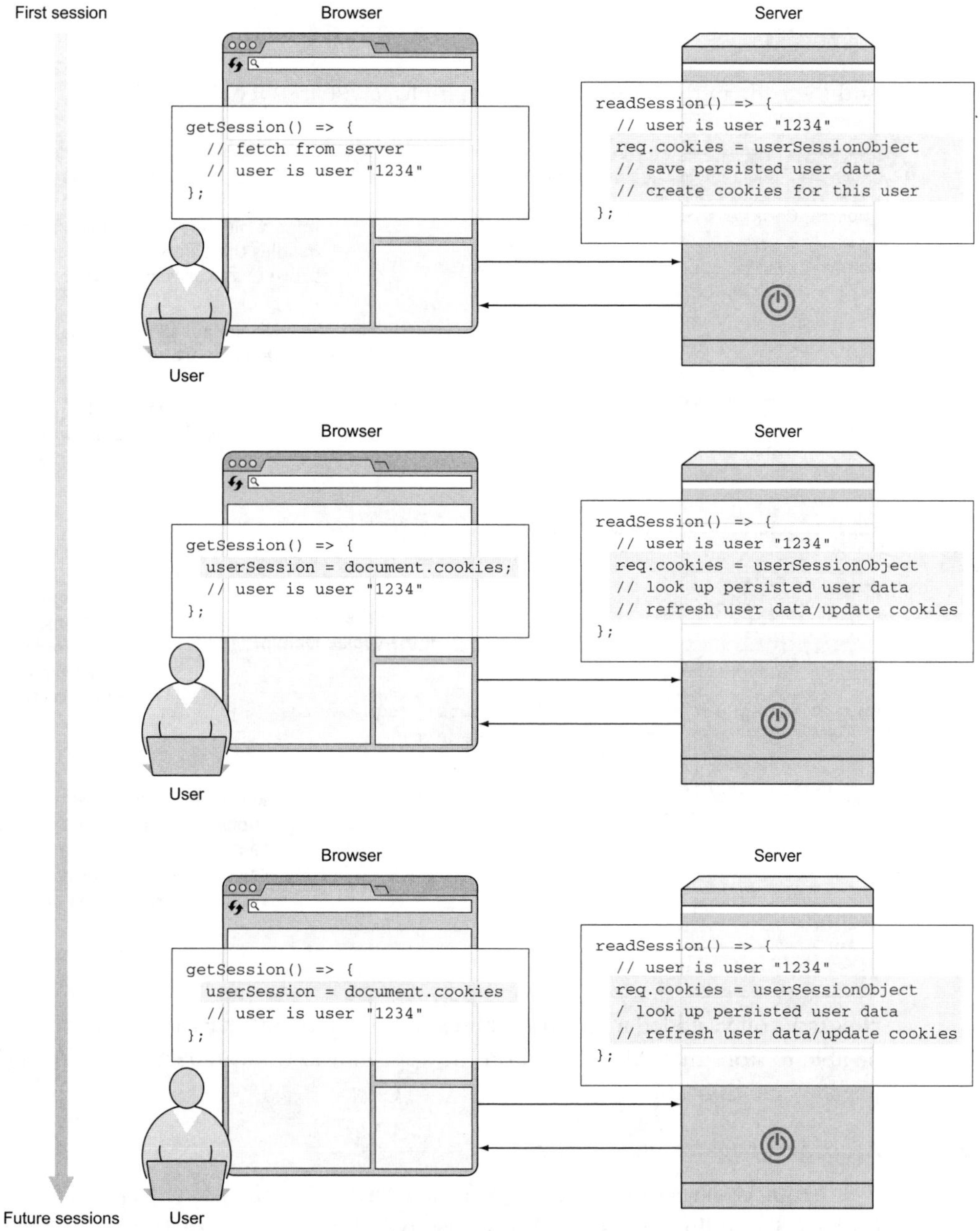
First session
Browser
Server
getSession() => {
// fetch from server
// user is user "1234"
};
readSession() => {
// user is user "1234"
req.cookies = userSessionObject
// save persisted user data
// create cookies for this user
};
User
Browser
Server
getSession() => {
userSession = document.cookies;
// user is user "1234"
};
readSession() => {
// user is user "1234"
req.cookies = userSessionObject
// look up persisted user data
// refresh user data/update cookies
};
User
Browser
Server
getSession() => {
userSession = document.cookies
// user is user "1234"
};
readSession() => {
// user is user "1234"
req.cookies = userSessionObject
/ look up persisted user data
// refresh user data/update cookies
};
Future sessions
User

Figure 11.5 Repeat visits by the same user on the server. Saving cookies lets you store information about the user that can be retrieved during future sessions.

Listing 11.9 shows an example module that handles both the browser and server cookie parsing for you. It uses Universal Cookie to help manage the cookies in both environments: www.npmjs.com/package/universal-cookie. You need to install this library for the code to work:

```
$ npm install --save universal-cookie
```

Add the code in this listing to a new module src/shared/cookies.es6.

Listing 11.9 Using isomorphic cookie module—src/shared/cookies.es6

```
import Cookie from 'universal-cookie';

const initCookie = (reqHeaders) => {
  let cookies;
  if (process.env.BROWSER) {
    cookies = new Cookie();
  } else if (reqHeaders.cookie) {
    cookies = new Cookie(reqHeaders.cookie);
  }
  return cookies;
};

export const get = (name, reqHeaders = {}) => {
  const cookies = initCookie(reqHeaders);
  if (cookies) {
    return cookies.get(name);
  }
};

export const set = (name, value, opts, reqHeaders = {}) => {
  const cookies = initCookie(reqHeaders);
  if (cookies) {
    return cookies.set(name, value, opts);
  }
};

export default {
  get,
  set
};
```

- Import the universal cookie library, which handles the differences between accessing browser and server cookies for you.
- Check the environment to determine whether reqHeaders are needed.
- If the headers have cookies, pass this into the cookie constructor.
- In the getter and setter functions, initialize the cookie object, passing in reqHeaders so it works on the server.
- Return the result of the cookie lookup.
- Return the result of setting the cookie. In addition to a name and value, you can pass in all standard cookie options. In most cases you'll call set from the browser.

Now that you've added a way to get and set cookies in both environments, you need to be able to store that information on the app state so you can access it in a consistent way in your application.

11.4.1 Accessing cookies universally

By fetching cookies with an action, you can standardize the way the app interacts with cookies. The following listing shows how to add a `storeUserId` action to fetch and store the user ID. Add this code to the app-action-creators file.

Listing 11.10 Accessing cookies on the server—src/shared/app-action-creators.es6

```
import UAParser from 'ua-parser-js';
import cookies from './cookies.es6';                        <-- Import the cookie module.

export const PARSE_USER_AGENT = 'PARSE_USER_AGENT';
export const STORE_USER_ID = 'STORE_USER_ID';              <-- Add a type for the new action.

export function parseUserAgent(requestHeaders) {}

export function storeUserId(requestHeaders) {              <-- Add the action, which takes in requestHeaders so that it works on the server.
  const userId = cookies.get('userId', requestHeaders);    <-- Pass the cookie name and requestHeaders to the cookie module.
  return {
    userId,                                                <-- Put the userId value on the action.
    type: STORE_USER_ID
  };
}

export default {
  parseUserAgent,
  storeUserId
};
```

Now you have access to the user ID in your application! It'll be fetched on the server and can be updated later in the browser as needed. You can apply this concept to any and all user session information. Managing user sessions as a whole is beyond the scope of this chapter.

11.4.2 Edge caching and users

When I first started building isomorphic applications, user management seemed simple. You used cookies to track user sessions in the browser as you would in a single-page application. Adding in the server complicates this, but you can read the cookies on the server. As you add in caching strategies, this becomes less straightforward.

Both the in-memory and persisted storage caching strategies work better with user sessions, as each user request still goes to the server, allowing the user's information to be gathered. You can add the user's identifying information into your cache key.

But edge caching doesn't work as well. That's because for each unique user, you must keep a unique copy of each page that has user-specific data on it. If you don't, you could end up showing user 1's information to user 2. That would be bad! Figure 11.6 illustrates this concept.

If you need to use edge caching and you have user data, you can employ one or more of the following strategies (depending on your content type and your traffic patterns):

- Create pages that have either user content or general consumption content (public). Then cache only the pages that are public on your edge servers.
- Save a cookie that tells the edge server whether the user is in an active user session. Use this information to determine whether to serve a cached page or send the request to the server (pass through).
- Serve pages with placeholder content (solid shapes that show where content will load) and then decide what content to load in the browser.

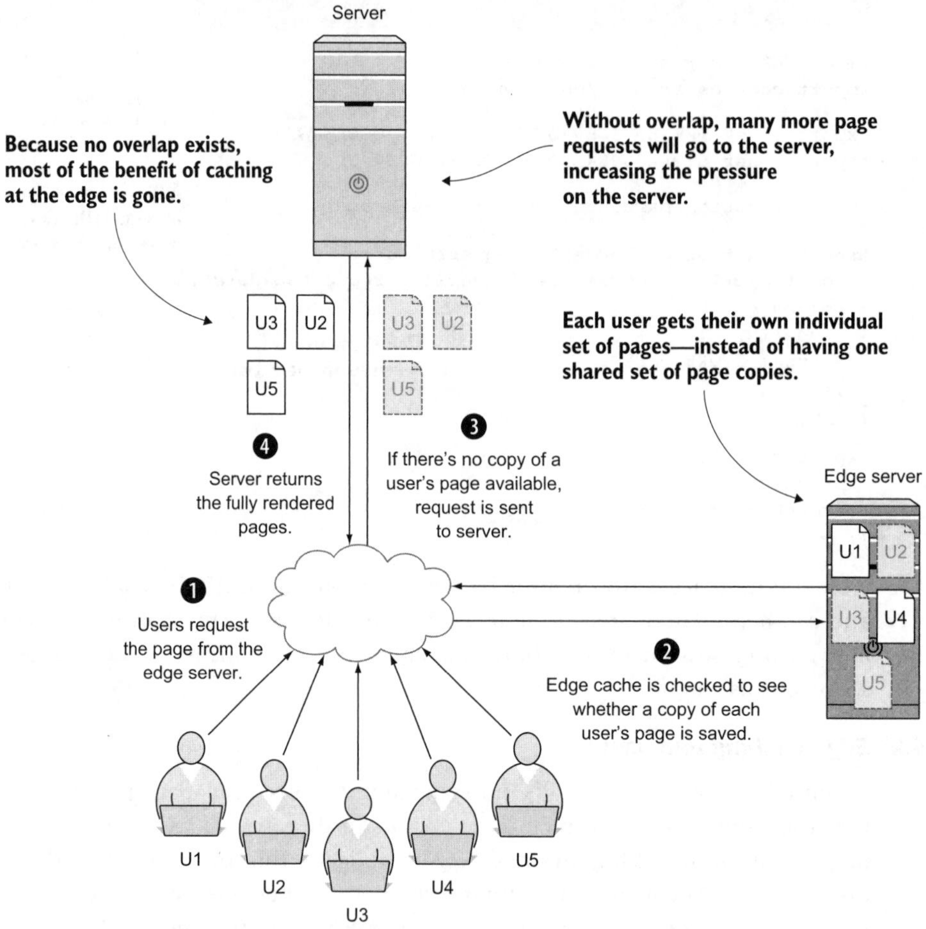
Server
Because no overlap exists, most of the benefit of caching at the edge is gone.
Without overlap, many more page requests will go to the server, increasing the pressure on the server.
U3
U2
U5
U3
U2
U5
Each user gets their own individual set of pages—instead of having one shared set of page copies.
4
Server returns the fully rendered pages.
3
If there's no copy of a user's page available, request is sent to server.
Edge server
U1
U2
U3
U4
U5
1
Users request the page from the edge server.
2
Edge cache is checked to see whether a copy of each user's page is saved.
U1
U2
U3
U4
U5

Figure 11.6 When the edge has to cache pages per user, the benefit of overlapping requests is lost.

Summary

This chapter covered several topics that will make your production isomorphic app run better, including performance and caching. You also learned about the complexities of adding certain types of caching to an isomorphic app that deals with user sessions.

- Use webpack chunking to improve browser performance.
- Optimize render cycles with `shouldComponentRender`.
- Improve the server's performance with streaming and connection pooling.
- Apply one of three caching strategies (in-memory, persisted, or edge) to improve render times on the server.
- Manage user sessions via cookies on the browser and the server.
- Understand the effects of caching strategies on user session management.

Part 4

Applying isomorphic architecture with other tools

React is a great choice for many types of front-end applications, but it's not the only choice. The skills taught in this book so far are a subset of what's out there to learn on your way to being a great front-end or full-stack developer. This last part covers additional technologies such as Angular and Ember and suggests how you can use them to build an isomorphic application. It also includes a brief chapter focused on additional skills and areas of expertise you should explore that will complement what you've learned in this book.

12 Other frameworks: implementing isomorphic without React

This chapter covers

- Using Ember's convention-over-configuration implementation to quickly implement a universal application
- Implementing the isomorphic parts of an Angular application with TypeScript
- Running an isomorphic app with Next.js, which gives you an out-of-the-box React implementation with server rendering built in

Each section in this chapter covers a framework that lets you get up and running with isomorphic rendering. This chapter doesn't teach you these other technologies, although it does provide links to resources if you want to dive deeper. Instead, each section highlights the key parts of each framework:

- Setting up and implementing server-side rendering in each framework
- Enabling hydration of the DOM with the server state in each framework
- Understanding the pros and cons to each approach

12.1 Blog example project

In each section of this chapter, you'll be working on the same sample application. Figure 12.1 shows the homepage view of the blog. It's a basic homepage with a header and a list of blog posts. Each blog post links to a Post Detail page, which shows the post body in full and a list of comments.

All code for this chapter is in its own GitHub repo at https://github.com/isomorphic-dev-js/chapter12-frameworks, which you can clone (`git clone https://github.com/isomorphic-dev-js/chapter12-frameworks`). There's a top-level folder for each section of this chapter and a folder for the data server that provides the stubbed APIs for all three apps:

- *angular2*—Code for section 12.2. This is a complete Angular app.
- *ember-universal*—Code for section 12.3. This is a complete Ember app.
- *nextjs*—Code for section 12.4. This is a complete isomorphic React app built with the Next.js framework.
- *server*—The code in this folder runs a simple data API.

12.1.1 UI and component breakdown

Before we get into the various isomorphic implementations, let's review how the blog works. It's made up of two routes: a home route (/) and a post detail route (/post). Figure 12.1 shows the homepage.

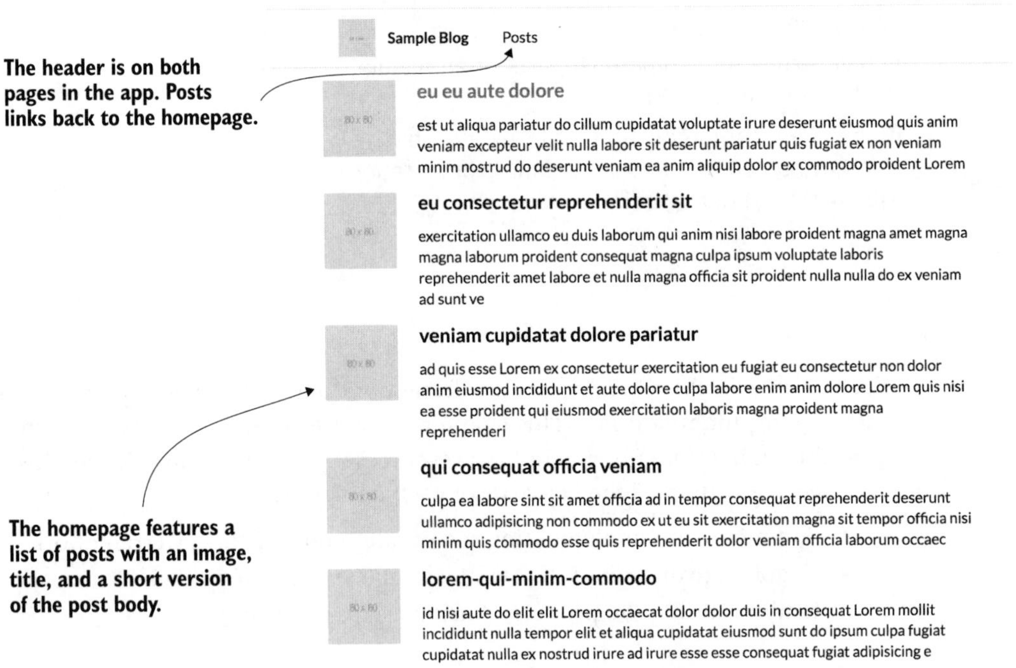
Sample Blog
Posts
The header is on both pages in the app. Posts links back to the homepage.
eu eu aute dolore
est ut aliqua pariatur do cillum cupidatat voluptate irure deserunt eiusmod quis anim veniam excepteur velit nulla labore sit deserunt pariatur quis fugiat ex non veniam minim nostrud do deserunt veniam ea anim aliquip dolor ex commodo proident Lorem
eu consectetur reprehenderit sit
exercitation ullamco eu duis laborum qui anim nisi labore proident magna amet magna magna laborum proident consequat magna culpa ipsum voluptate laboris reprehenderit amet labore et nulla magna officia sit proident nulla nulla do ex veniam ad sunt ve
veniam cupidatat dolore pariatur
ad quis esse Lorem ex consectetur exercitation eu fugiat eu consectetur non dolor anim eiusmod incididunt et aute dolore culpa labore enim anim dolore Lorem quis nisi ea esse proident qui eiusmod exercitation laboris magna proident magna reprehenderi
qui consequat officia veniam
culpa ea labore sint sit amet officia ad in tempor consequat reprehenderit deserunt ullamco adipisicing non commodo ex ut eu sit exercitation magna sit tempor officia nisi minim quis commodo esse quis reprehenderit dolor veniam officia laborum occaec
lorem-qui-minim-commodo
id nisi aute do elit elit Lorem occaecat dolor dolor duis in consequat Lorem mollit incididunt nulla tempor elit et aliqua cupidatat eiusmod sunt do ipsum culpa fugiat cupidatat nulla ex nostrud irure ad irure esse esse consequat fugiat adipisicing e
The homepage features a list of posts with an image, title, and a short version of the post body.

Figure 12.1 The homepage of the app that shows all the posts

The Post Detail page features the full post text with title and image.
Sample Blog
Posts
lorem-qui-minim-commodo
id nisi aute do elit elit Lorem occaecat dolor dolor duis in consequat Lorem mollit incididunt nulla tempor elit et aliqua cupidatat eiusmod sunt do ipsum culpa fugiat cupidatat nulla ex nostrud irure ad irure esse esse consequat fugiat adipisicing ex culpa et nulla deserunt ullamco aute magna et et nisi cillum velit culpa duis magna ut et deserunt exercitation fugiat commodo aliquip commodo sint esse deserunt ea qui ullamco qui qui culpa eiusmod deserunt eiusmod sit sunt aliquip consequat enim ea ullamco irure eiusmod et officia velit cillum laboris et aliquip reprehenderit dolor aliquip nostrud non ut reprehenderit ut in aute est anim amet minim exercitation velit esse cillum consequat exercitation commodo do ea enim et duis anim nisi quis veniam pariatur excepteur eu ullamco laborum occaecat reprehenderit aute aute minim aute nisi ad incididunt voluptate minim est ullamco consectetur incididunt nostrud exercitation cupidatat dolore consequat nisi consequat ipsum in non ex id Lorem cillum labore in proident esse in dolor consectetur labore do Lorem nulla officia et enim id ut exercitation aliquip cillum non et id magna in culpa enim non reprehenderit tempor occaecat amet reprehenderit ea reprehenderit aliquip duis do reprehenderit et aliquip anim exercitation laborum velit
Comments
enim dolor excepteur ea mollit ad deserunt
eu sint sunt elit amet ullamco ex reprehenderit do eiusmod exercitation dolore cillum dolor et ea est cupidatat reprehenderit ea dolore veniam ea labore mollit et eu dolor ullamco aute eu esse ex ut nisi exercitation ullamco eu dolore non ad consequat irure commodo est sunt officia laboris culpa occaecat laborum et commodo cupidatat nostrud
User: Juliet
id dolor pariatur nostrud consequat dolore culpa
tempor proident pariatur incididunt quis nostrud cupidatat dolor cillum irure
Below the post is the list of comments that have been made on this blog post. This includes the user's profile photo and name.

Figure 12.2 The Post Detail page with the corresponding comments

As you can see, the homepage is straightforward. A simple header has the Posts link that takes you back to the homepage. The list of posts is directly below the header. When you click any of the posts on the homepage, the app loads the corresponding Post Detail page. Figure 12.2 shows what this page looks like.

Now that you've seen what the app looks like, we'll go over the mock data server that provides the posts and comments data.

12.1.2 Shared stubbed data API

The repo includes a server that serves mock data for each of the sample apps. There are two data types in the blog app: posts and comments. To run the server (which needs to be running in order for the other apps to work), you should change into the server directory, run `npm install`, and then run the server:

```
$ cd server
$ npm install
$ npm start
```

After you've done that, you can fetch the mock data on the various endpoints provided:

- http://localhost:3535/posts
- http://localhost:3535/post/eu-eu-aute-dolore
- http://localhost:3535/post/1/comments

The mock data for these endpoints is provided by two JSON files that I've already provided in the repo. The following listing shows what an individual post looks like in posts.json.

Listing 12.1 Posts mock data—server/data/posts.json

```
[
  {
    "id": 1,                                          <- ID of post
    "image": "http://placehold.it/80x80",             <- Image for post
    "title": "eu eu aute dolore",                     <- Title of post
    "urlSlug": "eu-eu-aute-dolore",                   <- URL slug of post (title with dashes—posts can be looked up by urlSlug)
    "body": "est ut aliqua pariatur do cillum cupidatat voluptate irure
     deserunt eiusmod quis anim veniam excepteur velit nulla labore sit
     deserunt pariatur quis fugiat ex non veniam minim nostrud do deserunt
     veniam ea anim aliquip dolor ex commodo proident Lorem esse pariatur
     dolor elit non commodo commodo fugiat..."        <- Body of post
  },
  {},
  ...
]
```

To fetch all posts, you use the /posts endpoint. This is used on the homepage to display all the posts. The server can also get individual posts by fetching them with `urlSlug`, which allows the URLs to be readable. Individual posts are fetched on the Post Detail page.

In addition, you can fetch comments. The following listing shows the JSON for an individual comment. This code is already provided in the repo.

Listing 12.2 Comments mock data—server/data/comments.json

```
[
  {
    "message": "eu sint sunt elit amet ullamco ex
    ➥ reprehenderit do eiusmod exercitation dolore
    ➥ cillum dolor et ea est cupidatat reprehenderit...",   <- Main message body of comment
    "userImage": "http://placehold.it/32x32",                <- Image of user who wrote comment
    "user": "Juliet",                                        <- User's name
    "postId": 2,                                             <- ID for post that comment is associated with
    "id": 0                                                  <- ID of comment
  },
  {},
  ...
]
```

To fetch all the comments for a post, you use the post/:id/comments endpoint. This is used on the Post Detail page to display the blog post comments.

Now that you've seen how the app works and learned how to use the mock data server, let's build the first version.

12.2 Server rendering with Ember FastBoot

Ember is a popular convention-based web framework. Using Ember with its isomorphic implementation (called FastBoot) is straightforward. The implementation is well documented and nearly identical to what you do in a single-page application (SPA) with Ember. A couple of key differences exist:

- Install additional libraries such as ember-cli-fastboot to add support for server rendering.
- Use Ember Fetch to get data instead of Ember Data. If you're used to the automatic data handling provided by Ember Data, this requires a shift in thinking.

Figure 12.3 shows the isomorphic application diagram you've seen in previous chapters. Let's review it again so you can see the detail on using Ember's isomorphic implementation.

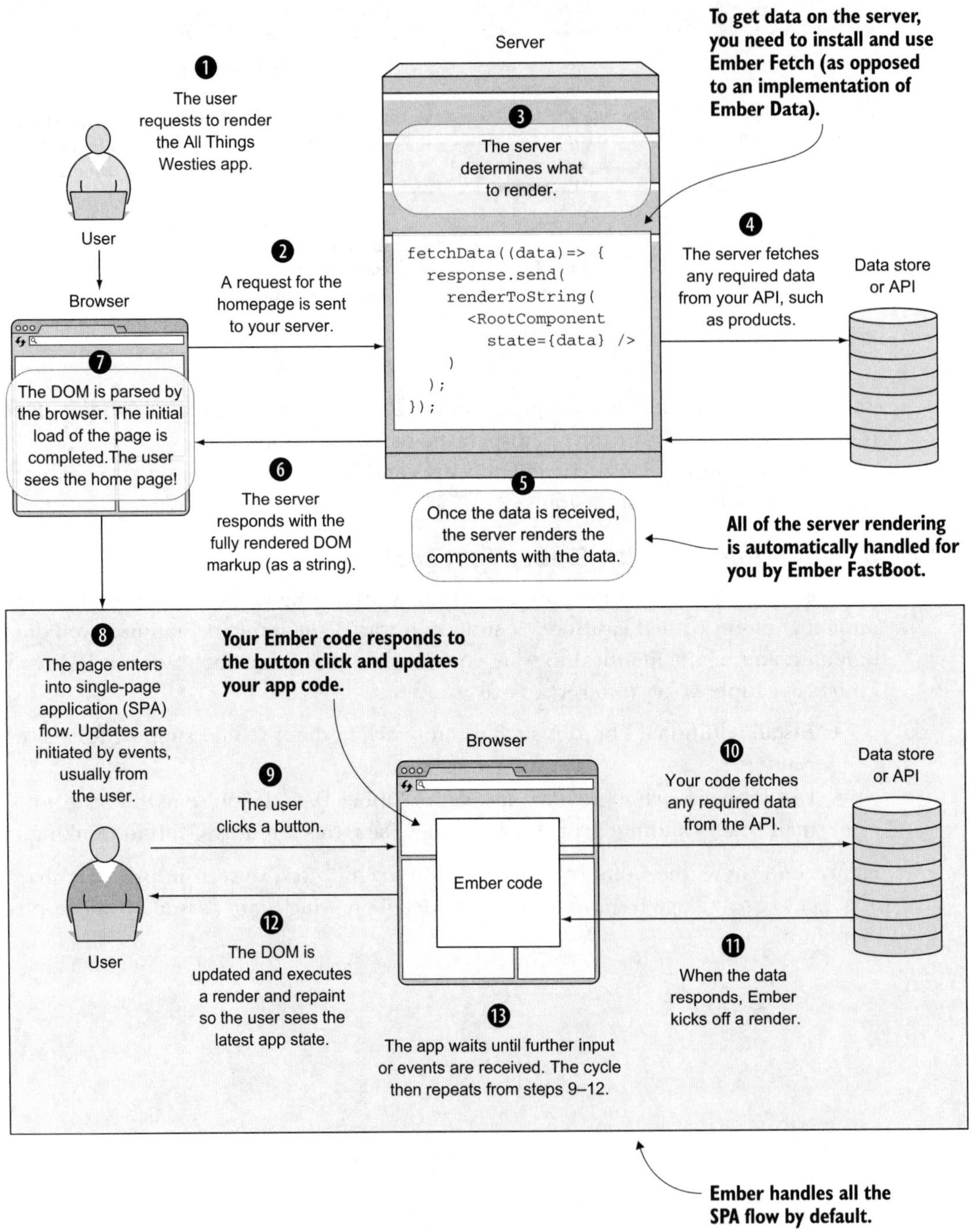
Server
To get data on the server, you need to install and use Ember Fetch (as opposed to an implementation of Ember Data).
1
The user requests to render the All Things Westies app.
User
Browser
3
The server determines what to render.
2
A request for the homepage is sent to your server.
fetchData((data)=> {
response.send(
renderToString(
<RootComponent
state={data} />
)
);
});
4
The server fetches any required data from your API, such as products.
Data store or API
7
The DOM is parsed by the browser. The initial load of the page is completed.The user sees the home page!
6
The server responds with the fully rendered DOM markup (as a string).
5
Once the data is received, the server renders the components with the data.
All of the server rendering is automatically handled for you by Ember FastBoot.
8
The page enters into single-page application (SPA) flow. Updates are initiated by events, usually from the user.
Your Ember code responds to the button click and updates your app code.
Browser
9
The user clicks a button.
10
Your code fetches any required data from the API.
Data store or API
Ember code
User
12
The DOM is updated and executes a render and repaint so the user sees the latest app state.
11
When the data responds, Ember kicks off a render.
13
The app waits until further input or events are received. The cycle then repeats from steps 9–12.
Ember handles all the SPA flow by default.

Figure 12.3 Isomorphic app flow with Ember—Ember specifics are highlighted in bold.

```
→ ember-universal git:(ember-starter) ✗ ember serve
Could not start watchman
Visit https://ember-cli.com/user-guide/#watchman for more info.
Livereload server on http://localhost:49153

Build successful (1592ms) – Serving on http://localhost:4200/


Slowest Nodes (totalTime => 5% )              | Total (avg)
----------------------------------------------+---------------------
Babel (15)                                    | 611ms (40 ms)
EslintValidationFilter (2)                    | 299ms (149 ms)
Concat (8)                                    | 227ms (28 ms)
TreeMerger (allTrees) (1)                     | 163ms
```

Running ember serve starts the server.

This build uses webpack dev server, which runs on its own port.

The server runs on port 4200.

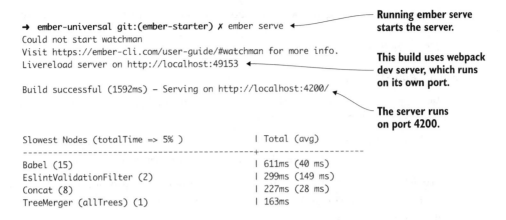

Figure 12.4 Run `ember serve` to start the app.

To follow along, check out the ember-starter branch in the GitHub repo (`git checkout ember-starter`). To run the app, you need to switch to the Ember directory (ember-universal), install the npm packages, and run the app with the Ember CLI. Figure 12.4 shows the output of running Ember:

```
$ cd ember-universal
$ npm install
$ ember serve
```

Ember has a tool called the Ember CLI that lets you get up and running quickly (I've already included it for you). You use the Ember CLI to run the app by calling `ember serve`. You can also use it to generate most of the types of files you use in an Ember app.

Ember resources

If you'd like to learn more about building web apps with Ember, here are some resources to help you get started:

- The Ember documentation site provides a getting started tutorial at https://guides.emberjs.com/v2.14.0/tutorial/ember-cli/.
- You can also check out the Quick Start guide at https://guides.emberjs.com/v2.14.0/getting-started/quick-start/.
- You'll find several other Ember tutorials at http://emberwatch.com/tutorials.html.
- The guide to server-rendered Ember is at https://ember-fastboot.com/quickstart.

The app will run at http://localhost:4200/. Remember to start the data server in the server folder as well.

Next, we'll review the structure of the Ember app.

12.2.1 Ember app structure

Ember apps use convention instead of configuration. To add a new file, you add it in the correct directory type. For example:

- When making a new component, you add it to the components folder.
- If you need to add a model, you add it in the models directory.

Figure 12.5 shows the app directory for the Ember app. Additional folders and files are in the ember-universal directory, but the ones in figure 12.5 are what you need to know about to get started.

I've already set up the main part of the app so you can focus on the isomorphic parts.

Next, we'll review the routes and components so you understand what you're working with.

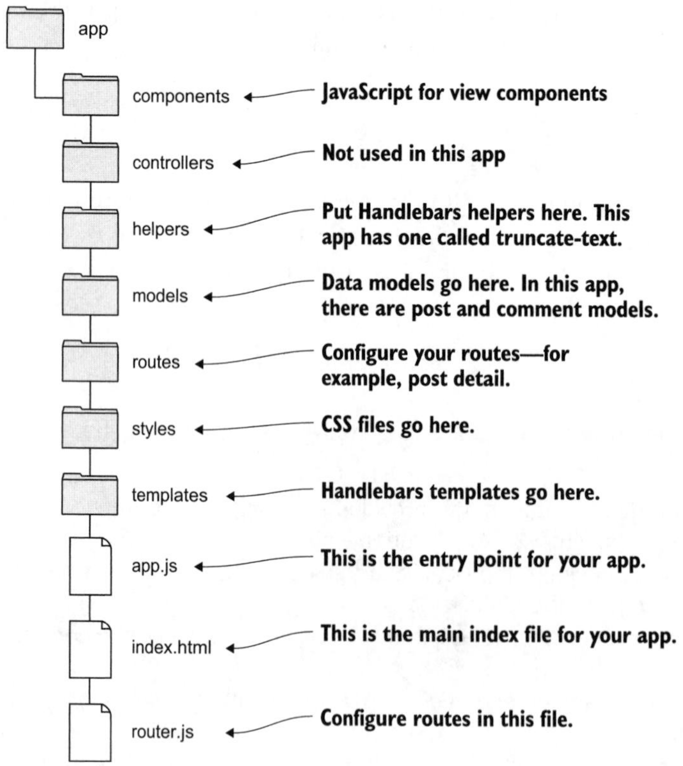
app
components
JavaScript for view components
controllers
Not used in this app
helpers
Put Handlebars helpers here. This app has one called truncate-text.
models
Data models go here. In this app, there are post and comment models.
routes
Configure your routes—for example, post detail.
styles
CSS files go here.
templates
Handlebars templates go here.
app.js
This is the entry point for your app.
index.html
This is the main index file for your app.
router.js
Configure routes in this file.

Figure 12.5 The app directory and files that are used in this Ember app

12.2.2 Routes in Ember

First let's look at the two top-level routes the app has. One is the root, or homepage route, and the other is the post detail route (/post/[post.urlSlug]). The routes will also be where all the data fetching happens. The following listing shows the routes file provided in the repo.

Listing 12.3 Routes—ember-universal/app/router.js

```
import Ember from 'ember';
import config from './config/environment';

const Router = Ember.Router.extend({
  location: config.locationType,
  rootURL: config.rootURL
});

Router.map(function() {
  this.route('post-detail', { path: '/post/:id' });
});

export default Router;
```

- Import the app config.
- Initialize the router with rootUrl and location type based on config (here, these are the same as the defaults set up by ember-cli).
- Add a second route for the Post Detail page—takes name and URL path.

In addition to the router, the app needs to provide the index (home) route. The following listing shows the code from index.js.

Listing 12.4 Index Route (Home)—ember-universal/app/routes/index.js

```
import Ember from 'ember';

export default Ember.Route.extend({
});
```

- Import Ember.
- Extend Route object on Ember.

As long as you follow Ember naming conventions and put the file in the right folder, you don't have to do anything else to get an initial route working. The post detail route also looks like this. You can check it out at ember-universal/app/routes/post-detail.js.

Next, let's look at the components that make up this app.

12.2.3 Components

Ember components consist of two files: a JavaScript file with a component class and a Handlebars template file that provides the view part of the component.

> **INFO** Handlebars is a JavaScript template language. You can learn more about it at http://handlebarsjs.com.

In the blog app, the JavaScript classes don't have to do much. Listing 12.5 shows what the post controller looks like. The other component classes look just like this in their own files (comment-component, header-component, post-list). All this code is already provided in the repo.

Listing 12.5 Post component—ember-universal/app/components/post-component.js

```
import Ember from 'ember';                          // Import Ember.

export default Ember.Component.extend({             // Extend component to make your Post component class.
});
```

All the components are already created in the application for you. If you want to add your own components, rather than add components by hand you generate them with the CLI:

```
$ ember generate component [name-of-component]
```

Each component also has its Handlebars template file. The following listing shows the Handlebars template file for the post component. You can find all the template files for the app inside the /templates directory.

Listing 12.6 Post component Handlebars template—ember-universal/app/templates/components/post-component.hbs

```
<div class="item">
  <div class="ui tiny image">
    <img src={{post.image}} />                     <!-- Places post image in template. -->
  </div>
  <div class="content">
    <div class="header">{{post.title}}</div>       <!-- Places post title in template -->
    <div class="description">
      <p>{{truncate-text post.body limit}}</p>    <!-- Passes body of post to helper function, which truncates text based on the limit value (also passed in). -->
    </div>
  </div>
</div>
```

The Post component is used on both routes in the application. It's used on the homepage to show the blog snippet and on the Post Detail page in full. The `truncate` helper function in the Handlebars template in listing 12.6 makes the component reusable in multiple cases. Listing 12.7 shows the template for the post detail route. Using Handlebars template notation, place the Post component on the route. Data is fed to each route via the model, so you can access it off the model. You'll set up the data fetching in the next section.

Listing 12.7 Post detail route template—ember-universal/app/templates/post-detail.hbs

```
{{post-component post=model.post}}                  <!-- Pass post data into the component -->
<div class="ui comments">
  <h3 class="ui dividing header">Comments</h3>      <!-- Render a dividing header for post comments. -->
  {{#each model.comments as |comment|}}             <!-- Use Handlebars helper each to loop over every comment (comments such as post data are stored on the model). -->
```

```
    {{comment-component comment=comment}}
  {{/each}}
</div>
```

Close the each helper.

Render a comment component for each comment returned on the model.

All the routes are loaded into the root template: application. This template renders the header and a placeholder for where the routes will be dynamically rendered. The following listing shows the template file for application.

Listing 12.8 Application template—ember-universal/app/templates/application.hbs

```
{{header-component}}
<div class="ui main text container offset" >
  {{outlet}}
</div>
```

Place header component into the root template, this will render on every page.

Special placeholder router knows to pass components down to children, handled automatically.

By now, you should have a good understanding of the blog app's code. Next, we'll make the Ember app isomorphic.

12.2.4 Implement isomorphic Ember

Now let's set up the two parts of this app that will make it isomorphic. Figure 12.6 shows what you should see at the end of this section when JavaScript is disabled in the browser.

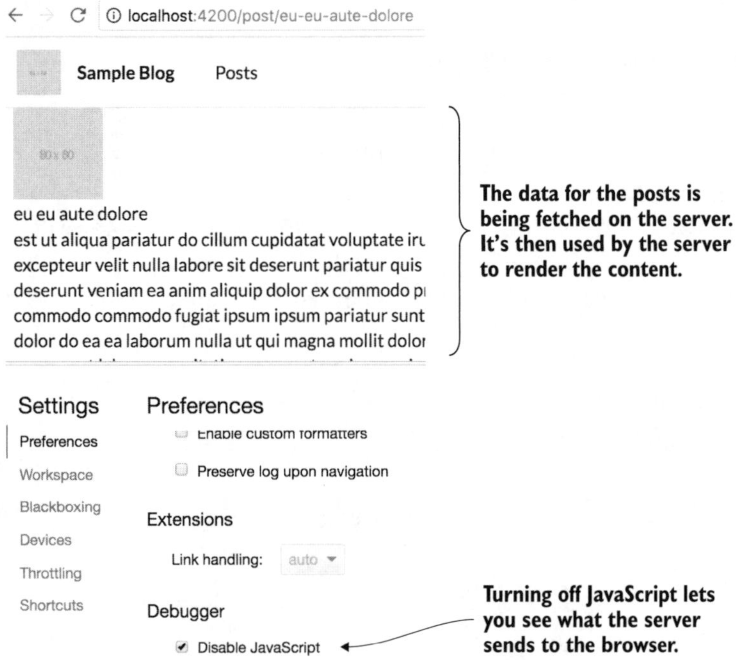
localhost:4200/post/eu-eu-aute-dolore
Sample Blog
Posts
eu eu aute dolore
est ut aliqua pariatur do cillum cupidatat voluptate iru
excepteur velit nulla labore sit deserunt pariatur quis
deserunt veniam ea anim aliquip dolor ex commodo pi
commodo commodo fugiat ipsum ipsum pariatur sunt
dolor do ea ea laborum nulla ut qui magna mollit doloi
The data for the posts is being fetched on the server. It's then used by the server to render the content.
Settings
Preferences
Preferences
Enable custom formatters
Workspace
Preserve log upon navigation
Blackboxing
Extensions
Devices
Link handling:
auto
Throttling
Shortcuts
Debugger
Disable JavaScript
Turning off JavaScript lets you see what the server sends to the browser.

Figure 12.6 The server-rendered app after you've added all of the isomorphic pieces

STEP 1: EMBER FASTBOOT

First, install the Ember CLI FastBoot library. Run the following command:

```
$ npm install --save-dev ember-cli-fastboot
```

Now if you run the server and disable JavaScript in the browser, you'll see the header rendered. To disable JavaScript, open the Options menu in the upper-right corner of the Chrome DevTools window and click Settings. Under Debugger, select the Disable JavaScript check box. Figure 12.7 shows this in action.

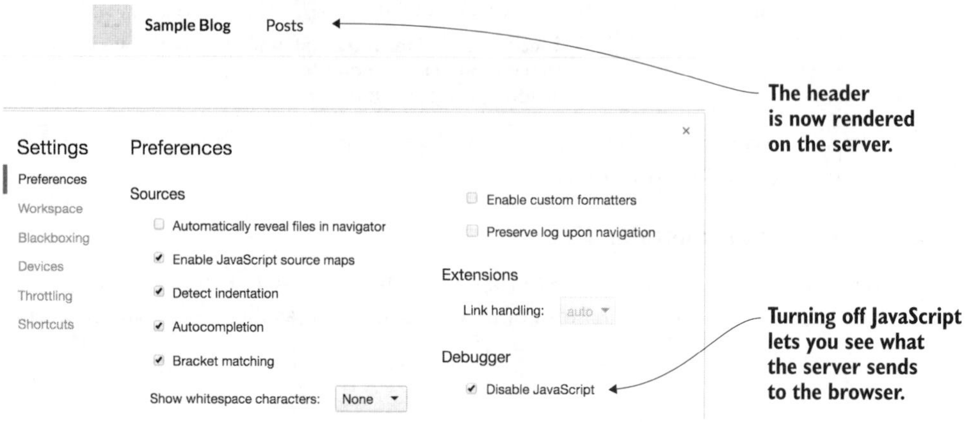
Sample Blog
Posts
The header is now rendered on the server.
Settings
Preferences
Preferences
Workspace
Blackboxing
Devices
Throttling
Shortcuts
Sources
Automatically reveal files in navigator
Enable JavaScript source maps
Detect indentation
Autocompletion
Bracket matching
Show whitespace characters:
None
Enable custom formatters
Preserve log upon navigation
Extensions
Link handling:
auto
Debugger
Disable JavaScript
Turning off JavaScript lets you see what the server sends to the browser.

Figure 12.7 The header now renders on the server.

Next we'll go over how to fetch data in the app.

STEP 2: ISOMORPHIC DATA FETCHING

To ensure that you can fetch the data for the app on the server and in the browser, you'll need to use an implementation of fetch that works in both environments. Ember has a library you can install, called ember-fetch. Go ahead and install it now:

```
$ npm install ember-fetch --save
```

After this is installed, you can add a fetch call to the main route. The following listing shows the code to add to routes/index.js.

Listing 12.9 Index route (home)—ember-universal/app/routes/index.js

```
import Ember from 'ember';
import fetch from 'ember-fetch/ajax';          <- Include Ajax module from ember-fetch.

export default Ember.Route.extend({
  model() {
    return fetch('http://localhost:3535/posts')     <- Fetch posts from posts endpoint.
      .then((response) => {
```

```
        return response;
      });
    }
});
```

Return response as is—JSON response in an array (view expects data in this format).

Navigate to the homepage and you'll see the list of blog posts. To also get the data working for the Post Detail page, add the code in the following listing to the post detail route.

Listing 12.10 Post detail route—ember-universal/app/routes/post-detail.js

```
import Ember from 'ember';
import fetch from 'ember-fetch/ajax';

export default Ember.Route.extend({
  model(params) {
    return fetch(
    ➥ `http://localhost:3535/post/${params.id}`)
      .then((response) => {
        return fetch(`http://localhost:3535/post/${response.id}/comments`)
          .then((comments) => {
            return {
              post: response,
              comments: comments
            };
          });
      });
  }
});
```

If route will have params, these get passed into the model function.

Call individual post endpoint with ID from URL (URL slug).

After post has returned, get associated comments based on ID.

Send both post and array of comments to the view.

That's all there is to getting the Ember app converted to an isomorphic app! (If you'd like to see the complete code, it's in the ember-complete branch.) Figure 12.8 shows what happened in the DOM during the Ember isomorphic render.

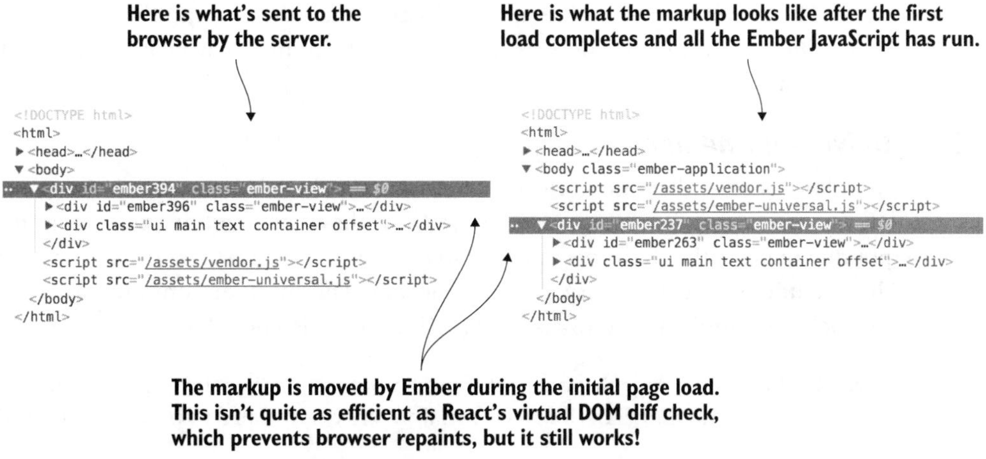

Here is what's sent to the browser by the server.
Here is what the markup looks like after the first load completes and all the Ember JavaScript has run.
<!DOCTYPE html>
<html>
<head>…</head>
<body>
<div id="ember394" class="ember-view"> == $0
<div id="ember396" class="ember-view">…</div>
<div class="ui main text container offset">…</div>
</div>
<script src="/assets/vendor.js"></script>
<script src="/assets/ember-universal.js"></script>
</body>
</html>
<!DOCTYPE html>
<html>
<head>…</head>
<body class="ember-application">
<script src="/assets/vendor.js"></script>
<script src="/assets/ember-universal.js"></script>
<div id="ember237" class="ember-view"> == $0
<div id="ember263" class="ember-view">…</div>
<div class="ui main text container offset">…</div>
</div>
</body>
</html>
The markup is moved by Ember during the initial page load. This isn't quite as efficient as React's virtual DOM diff check, which prevents browser repaints, but it still works!

Figure 12.8 Ember replaces the DOM completely, but it's imperceptible to the user.

Finally, let's review the benefits and costs associated with using Ember for isomorphic rendering.

12.2.5 Pros and cons of isomorphic Ember

As you've seen in this section, setting up an Ember app to server render is almost as simple as setting up an Ember app. That means getting up and running with isomorphic Ember is relatively fast. An added bonus is that the Ember CLI lets you autogenerate the basics of the app. The following list evaluates the pros and cons of using Ember to build your isomorphic app.

Pros

- It's easy to set up isomorphic parts of the app. Install two extra libraries (ember-cli-fastboot and ember-fetch).
- The Ember CLI (along with FastBoot) makes the time between installation and a working app extremely short.
- Convention over configuration makes it easy to wire things together and can be beneficial for teams of all sizes.
- Ember FastBoot already supports the majority of isomorphic use cases, including cookies in different environments and dynamic metatags based on routes. The overall documentation and user guide is good (https://ember-fastboot.com/docs/user-guide).

Cons

- Replacing the DOM rather than calculating that a DOM update isn't needed on the first render adds additional cost to the initial render.
- Ember's focus on convention isn't for everyone and may not fit your needs.
- It takes time to master Ember. Many things can appear magical for developers who are new to the framework.
- The current best practice around FastBoot doesn't have an Ember Data integration, which means you lose out on one of the powerful features of the Ember framework.

12.3 Universal Angular

Angular has gone through quite an evolution over the last few years. Although most of the core concepts from Angular.js (Angular 1) have survived, it has evolved to incorporate concepts that have become popular in other libraries and frameworks. Luckily, this includes support for server-side rendering. The Angular community has decided to label their implementation as *universal* instead of isomorphic.

NOTE Officially, Angular now refers to Angular 1 as *Angular.js* and the newer iterations as *Angular*. This allows for major version updates to be smoother and continuous without your having to remember whether you should be using Angular 2 or Angular 4. The code in the repo uses Angular version 4.0.0.

In this section, I'm going to walk you through setting up a universal Angular app. If you're new to Angular, I highly recommend getting up to speed on Angular basics first. The Angular documentation site has a high-quality tutorial at https://angular.io/tutorial. If you want to go in depth with Angular, I recommend checking out *Angular in Action* by Jeremy Wilken (Manning, 2018). Finally, if you want to learn more about the Angular CLI tool, you can check out its GitHub repo at https://github.com/angular/angular-cli.

Best of friends: TypeScript and Angular

Angular is written with TypeScript, a superset of JavaScript that introduces the ability to enforce typing information. It can be used with any version of JavaScript, so you can use it with anything ES3 (that's not a typo) or newer.

The basic value of TypeScript is to enforce that variables are restricted to a specific type of value, such as: a variable may hold only a number or an array of strings. JavaScript has types (don't let anyone tell you otherwise!), but variables aren't typed, so you can store any type of value on any variable. This also gave birth to the many types of comparison operators, such as `==` for loose equality or `===` for strict equality.

TypeScript can help catch many simple syntax errors before they affect your application. Sometimes you can write valid JavaScript, but the real world shows that valid syntax doesn't always mean valid behavior. Take this example:

```
var bill = 20;?
var   tip   =   document.getElementById('tip').value;   //   Contains  '5'
console.log(bill + tip); // 205
```

This snippet shows a simple tip calculator example: you take the value from an input element and add it to the bill to get the total payment amount. But the problem here is that the `tip` variable is a string (because it's a text input). Adding a number and a string together is perhaps one of the most common pitfalls for new JavaScript developers, but it still can happen to anyone! If you used TypeScript to enforce types, this code could be written to alert about this common error:

```
var bill: number = 20;
var tip: number = document.getElementById('tip').value;
// 5, error!
var total: number = bill + tip; // error!
```

Here you're using TypeScript to declare that all these variables must each hold a number value by using `number`. This is a simple syntax that sits inside JavaScript to tell TypeScript the type of value the variable should hold. The tip value will error because it's being assigned a string, and then the total value will error because it attempts to add a number and string type, which results in a string.

(continued)

This may seem like an obvious error to a seasoned JavaScript developer, but how often do you have new developers work on your code base? How often do you refactor your code? Can you still ensure that your application is passing around the same value types as you continue to maintain the application? Without TypeScript, you're responsible for doing a strict comparator check of every value before it's used.

Many developers wonder why they should bother learning and using TypeScript. Here are the primary reasons to use TypeScript, in my humble opinion:

- *It adds clarity to your code*—Variables that have types are easier to understand, because other developers (or yourself in six months) don't have to think very hard about what the variable should be.
- *It enables a smarter editor*—When you use TypeScript with a supported editor, you'll get automatic IntelliSense support for your code. As you write, the editor can suggest known variables or functions and tell you the type of value it expects.
- *It catches errors before you run code*—TypeScript will catch syntax errors before you run the code in the browser, helping to reduce the feedback loop when you write invalid code.
- *It's entirely optional*—You can use types when you want and optionally leave it out where it doesn't matter.

Hopefully you're sold on the value of TypeScript. If not, don't worry—I won't judge. But this book will use it in examples because it'll help provide more clarity and will also help further demonstrate the power of TypeScript. I'll try to provide additional insight into TypeScript features and functionality as we use features in the examples, but you can always learn all there is to know at www.typescriptlang.org/docs/tutorial.html. Even if you choose not to use TypeScript for type enforcement in your application, you can use TypeScript to compile your application. Because the Angular CLI already uses TypeScript internally, you may be using it without even knowing. If you decide to build your own build tooling, TypeScript is still a worthwhile compiler option.

Figure 12.9 shows the isomorphic application diagram you've seen in previous chapters. I've called out all the pieces you must implement yourself when using Angular to build an isomorphic app. Angular handles some parts of the flow for you. For example, the data fetching will work out of the box if you handle your server initialization correctly, but you still need to configure a browser entry point and a server entry point.

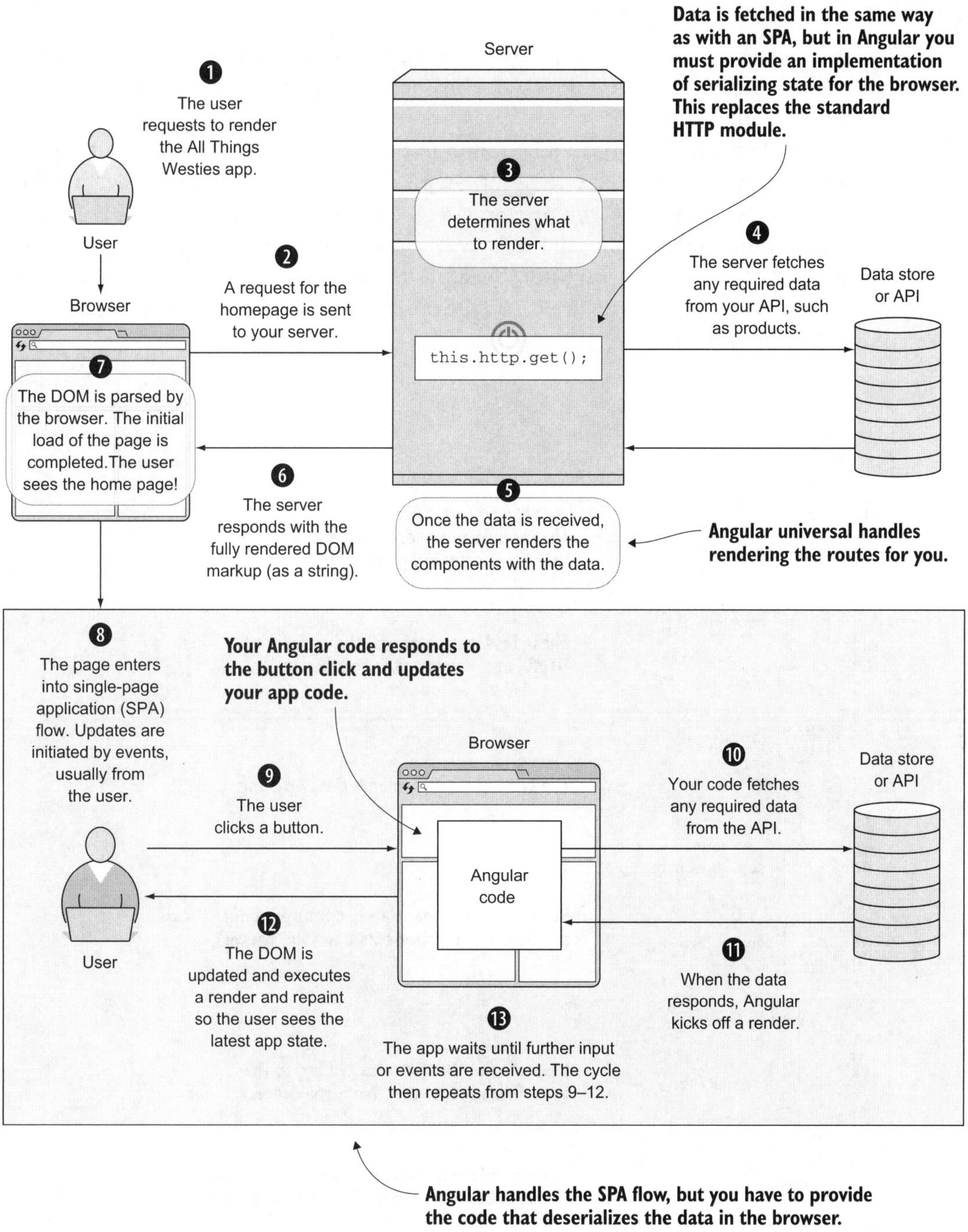
Data is fetched in the same way as with an SPA, but in Angular you must provide an implementation of serializing state for the browser. This replaces the standard HTTP module.
Server
1 The user requests to render the All Things Westies app.
User
Browser
2 A request for the homepage is sent to your server.
3 The server determines what to render.
4 The server fetches any required data from your API, such as products.
Data store or API
this.http.get();
7 The DOM is parsed by the browser. The initial load of the page is completed.The user sees the home page!
6 The server responds with the fully rendered DOM markup (as a string).
5 Once the data is received, the server renders the components with the data.
Angular universal handles rendering the routes for you.
8 The page enters into single-page application (SPA) flow. Updates are initiated by events, usually from the user.
Your Angular code responds to the button click and updates your app code.
Browser
9 The user clicks a button.
Angular code
10 Your code fetches any required data from the API.
Data store or API
User
12 The DOM is updated and executes a render and repaint so the user sees the latest app state.
11 When the data responds, Angular kicks off a render.
13 The app waits until further input or events are received. The cycle then repeats from steps 9–12.
Angular handles the SPA flow, but you have to provide the code that deserializes the data in the browser.

Figure 12.9 The universal flow in Angular

12.3.1 Building blocks: components

I've already set up most of the app structure for you, so you can focus on learning how to enable Angular to be universal. In this section, I'll briefly walk you through the structure of this code.

The code for this section can be found in the branch angular-starter, and you can switch to it by running `git checkout angular-starter`. You also need to switch to the angular2 folder and run `npm install`. Note that at this point, this is a single-page application (SPA). You can run it by executing the `npm start` command in your terminal. The app will run on http://localhost:4100.

First let's review the structure of the files already in the app. Figure 12.10 shows the main folders and files.

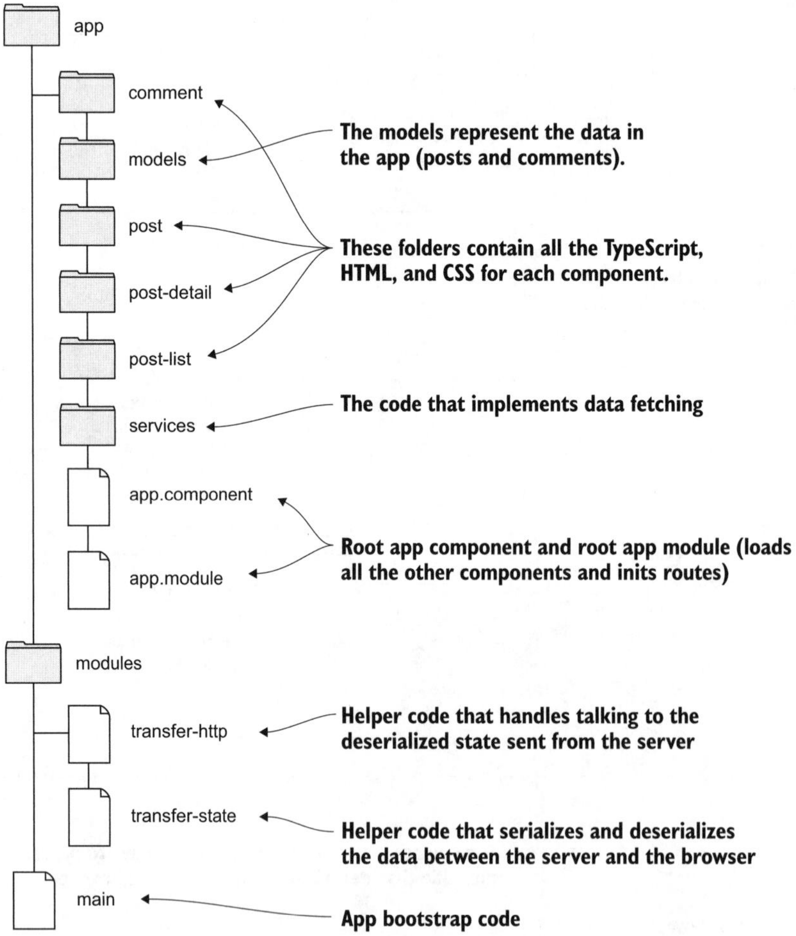
app
comment
models
post
post-detail
post-list
services
app.component
app.module
modules
transfer-http
transfer-state
main
The models represent the data in the app (posts and comments).
These folders contain all the TypeScript, HTML, and CSS for each component.
The code that implements data fetching
Root app component and root app module (loads all the other components and inits routes)
Helper code that handles talking to the deserialized state sent from the server
Helper code that serializes and deserializes the data between the server and the browser
App bootstrap code

Figure 12.10 The app folder and files that make up the SPA. It also includes the helper modules for universal state transfer and data fetching.

Each component is made up of three files: the TypeScript file with the component definition, a component CSS file, and the HTML file that provides the component template. The app component has app.component.ts, app.component.css, and app .component.html. All the components in the Angular app mirror the components in the Ember app but are implanted with Angular patterns instead.

Currently, the app flow works like this:

1. The user navigates to the page, and index.html loads the webpack-bundled files. This executes the code from the app entry point (main.ts), which bootstraps the application.
2. This app has one module (AppModule) that's loaded when the app bootstraps.
3. AppModule includes all the component dependencies. These are now loaded, and the current route is rendered.

Next you want to add the server-rendering libraries and logic.

12.3.2 Converting to universal: dependencies

To get server-side rendering working, first you need to install dependencies. The first thing you need to add are libraries:

```
$ npm install --save @angular/platform-server
```

To run universal Angular, you also need to provide a state transfer module, as this isn't provided for you. You also need to provide an HTTP implementation that's compatible with this state transfer module. Some packages can help with this, but the current best implementation that I've found comes from a universal example repo: https://github .com/FrozenPandaz/ng-universal-demo. The code can be found in the angular2/src/ modules folder, as it's already included in the repo.

The code is made up of two modules: transfer-state and transfer-http. Transfer State is a module that handles serializing and deserializing the JSON. Transfer HTTP is a module that has logic to look up the app state from the Transfer State module before trying to fetch the requested data. It automatically uses keys extrapolated from your requests, so you use the Transfer HTTP module just like the regular Angular HTTP module.

12.3.3 Converting to universal: server and browser code

The next step in converting the app to universal is to create two entry points instead of the one currently implemented with AppModule. First, you should create the browser entry point. The following listing shows the code to put in the browser.module.ts file.

Listing 12.11 Browser module—angular2/src/browser.module.ts

```
import { BrowserModule } from '@angular/platform-browser';
import { NgModule } from '@angular/core';
```

Import Angular dependencies.

```
import { AppComponent } from './app/app.component';
import { AppModule } from './app/app.module';
import { BrowserTransferStateModule } from './modules/
    transfer-state/browser-transfer-state.module';
    //

@NgModule({
  imports: [
    BrowserModule.withServerTransition({
      appId: 'ng-universal-example'
    }),
    BrowserTransferStateModule,
    AppModule
  ],
  providers: [],
  bootstrap: [AppComponent]
})
export class AppBrowserModule { }
```

Import app component, the root component that gets passed into bootstrap array.

Import AppModule so dependencies get set up properly for dependency injection.

Import browser transfer state helper module.

Initialize browserModule with server transition.

When you initialize the `browserModule`, make sure the `appId` property matches what's in the server module (you'll add this in listing 12.13).

Now you need to load the browser entry in main.ts, which bootstraps the application. This is just a change of the module that's currently imported (AppModule). The following listing shows the code to replace.

Listing 12.12 Update the main.ts file—angular2/src/main.ts

Import browser module instead of app.module.

```
// remove this line: import { AppModule } from './app/app.module';
import { AppBrowserModule } from './browser.module';

platformBrowserDynamic().bootstrapModule(AppBrowserModule);
```

Use AppBrowserModule to bootstrap app.

Next, you need to create a server entry module. This will be similar to your browser module but will set up injecting the server state. The following listing shows what to add with an app.server.module.ts file.

Listing 12.13 Server entry module—angular2/src/app.server.module.ts

```
import { NgModule, APP_BOOTSTRAP_LISTENER, ApplicationRef } from '@angular/
    core';
import 'rxjs/Rx';
import { BrowserModule } from '@angular/platform-browser';
import { ServerModule } from '@angular/platform-server';
import {
  ServerTransferStateModule
  } from
```

Import Angular and supporting dependencies.

```
➥ './modules/transfer-state/server-transfer-state.module';
import {
  TransferState
} from './modules/transfer-state/transfer-state';

import { AppComponent } from './app/app.component';
import { AppModule } from './app/app.module';

export function onBootstrap(appRef:
     ApplicationRef, transferState: TransferState) {
  return () => {
    appRef.isStable
      .filter(stable => stable)
      .first()
      .subscribe(() => {
        transferState.inject();
      });
  };
}

@NgModule({
  providers: [
    {
      provide: APP_BOOTSTRAP_LISTENER,
      useFactory: onBootstrap,
      multi: true,
      deps: [
        ApplicationRef,
        TransferState
      ]
    }
  ],
  imports: [
    ServerModule,
    BrowserModule.withServerTransition({
      appId: 'ng-universal-example'
    }),
    ServerTransferStateModule,
    AppModule
  ],
  bootstrap: [
    AppComponent
  ]
})
export class AppServerModule {}
```

Include TransferState module so you can inject the state into it after the app is bootstrapped.

Include ServerTransferState-Module, which implements the server version of app state.

Server module needs to import the root AppModule and component.

Set up server transition appId to match the one you added in browser module file.

Finally, you need to add a server configuration file that will handle incoming routes and then load Angular and render it. The following listing shows the code you need to add to the main.server.ts file.

Listing 12.14 Node.js server—main.server.ts

```
import 'reflect-metadata';
import 'zone.js/dist/zone-node';
```

```
import { platformServer, renderModuleFactory } from '@angular/platform-
     server';
import { enableProdMode } from '@angular/core';
import {
  AppServerModuleNgFactory
} from './app.server.module.ngfactory';
import * as express from 'express';
import { readFileSync } from 'fs';
import { join } from 'path';

const PORT = 4000;

enableProdMode();

const app = express();

const template = readFileSync(join(__dirname, '..', 'dist',
     'index.html')).toString();

app.engine('html', (_, options, callback) => {
  const opts = { document: template, url: options.req.url };

  renderModuleFactory(AppServerModuleNgFactory, opts)
    .then(html => callback(null, html));
});

app.set('view engine', 'html');
app.set('views', 'src');

app.get('*.*', express.static(join(__dirname, '..', 'dist')));

app.get('*', (req, res) => {
  res.render('index', { req });
});

app.listen(PORT, () => {
  console.log(`listening on http://localhost:${PORT}!`);
});
```

Module factory is passed to the render function so Angular can properly handle routes.

Set up HTML rendering engine.

Make sure view engine points at HTML.

When route is received, call res.render.

At this point, you can successfully run the code. You use a different server command than for the SPA version. This command builds and starts both the server and the browser code:

```
$ npm run start-isomorphic
```

At this point, the app is set up but doesn't have data. The server will load, and you'll see the app header but no content. The next section covers data fetching, which is needed to load the full content.

12.3.4 Fetching data in universal

To successfully fetch data and pass it down to the browser, you also need to use the Transfer HTTP library in the services that fetch the data. The following listing shows how to import the module into the App module.

Listing 12.15 App module with Transfer HTTP—angular2/src/app/app.module.ts

```
//...more imports
// remove { Http } import
import { TransferHttpModule } from '../modules/transfer-http/
     transfer-http.module';
//...more imports

@NgModule({
  declarations: [],
  imports: [
    // remove HttpModule and BrowserModule
    TransferHttpModule,
    CommonModule,
    RouterModule.forRoot([])
  ],
  providers: [
],
  bootstrap: [AppComponent]
})
export class AppModule { }
```

Import module and add it to Angular imports—make sure to take out old HTTP module and Browser module.

Now that you've included the module into the App module, you can import the TransferHttp library into your services. The following listing shows how to update the Posts service.

Listing 12.16 Update Posts service—angular2/src/app/services/posts.service.ts

```
import { Injectable } from '@angular/core';
// remove the Http import
import {
  TransferHttp
} from '../../modules/transfer-http/transfer-http';

const service = 'http://localhost:3535'

@Injectable()
export class PostsService {

  constructor(private http: TransferHttp) {}

  getPosts(): any {
    return this.http.get(`${service}/posts`);
  }

  getPostByUrlSlug(urlSlug): any {
    return this.http.get(`${service}/post/${urlSlug}`);
  }
}
```

Change Http import to TransferHttp import, then use in constructor instead of Http.

You also need to make this same update in the comments service. The following listing shows what to change in the comments service file.

Listing 12.17 Update Comments service—angular2/src/app/services/comments.service.ts

```
import { Injectable } from '@angular/core';
import {
  TransferHttp
} from '../../modules/transfer-http/transfer-http';

const service = 'http://localhost:3535'

@Injectable()
export class CommentsService {

  constructor(private http: TransferHttp) {}

  getCommentsForPost(postId): any {
    return this.http.get(`${service}/post/${postId}/comments`);
  }
}
```

Change Http import to TransferHttp import, then use in constructor instead of Http.

At this point, the full universal flow is working. You can go through the same exercise you did with Ember: disable JavaScript in the browser via Chrome DevTools and observe the HTML that's loaded. You can also get the full code in the angular-complete branch.

12.3.5 Pros and cons of universal Angular

Using universal Angular has the following pros and cons:

Pros

- Uses dependency injection, which allows you to swap out dependencies as needed
- Access to Angular CLI, which lets you generate components
- Less magic—you have control over the server and the data hydration

Cons

- Requires implementation of state transfer logic
- Requires setting up your own server
- Requires setting up your own browser and server entry points

12.4 Next.js: React isomorphic framework

If you're looking for an all-in-one solution that uses React, Next.js is a strong option. Isomorphic by default, Next.js uses a convention-driven approach to building a React app. Even if you decide not to use Next.js in production, you may find it a good tool for building isomorphic prototypes or proofs of concept (*pocs*). It could aid you in selling the idea of isomorphic to your team or boss.

To run the Next.js example, check out the master branch (`git checkout master`). Change into the nextjs directory, install the Node.js packages, and then run the webpack dev server:

```
$ cd nextjs
$ npm install
$ npm run dev
```

Figure 12.11 walks through the isomorphic flow as implemented by Next.js. Next.js is server rendered by default, so you don't have to configure anything!

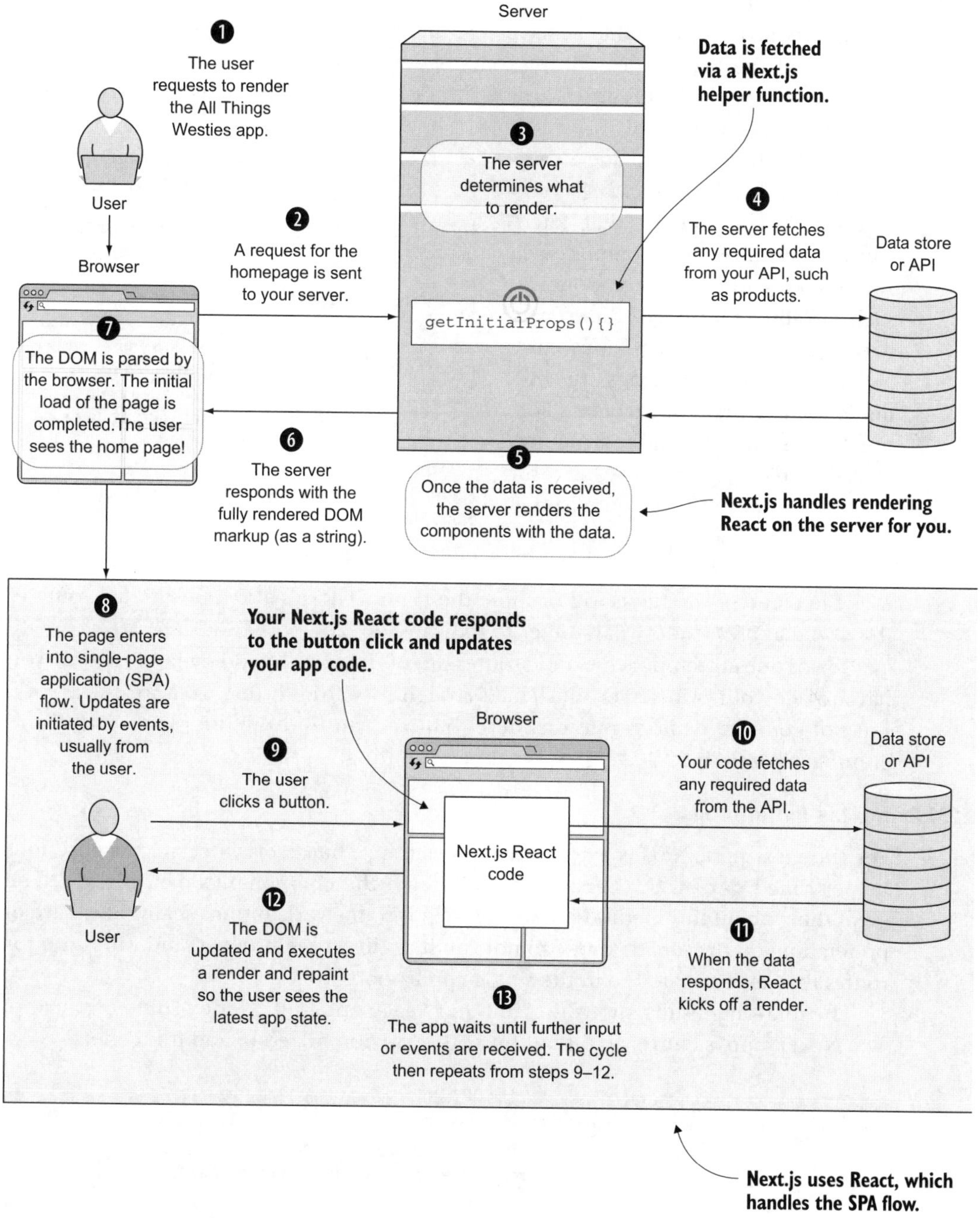
Server
1
The user requests to render the All Things Westies app.
User
Browser
Data is fetched via a Next.js helper function.
3
The server determines what to render.
2
A request for the homepage is sent to your server.
4
The server fetches any required data from your API, such as products.
Data store or API
getInitialProps(){}
7
The DOM is parsed by the browser. The initial load of the page is completed.The user sees the home page!
6
The server responds with the fully rendered DOM markup (as a string).
5
Once the data is received, the server renders the components with the data.
Next.js handles rendering React on the server for you.
8
The page enters into single-page application (SPA) flow. Updates are initiated by events, usually from the user.
Your Next.js React code responds to the button click and updates your app code.
Browser
9
The user clicks a button.
10
Your code fetches any required data from the API.
Data store or API
Next.js React code
User
12
The DOM is updated and executes a render and repaint so the user sees the latest app state.
11
When the data responds, React kicks off a render.
13
The app waits until further input or events are received. The cycle then repeats from steps 9–12.
Next.js uses React, which handles the SPA flow.

Figure 12.11 The isomorphic flow with Next.js

Now let's walk through the Next.js app. We'll review the parts that make it isomorphic out of the box.

12.4.1 Next.js structure

Next.js uses an opinionated React implementation that comes with many standard features out of the box (code splitting, built-in router, server rendering, Webpack Dev Server, and more). Next.js also provides a set of scripts for building and serving your application in production.

Next.js projects are made up of components and pages. *Pages* are con- tainer components that fetch data and compose child components. You could easily add components such as Redux. One major difference between standard React apps and Next.js is that in Next.js they've implemented their own router. Figure 12.12 shows the folder structure of this simple application.

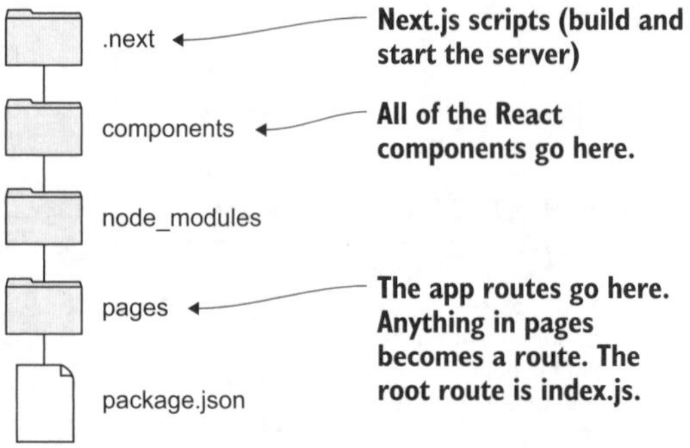
.next
Next.js scripts (build and start the server)
components
All of the React components go here.
node_modules
pages
The app routes go here. Anything in pages becomes a route. The root route is index.js.
package.json

Figure 12.12 The folders and files that make up a basic Next.js app

Notice that to add a route to the app, you create a new React component in the pages directory. Whatever the name of the file is will become the route. There's also a post detail route in this app that uses a query parameter to indicate the blog post URL slug.

Next.js doesn't support dynamic routes out of the box. To add dynamic routes, you have to add your own server file. That's straightforward but does require extra work. I'm not going to demonstrate this here, but you can find the docs for it at https://github.com/zeit/next.js/#custom-server-and-routing.

12.4.2 Next.js initial props

For the most part, Next.js is a standard React app, but it provides an asynchronous helper called `getInitialProps` that will fetch the component's data for you. The great thing about this method is that the Next.js framework automatically takes care of prefetching on the server, knows to not run it again on the browser, and will run it for routes that are navigated to in the single-application flow.

The following listing shows the `getInitialProps` in the index route of the app. The Next.js app is entirely built out for you—you don't need to add this code.

Listing 12.18 Index route data fetching—nextjs/pages/index.js

Define function as async function—Next.js Babel presets are already configured to use ES7 features.

```
IndexPage.getInitialProps = async ({ req }) => {
  let res, json;
```

```
  try {
    res = await fetch('http://localhost:3535/posts');   <-- Add await function to fetch list of posts.
    json = await res.json()                             <-- Add await function to get JSON response.
  } catch (e) {
    console.log("e", e);                                <-- If there's an error, log it—async await doesn't support promise error catching, so use a try/catch block.
  }
  return { posts: json || [] }                          <-- Return posts results.
}
```

12.4.3 Pros and cons of Next.js

Overall, Next.js provides a great solution if you want to try something quickly or if you have a simple app with just a few pages. For complex apps with dynamic routing, Next.js requires more time investment to get up and running.

Pros

- Works out of the box as long as you don't need dynamic routes.
- Provides all dev build scripts and support for production builds.
- Convention-based routing system.
- Isomorphic data-fetching implementation supplied for you. You just add your code for fetching the data from your back ends.

Cons

- More-complex apps require doing additional work to set up Redux and dynamic routing.
- Some parts of the framework are custom, such as the router, meaning you have to learn yet another router.
- Originally built with smaller static sites in mind.

12.5 Comparing the options

You've seen several ways to build isomorphic apps with popular JavaScript frameworks. Table 12.1 compares the three frameworks.

Table 12.1 Comparison of Ember, Angular, and Next.js

	Ember	Angular	Next.js
Learning curve for framework	Medium: Get started quickly, but steep learning curve for advanced knowledge.	Medium: Requires solid grasp of Angular's MVC implementation.	Easy (if you know React): Requires ramp-up on framework conventions.
Easy to get into production?	Yes	More steps required than other two options	Yes
Isomorphic code works by default?	Yes, but requires nonstandard Ember data fetching	Requires added code module to override default HTTP behavior	Yes
Size of app?	Any	Any	Ideal for small or static apps

Table 12.1 Comparison of Ember, Angular, and Next.js *(continued)*

	Ember	Angular	Next.js
Approach to initial load of the browser app (handoff between server and browser)	Full replace	Calculated replace	Virtual DOM with React, no replacement or DOM updates

Summary

This chapter provided an overview of three ways to get up and running with isomorphic (or universal) apps. You learned about Ember FastBoot, universal Angular, and Next.js. Each provides a good implementation that may work for your situation.

- Build a convention-driven app using Ember and Ember FastBoot. Ember provides most of the implementation for you, so getting an app running is fast.
- Use Angular to server-render your app. Angular requires more code to get the state transfer working properly between the server and the browser.
- Next.js is a React framework that's isomorphic out of the box, for an app without dynamic pages.

13 Where to go from here

This chapter covers

- Additional isomorphic tools and frameworks
- The skills that you'll want to acquire to become an expert at building isomorphic applications
- Where to learn more about related areas of focus such as GraphQL, search engine optimization (SEO), and performance

Throughout this book, you've learned about many tools, libraries, and frameworks. You've been exposed to best practices in building isomorphic apps. Most important, you're comfortable thinking isomorphically: you can navigate the server/browser handoff and are familiar with the technology that makes this possible. You've also been exposed to how other technologies such as Ember and Angular implement server rendering. And you've seen an all-in-one isomorphic framework (Next.js).

Now it's time to go over some resources for learning more about isomorphic apps, the various technologies presented in this book, and even related topics that you may need in order to build practical, real-world apps.

13.1 Additional tools and frameworks

This book has covered many of the most popular libraries used in web development today. But if you've spent even a month as a web developer, you know that the JavaScript community is always evolving ideas, and there are far more useful topics than can be covered in a single book. This section provides an overview of Webpack Dev Server, suggests where to learn more about implementing it, and goes over additional isomorphic frameworks. Webpack Dev Server is a tool that makes your development environment easier to work with when building webpack-configured applications.

13.1.1 Webpack Dev Server

Webpack Dev Server is the development environment provided by webpack. It enables Hot Module Replacement, which takes an updated build and automatically replaces the parts of your running application that have changed. Here's a walk-through of how it works:

1. Start the first build and output the initial file, served from the dev server.
2. Enable a watcher.
3. A build is triggered by the watcher output, which outputs a new version on the dev server.
4. Use Hot Module Replacement to update the code running in the browser.

This becomes extremely helpful in a development environment and significantly speeds up your ability to compile and see changes. I highly recommend setting it up for all your webpack projects.

To learn about Webpack Dev Server, you can visit webpack's documentation: https://webpack.js.org/guides/hot-module-replacement/. You have to set up some things specifically for React. The URL for the Hot Module Replacement guide includes links (see the Other Code and Frameworks section of the documentation site at https://webpack.js.org/guides/hot-module-replacement/#other-code-and-frameworks).

Implementing this in an isomorphic environment isn't trivial—especially when using a Node.js server with a webpack bundle on the front end (as opposed to also using webpack to build your Node.js server, which I don't recommend). Webpack Isomorphic Tools can help you get going with this: https://github.com/halt-hammerzeit/webpack-isomorphic-tools.

13.1.2 Isomorphic frameworks

Besides Next.js, at least two other isomorphic React frameworks are worth looking into (if you want to use a prebuilt option instead of building up your own):

- Walmart Labs Electrode (www.electrode.io)
- React Server from Redfin (https://react-server.io)

Almost every new JavaScript framework provides the ability to do server rendering. Whether you want to try Vue.js (https://vuejs.org), Aurelia (https://github.com/AureliaUniversal/universal), or something else, it probably supports isomorphic rendering.

13.2 Up your game: building on isomorphic skills

This book gives you a solid foundation in several areas, including React architecture and server rendering with Node.js. Although you have a good start on these skills, this section tells you where you can find more resources to continue improving these skills.

13.2.1 React best practices

If you're going to build isomorphic React apps in production, becoming an expert at React architecture is an area where you'll want to improve your knowledge. Luckily for you, React has a strong community and many resources:

- GitHub repo with links to various blogs and resources about React (http://mng.bz/XEXE)
- Egghead.io courses—some are free, and others require a subscription (https://egghead.io/technologies/react). I'm a big fan of the way Egghead splits its courses into tiny consumable concepts:
  - React/Redux cheat sheets (https://egghead.io/react-redux-cheatsheets)
  - Learn React Router v4 (http://mng.bz/YHFN)
  - Add internationalization to a React app (http://mng.bz/g5On)
- Additional React books:
  - *React in Action* by Mark T. Thomas (Manning, 2017)
  - *React Quickly* by Azat Mardan (Manning, 2017)
  - *Redux in Action* by Marc Garreau and Will Faurot (Manning, 2018)

13.2.2 Up your Node.js game

If you don't have much experience with Node.js, I suggest improving your Node.js skills by doing the following:

- Learning about Node.js's I/O model (https://nodejs.org/en/docs/guides/blocking-vs-non-blocking/ and http://mng.bz/NR1f)
- Building a simple REST API with Node.js:
  - Loopback framework (https://loopback.io/doc/en/lb3/Tutorials-and-examples.html)
  - Tutorial with Node.js, Express, MongoDB, Mongoose, and Postman (http://mng.bz/1qSO)
- Learning how to harden Node.js to make a more secure server:
  - Blog post on hardening Node.js (https://blog.risingstack.com/node-js-security-checklist/)

  - Express documentation on security (https://expressjs.com/en/advanced/best-practice-security.html)

To practice, I suggest building a CRUD app of some kind. Building some of the examples in this book would work well—a recipes app that allows users to upload a recipe would be a good practice app. Building a chat app is another good way to practice because it covers several important topics (REST API, WebSocket, security because it requires accounts, and so forth).

13.2.3 Infrastructure

Because an isomorphic app will always have a server component, acquiring proficiency in build tools and server management will help you when running production apps. Additionally, understanding CDNs and being able to use them is an important skill in any web developer's tool belt. This blog post is a good place to get started deploying React apps using Docker with Amazon Web Services (AWS): http://mng.bz/9Na2.

Here's a list of general skills you'll need to get started:

- Containers: Docker (https://docs.docker.com/get-started/)
- CI tool: CircleCI (https://circleci.com) or TravisCI (https://travis-ci.org) are good starting places
- Cloud hosting: AWS, Google, Heroku, Digital Ocean, and more
- A good explanation of CDNs (http://mng.bz/k6qG)
- There are many CDN providers you can check out: Amazon Cloud Front, CloudFlare, Fastly, Akamai
- SSL/TLS (https://blog.talpor.com/2015/07/ssltls-certificates-beginners-tutorial/)
- CORS (https://developer.mozilla.org/en-US/docs/Web/HTTP/Access _control _CORS)

One of the best ways you can practice these skills is to deploy a personal website or practice app with AWS. That will force you to go through the process of using several of the tools listed here (for example, you could build an app with Docker and deploy it to Elastic Beanstalk in AWS).

13.3 All the things: data, SEO, and performance

This book focuses on a narrow slice of web development. But adding deep knowledge in at least one of the following areas will improve your ability to execute real-world apps (and make you more hirable!).

13.3.1 Data: accessing services with GraphQL

As app ecosystems have evolved and microservice architecture has become more popular, many engineering organizations have come to realize the limits of REST architecture. (I recommend the Netflix technical video at https://netflix.github.io/falcor/starter/why-falcor.html if you want to understand more about the problem).

In response, both Netflix and Facebook have proposed solutions. You can think of their implementations—Falcor (https://netflix.github.io/falcor/) and GraphQL (http://graphql.org/)—as front-end services for all your back-end services. Both allow the client application to request the data required for a view without knowing the underlying implementations.

For example, say I have a chat application. While chatting, the app needs to fetch chat data and user data, which will likely live on different services or endpoints in a REST application. These frameworks allow you to request all the data you need in a single request. They contain the business logic indicating where to fetch the data from so the client apps don't have to.

13.3.2 Search engine optimization

One of the main reasons you'd want to build an isomorphic application is to server-render your application's pages for searchbots. If this is a reason relevant to your situation, learning more about what makes good SEO strategy and how to perform the technical implementations of SEO is a requirement.

Understanding SEO best practices

Whole books and websites have been devoted to SEO strategy. If you're new to SEO or want to up your game, a variety of tools and resources can help you get started:

- SEO 101 from Moz (https://moz.com/beginners-guide-to-seo)
- Moz, an SEO tracking tool, subscription (https://moz.com)
- Moz Blog (https://moz.com/blog)
- Google Webmasters Blog (https://webmasters.googleblog.com)
- Google Trends (https://trends.google.com/trends/)
- SERPs Keyword Search Tool, subscription (https://serps.com/tools/keyword-research/)

Technical implementation of SEO

The more technical side of SEO involves implementing best practices and using Google's tracking tools to monitor and improve SEO. Things like building sitemaps also fall in this category:

- Google Search Console (www.google.com/webmasters/tools/home)—you have to verify your web properties before getting started
- Schema.org (http://schema.org/docs/schemas.html and https://moz.com/learn/seo/schema-structured-data)
- Use good header practices (www.hobo-web.co.uk/headers/)
- Internal linking (https://moz.com/learn/seo/internal-link)
- Sitemaps (https://moz.com/blog/xml-sitemaps)

13.3.3 Web performance

One of the other reasons for building isomorphic apps is to have good perceived performance for your users. But you still want to adhere to best practices around web performance. There are many things to learn in this area.

The best way to get started learning about performance is to take an app you have in production and make performance improvements. Before you start, make sure you have a way to measure your web app's performance (many third-party tools are available for this—you can try Pingdom or New Relic).

Here are some resources on how to improve web performance:

- Google's Lighthouse tools (https://developers.google.com/web/tools/lighthouse/)
- Web performance best practices (www.manning.com/books/web-performance-in-action)
- HTTP2 (https://http2.github.io/0)
- Service workers (http://mng.bz/tLwh)
- React performance case study (http://mng.bz/sNeU)

You might also consider looking into Preact (https://github.com/developit/preact). This library provides a "React lite" implementation with the same virtual DOM concepts you've learned in React. If you're looking for performance gains, this is worth exploring.

Summary

In this chapter, we reviewed several topics that will help you continue to improve your web app skills and contribute to your ability to build isomorphic apps in production environments:

- Where to go to find information that builds on the topics in this book, including webpack and more isomorphic frameworks.
- Resources for improving your Node.js and React skills.
- Topics you may want to learn in the future if you build isomorphic web apps. These include data services such as GraphQL, SEO, and infrastructure skills.

appendix A
React Router 4 basics

This appendix covers

- Using declarative routing in your components
- Using configurable routing to create a single source of truth
- Moving code from React Router 3 lifecycle events into a higher-order component
- Prefetching data in the browser by using a higher-order component

React Router 4 represents a big change in thinking from React Router 3. It moves from a standard static router implementation in which you define your routes in a single file to a dynamic implementation in which routes are created within React components. This also allows you to move most lifecycle logic out of React Router lifecycle methods and into React's lifecycle. Let's start by reviewing how you switch your components over to use React Router's decentralized routing pattern. The code examples in this appendix assume you've reviewed the React Router 3 version and want to see the differences. Each listing assumes that code presented in the related chapter is familiar to you. I've listed new code in bold.

A.1 Browser-only routing with React Router 4

In this section, I'll walk you through making routes work in a single-page application (SPA) architecture so you understand the basics of React Router 4. The code for the examples in this section can be found in the repo for the complete isomorphic example at http://mng.bz/zRGa. The code can also be found in the branch chapter-4-react-router-basic-routes (`git checkout chapter-4-react-router-basic-routes`).

First, you need to install the React Router 4 packages to have the correct code for this section. React Router now follows the React convention of separating DOM-related code into its own package. Make sure to upgrade react-router and install react-router-dom:

```
$ npm install react-router@4.2.0
$ npm install react-router-dom
```

After you've done this, you need to set up React Router in main.jsx.

A.1.1 Creating the app

The way you instantiate the main Router is slightly different in React Router 4 than in it was in version 3. Instead of taking the router and passing in routes and history, you pick the router that's appropriate to the use case. In this case, you want to use `BrowserRouter` so you can take advantage of the browser history API in your app. The following listing shows how to change the code in main.jsx to work with React Router 4.

Listing A.1 Set up the router—main.jsx

```
import React from 'react';
import ReactDOM from 'react-dom';
import { BrowserRouter } from 'react-router-dom';
import App from './components/app';

ReactDOM.render(
  <BrowserRouter>
    <App />
  </BrowserRouter>,
  document.getElementById('react-content')
);
```

Uses the BrowserRouter component as the root component

App should be the child of BrowserRouter. You'll put the routes into the App component.

Even though you've instantiated the router, you still need to update your components to handle the routes. The next section walks you through how to do this.

A.1.2 Routing in components

The basics of React Router 4 are similar to those of React Router 3. You declare your routes using a Route component. You give it a path and a component to render. The big change is in where you declare your routes. In version 3, you have a single, centralized routes file. In version 4, you declare your routes inside the appropriate component.

The following listing shows how you'd take the routes from the sharedRoutes.jsx file and put them in app.jsx instead.

Listing A.2 Declare the routes—components/app.jsx

```
// ... other code
import {
  Link, Route, withRouter
} from 'react-router-dom';
import Cart from '../components/cart';
import Products from '../components/products';
import Profile from '../components/profile';
import Login from '../components/login';

const App = (props) => {
  return (
    <div>
      <div className="ui fixed inverted menu">
        <h1 className="header item">All Things Westies</h1>
        <Link to="/products" className="item">Products</Link>
        <Link to="/cart" className="item">Cart</Link>
        <Link to="/profile" className="item">Profile</Link>
      </div>
      <div className="ui main text container">
        <Route path="/" exact component={Products} />
        <Route path="/products" component={Products} />
        <Route path="/cart" component={Cart} />
        <Route path="/profile" component={Profile} />
        <Route path="/login" component={Login} />
      </div>
    </div>
  );
};

export default withRouter(App);
```

- Imports the Route component and the withRouter higher-order component
- Imports the various app components used in the routes
- For paths that would result in multiple matches, make sure to use the exact option.
- Each Route takes a path and a component.
- Wraps App in the HOC withRouter. This ensures your components have access to the history and location props.

Now that you've moved the routes to the correct place, your app works! Note that the Link component works the same way in both versions. You declare a link by providing the Link component a `to` prop.

> **NOTE** In React Router 3, you could define a parent route with / and then define the child routes without the leading slash (for example, `products`). This is no longer supported. Instead, on a parent route, you need to use the `exact` option. For your root route /, you'll want to set `exact: true`.

Next, you'll learn how to create routes in a way that works well for an isomorphic app.

A.2 *Creating a single source of truth*

Now that you have React Router 4 working in the app, let's apply the same principles that you applied in React Router 3; the goal is to have a single source of truth for your routes. All the code in this section can be found in the branch chapter-4-react-router-v4 (`git checkout chapter-4-react-router-v4`).

You need a way to define your routes in a single object that can be used right now in the browser and again later on the server. The good news is that the React Router creators have created a beta library for addressing this problem: React Router Config (http://mng.bz/33Vu). This is a utility library that provides two functions for you to use to make server rendering and matching easier:

- `matchRoutes(routes, pathname)`—Determines whether the current route matches one of the routes in the provided configuration.
- `renderRoutes(routes, extraProps)`—Renders the provided routes into the component where the function is called. This method must be used instead of the Route component to ensure that the browser render matches the server-side render.

Install this library so you can import it:

```
$ npm install react-router-config
```

Next, you'll set up your routes with a configuration object instead of declaring them in the App component directly.

A.2.1 Routes as config

Rather than declare the routes in the App component as subcomponents, you'll now create a JavaScript object that represents the routes. As with React Router 3, you'll do this in a sharedRoutes file. So that you can differentiate and compare, I've called this file sharedRoutesv4.jsx.

The following listing shows the code that makes up this module.

Listing A.3 Route configuration—shared/sharedRoutesv4.es6

```
import App from '../components/app';
import Cart from '../components/cart';
import Products from '../components/products';
import Profile from '../components/profile';
import Login from '../components/login';

const routes = [
  {
    component: App,
    routes: [
      {
        path: '/',
        exact: true,
        component: Products
      },
      {
        path: '/cart',
        component: Cart
      },
      {
        path: '/products',
```

- Imports the components used in the routes
- Declares your root component
- Declares the subroutes in the routes array for the App component
- You can still declare the exact option by adding this property.
- Every route has a path and a component.

```
        component: Products
      },
      {
        path: '/profile',
        component: Profile
      },
      {
        path: '/login',
        component: Login
      }
    ]
  }
]

export default routes;
```

Every route has a path and a component.

Now that you've declared your routes, you need to use this route configuration instead of the Route components from the previous section.

A.2.2 Configuring the routes in the components

Using the React Router Config library, you can easily set up your app to use the routes from the previous section. To get everything working properly, you need to call the `renderRoutes` function from this library in main.jsx and in your top-level App component. The following listing shows how to declare this function in main.jsx.

Listing A.4 Use the configured routes—main.jsx

```
import from 'react';
import ReactDOM from 'react-dom';
import { BrowserRouter } from 'react-router-dom';
import { renderRoutes } from 'react-router-config';
import routes from './shared/sharedRoutesv4.es6';

ReactDOM.render(
  <BrowserRouter>
    { renderRoutes(routes) }
  </BrowserRouter>,
  document.getElementById('react-content')
);
```

- Imports renderRoutes
- Imports the route configuration object
- Calls renderRoutes and passes in the routes configuration. This replaces the App component declaration.

Next you need to also declare these routes inside the App component—you need to declare routes anytime you have a component that has subroutes. This replaces the Route component declarations you made previously. The following listing shows how to update the code.

Listing A.5 Use the configured routes—components/app.jsx

```
import { Link } from 'react-router-dom';
import {
  renderRoutes
} from 'react-router-config';
```

- Imports renderRoutes

```
const App = (props) => {
  return (
    <div>
      // ...more code
      <div className="ui main text container">
        {
          renderRoutes(
            props.route.routes,
            { history: props.history }
          )
        }
      </div>
    </div>
  );
};
```

- **Calls renderRoutes. Passes in the routes object provided via props because you declared them in main.jsx.**
- **Passes the history object in as a prop so child components have access as needed.**

At this point, your routes should work as expected. Next we'll review the changes to the React lifecycle.

A.3 Handling lifecycle events

Another major change between React Router 3 and 4 is the way lifecycle events are handled. In React Router 3, the Router had its own independent lifecycle. You had to manage React's lifecycle and React Router's lifecycle, which often became complex. You added code in the sharedRoutes file that handled code that happens at specific points in the lifecycle. Now you need to do that in a different way.

In React Router 4, you use React's lifecycle to do updates based on the route changing. A good way to facilitate this is to create a higher-order component (HOC).

A.3.1 Using higher-order components to manage route changes

To create your own higher-order component, you create a function that returns a React component. Then you can hook into the React lifecycle and do updates based on the route changing. The following listing shows how to do this. It includes the example from chapter 4, where you add page tracking on every update.

Listing A.6 `onRouteChange` higher-order component—components/onRouteChange.jsx

```
const onRouteChange = (WrappedComponent) => {
  return class extends React.PureComponent {

    trackPageView() {
      // In real life you would hook this up to your analytics tool of
      choice console.log('Tracked a pageview');
    };

    componentDidMount() {
      this.trackPageView();
    }
```

- **Creates a function that takes in a component**
- **This function represents tracking a page view.**
- **Calls the trackPageView function from componentDidMount. This replaces the onEnter call in the old sharedRoutes file.**

```
    componentWillReceiveProps(nextProps) {
      const navigated = nextProps.location !== this.props.location;

      if (navigated) {
        this.trackPageView();
      }
    }

    render() {
     return <WrappedComponent {...this.props} />;
    }
  }
}
```

Checks whether the route has changed

Calls trackPageView if the route has changed. Calling it in componentWillReceiveProps replaces the onChange call in the old sharedRoutes file.

After you've created this HOC, you need to use it in your root component, App. The following listing shows how to import and apply it.

Listing A.7 Use the configured routes—components/app.jsx

```
// no longer using withRouter HOC
import onRouteChange from './onRouteChange';

const App = (props) => {};

// no longer using withRouter HOC
export default onRouteChange(App);
```

Imports onRouteChange

To have the onRouteChange HOC manage your routes, you need to wrap your root component with it.

Now that you've wrapped the root component in `onRouteChange`, you can easily add the code to prefetch data when navigating around the app.

A.3.2 Prefetching the data for the view

Chapter 8 teaches you how to prefetch the data when navigating around the site in the browser. With the removal of React Router lifecycle events in version 4, you need to take a different approach. This is handled the same way you handle page-tracking events in the previous section.

The code for this example can be found on GitHub (`git checkout chapter-8-complete-react-router-4`).

The following listing shows how to prefetch data in the browser when navigating between routes. It uses the `onRouteChange` HOC you created in the previous section.

Listing A.8 Prefetch the data—components/onRouteChange.jsx

```
import { matchRoutes } from 'react-router-config';
import routes from '../shared/sharedRoutesv4.es6';

const onRouteChange = (WrappedComponent) => {
  return class extends React.PureComponent {
    // ... other code

    fetchData(nextProps) {
```

Imports matchRoutes so you can pull out all the components used in the current route. Gets the routes from the configured routes in sharedRoutesv4.

```
  const { route, location } = nextProps;
  const { routes } = route;
  const matches = matchRoutes(
                              routes,
                              location.pathname
                            );
  let results = matches.map(({match, route}) => {
    const component = route.component;
    if (component) {
      if (component.displayName &&
          component.displayName.toLowerCase().indexOf('connect') > -1
      ) {
        let parentComponent = component.WrappedComponent;
        if (parentComponent.prefetchActions) {
          return parentComponent.prefetchActions (
            location.pathname.substring(1)
          );
        } else if (parentComponent.wrappedComponent &&
parentComponent.wrappedComponent().prefetchActions ) {
          return parentComponent.wrappedComponent().prefetchActions (
            location.pathname.substring(1)
          );
        }
      } else if (component.prefetchActions) {
        return component.prefetchActions (
          location.pathname.substring(1)
        )
      }
    }
    return [];
  });

  const actions = results.reduce((
                                  flat,
                                  toFlatten
                                  ) => {
    return flat.concat(toFlatten);
  }, []);

  const promises = actions.map((initialAction) => {
    return this.props.dispatch(initialAction());
  });
  Promise.all(promises);
}

componentDidMount() {}

componentWillReceiveProps(nextProps) {
  this.fetchData(nextProps);
  //... other code
}
```

Calls matchRoutes with the routes and location from props

Iterates over each item in the matches array. This represents each component being rendered on this route—anything you declared in sharedRoutesv4.

This block is almost identical to the one in chapter 7. You look for the base component and call prefetchActions if the function exists.

The major difference is you have to handle the case where you wrapped App in two HOCs.

Flattens the results of getting the actions into a single array

Gets ready to execute the actions by passing them into the dispatch function from Redux

Call of the actions

You call the fetchData function from componentWillReceiveProps, so it will run every time except the initial load.

Because you're using `dispatch` in the preceding code, you need to wrap your App component with the connect HOC. The following listing shows how to do this.

Listing A.9 Use the configured routes—components/app.jsx

```
import { connect } from 'react-redux';

const App = (props) => {};

export default connect()(onRouteChange(App));
```

Imports connect

To have access to the dispatch function in onRouteChange, you must first wrap it in the connect HOC.

Now the app will run! It prefetches the data when needed. Try navigating from /products to /cart to see this in action.

appendix B
Server-side React Router

From an isomorphic app standpoint, one of the difficult parts of moving to React Router 4 is that the maintainers and community at large have yet to arrive at a consistent set of best practices for data prefetching patterns. You'll see this sentiment over and over in the documentation; for instance, the React Router Config readme file states: "There are a lot of ways to do server rendering with data and pending navigation, and we haven't settled on one."

Chapter 7 teaches you how to prefetch data on the server so that it's available at render time. This appendix shows you how to do that with React Router 4. The code for the example here can be found in the repo at http://mng.bz/S3N0, in branch chapter-7-complete-react-router-4 (`git checkout chapter-7-complete-react-router-4`).

React Router 4 allows you to prefetch your data on the server before rendering. In the setup I suggest in appendix A, you use `matchRoutes` from React Router Config to prefetch data in the browser. You do the same thing on the server! This allows you to have consistency on the server and the browser because you're using the same approach via the utility functions provided in the library. This function is synchronous, unlike the asynchronous route match function in React Router 3. (If you want consistency for your Node.js app, you could always wrap it so it returns asynchronously.) The following listing shows how to update the code to work with React Router 4.

Listing B.1 Fetching data on the server—middleware/renderView.jsx

```
//...other code
import { StaticRouter } from 'react-router';        // Imports the dependencies
import {
  matchRoutes, renderRoutes
} from 'react-router-config';
import routes from '../shared/sharedRoutesv4';      // Imports the dependencies
```

```
export default function renderView(req, res, next) {
  const matches = matchRoutes(routes, req.path);
  const context = {};

  if (matches) {
    const store = initRedux();
    let actions = [];
    matches.map(({match, route}) => {
      const component = route.component;
      if (component) {
        if (component.displayName &&
            component.displayName.toLowerCase().indexOf('connect') > -1
        ) {
          let parentComponent = component.WrappedComponent;
          if (parentComponent.prefetchActions) {
            actions.push(parentComponent.prefetchActions());
          } else if (parentComponent.wrappedComponent &&
     parentComponent.wrappedComponent().prefetchActions) {
        actions.push(parentComponent.wrappedComponent().prefetchActions());
          }
        } else if (component.prefetchActions) {
          actions.push(component.prefetchActions());
        }
      }
    });
    actions = actions.reduce((flat, toFlatten) => {
      return flat.concat(toFlatten);
    }, []);

    const promises = actions.map((initialAction) => {
      return store.dispatch(initialAction());
    });
    Promise.all(promises).then(() => {
      const app = renderToString(
        <Provider store={store}>
          <StaticRouter
            location={req.url}
            context={context}>
            { renderRoutes(routes) }
          </StaticRouter>
        </Provider>
      );

      if (!context.url) {
        const html = renderToString(<HTML renderedToStringComponents={app} />);
        res.send(`<!DOCTYPE html>${html}`);
      }
    });
  } else {
    next();
  }
}
```

Calls matchRoutes to find out which components are being loaded

Creates a context object used to determine whether there's a route redirect

Iterates through the matches so you can call the prefetchActions function. Most of this method is the same as in chapter 7.

This is the major difference in the code. Because App is wrapped in two HOCs, you have to check two levels down to access the root component.

Uses the StaticRouter on the server instead of the BrowserRouter, as you don't need a history. Passes in the location and context object.

Calls renderRoutes just as in main.jsx

Checks the context to make sure there isn't a redirect

appendix C
Additional React Router 4 use cases

This appendix covers

- Handling third-party libraries such as an analytics module in React Router 4
- Adding routes dynamically at runtime
- Code splitting with webpack and React Router 4

Chapters 10 and 11 show you how to do several things that affect the way the React Router code and the rest of the app work together. This appendix goes over several of those examples with React Router 4.

All the examples in this appendix live in the react-router-4 branch (`git checkout react-router-4`) of the main example repo, http://mng.bz/S3N0. The code in this branch is also updated so you can see a complete example of the way React Router 4 works with the final version of the code as it exists at the end of chapter 11. This builds off the code changes presented in appendix A and appendix B.

C.1 Moving analytics to onRouteChange

The first update you need to make is to move the analytics code into the `onRouteChange` HOC. Previously, this was handled in the React Router 3 lifecycle methods. Now you'll handle it like page tracking and prefetching data are in appendix A. The following listing demonstrates how this is done. This change is from chapter 10, section 10.1.

Listing C.1 Add analytics to `onRouteChange`—components/onRouteChange.jsx

```
import { sendData } from '../analytics.es6';

const onRouteChange = (WrappedComponent) => {
  return class extends React.PureComponent {
    trackPageView(location) {
      this.sendAnalytics(location);
      console.log('Tracked a pageview');
    };

    fetchData(nextProps) {}

    sendAnalytics(location) {
      sendData({
        location: location && location.pathname,
        type: 'navigation'
      });
    }

    componentDidMount() {
      this.trackPageView(this.props.location);
    }

    componentWillReceiveProps(nextProps) {
      //...other code

      if (navigated) {
        this.trackPageView(nextProps.location);
      }
    }
  }
}
```

- Imports sendData from the analytics module
- Passes location into the function. Calls sendAnalytics.
- Creates a sendAnalytics function that calls sendData. The location will be passed in.
- Calls trackPageView each time the route changes. Make sure to pass in the correct location.

Calling `sendAnalytics` from `componentWillReceiveProps` replaces the `onEnter` call in `sharedRoutes`. Additionally, calling `sendAnalytics` from `componentDidMount` replaces the `onEnter` call in `sharedRoutes`.

C.2 Adding dynamic routes

Chapter 10 also demonstrates how to add dynamic routes based on an environment variable or other flag. To do this in the new sharedRoutesv4 file, you need to update the routes array before exporting it. The following listing shows how to do this.

Listing C.2 Adding a dynamic route—sharedRoutesv4.es6

```
const routes = [
  {
```

```
    component: App,
    routes: [
      //...other code
    ]
  }
]

if (process.env.NODE_ENV !== 'production') {
  routes[0].routes.push({
    path: '/dev-test',
    component: Products
  });
}

export { routes };

export default routes;
```

Checks for the environment. If it isn't production, adds this dev-only route.

Pushes the new route into the routes array. Remember, the routes array is a child of the root App component in the routes object.

Now you have an additional route in dev!

C.3 Code splitting: React Loadable

The last example that touches on React Router is code splitting from chapter 11. The good news is that it's somewhat easier with React Router 4. The community has definitely caught up here and provides a library to handle all your code-splitting needs. The library is called React Loadable, and it's easy to use and well documented.

The React community has thought of everything, including handling an isomorphic app. They've provided good documentation at http://mng.bz/3hJg. I'm not going to reproduce all their examples here.

A few cool things about React Loadable:

- You can provide a component that's shown while your components are being loaded (http://mng.bz/518M).
- The library ships with an option to preload components (which is always used on the server) and can be used on the browser for optimistic loading (http://mng.bz/081O).
- Instead of installing all the correct Babel plugins and having to set up webpack properly, the library handles all that for you. It provides a Babel package for you (http://mng.bz/91mV). It also ships with a webpack plugin and a related utility for server-side rendering (http://mng.bz/34vL).

index

Symbols

A

B

C

D

S

T

U